D1535271

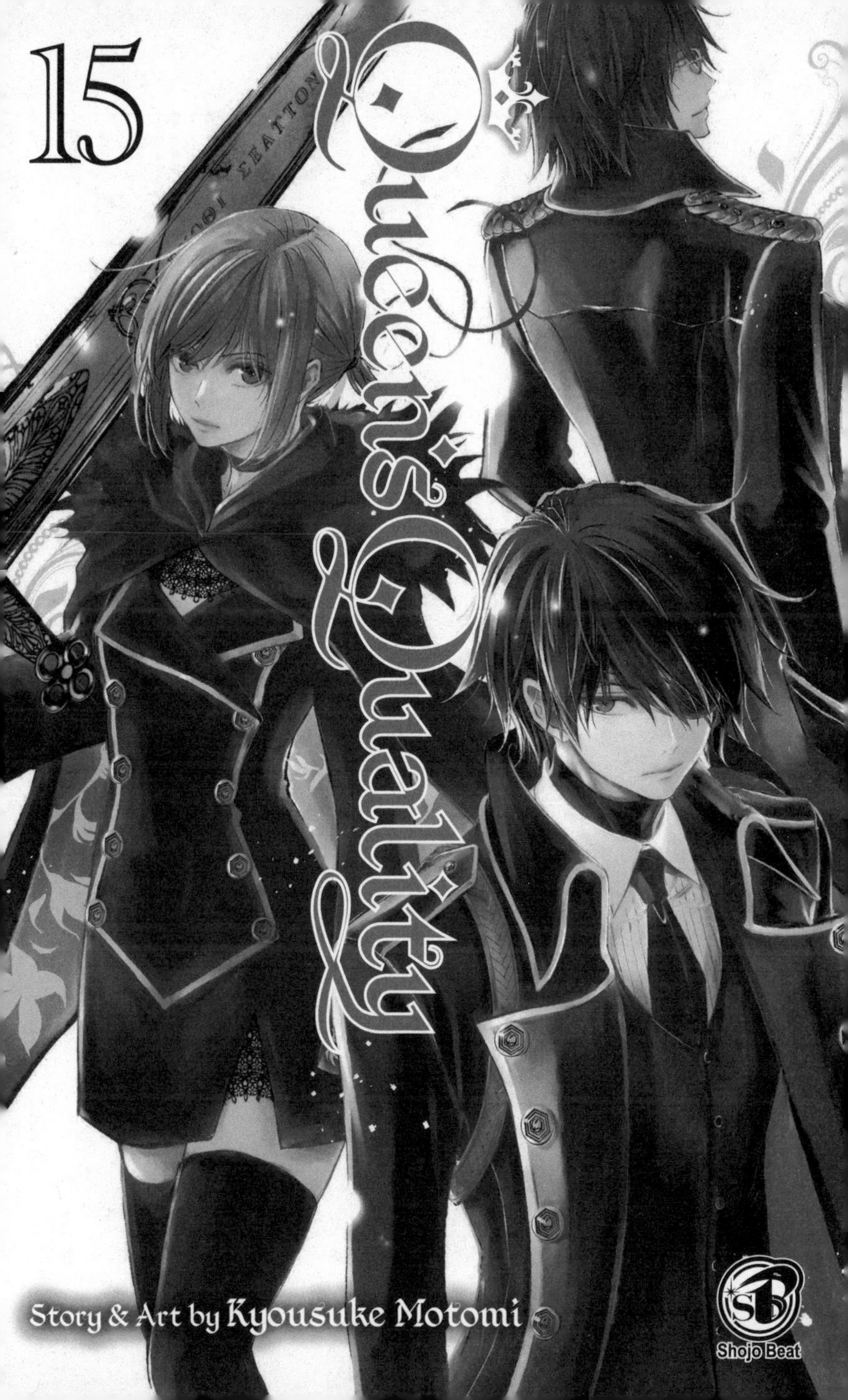
15
Queen's Quality
Story & Art by Kyousuke Motomi
Shojo Beat

Queen's Quality

CONTENTS

15

◇ Cast of Characters ◆

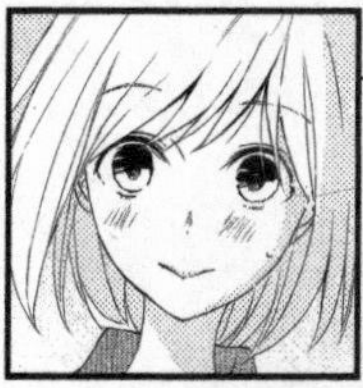

Fumi Nishioka

An apprentice Sweeper with the powers of a Queen, this second-year high school student dreams of finding her very own Prince Charming.

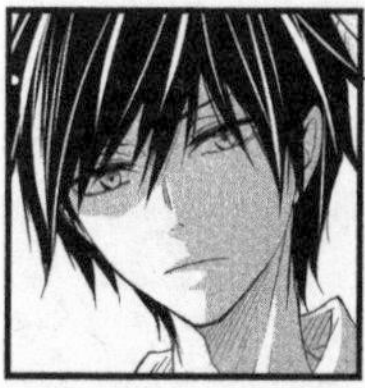

Kyutaro Horikita

A mind Sweeper who cleanses people's minds of dangerous impurities. Although incredibly awkward with people, he and Fumi are now dating.

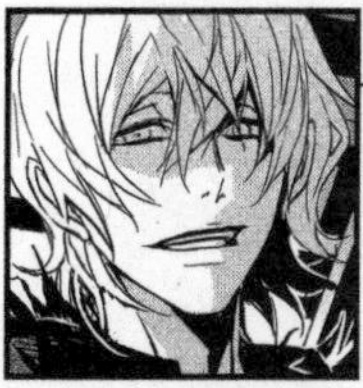

Ataru Shikata

A former bug handler who uses bugs to manipulate people. Saved by Fumi and Kyutaro, he has joined the Genbu Clan.

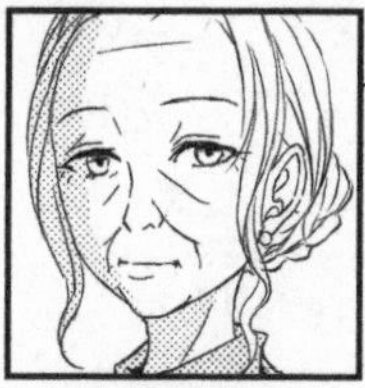

Miyako Horikita

The prior head of the Genbu Gate Sweepers. She can be both strict and kind, and she watches over and advises Fumi.

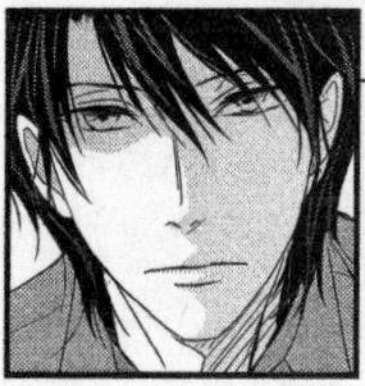

Koichi Kitagawa

The chairman of the school Fumi and Kyutaro attend. He's a Sweeper as well as being Kyutaro's brother-in-law.

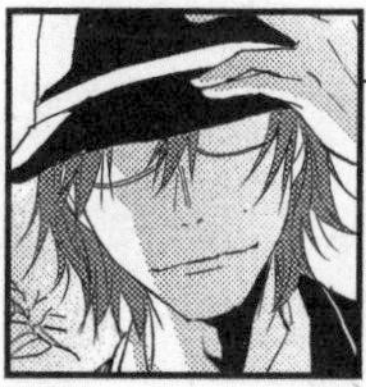

Takaya Kitahara

One of the Genbu Clan, he was originally a member of the main Byakko Clan. He's an expert with suggestive therapy and is actually Fumi's uncle.

◇ Story Thus Far ◆

The Horikitas are a family of Sweepers—people who cleanse impurities from human hearts. After seeing Fumi's potential, they take her on as an assistant and trainee. Within Fumi dwells the power of both the White and the Dark-Gray queens, both of whom have the ability to give people immense power.

Having both paid the compensation demanded by the White Queen and completed their training in Seichi, Fumi and Kyutaro are now in a relationship! Soon after, when it becomes clear that a snake is dwelling within Kyutaro, Fumi defeats the snake and attains the powers of the True Queen.

Peace has barely descended when disaster strikes again—Yanagi of the Suzaku, the mastermind behind the recent crises, steals Ataru's spirit away! The Genbu and Seiryu clans work together to save him, but at a high cost to Kyutaro... Unfortunately, the Suzaku have even more dastardly plans in store!

MONTHLY BETSUCOMI SALE DATE NOTICE ON TWITTER AND INSTAGRAM

CHAPTER 66

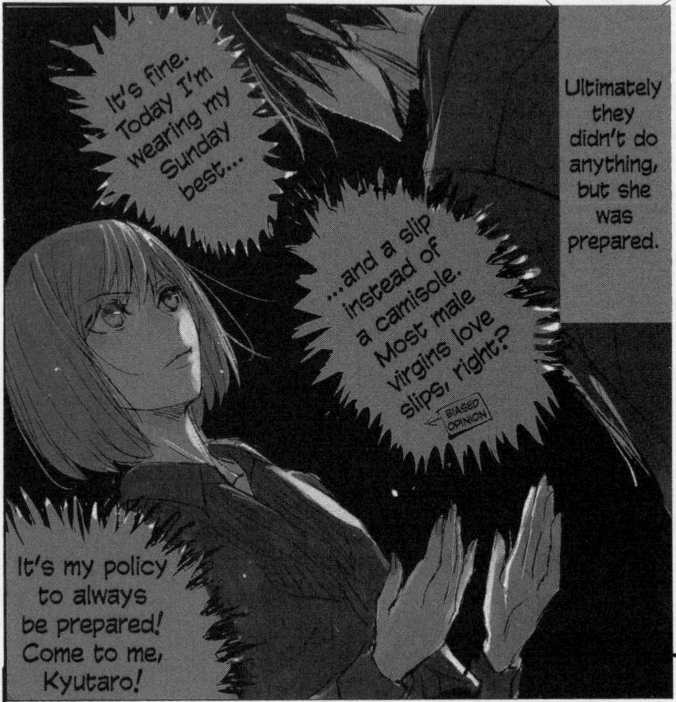
Ultimately they didn't do anything, but she was prepared.
It's fine. Today I'm wearing my Sunday best...
...and a slip instead of a camisole. Most male virgins love slips, right?
BIASED OPINION
It's my policy to always be prepared! Come to me, Kyutaro!

FUMI IS BIASED, BUT I THINK KYUTARO REALLY LIKES IT (THE SLIP) TOO.

LET'S SEE... WHAT'S UP IN *QUEEN'S QUALITY* THIS MONTH?
1) FUMI NEVER CLOSES HER CURTAINS, DOES SHE?
2) I WANTED THEM TO LOOK LIKE SEA ANGELS BUT DIDN'T GET THEM QUITE RIGHT.
3) I WONDERED IF IT WAS OKAY FOR THERE TO BE SO MUCH BONDAGE IN A MANGA, BUT THERE WAS ALREADY PLENTY OF IT IN VOLUME 4 (BY SNAKES).

THEY'RE GOING AT IT HARD, BUT THEY'RE NOT DOING ANYTHING OBSCENE IN THIS CHAPTER!

I SEND OUT TWITTER UPDATES LIKE THIS EVERY MONTH. YOU CAN READ SOME OF MY OTHER MUTTERINGS THERE TOO.

@motomikyosuke

I'VE STARTED AN INSTAGRAM ACCOUNT TOO! (KYOSUKEMOTOMI)

Chapter 66

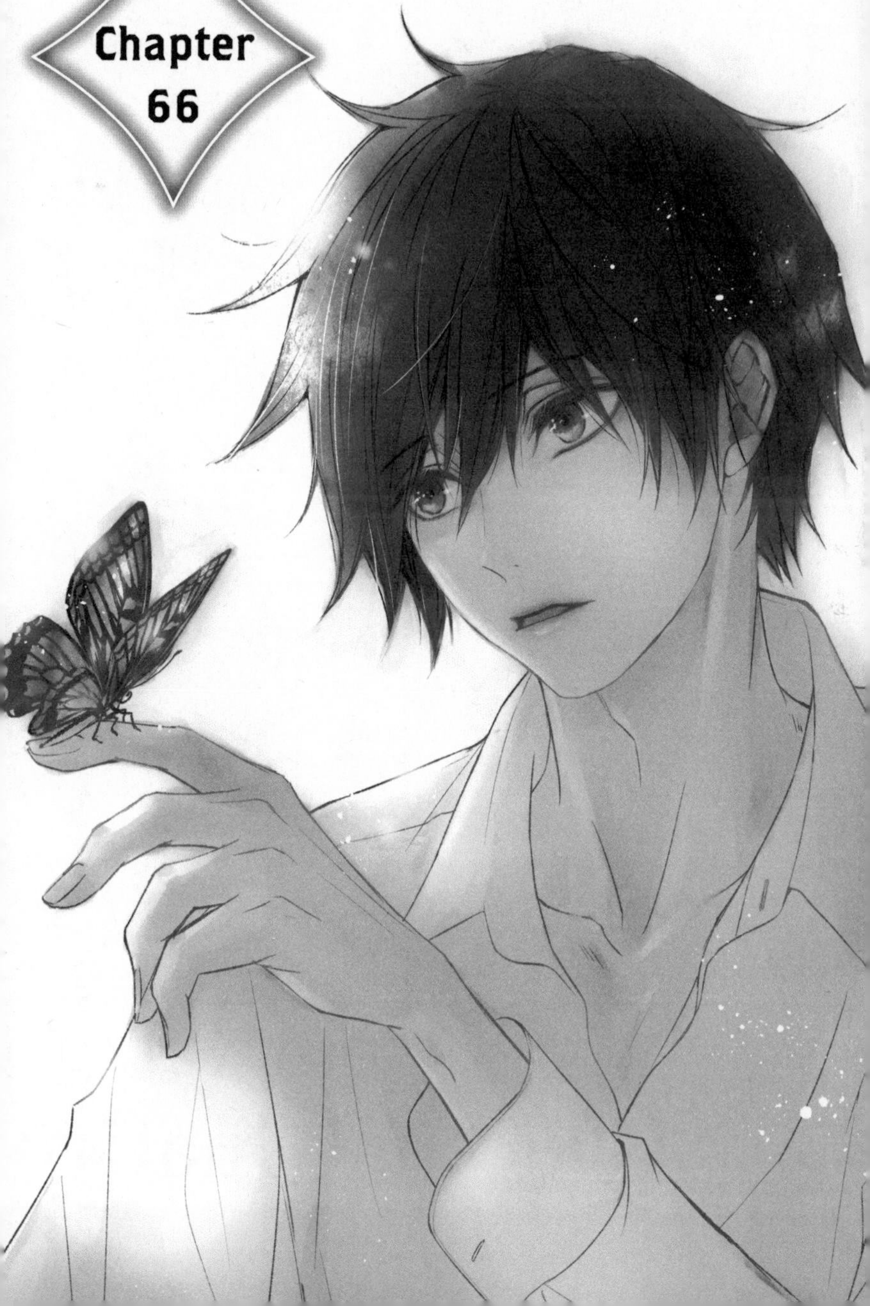

Queen's Quality

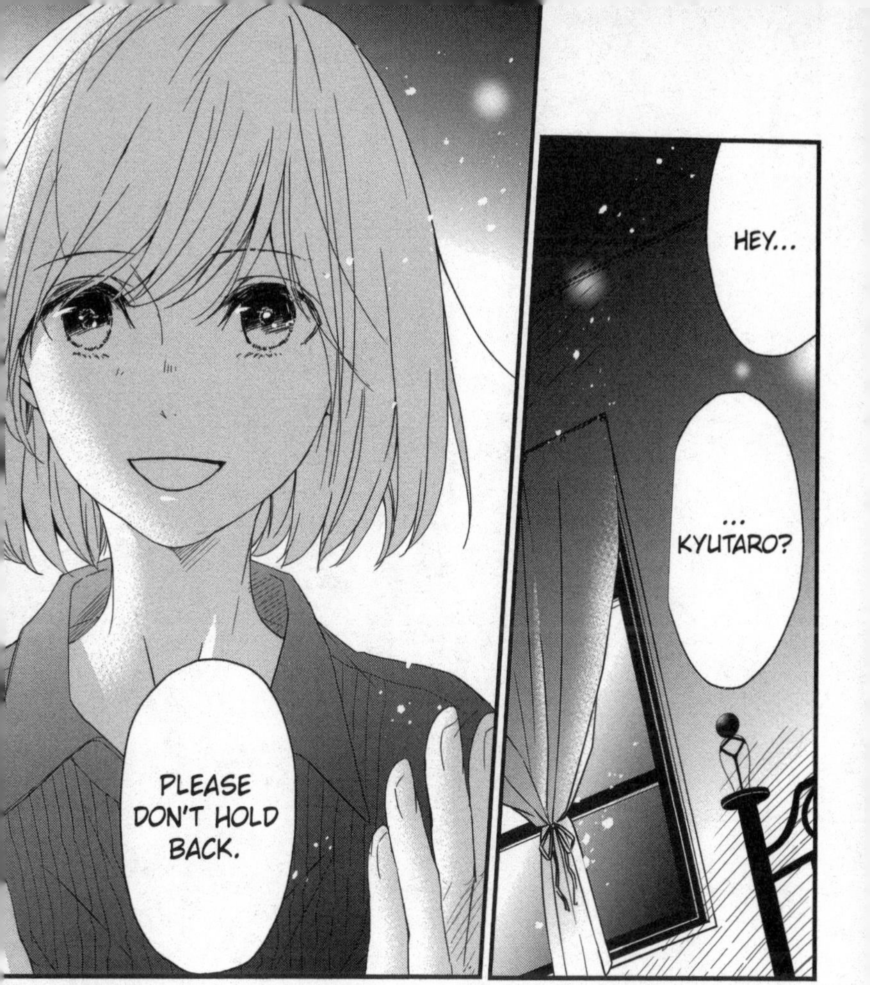
HEY...
...KYUTARO?
PLEASE DON'T HOLD BACK.

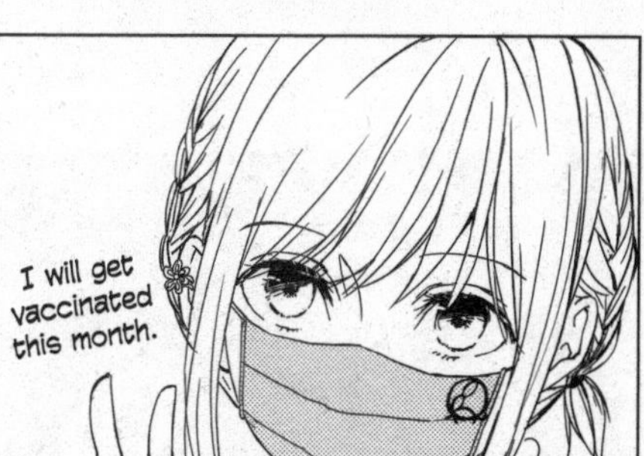
I will get vaccinated this month.

Hello, everyone! This is Kyousuke Motomi. Thank you for picking up volume 15 of Queen's Quality!

This marks the start of another new arc. I plan to reveal many secrets. I hope you'll enjoy it!

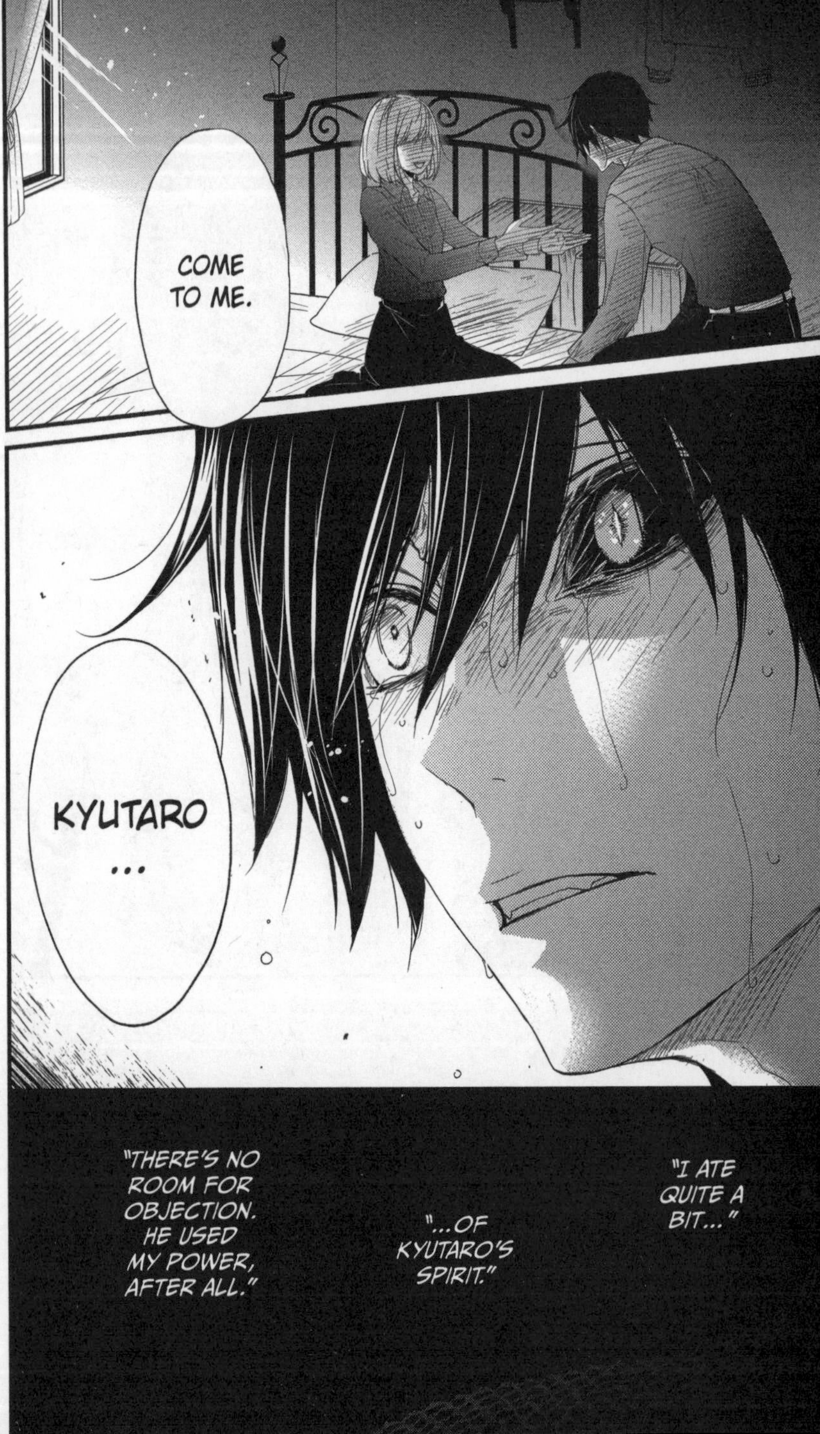
COME TO ME.
KYUTARO ...
"I ATE QUITE A BIT..."
"...OF KYUTARO'S SPIRIT."
"THERE'S NO ROOM FOR OBJECTION. HE USED MY POWER, AFTER ALL."

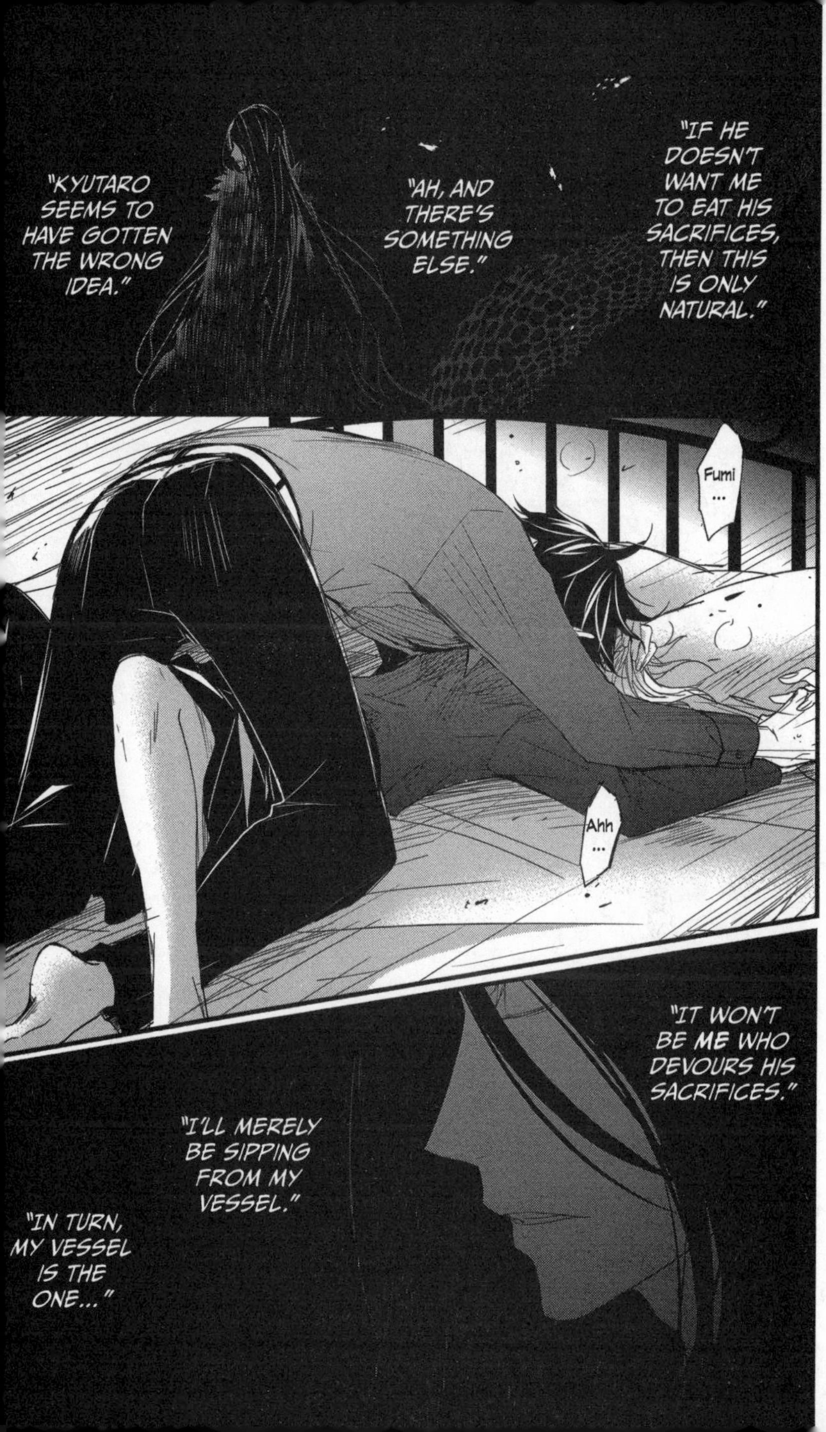
"IF HE DOESN'T WANT ME TO EAT HIS SACRIFICES, THEN THIS IS ONLY NATURAL."
"AH, AND THERE'S SOMETHING ELSE."
"KYUTARO SEEMS TO HAVE GOTTEN THE WRONG IDEA."
Fumi ...
Ahh ...
"IT WON'T BE **ME** WHO DEVOURS HIS SACRIFICES."
"I'LL MERELY BE SIPPING FROM MY VESSEL."
"IN TURN, MY VESSEL IS THE ONE..."

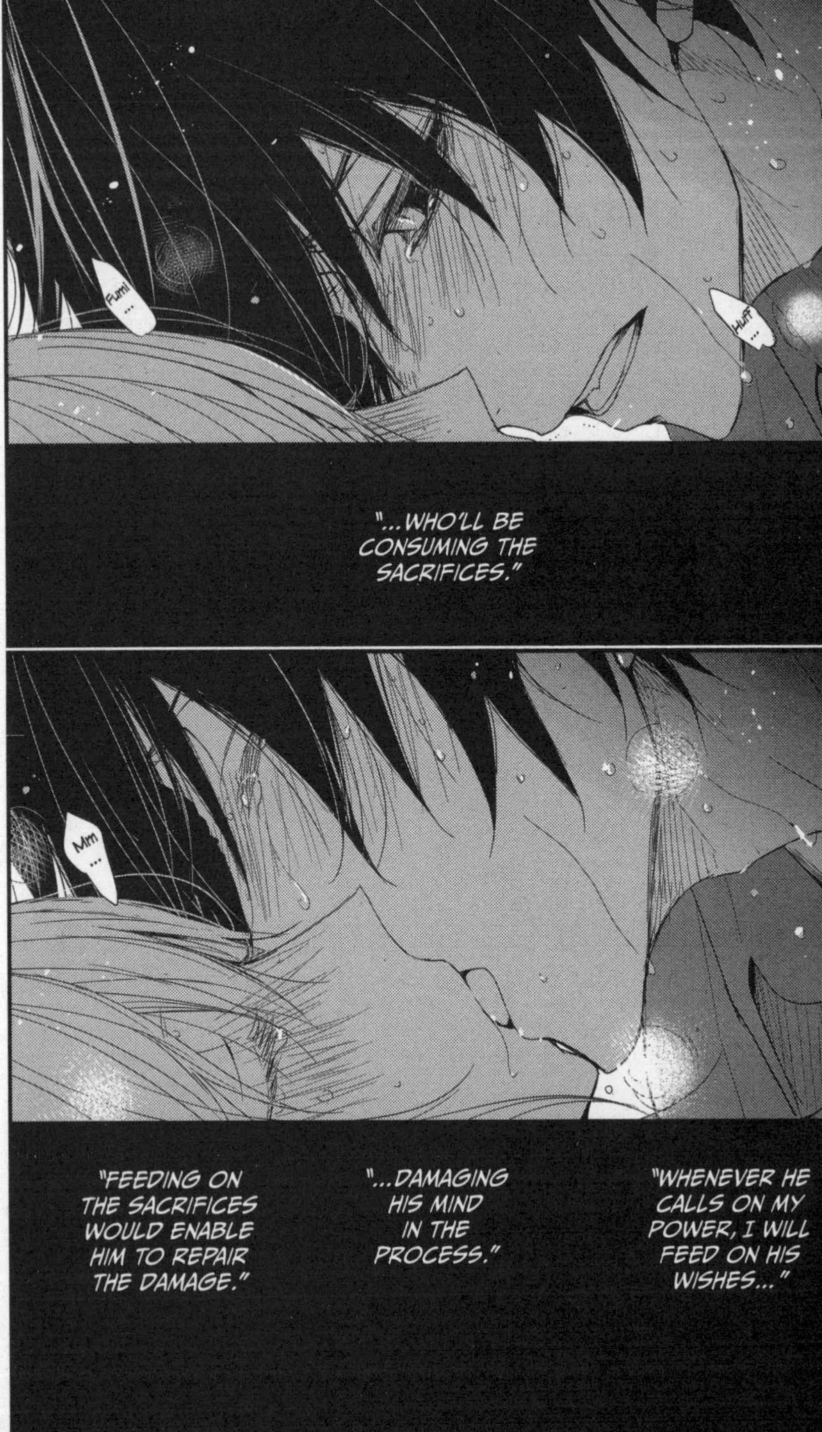
Huff ...
Fumi ...
"...WHO'LL BE CONSUMING THE SACRIFICES."
Mm ...
"WHENEVER HE CALLS ON MY POWER, I WILL FEED ON HIS WISHES..."
"...DAMAGING HIS MIND IN THE PROCESS."
"FEEDING ON THE SACRIFICES WOULD ENABLE HIM TO REPAIR THE DAMAGE."

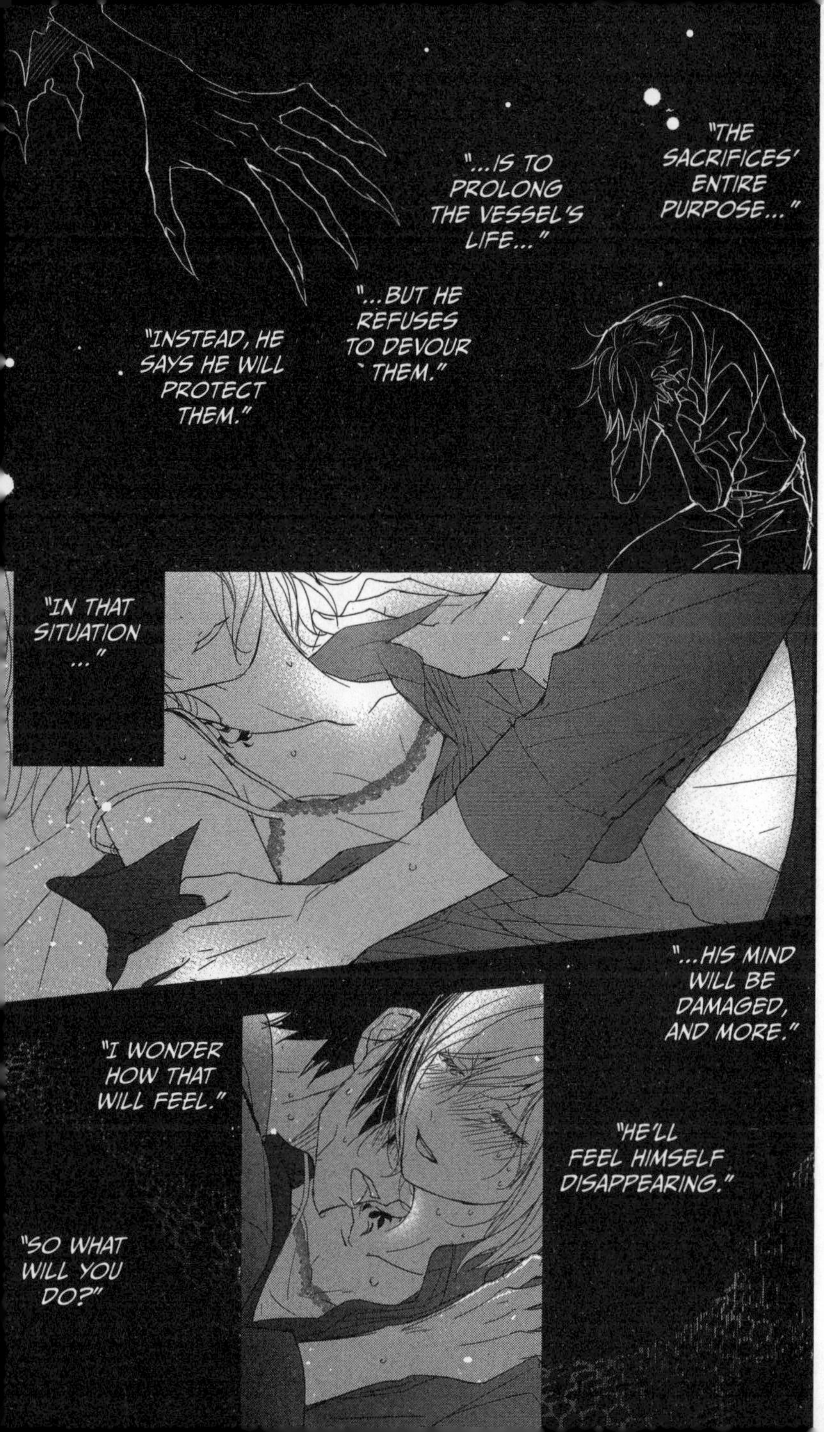
"THE SACRIFICES' ENTIRE PURPOSE..."
"...IS TO PROLONG THE VESSEL'S LIFE..."
"...BUT HE REFUSES TO DEVOUR THEM."
"INSTEAD, HE SAYS HE WILL PROTECT THEM."
"IN THAT SITUATION ..."
"...HIS MIND WILL BE DAMAGED, AND MORE."
"HE'LL FEEL HIMSELF DISAPPEARING."
"I WONDER HOW THAT WILL FEEL."
"SO WHAT WILL YOU DO?"

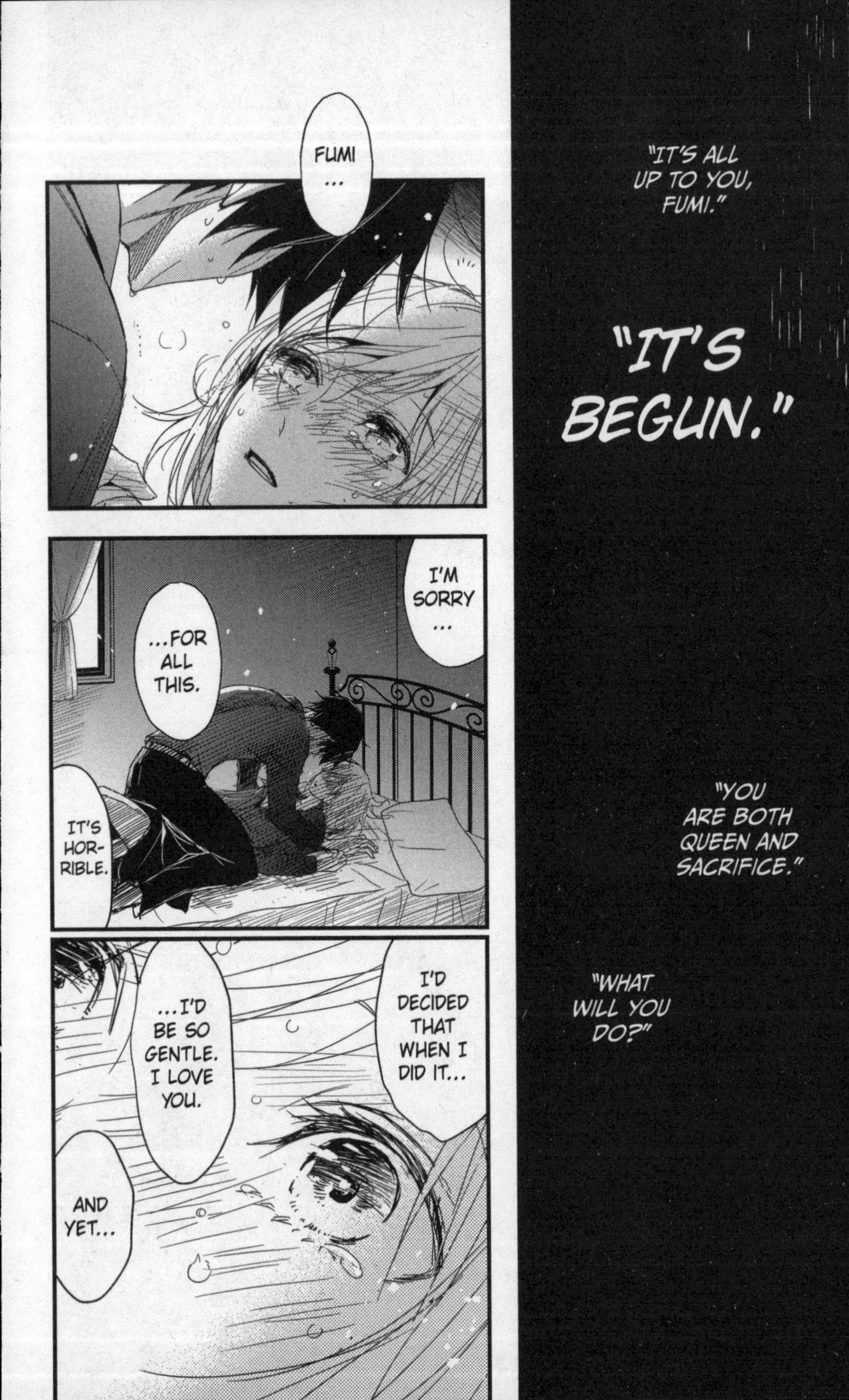
"IT'S ALL UP TO YOU, FUMI."
"IT'S BEGUN."
"YOU ARE BOTH QUEEN AND SACRIFICE."
"WHAT WILL YOU DO?"
FUMI ...
I'M SORRY ...
...FOR ALL THIS.
IT'S HOR-RIBLE.
I'D DECIDED THAT WHEN I DID IT...
...I'D BE SO GENTLE. I LOVE YOU.
AND YET...

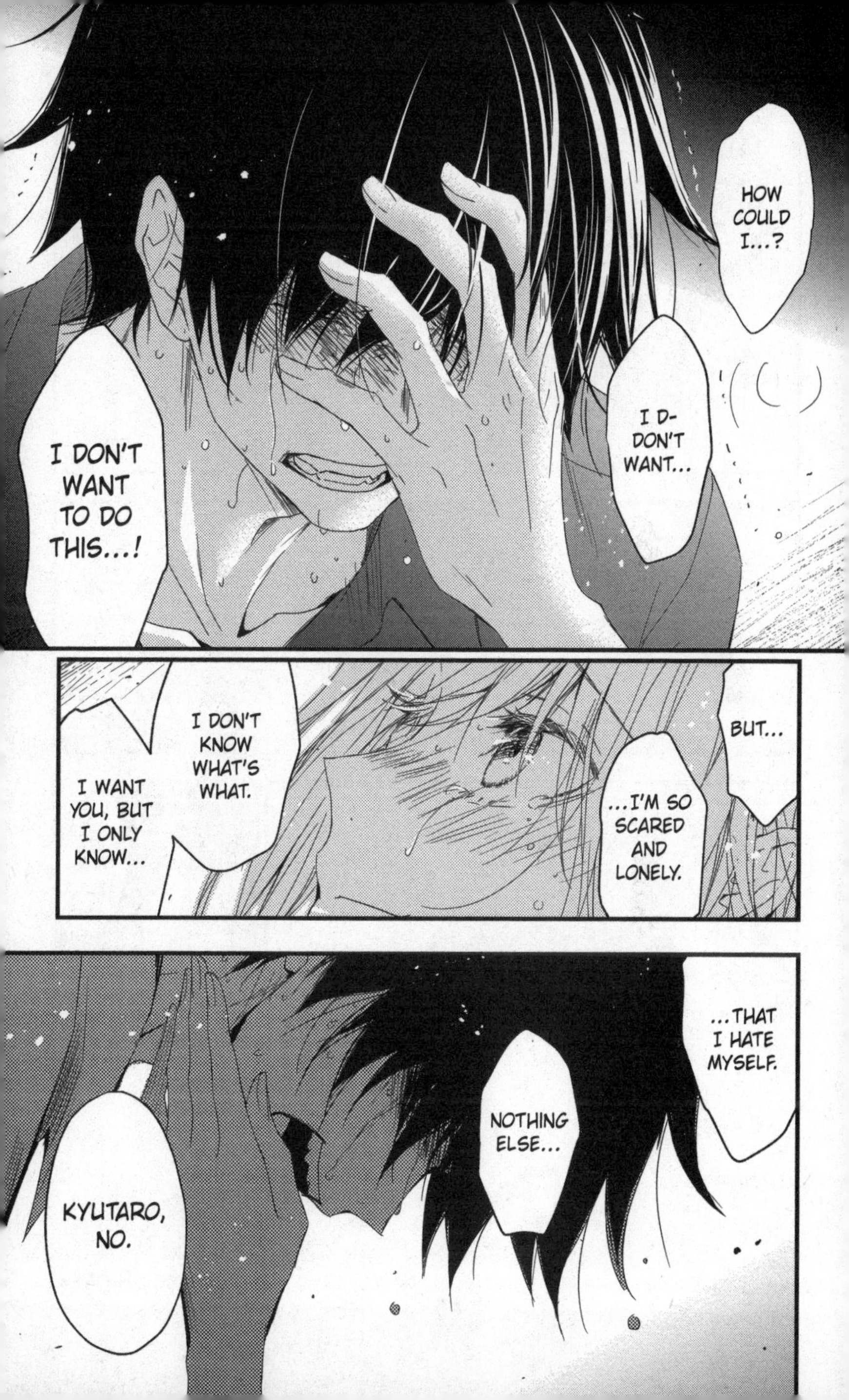
HOW COULD I...?
I D-DON'T WANT...
I DON'T WANT TO DO THIS...!
BUT...
...I'M SO SCARED AND LONELY.
I DON'T KNOW WHAT'S WHAT.
I WANT YOU, BUT I ONLY KNOW...
...THAT I HATE MYSELF.
NOTHING ELSE...
KYUTARO, NO.

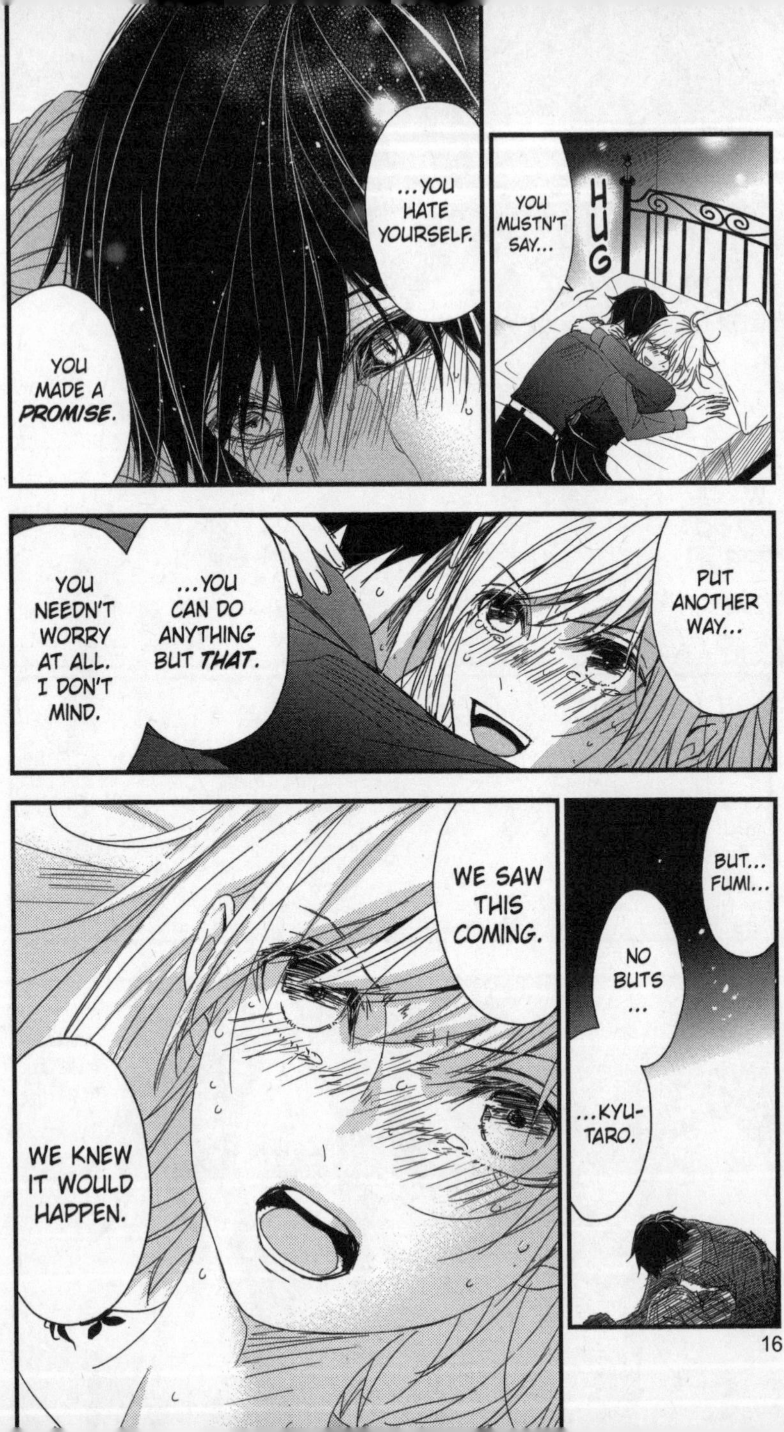
HUG
YOU MUSTN'T SAY...
...YOU HATE YOURSELF.
YOU MADE A **PROMISE**.
PUT ANOTHER WAY...
...YOU CAN DO ANYTHING BUT ***THAT***.
YOU NEEDN'T WORRY AT ALL. I DON'T MIND.
BUT... FUMI...
NO BUTS ...
...KYU-TARO.
WE SAW THIS COMING.
WE KNEW IT WOULD HAPPEN.

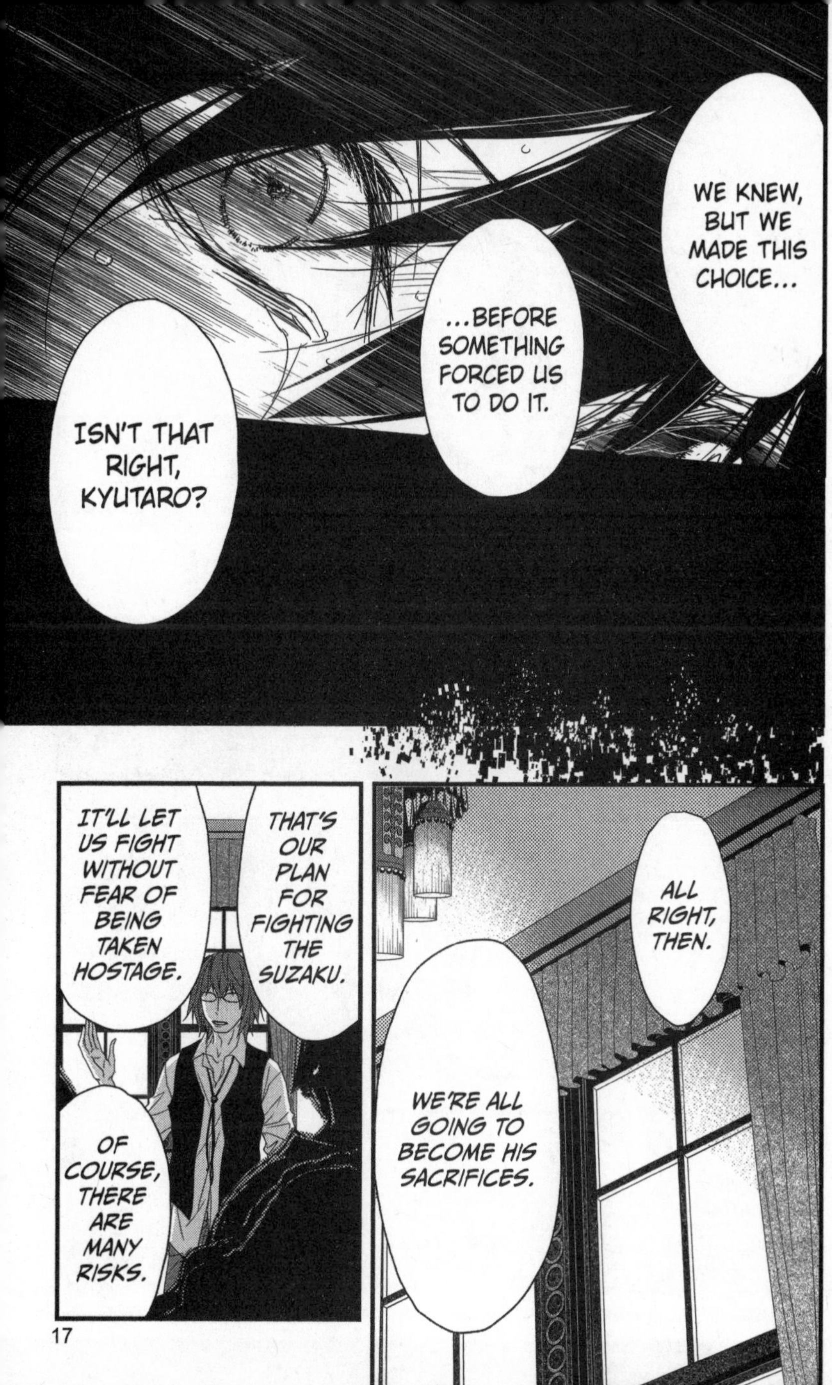
WE KNEW, BUT WE MADE THIS CHOICE...
...BEFORE SOMETHING FORCED US TO DO IT.
ISN'T THAT RIGHT, KYUTARO?
ALL RIGHT, THEN.
WE'RE ALL GOING TO BECOME HIS SACRIFICES.
THAT'S OUR PLAN FOR FIGHTING THE SUZAKU.
IT'LL LET US FIGHT WITHOUT FEAR OF BEING TAKEN HOSTAGE.
OF COURSE, THERE ARE MANY RISKS.

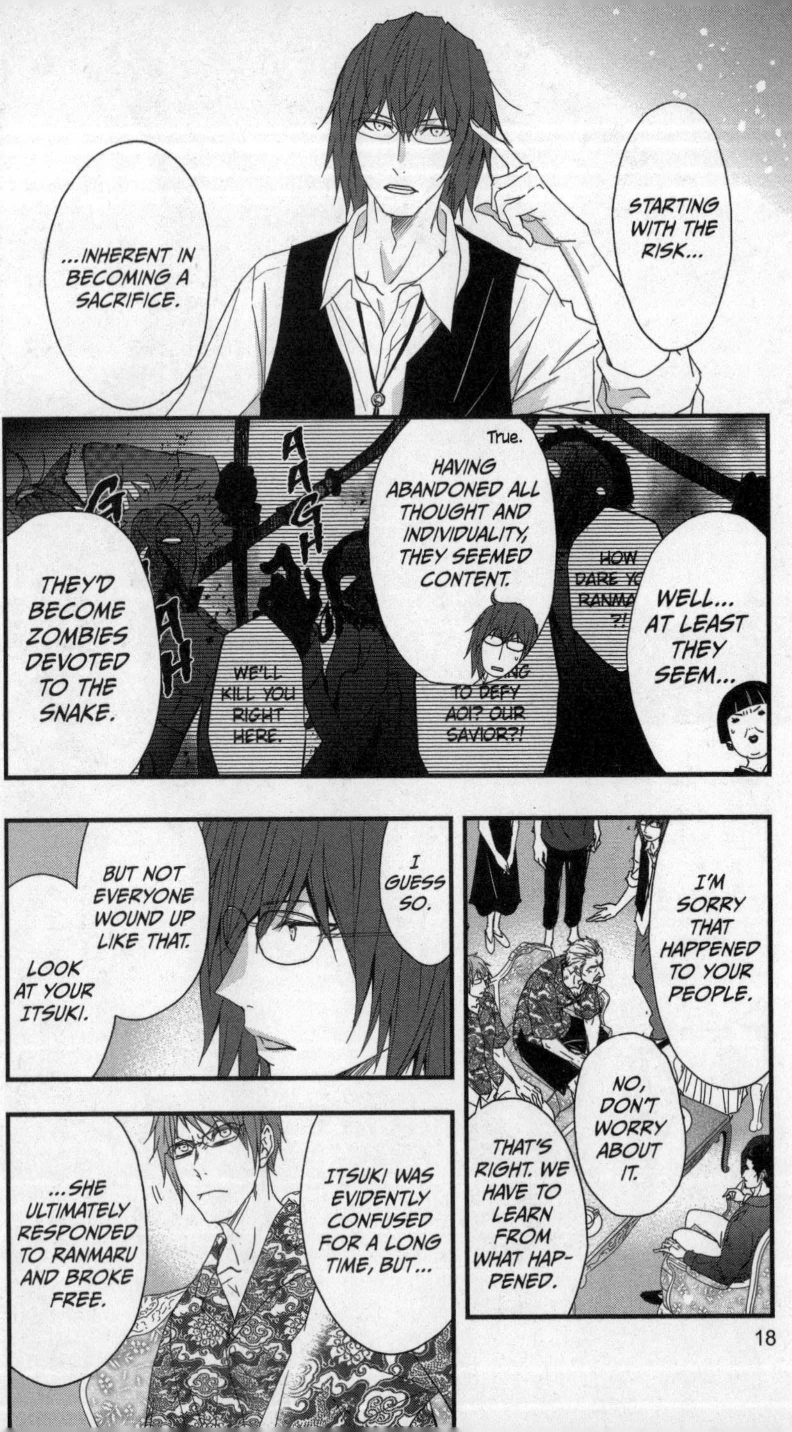
STARTING WITH THE RISK...
...INHERENT IN BECOMING A SACRIFICE.
WELL... AT LEAST THEY SEEM...
True.
HAVING ABANDONED ALL THOUGHT AND INDIVIDUALITY, THEY SEEMED CONTENT.
HOW
TO DEFY AOI? OUR SAVIOR?!
WE'LL KILL YOU RIGHT HERE.
AAGH
THEY'D BECOME ZOMBIES DEVOTED TO THE SNAKE.
I'M SORRY THAT HAPPENED TO YOUR PEOPLE.
NO, DON'T WORRY ABOUT IT.
THAT'S RIGHT. WE HAVE TO LEARN FROM WHAT HAPPENED.
I GUESS SO.
BUT NOT EVERYONE WOUND UP LIKE THAT.
LOOK AT YOUR ITSUKI.
ITSUKI WAS EVIDENTLY CONFUSED FOR A LONG TIME, BUT...
...SHE ULTIMATELY RESPONDED TO RANMARU AND BROKE FREE.

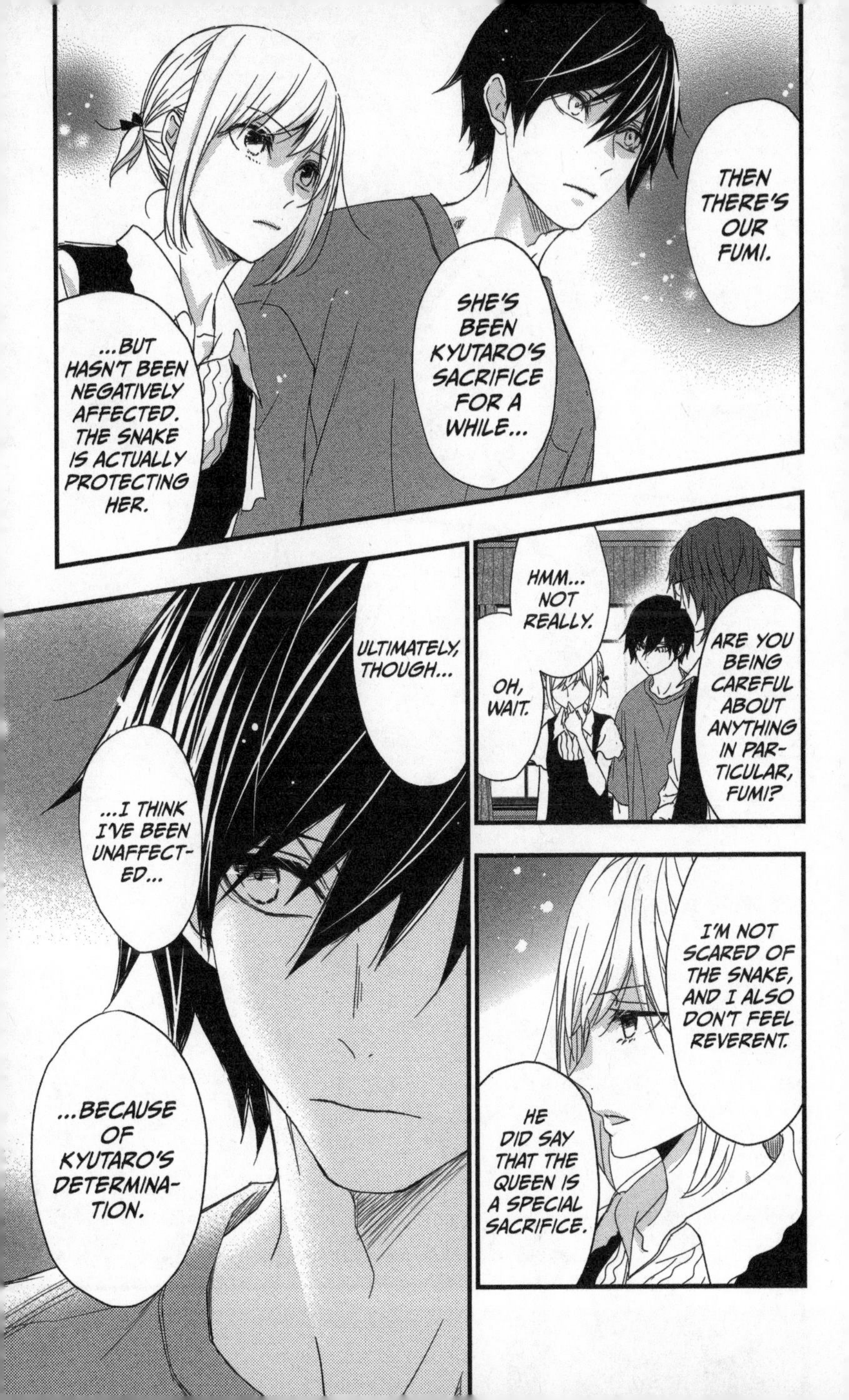
THEN THERE'S OUR FUMI.
SHE'S BEEN KYUTARO'S SACRIFICE FOR A WHILE...
...BUT HASN'T BEEN NEGATIVELY AFFECTED. THE SNAKE IS ACTUALLY PROTECTING HER.
ARE YOU BEING CAREFUL ABOUT ANYTHING IN PARTICULAR, FUMI?
HMM... NOT REALLY.
OH, WAIT.
I'M NOT SCARED OF THE SNAKE, AND I ALSO DON'T FEEL REVERENT.
HE DID SAY THAT THE QUEEN IS A SPECIAL SACRIFICE.
ULTIMATELY, THOUGH...
...I THINK I'VE BEEN UNAFFECTED...
...BECAUSE OF KYUTARO'S DETERMINATION.

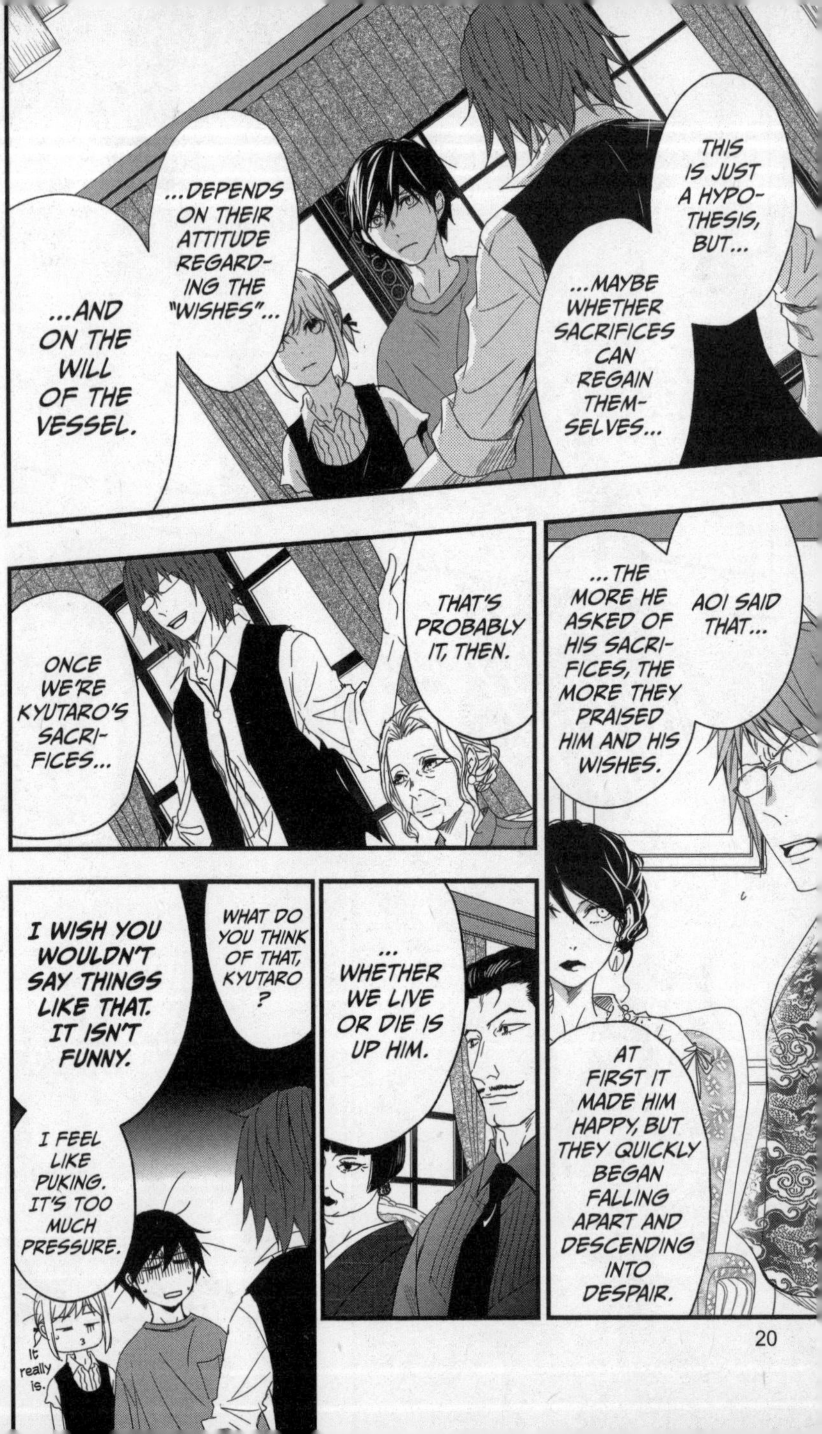
THIS IS JUST A HYPO-THESIS, BUT...
...MAYBE WHETHER SACRIFICES CAN REGAIN THEM-SELVES...
...DEPENDS ON THEIR ATTITUDE REGARD-ING THE "WISHES"...
...AND ON THE WILL OF THE VESSEL.
AOI SAID THAT...
...THE MORE HE ASKED OF HIS SACRI-FICES, THE MORE THEY PRAISED HIM AND HIS WISHES.
AT FIRST IT MADE HIM HAPPY, BUT THEY QUICKLY BEGAN FALLING APART AND DESCENDING INTO DESPAIR.
THAT'S PROBABLY IT, THEN.
ONCE WE'RE KYUTARO'S SACRI-FICES...
... WHETHER WE LIVE OR DIE IS UP HIM.
WHAT DO YOU THINK OF THAT, KYUTARO ?
I WISH YOU WOULDN'T SAY THINGS LIKE THAT. IT ISN'T FUNNY.
I FEEL LIKE PUKING. IT'S TOO MUCH PRESSURE.
It really is.

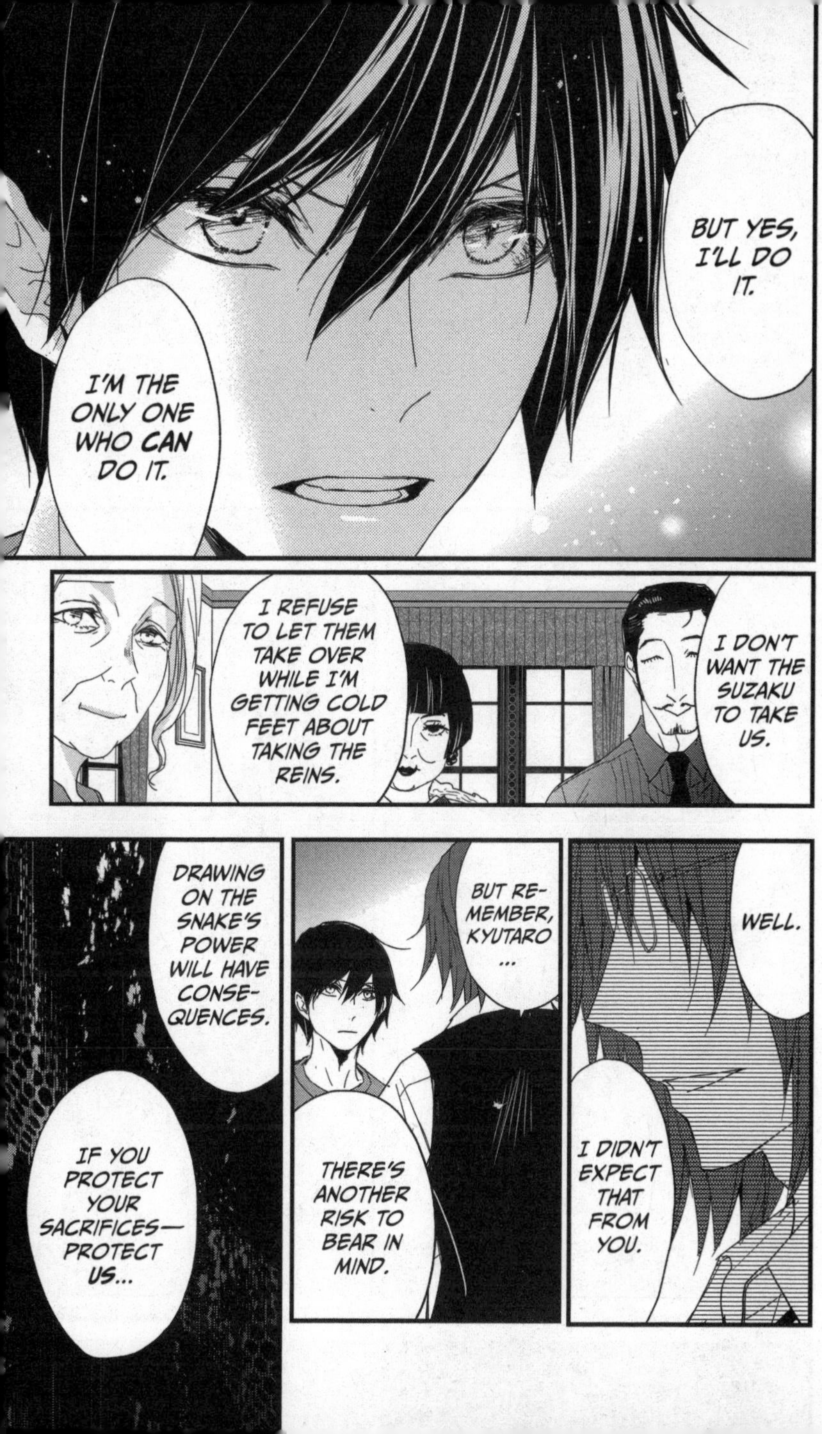
BUT YES, I'LL DO IT.
I'M THE ONLY ONE WHO CAN DO IT.
I DON'T WANT THE SUZAKU TO TAKE US.
I REFUSE TO LET THEM TAKE OVER WHILE I'M GETTING COLD FEET ABOUT TAKING THE REINS.
WELL.
I DIDN'T EXPECT THAT FROM YOU.
BUT RE-MEMBER, KYUTARO...
THERE'S ANOTHER RISK TO BEAR IN MIND.
DRAWING ON THE SNAKE'S POWER WILL HAVE CONSE-QUENCES.
IF YOU PROTECT YOUR SACRIFICES—PROTECT US...

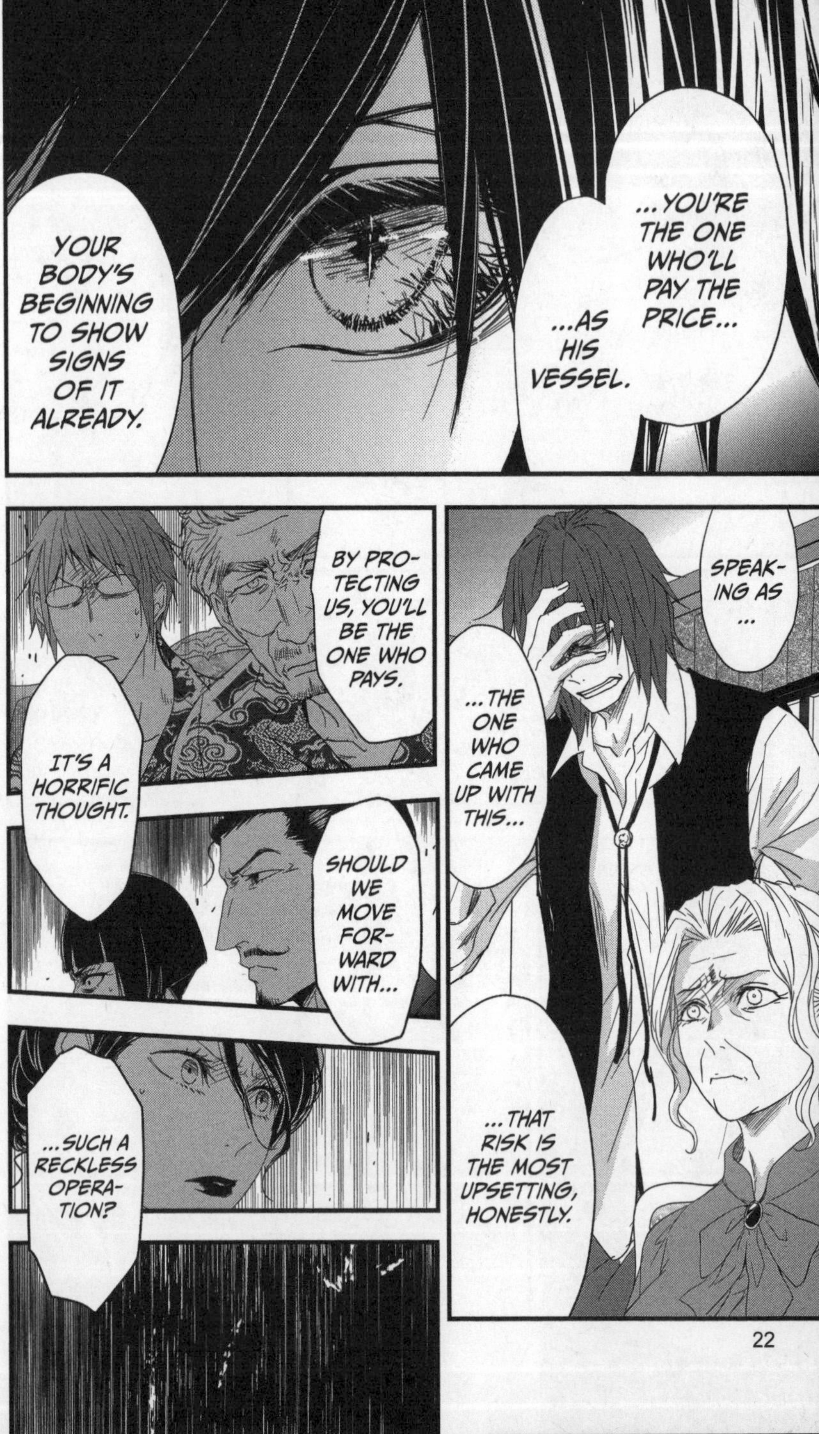
...YOU'RE THE ONE WHO'LL PAY THE PRICE...
...AS HIS VESSEL.
YOUR BODY'S BEGINNING TO SHOW SIGNS OF IT ALREADY.
SPEAK-ING AS ...
...THE ONE WHO CAME UP WITH THIS...
...THAT RISK IS THE MOST UPSETTING, HONESTLY.
BY PRO-TECTING US, YOU'LL BE THE ONE WHO PAYS.
IT'S A HORRIFIC THOUGHT.
SHOULD WE MOVE FOR-WARD WITH...
...SUCH A RECKLESS OPERA-TION?

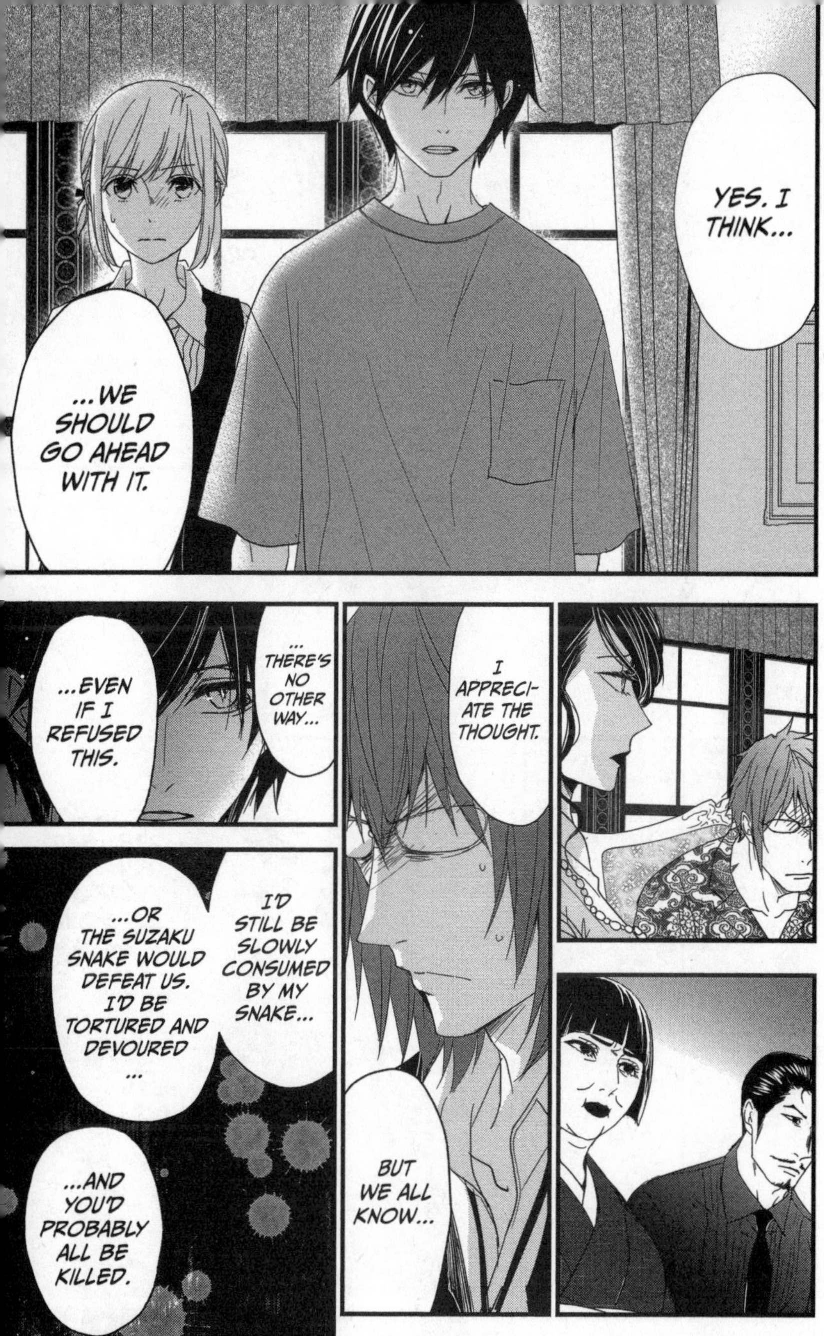
YES. I THINK...
...WE SHOULD GO AHEAD WITH IT.
I APPRECIATE THE THOUGHT.
BUT WE ALL KNOW...
...THERE'S NO OTHER WAY...
...EVEN IF I REFUSED THIS.
I'D STILL BE SLOWLY CONSUMED BY MY SNAKE...
...OR THE SUZAKU SNAKE WOULD DEFEAT US. I'D BE TORTURED AND DEVOURED...
...AND YOU'D PROBABLY ALL BE KILLED.

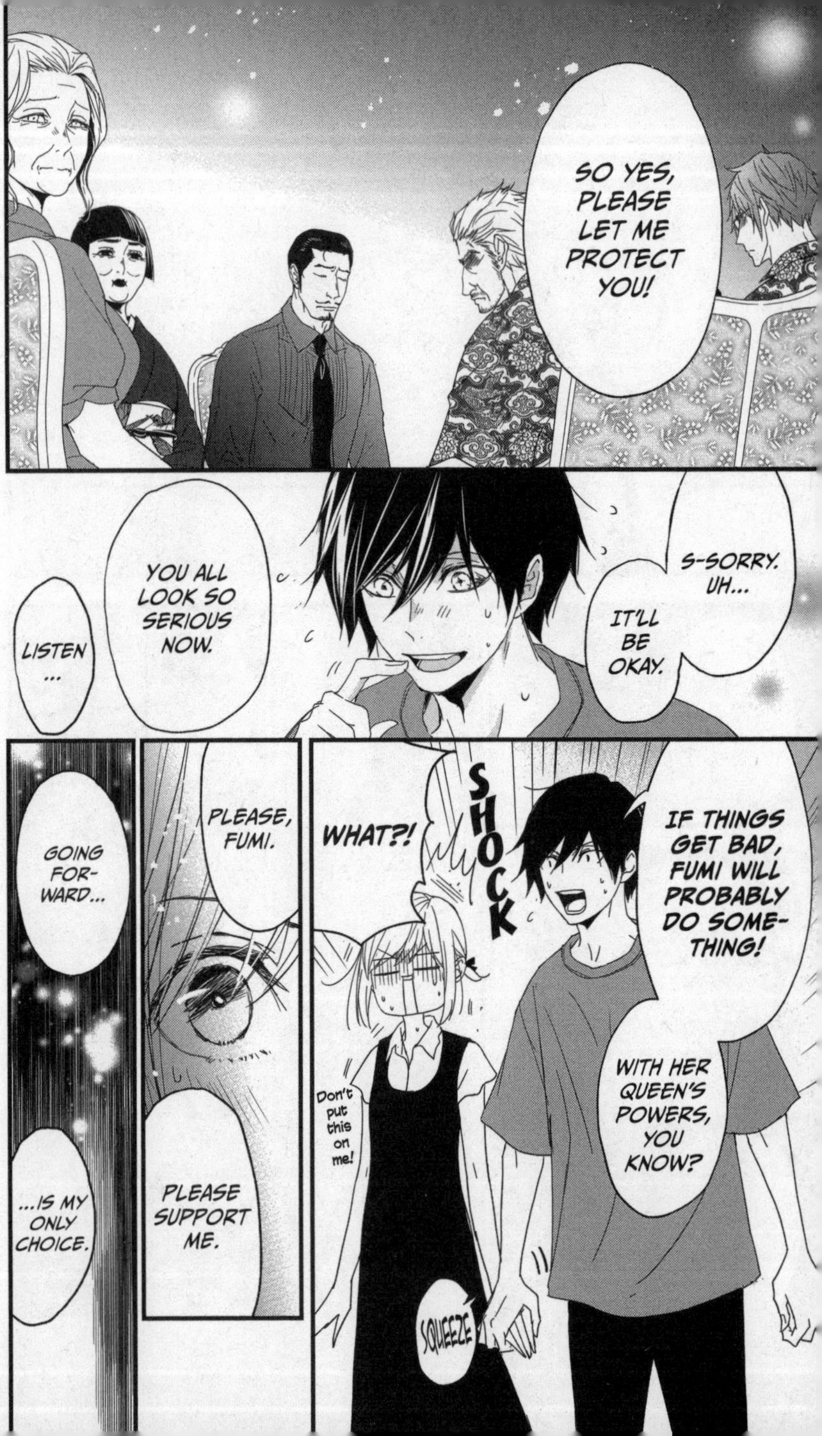
SO YES, PLEASE LET ME PROTECT YOU!
S-SORRY. UH...
IT'LL BE OKAY.
YOU ALL LOOK SO SERIOUS NOW.
LISTEN...
IF THINGS GET BAD, FUMI WILL PROBABLY DO SOME-THING!
SHOCK
WHAT?!
WITH HER QUEEN'S POWERS, YOU KNOW?
Don't put this on me!
SQUEEZE
PLEASE, FUMI.
PLEASE SUPPORT ME.
GOING FOR-WARD...
...IS MY ONLY CHOICE.

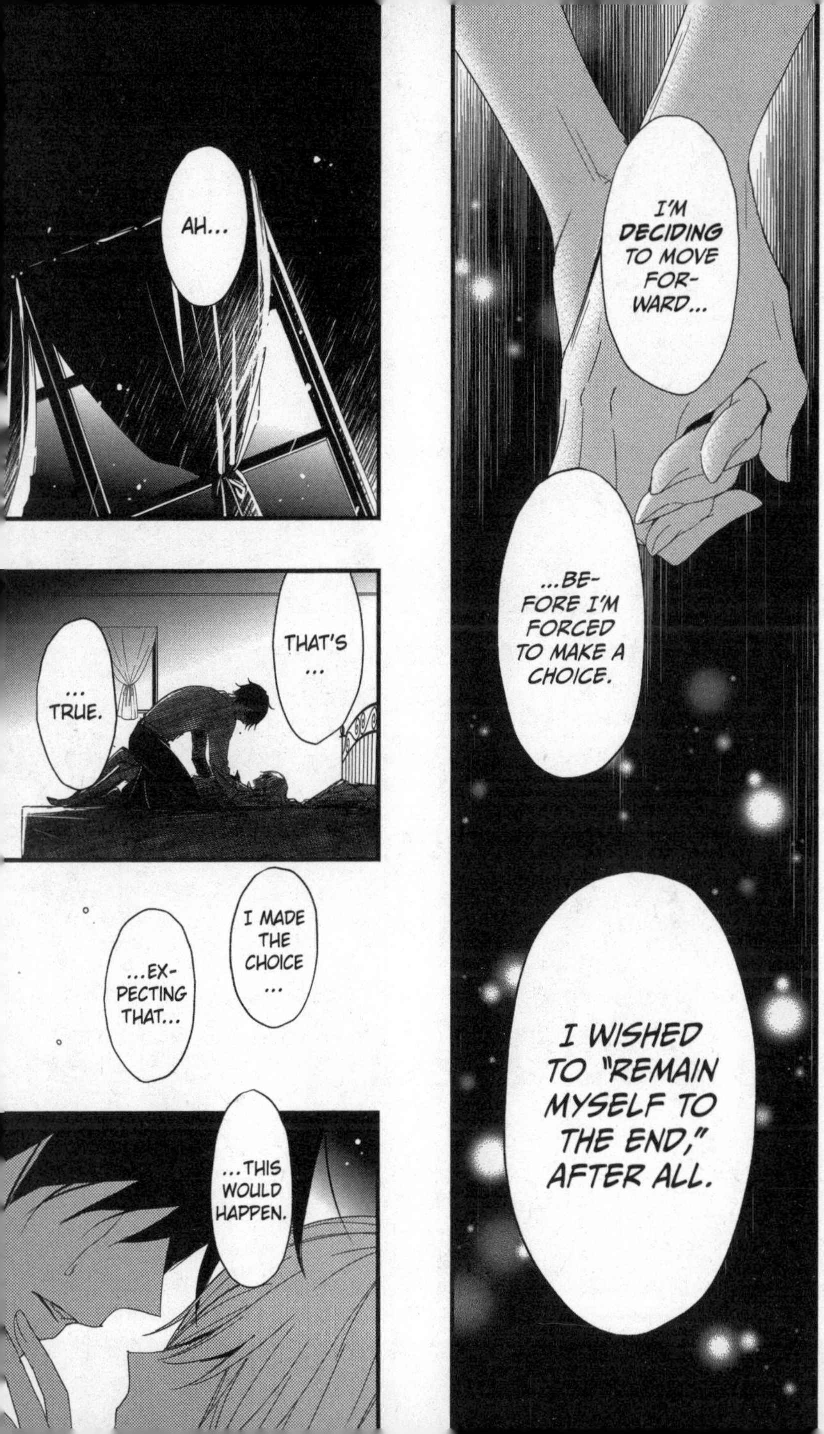
I'M DECIDING TO MOVE FOR-WARD...
...BE-FORE I'M FORCED TO MAKE A CHOICE.
I WISHED TO "REMAIN MYSELF TO THE END," AFTER ALL.
AH...
THAT'S ...
... TRUE.
I MADE THE CHOICE ...
...EX-PECTING THAT...
...THIS WOULD HAPPEN.

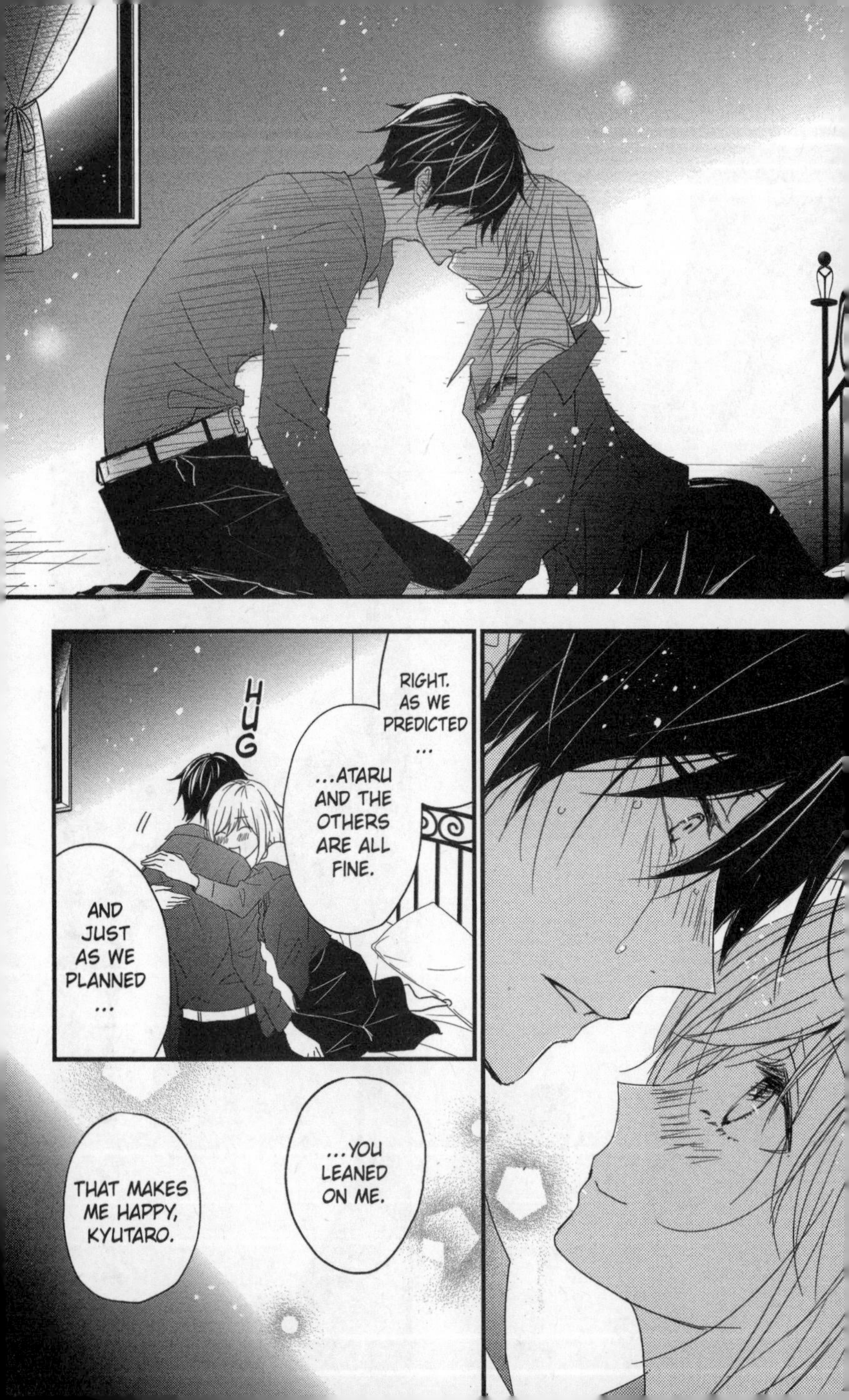
RIGHT. AS WE PREDICTED ...
...ATARU AND THE OTHERS ARE ALL FINE.
HUG
AND JUST AS WE PLANNED ...
...YOU LEANED ON ME.
THAT MAKES ME HAPPY, KYUTARO.

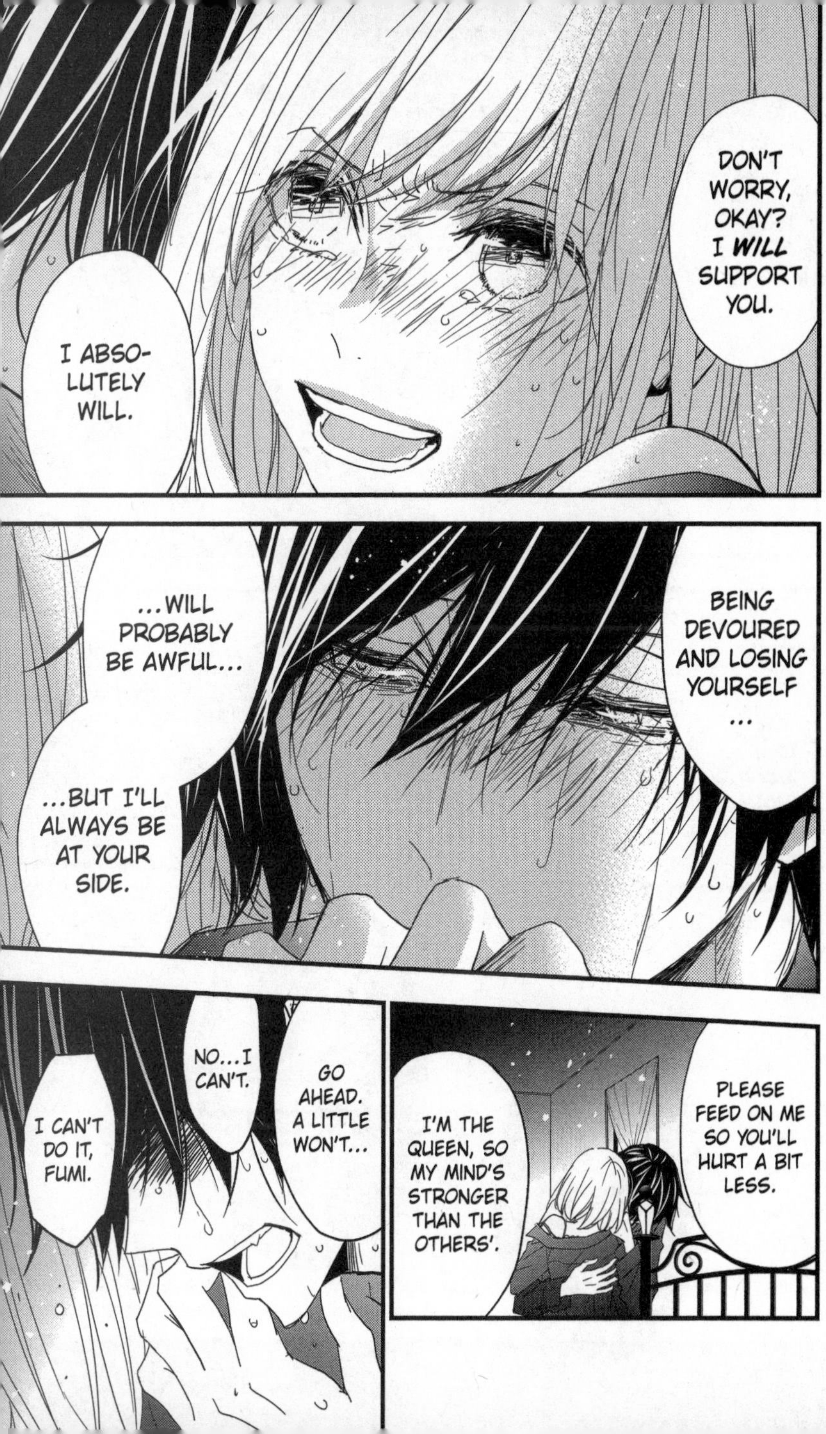
DON'T WORRY, OKAY? I WILL SUPPORT YOU.
I ABSOLUTELY WILL.
BEING DEVOURED AND LOSING YOURSELF ...
...WILL PROBABLY BE AWFUL...
...BUT I'LL ALWAYS BE AT YOUR SIDE.
PLEASE FEED ON ME SO YOU'LL HURT A BIT LESS.
I'M THE QUEEN, SO MY MIND'S STRONGER THAN THE OTHERS'.
GO AHEAD. A LITTLE WON'T...
NO...I CAN'T.
I CAN'T DO IT, FUMI.

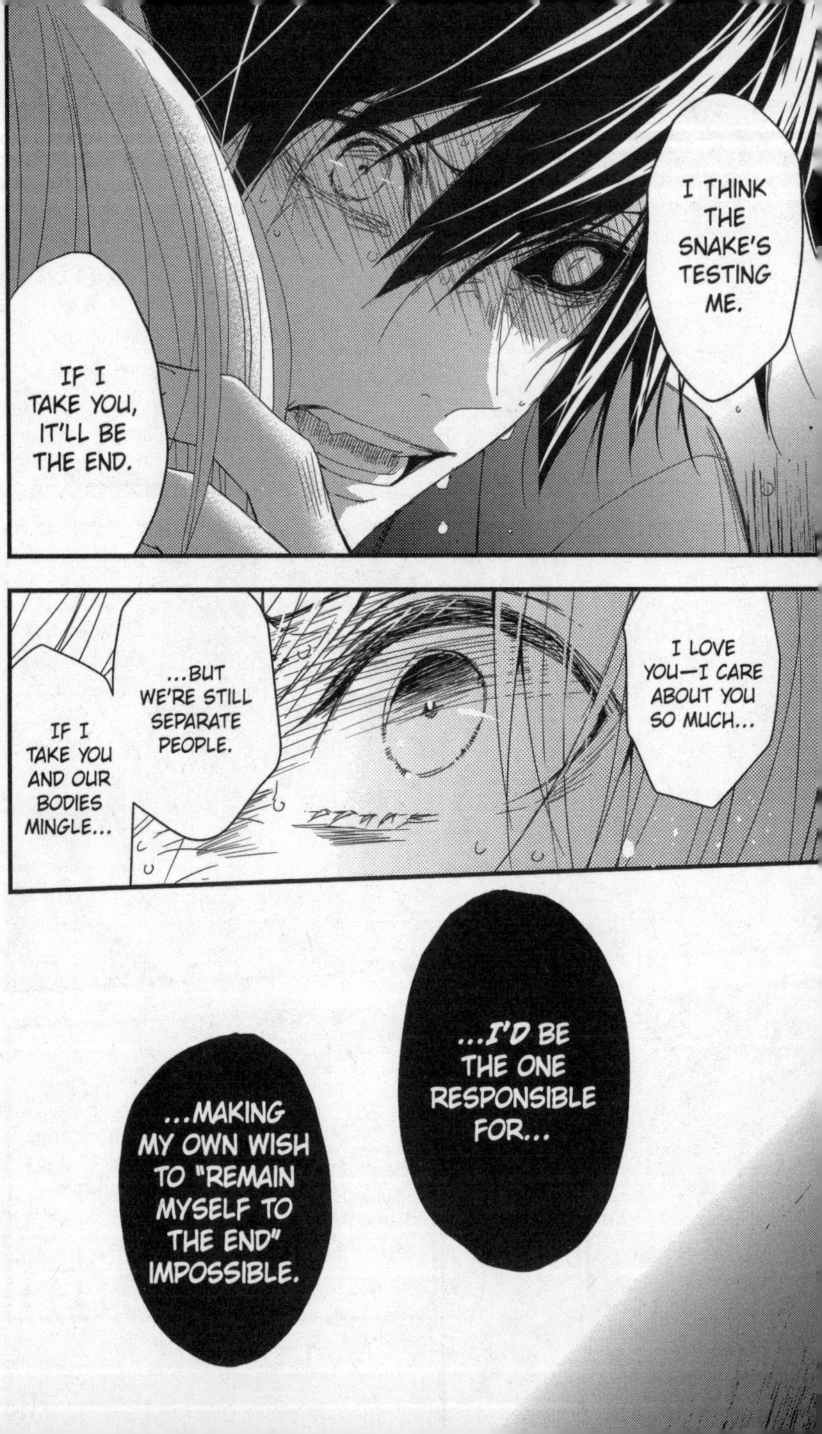
I THINK THE SNAKE'S TESTING ME.
IF I TAKE YOU, IT'LL BE THE END.
I LOVE YOU—I CARE ABOUT YOU SO MUCH...
...BUT WE'RE STILL SEPARATE PEOPLE.
IF I TAKE YOU AND OUR BODIES MINGLE...
...*I'D* BE THE ONE RESPONSIBLE FOR...
...MAKING MY OWN WISH TO "REMAIN MYSELF TO THE END" IMPOSSIBLE.

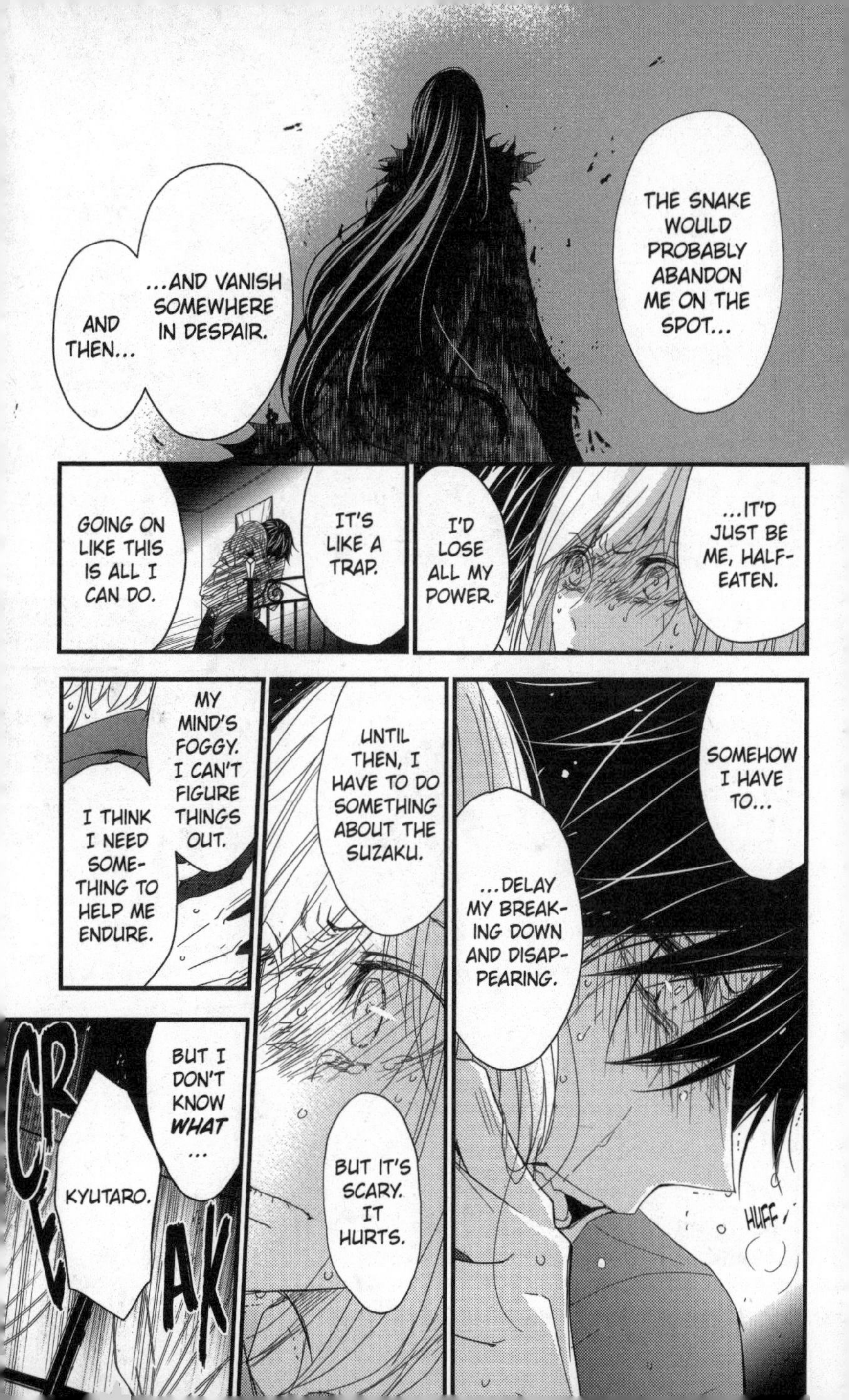
THE SNAKE WOULD PROBABLY ABANDON ME ON THE SPOT...
...AND VANISH SOMEWHERE IN DESPAIR.
AND THEN...
...IT'D JUST BE ME, HALF-EATEN.
I'D LOSE ALL MY POWER.
IT'S LIKE A TRAP.
GOING ON LIKE THIS IS ALL I CAN DO.
SOMEHOW I HAVE TO...
...DELAY MY BREAKING DOWN AND DISAPPEARING.
HUFF
UNTIL THEN, I HAVE TO DO SOMETHING ABOUT THE SUZAKU.
BUT IT'S SCARY. IT HURTS.
MY MIND'S FOGGY. I CAN'T FIGURE THINGS OUT.
I THINK I NEED SOMETHING TO HELP ME ENDURE.
BUT I DON'T KNOW ***WHAT***...
KYUTARO.
CREAK

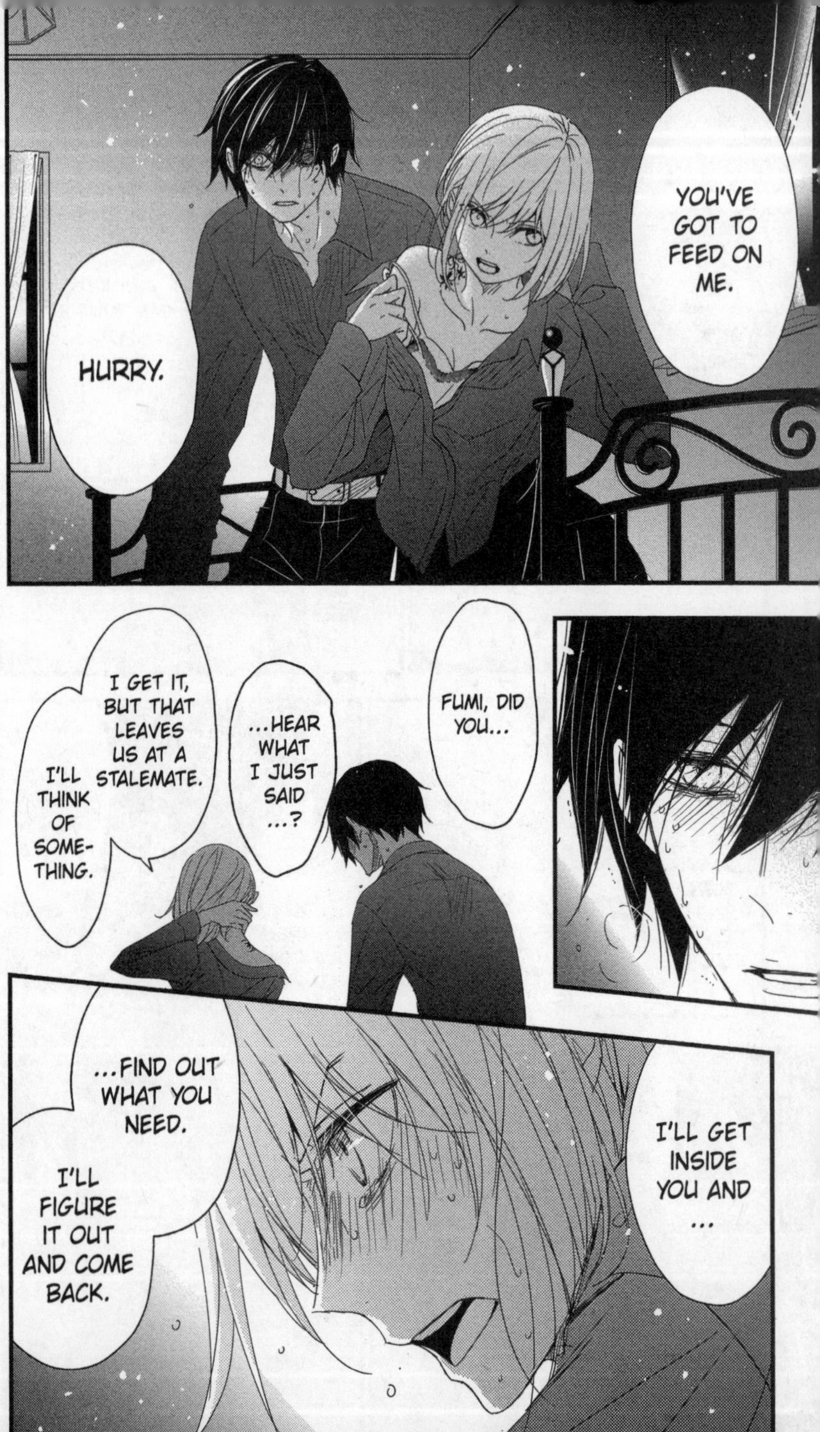
YOU'VE GOT TO FEED ON ME.
HURRY.
FUMI, DID YOU...
...HEAR WHAT I JUST SAID ...?
I GET IT, BUT THAT LEAVES US AT A STALEMATE.
I'LL THINK OF SOME-THING.
I'LL GET INSIDE YOU AND ...
...FIND OUT WHAT YOU NEED.
I'LL FIGURE IT OUT AND COME BACK.

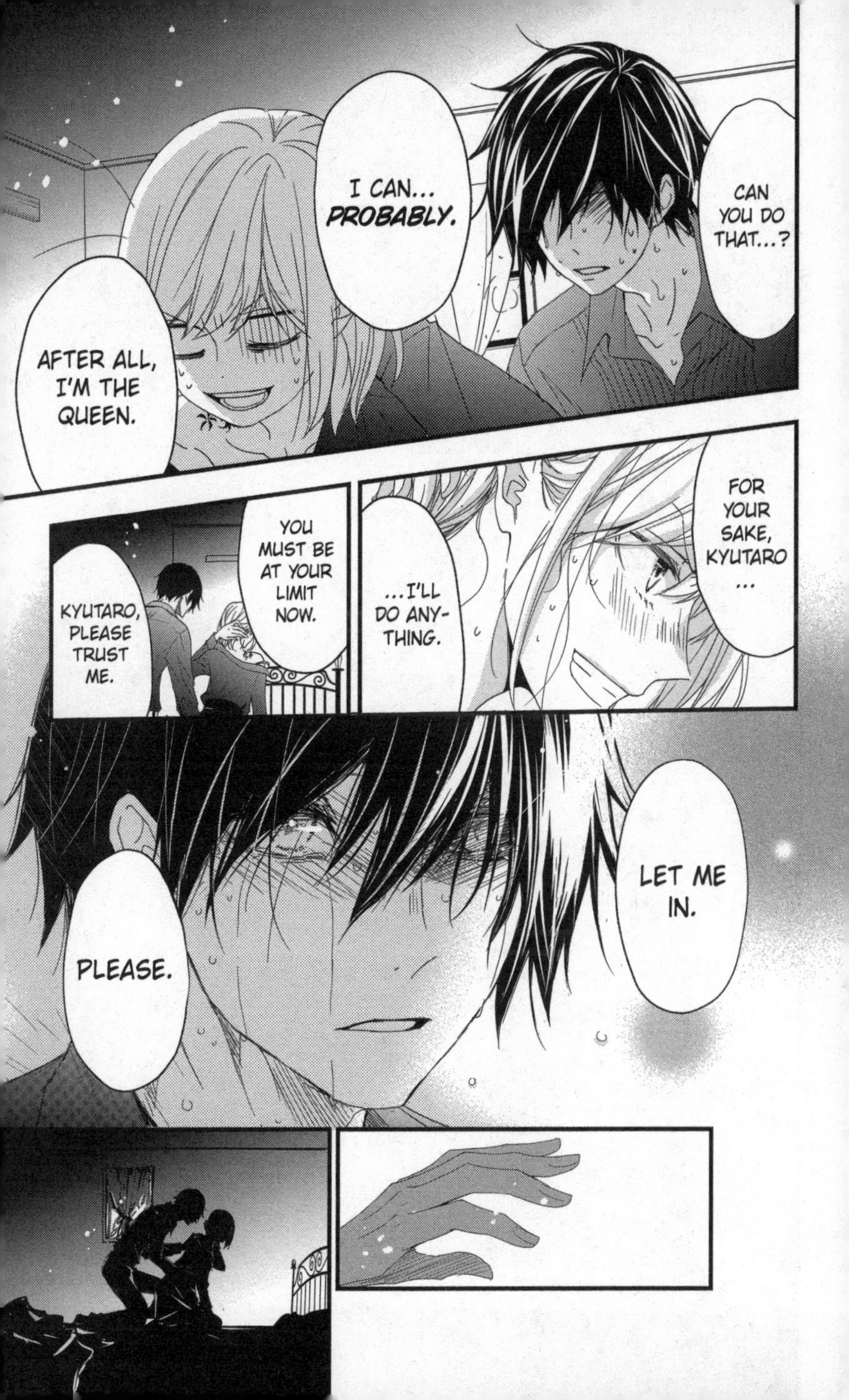
CAN YOU DO THAT...?
I CAN... *PROBABLY.*
AFTER ALL, I'M THE QUEEN.
FOR YOUR SAKE, KYUTARO...
...I'LL DO ANY-THING.
YOU MUST BE AT YOUR LIMIT NOW.
KYUTARO, PLEASE TRUST ME.
LET ME IN.
PLEASE.

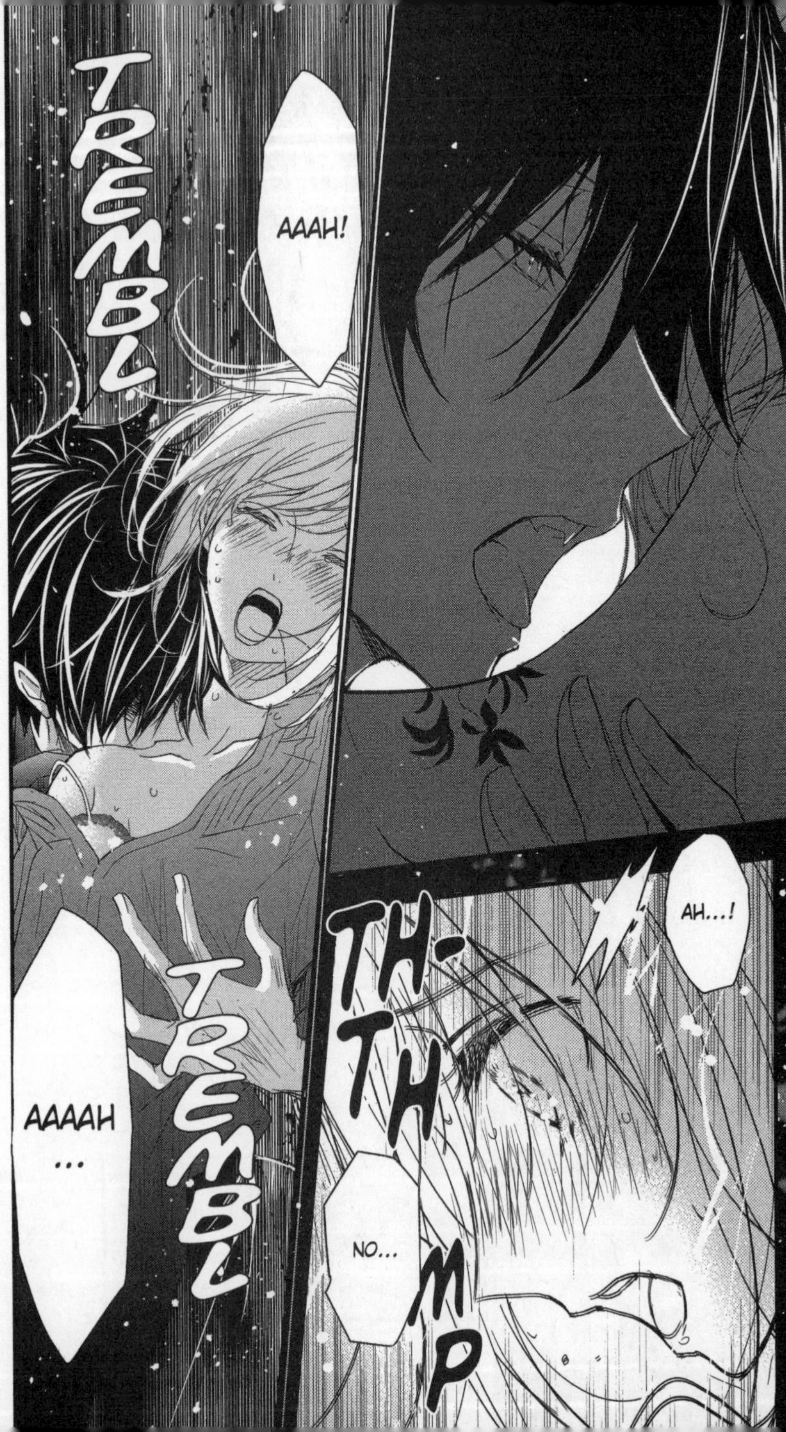
AH...!
TH-TH
NO...
MP
TREMBL
AAAH!
AAAAH ...
TREMBL

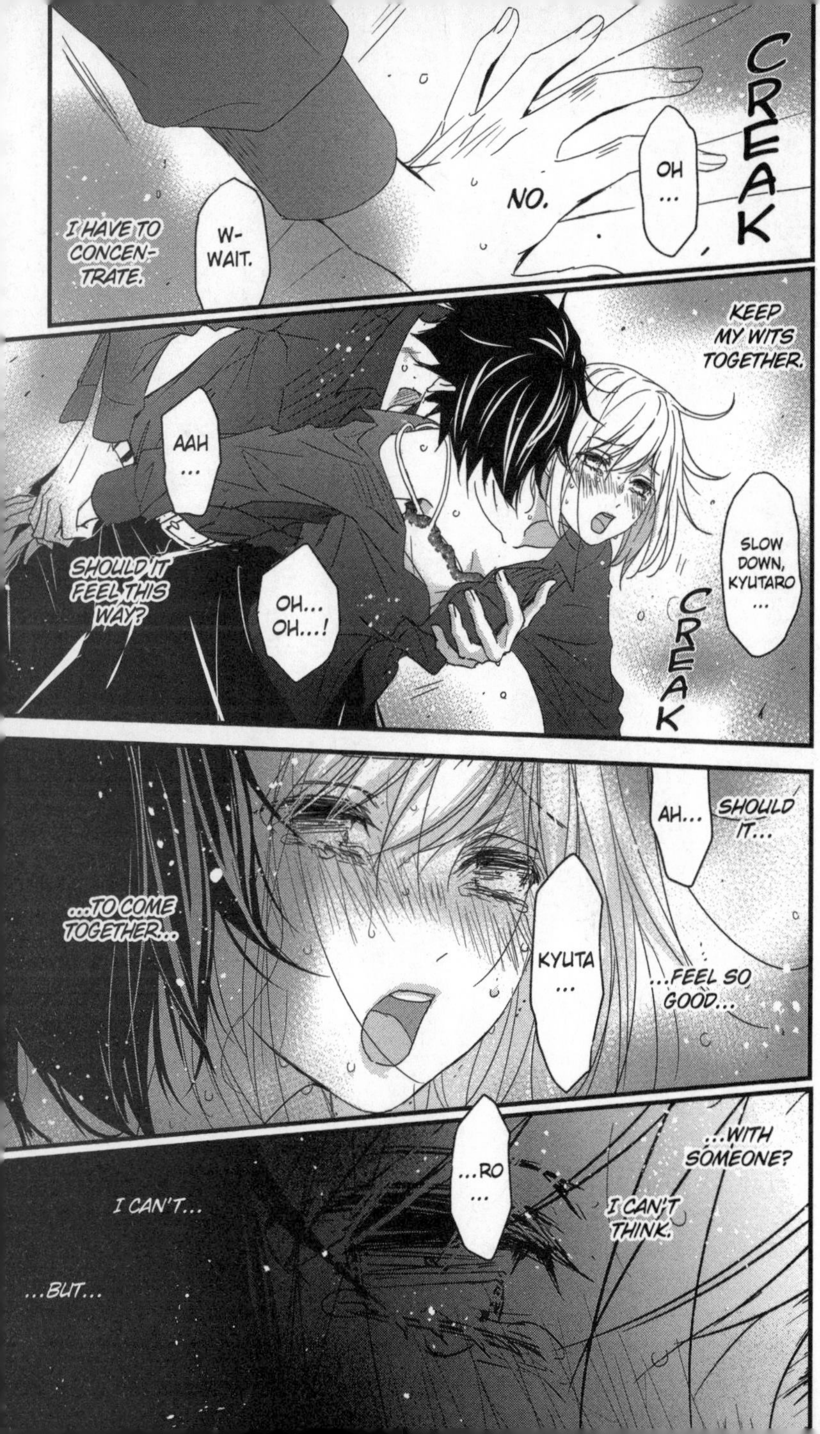
CREAK
OH ...
NO.
W-WAIT.
I HAVE TO CONCENTRATE.
KEEP MY WITS TOGETHER.
SLOW DOWN, KYUTARO ...
CREAK
AAH ...
OH... OH...!
SHOULD IT FEEL THIS WAY?
SHOULD IT...
AH...
...FEEL SO GOOD...
KYUTA ...
...TO COME TOGETHER...
...WITH SOMEONE?
...RO ...
I CAN'T THINK.
I CAN'T...
...BUT...

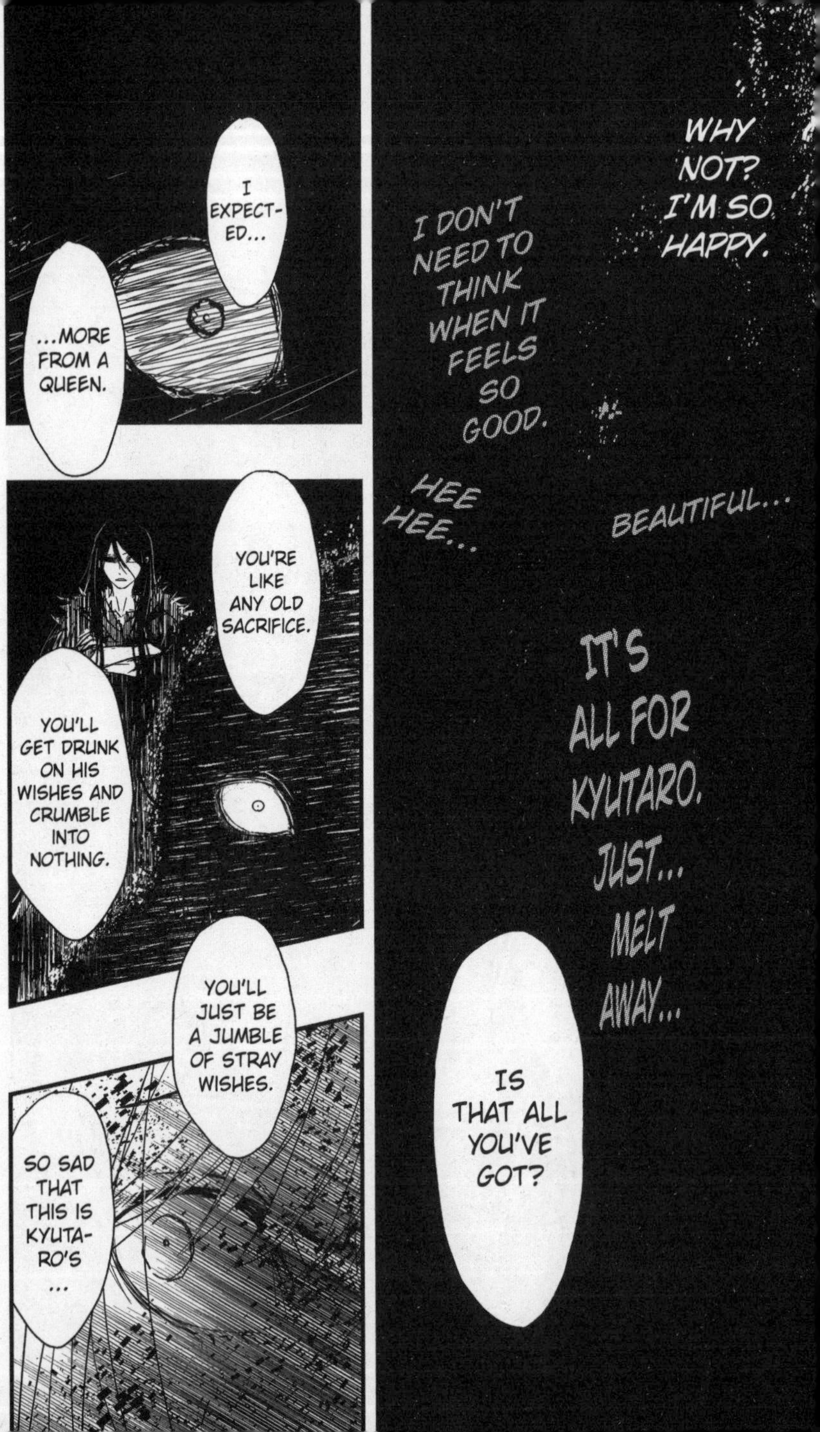
WHY NOT? I'M SO HAPPY.
I DON'T NEED TO THINK WHEN IT FEELS SO GOOD.
BEAUTIFUL...
HEE HEE...
IT'S ALL FOR KYUTARO. JUST... MELT AWAY...
IS THAT ALL YOU'VE GOT?
I EXPECTED...
...MORE FROM A QUEEN.
YOU'RE LIKE ANY OLD SACRIFICE.
YOU'LL GET DRUNK ON HIS WISHES AND CRUMBLE INTO NOTHING.
YOU'LL JUST BE A JUMBLE OF STRAY WISHES.
SO SAD THAT THIS IS KYUTARO'S ...

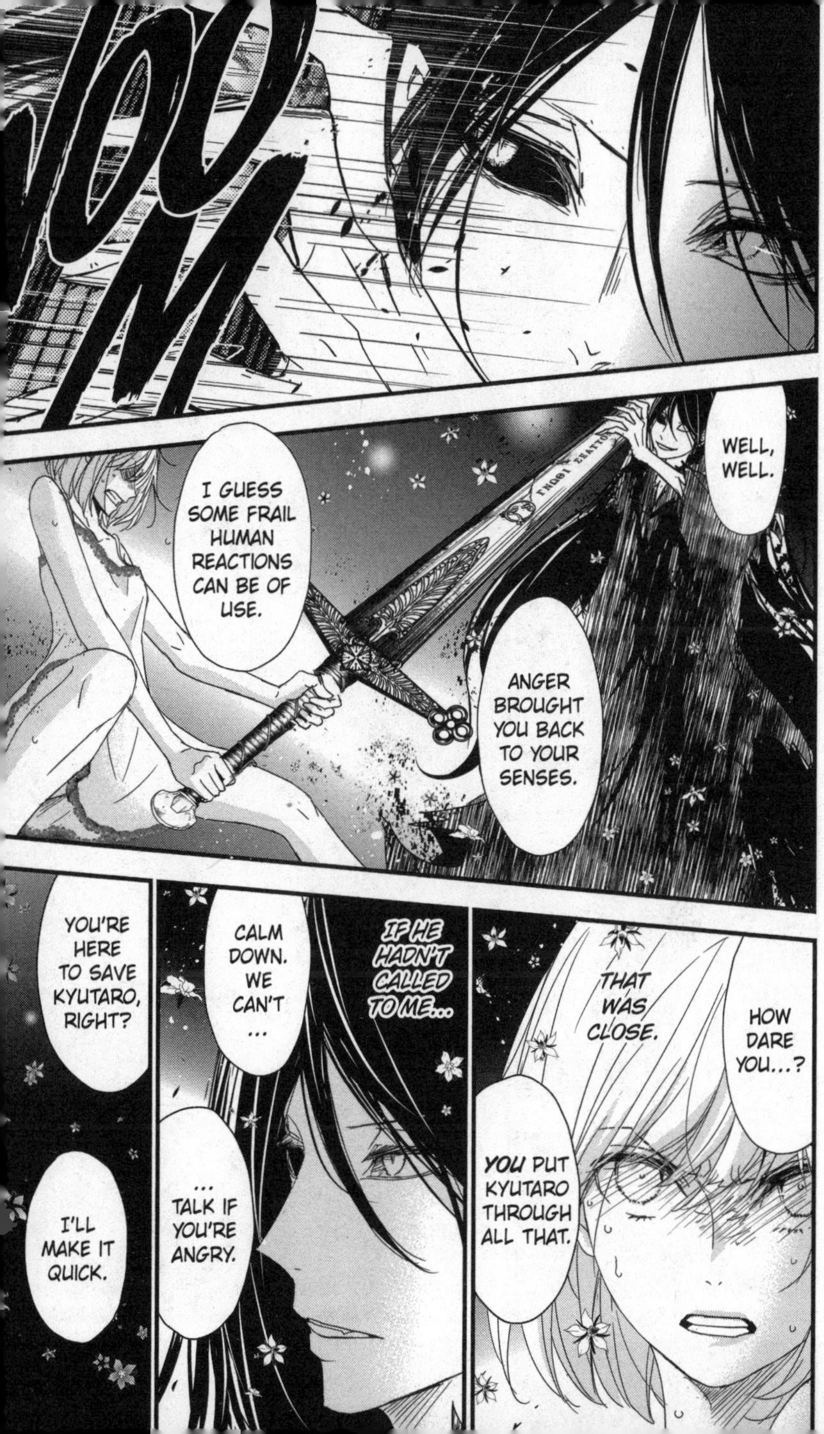
WELL, WELL.
ANGER BROUGHT YOU BACK TO YOUR SENSES.
I GUESS SOME FRAIL HUMAN REACTIONS CAN BE OF USE.
HOW DARE YOU...?
THAT WAS CLOSE.
YOU PUT KYUTARO THROUGH ALL THAT.
IF HE HADN'T CALLED TO ME...
CALM DOWN. WE CAN'T ...
... TALK IF YOU'RE ANGRY.
YOU'RE HERE TO SAVE KYUTARO, RIGHT?
I'LL MAKE IT QUICK.

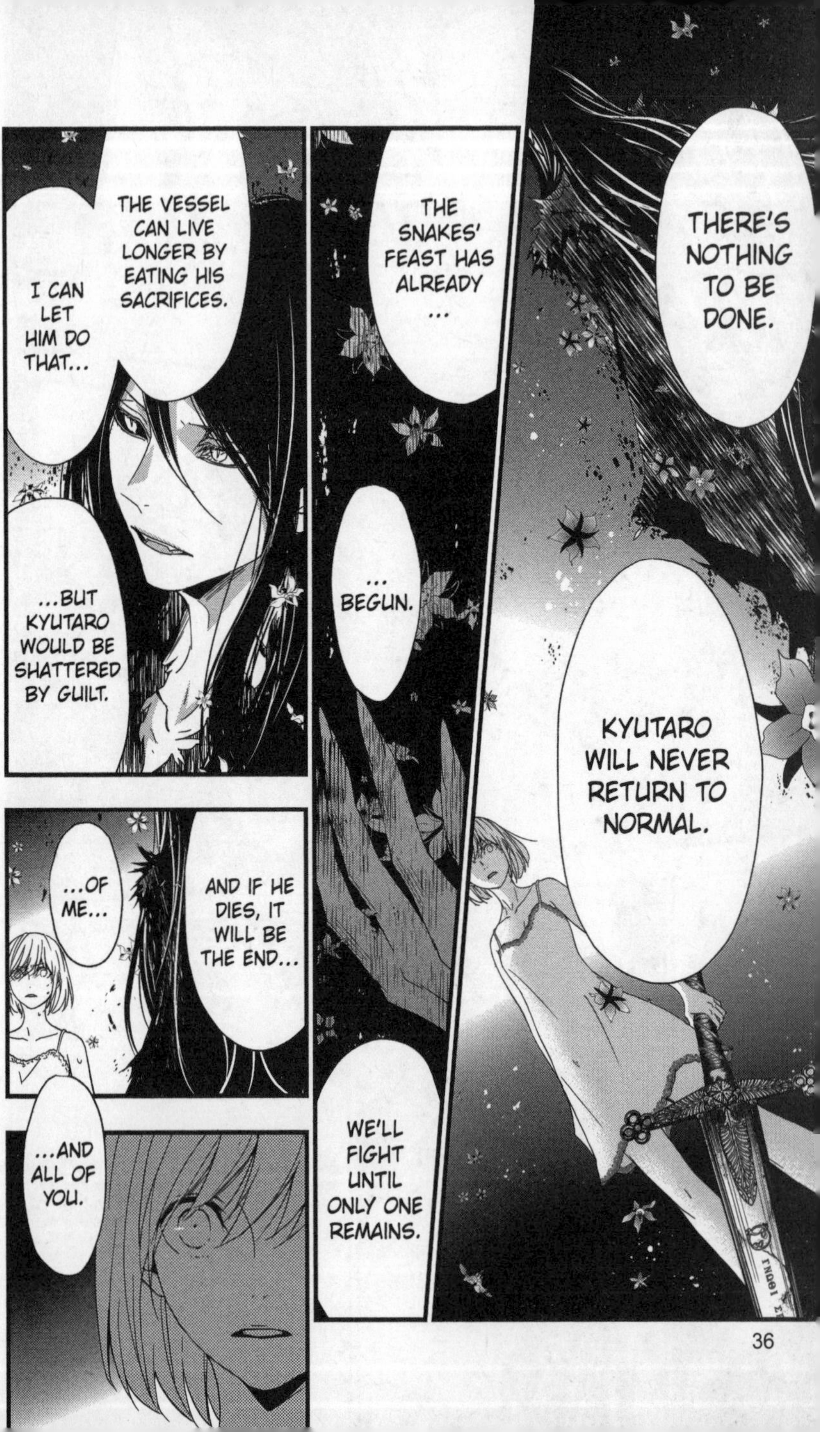
THERE'S NOTHING TO BE DONE.
KYUTARO WILL NEVER RETURN TO NORMAL.
THE SNAKES' FEAST HAS ALREADY ...
... BEGUN.
WE'LL FIGHT UNTIL ONLY ONE REMAINS.
THE VESSEL CAN LIVE LONGER BY EATING HIS SACRIFICES.
I CAN LET HIM DO THAT...
...BUT KYUTARO WOULD BE SHATTERED BY GUILT.
AND IF HE DIES, IT WILL BE THE END...
...OF ME...
...AND ALL OF YOU.

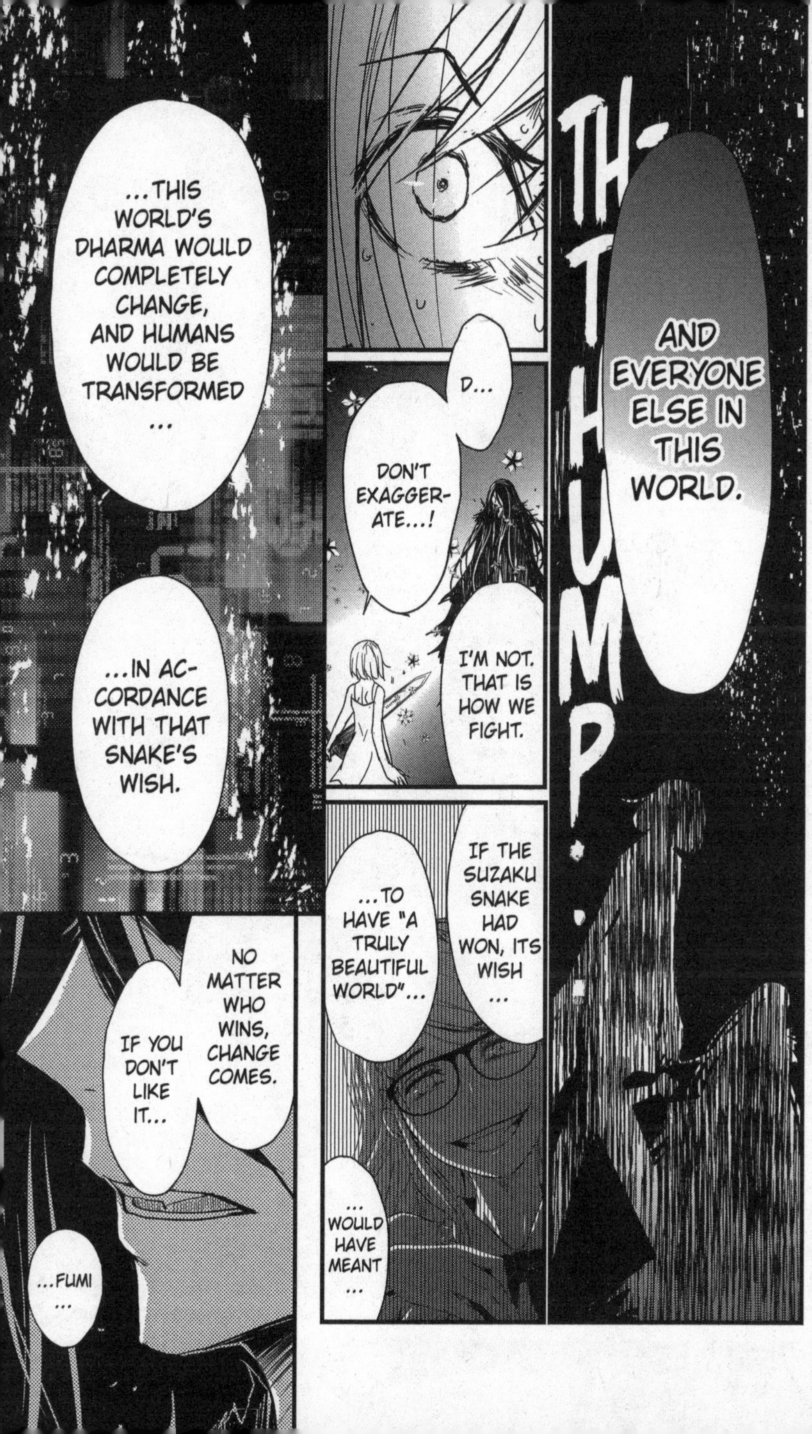
TH-THUMP
AND EVERYONE ELSE IN THIS WORLD.
D...
DON'T EXAGGERATE...!
I'M NOT. THAT IS HOW WE FIGHT.
IF THE SUZAKU SNAKE HAD WON, ITS WISH...
...TO HAVE "A TRULY BEAUTIFUL WORLD"...
...WOULD HAVE MEANT...
...THIS WORLD'S DHARMA WOULD COMPLETELY CHANGE, AND HUMANS WOULD BE TRANSFORMED...
...IN ACCORDANCE WITH THAT SNAKE'S WISH.
NO MATTER WHO WINS, CHANGE COMES.
IF YOU DON'T LIKE IT...
...FUMI...

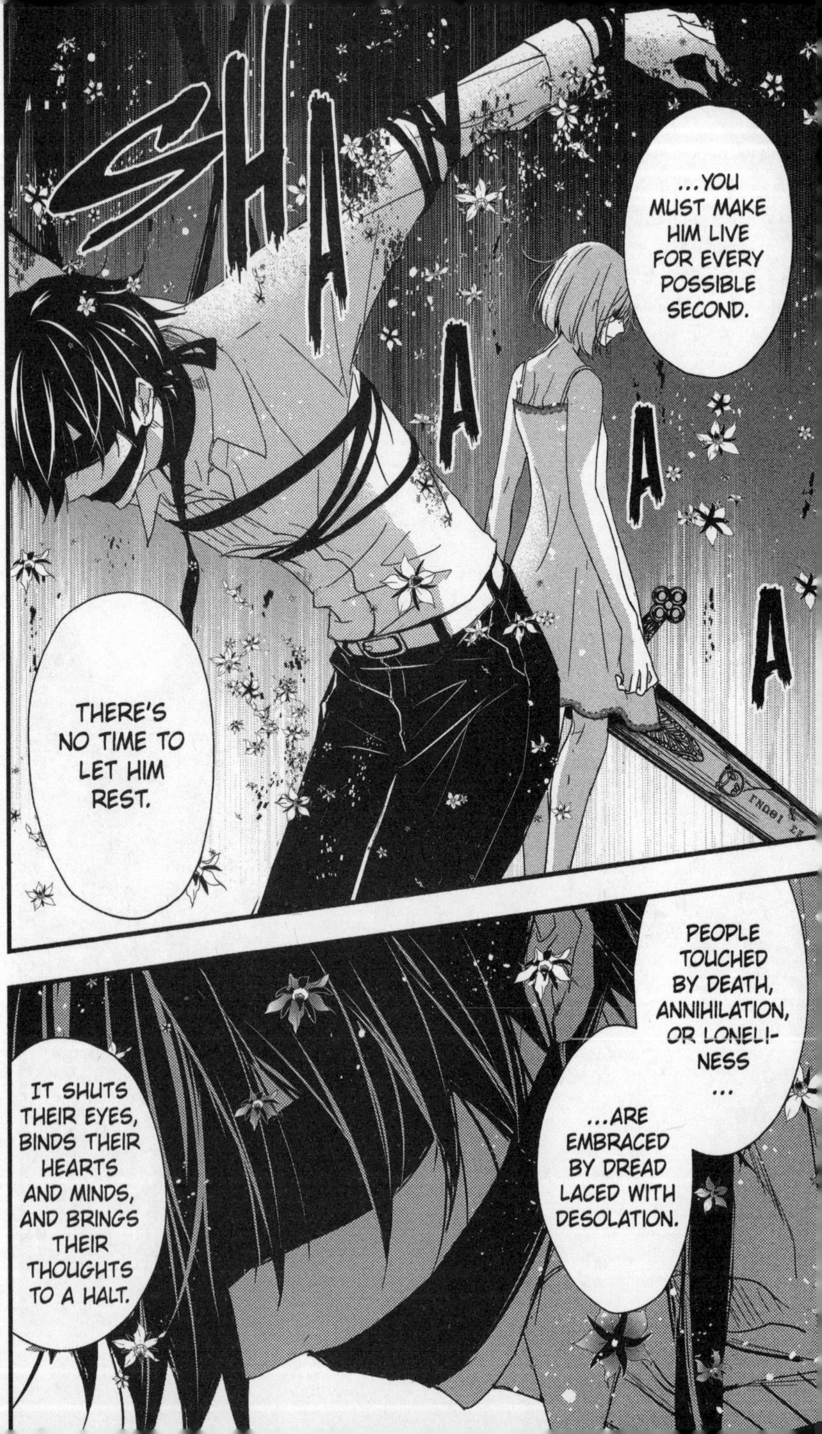
...YOU MUST MAKE HIM LIVE FOR EVERY POSSIBLE SECOND.
SHAAAA
THERE'S NO TIME TO LET HIM REST.
PEOPLE TOUCHED BY DEATH, ANNIHILATION, OR LONELI-NESS...
...ARE EMBRACED BY DREAD LACED WITH DESOLATION.
IT SHUTS THEIR EYES, BINDS THEIR HEARTS AND MINDS, AND BRINGS THEIR THOUGHTS TO A HALT.

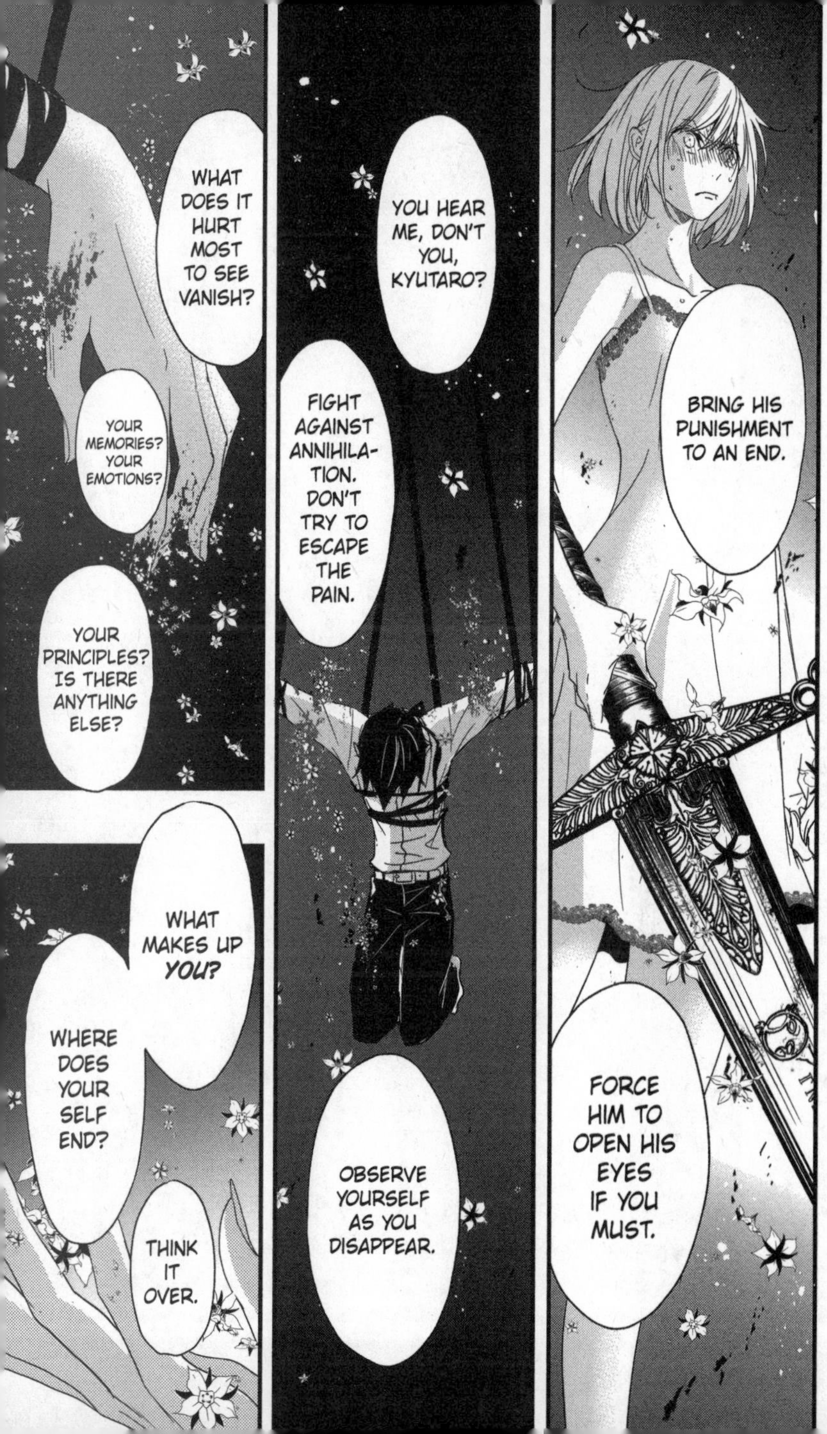
BRING HIS PUNISHMENT TO AN END.
FORCE HIM TO OPEN HIS EYES IF YOU MUST.
YOU HEAR ME, DON'T YOU, KYUTARO?
FIGHT AGAINST ANNIHILATION. DON'T TRY TO ESCAPE THE PAIN.
OBSERVE YOURSELF AS YOU DISAPPEAR.
WHAT DOES IT HURT MOST TO SEE VANISH?
YOUR MEMORIES? YOUR EMOTIONS?
YOUR PRINCIPLES? IS THERE ANYTHING ELSE?
WHAT MAKES UP *YOU?*
WHERE DOES YOUR SELF END?
THINK IT OVER.

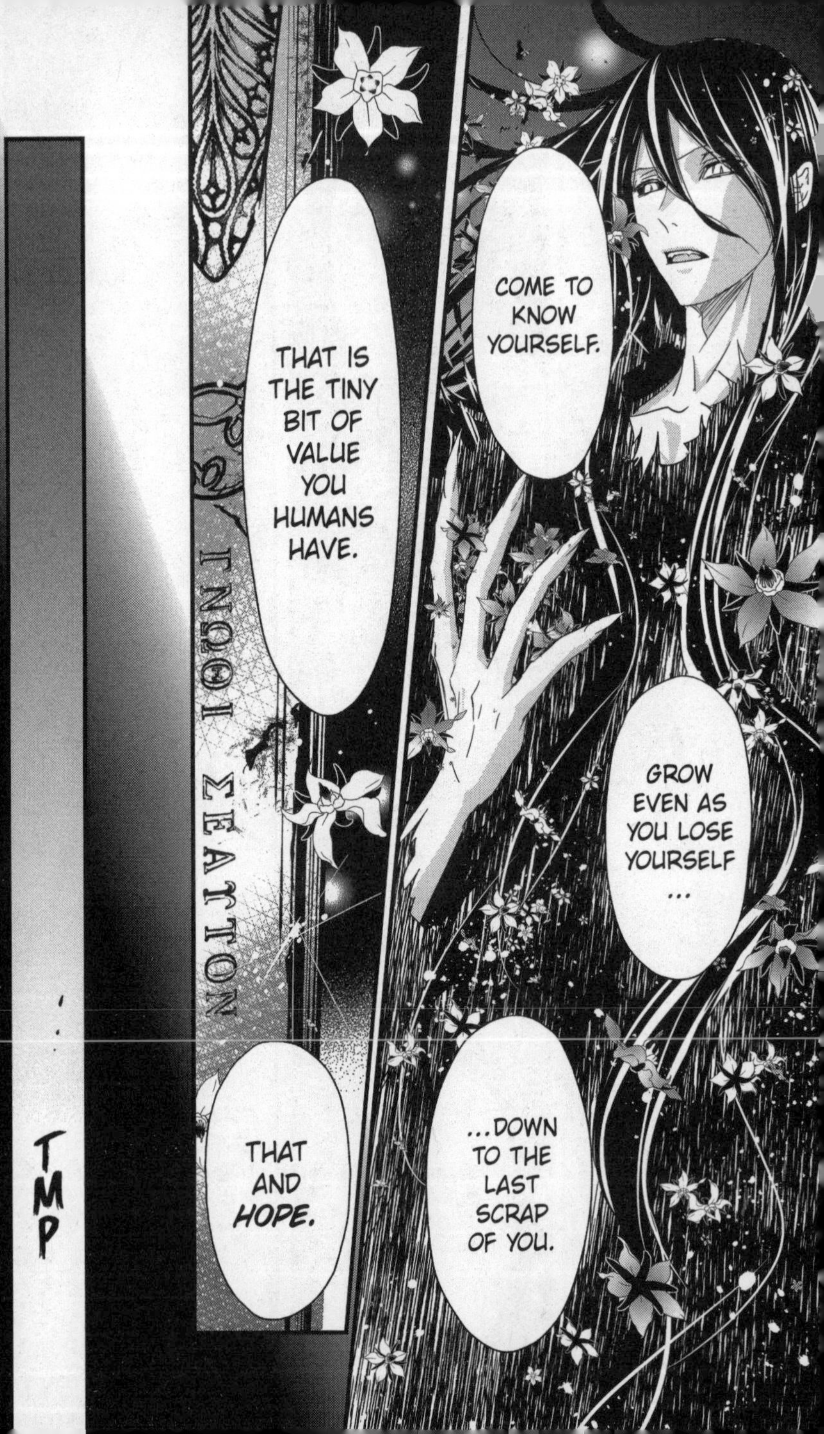
COME TO KNOW YOURSELF.
GROW EVEN AS YOU LOSE YOURSELF ...
...DOWN TO THE LAST SCRAP OF YOU.
THAT IS THE TINY BIT OF VALUE YOU HUMANS HAVE.
THAT AND *HOPE.*
...
TMP

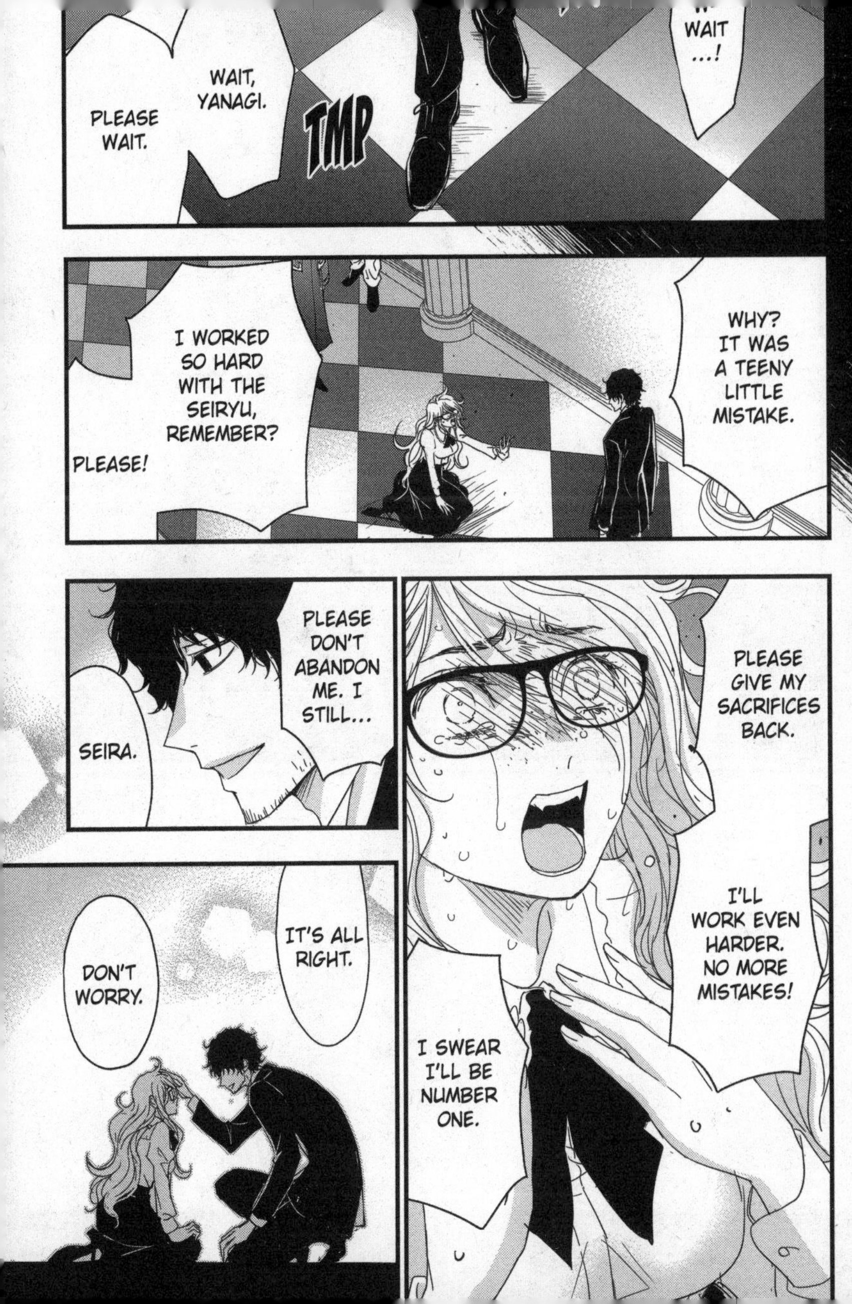
WAIT ...!
WAIT, YANAGI.
TMP
PLEASE WAIT.
WHY? IT WAS A TEENY LITTLE MISTAKE.
I WORKED SO HARD WITH THE SEIRYU, REMEMBER?
PLEASE!
PLEASE GIVE MY SACRIFICES BACK.
I'LL WORK EVEN HARDER. NO MORE MISTAKES!
I SWEAR I'LL BE NUMBER ONE.
PLEASE DON'T ABANDON ME. I STILL...
SEIRA.
IT'S ALL RIGHT.
DON'T WORRY.

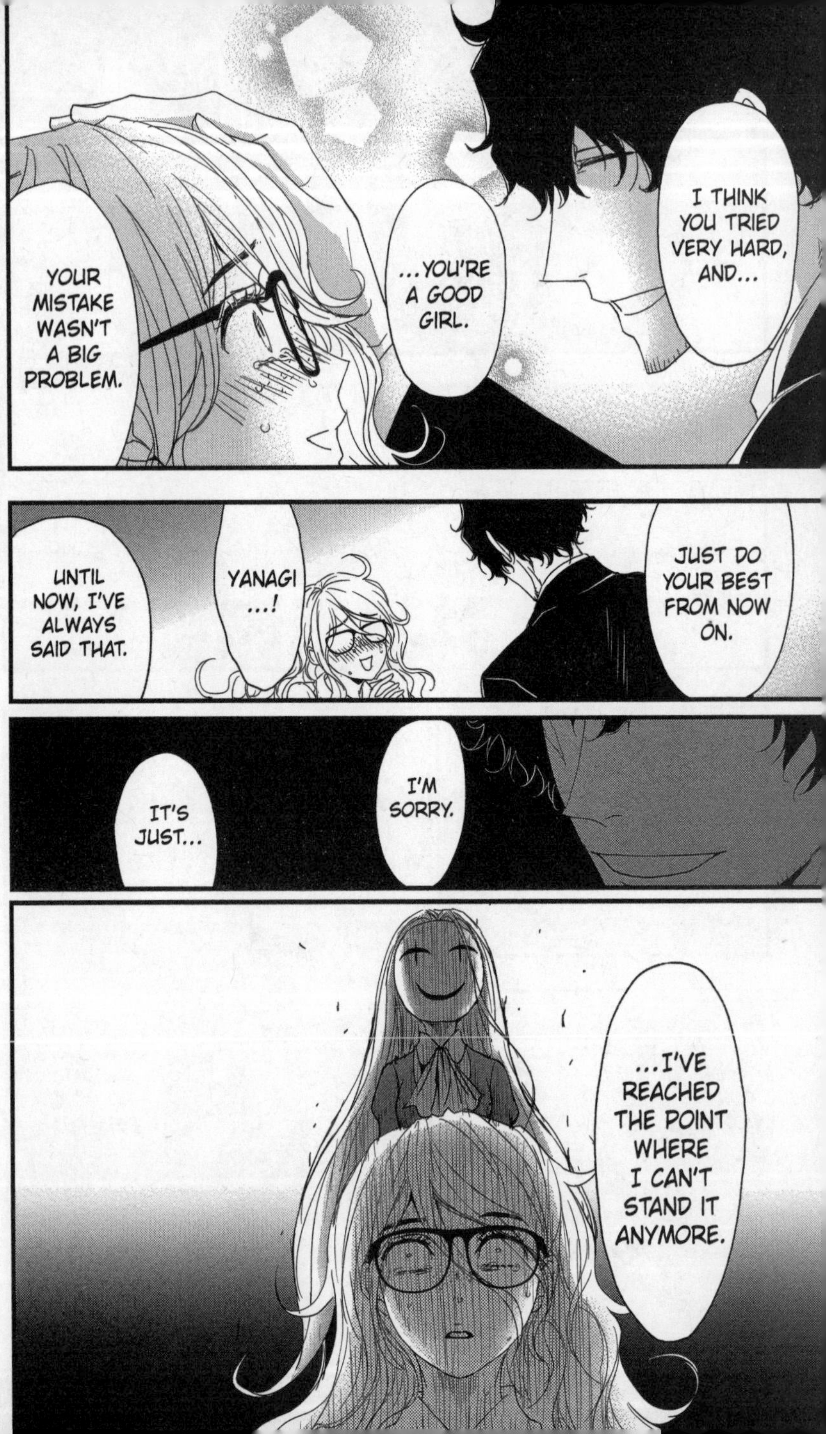
I THINK YOU TRIED VERY HARD, AND...
...YOU'RE A GOOD GIRL.
YOUR MISTAKE WASN'T A BIG PROBLEM.
JUST DO YOUR BEST FROM NOW ON.
YANAGI ...!
UNTIL NOW, I'VE ALWAYS SAID THAT.
I'M SORRY.
IT'S JUST...
...I'VE REACHED THE POINT WHERE I CAN'T STAND IT ANYMORE.

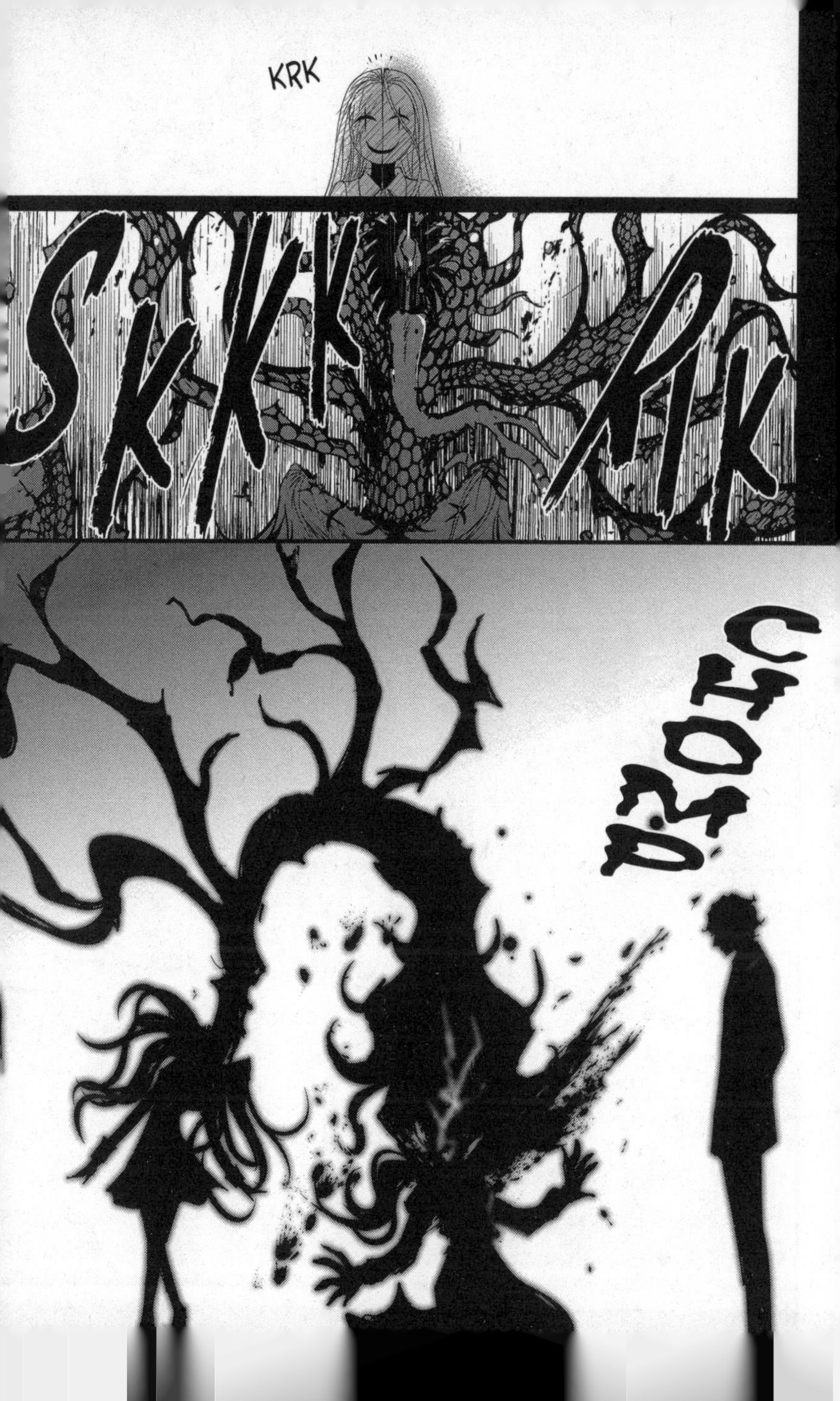
KRK
SKKK
CHOMP

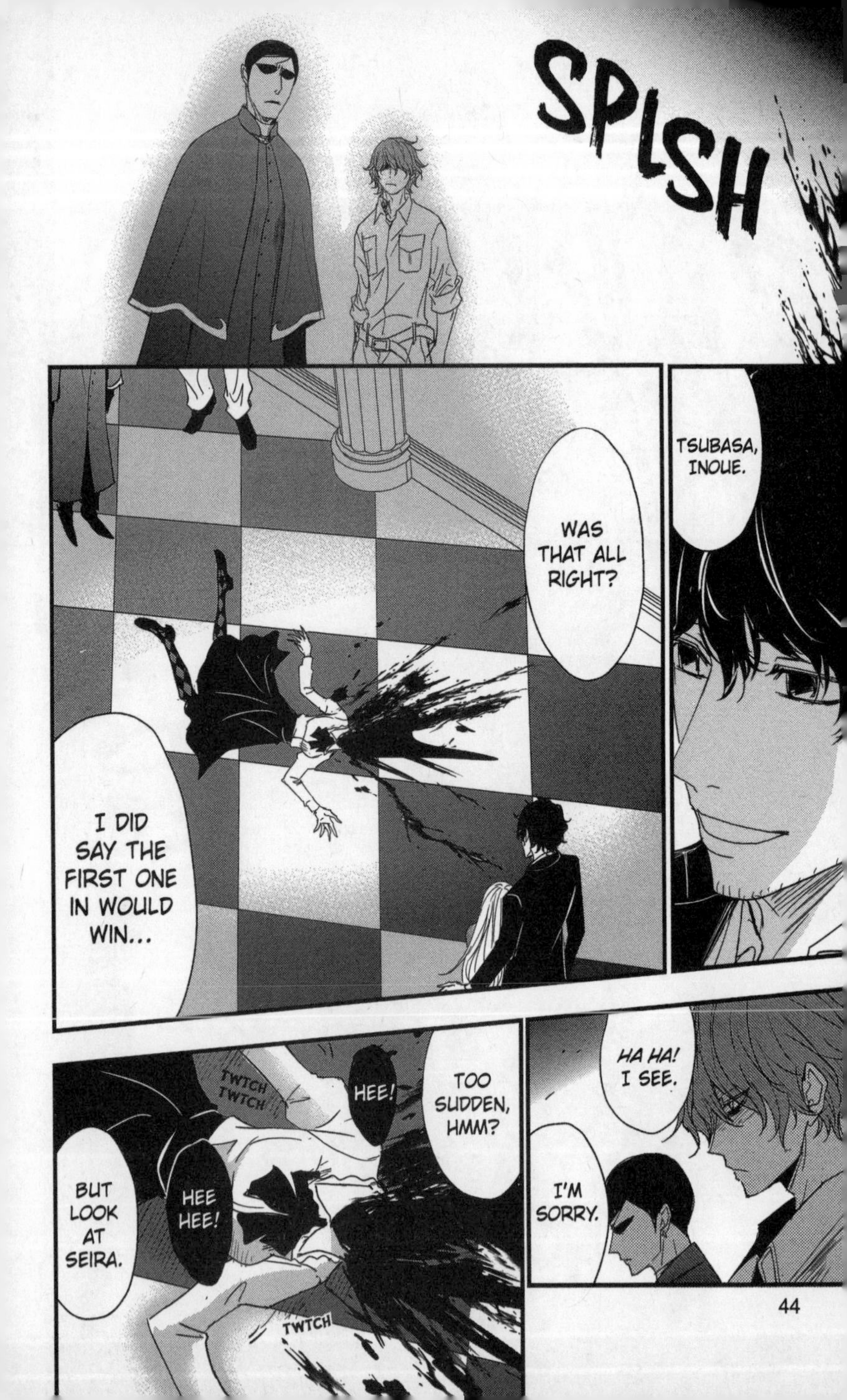
SPLSH
TSUBASA, INOUE.
WAS THAT ALL RIGHT?
I DID SAY THE FIRST ONE IN WOULD WIN...
HA HA! I SEE.
I'M SORRY.
TOO SUDDEN, HMM?
HEE!
TWTCH TWTCH
HEE HEE!
BUT LOOK AT SEIRA.
TWTCH

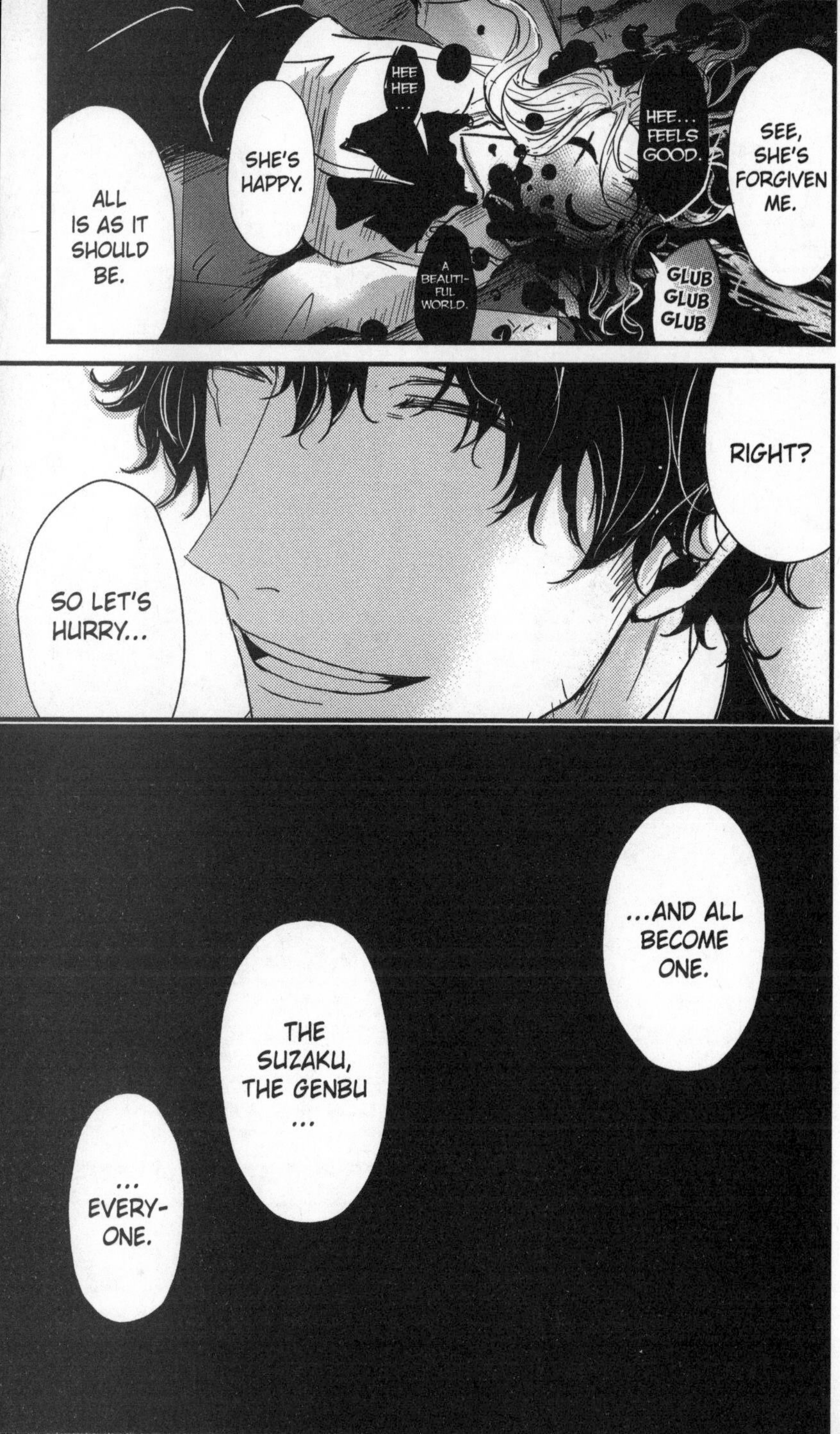
SEE, SHE'S FORGIVEN ME.
HEE... FEELS GOOD.
GLUB GLUB GLUB
HEE HEE ...
A BEAUTIFUL WORLD.
SHE'S HAPPY.
ALL IS AS IT SHOULD BE.
RIGHT?
SO LET'S HURRY...
...AND ALL BECOME ONE.
THE SUZAKU, THE GENBU ...
... EVERYONE.

CHAPTER 67

MONTHLY BETSUCOMI SALE DATE NOTICE ON TWITTER AND INSTAGRAM

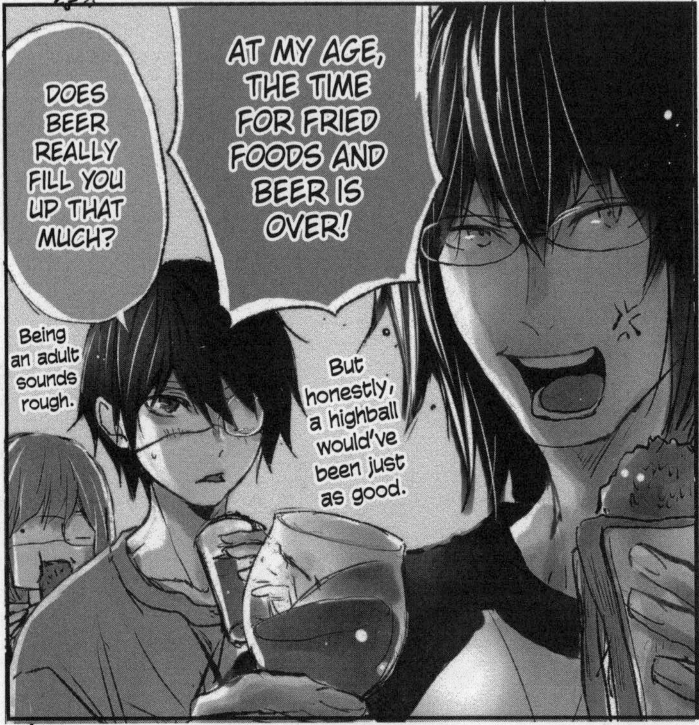
AT MY AGE, THE TIME FOR FRIED FOODS AND BEER IS OVER!
DOES BEER REALLY FILL YOU UP THAT MUCH?
But honestly, a highball would've been just as good.
Being an adult sounds rough.

LET'S SEE... WHAT'S UP IN *QUEEN'S QUALITY* THIS MONTH?
1) KYUTARO WAS BLINDFOLDED, SO HE DIDN'T GET TO SEE FUMI IN HER SLIP.
2) I THINK BEER PAIRS BETTER, BUT AS AN ADULT HE GETS WINE...
3) TSUBASA LOOKS A LOT DIFFERENT THAN HE DID AT THE BEGINNING. HASN'T HE BEEN SLEEPING?

KYUTARO'S HAIR IS PARTED A LITTLE DIFFERENTLY IN THIS CHAPTER!

I LOVE BEER, BUT IT SEEMS LIKE EVERY YEAR I HAVE TO DRINK LESS. IT'S SO SAD. WHEN PAIRING WINE WITH FRIED FOODS, YOU SHOULD THOROUGHLY CHILL THE WINE OR ADD ICE. (COMMENTS FROM A DRINKER)

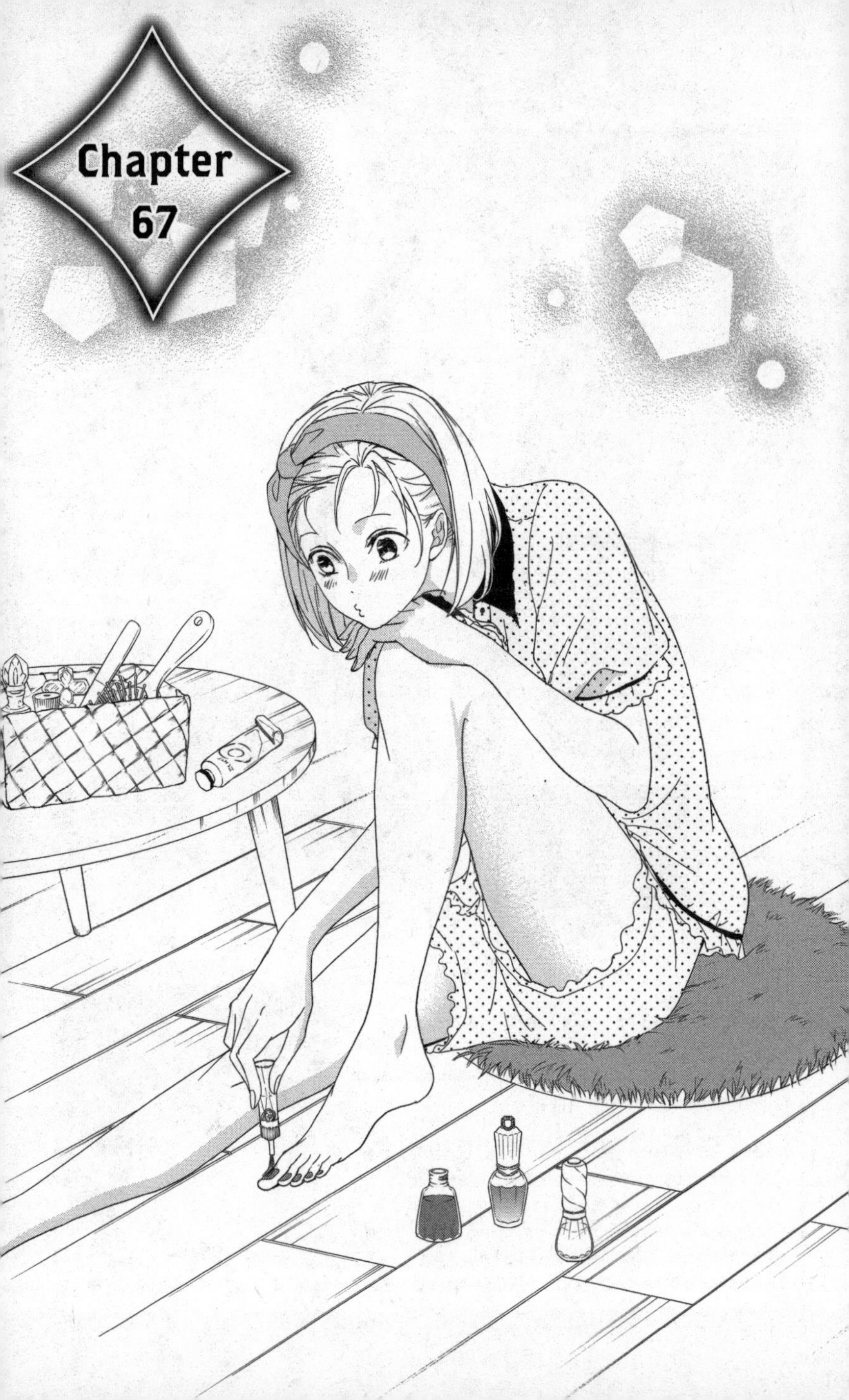
Chapter
67

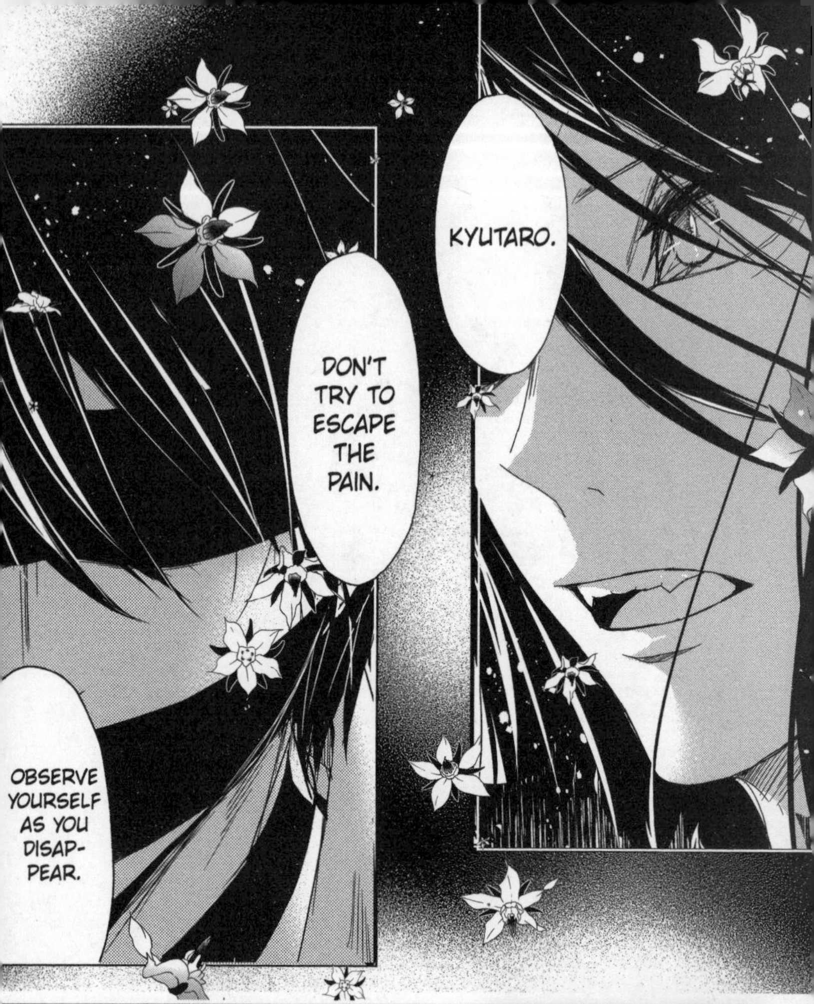
KYUTARO.
DON'T TRY TO ESCAPE THE PAIN.
OBSERVE YOURSELF AS YOU DISAP-PEAR.

Due to the kind of work I do, my eyes get very tired. They seem to get even drier when I use eyedrops. I wonder if my dry-eye disease is worse than I thought…

I can't let this continue, so I've decided to do eye exercises at the same time every day. I've built daily stretches and exercise into my routine and they seem to be doing some good, so I think eye exercises should help too! That's why I make sure to wink every day.

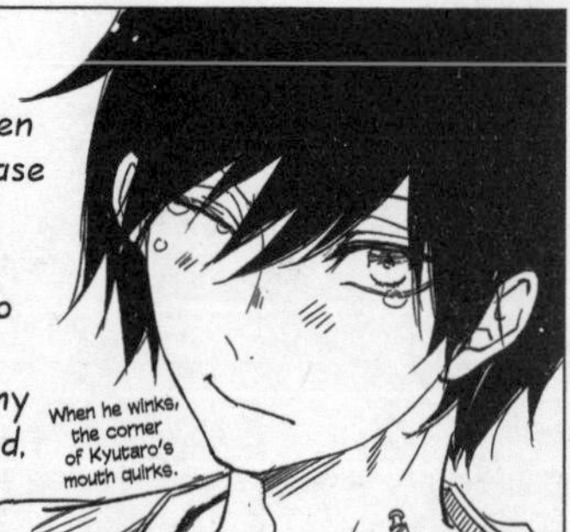
When he winks, the corner of Kyutaro's mouth quirks.

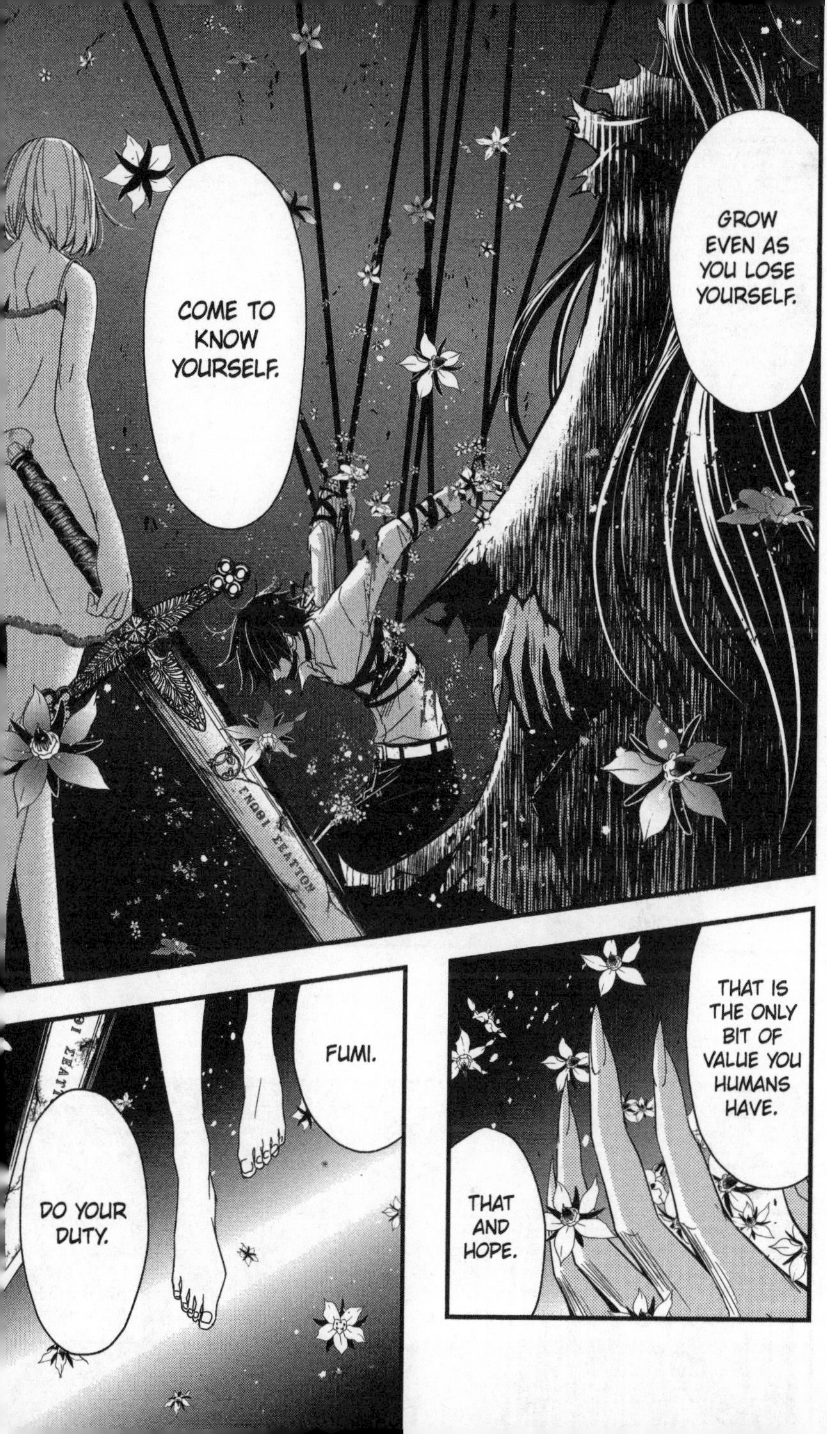
GROW EVEN AS YOU LOSE YOURSELF.
COME TO KNOW YOURSELF.
THAT IS THE ONLY BIT OF VALUE YOU HUMANS HAVE.
THAT AND HOPE.
FUMI.
DO YOUR DUTY.

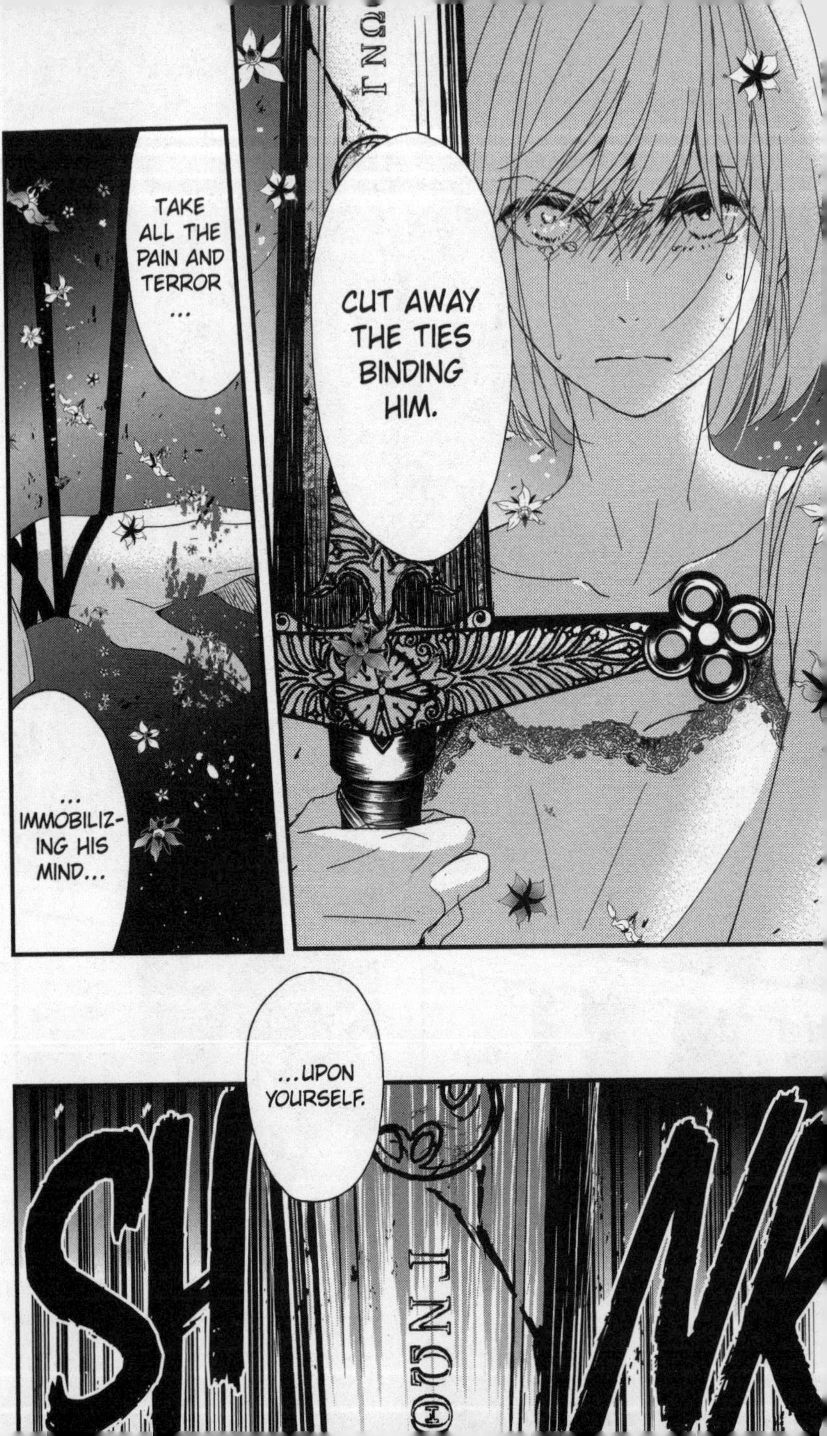
CUT AWAY THE TIES BINDING HIM.
TAKE ALL THE PAIN AND TERROR...
...IMMOBILIZING HIS MIND...
...UPON YOURSELF.
SHNK

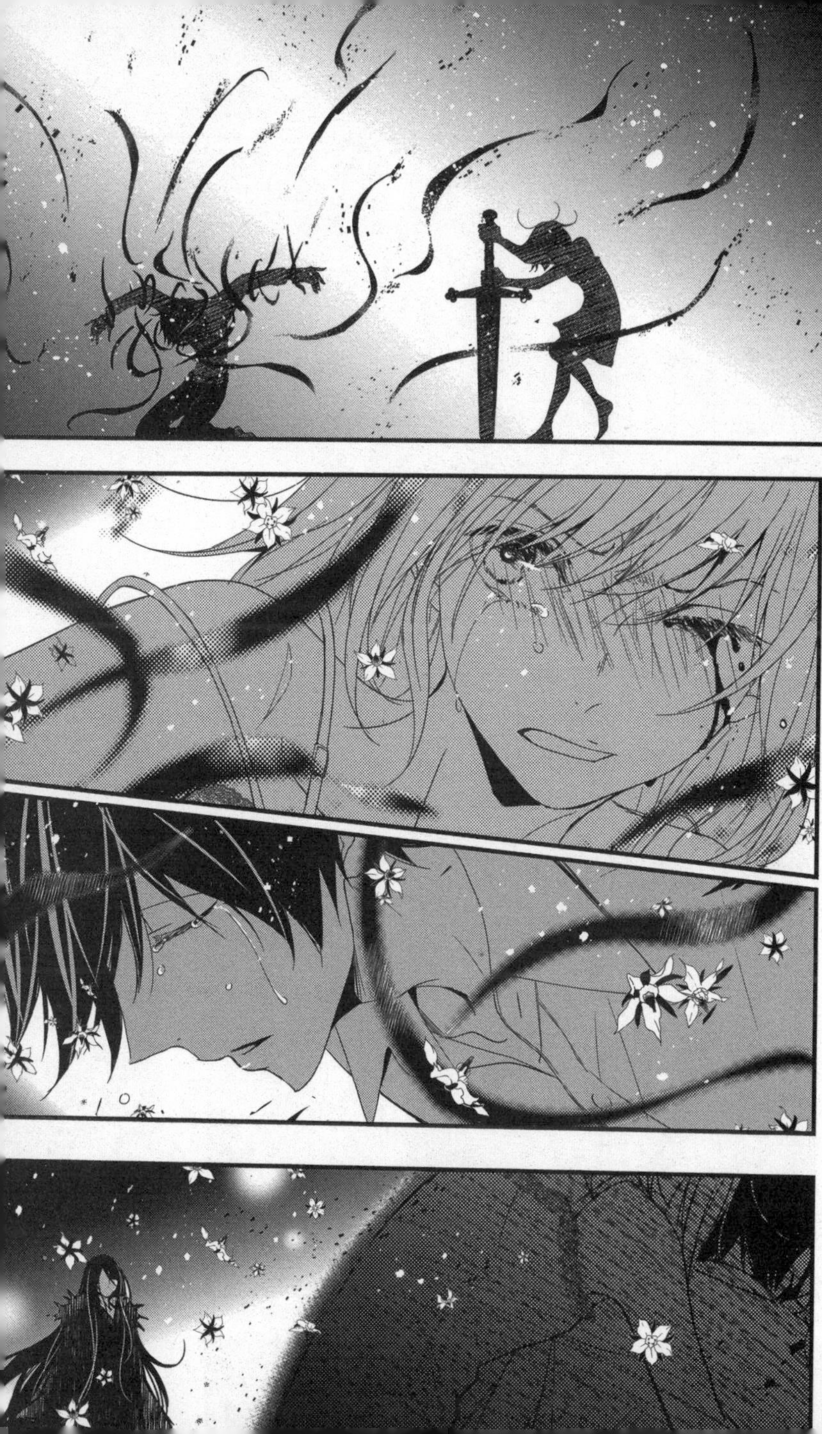

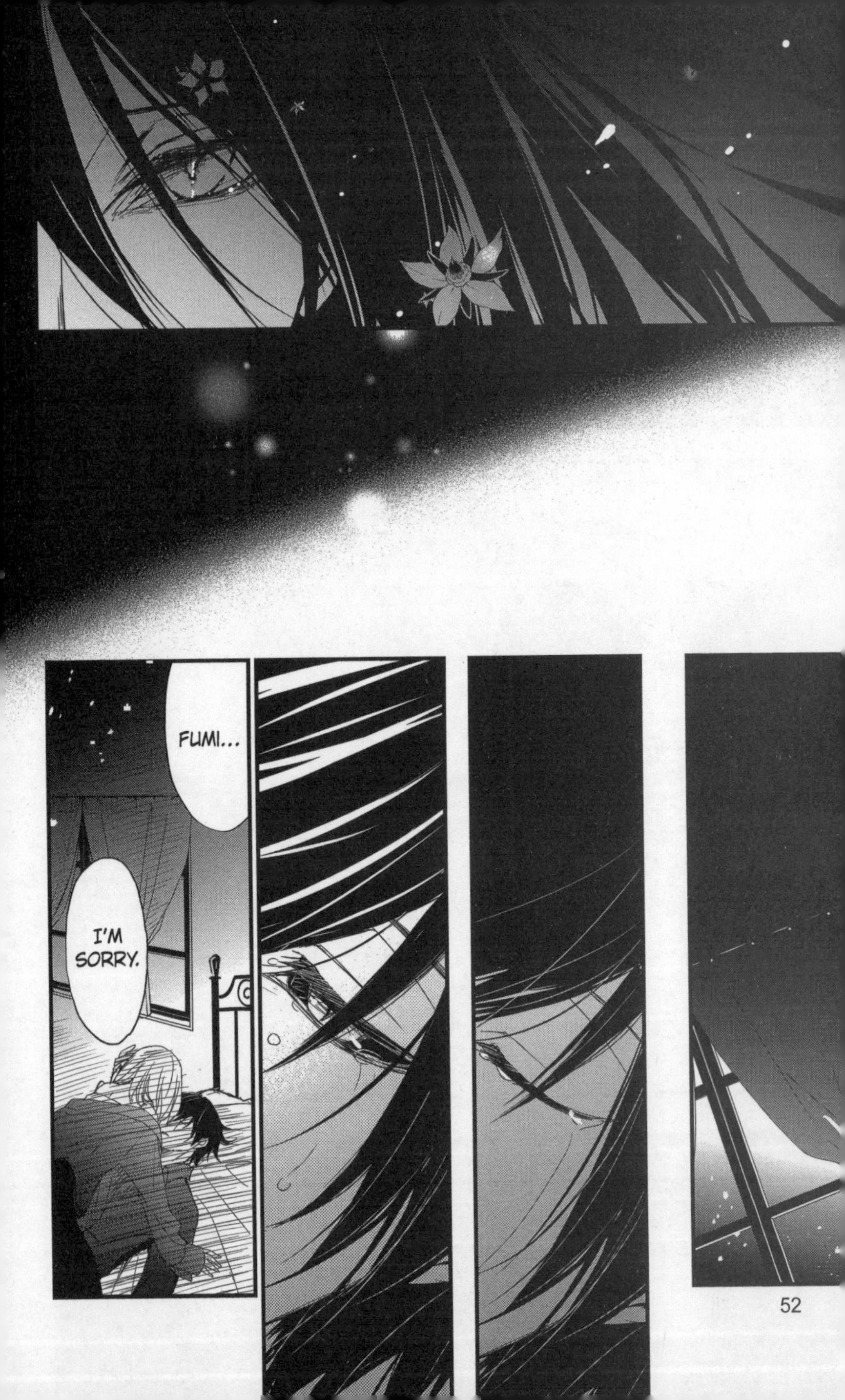
FUMI...
I'M SORRY.

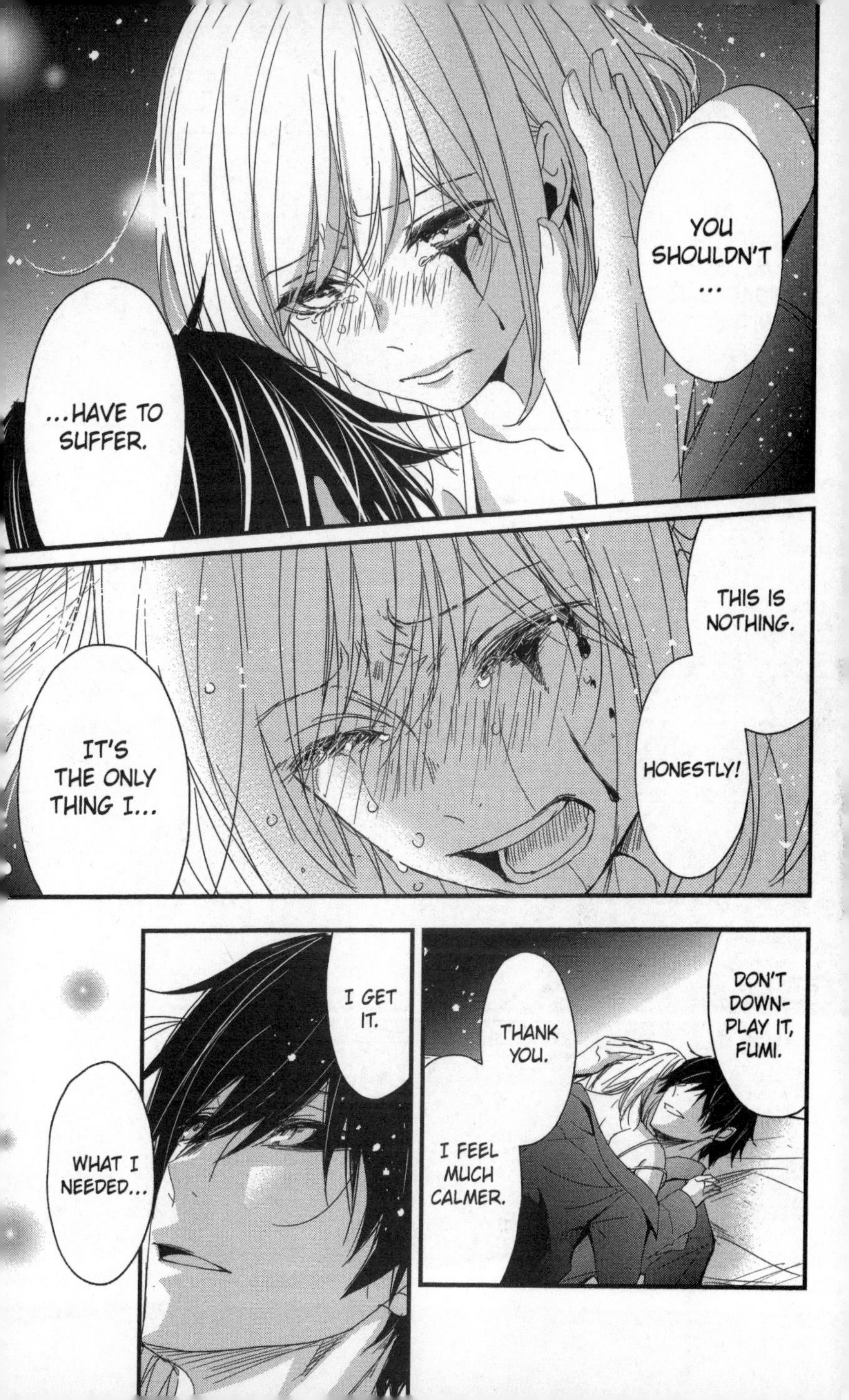
YOU SHOULDN'T ...
...HAVE TO SUFFER.
THIS IS NOTHING.
HONESTLY!
IT'S THE ONLY THING I...
DON'T DOWN-PLAY IT, FUMI.
THANK YOU.
I FEEL MUCH CALMER.
I GET IT.
WHAT I NEEDED...

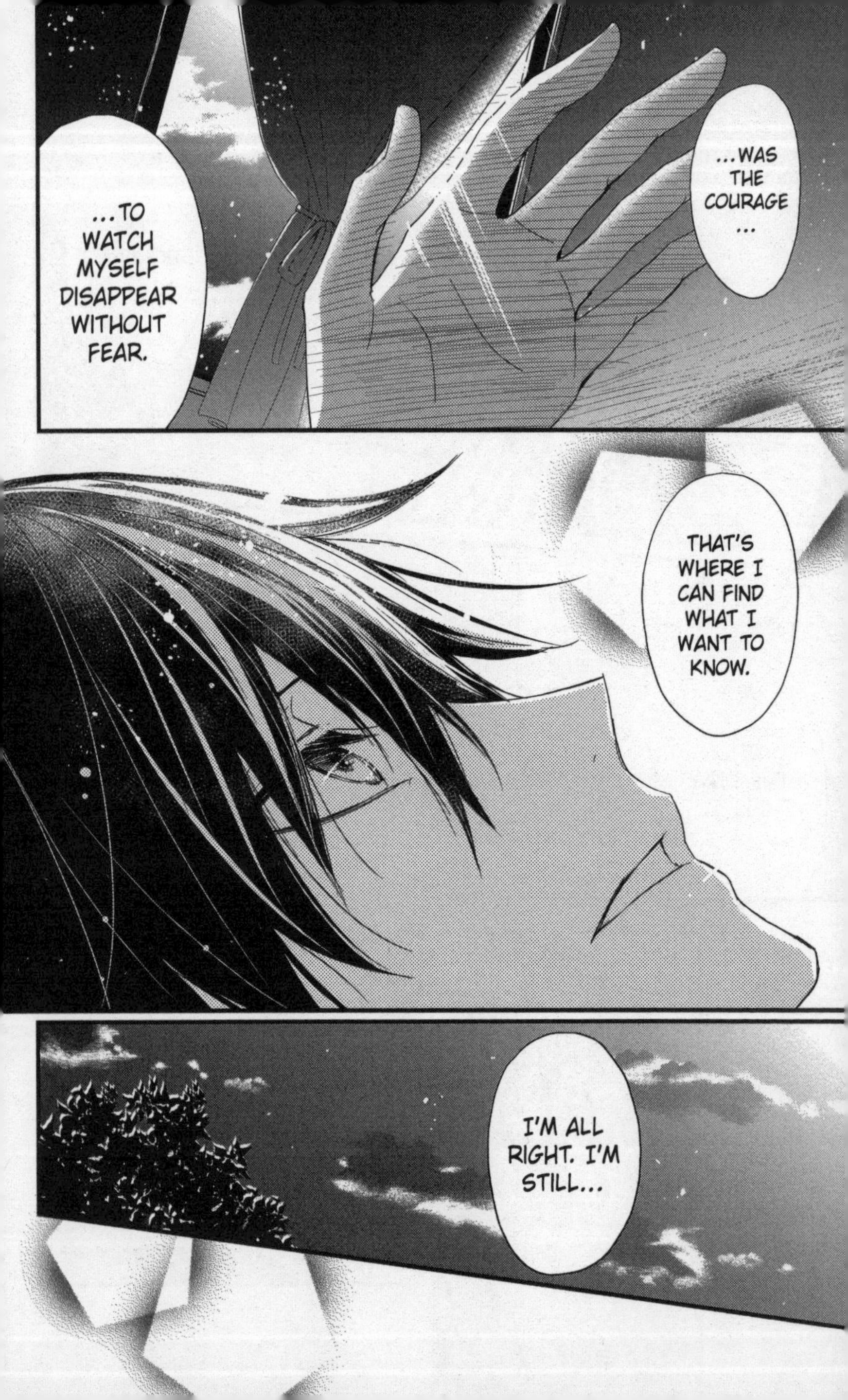
...WAS THE COURAGE...
...TO WATCH MYSELF DISAPPEAR WITHOUT FEAR.
THAT'S WHERE I CAN FIND WHAT I WANT TO KNOW.
I'M ALL RIGHT. I'M STILL...

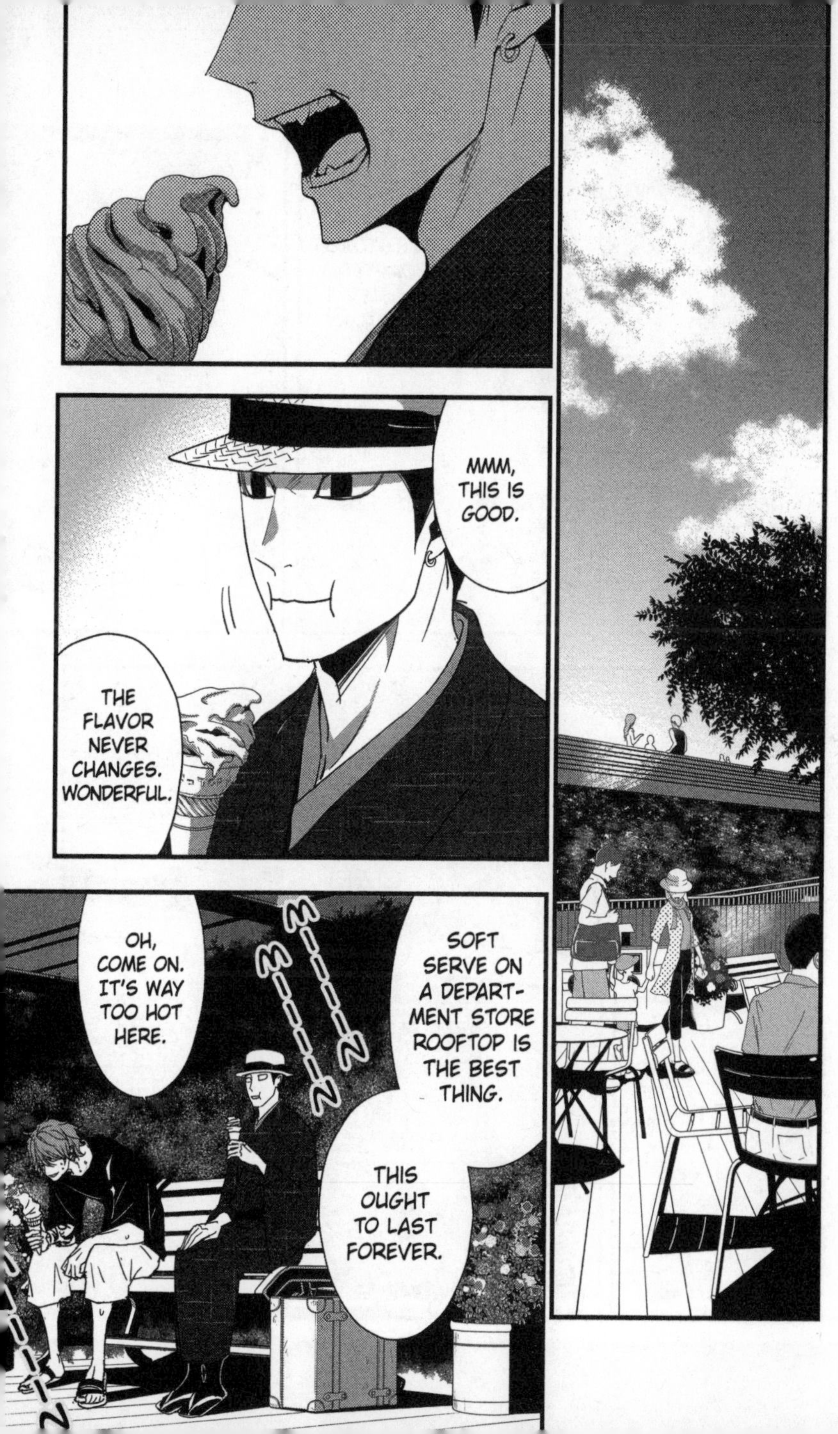
MMM, THIS IS GOOD.
THE FLAVOR NEVER CHANGES. WONDERFUL.
SOFT SERVE ON A DEPARTMENT STORE ROOFTOP IS THE BEST THING.
THIS OUGHT TO LAST FOREVER.
MIIIIIN
MIIIIIN
OH, COME ON. IT'S WAY TOO HOT HERE.

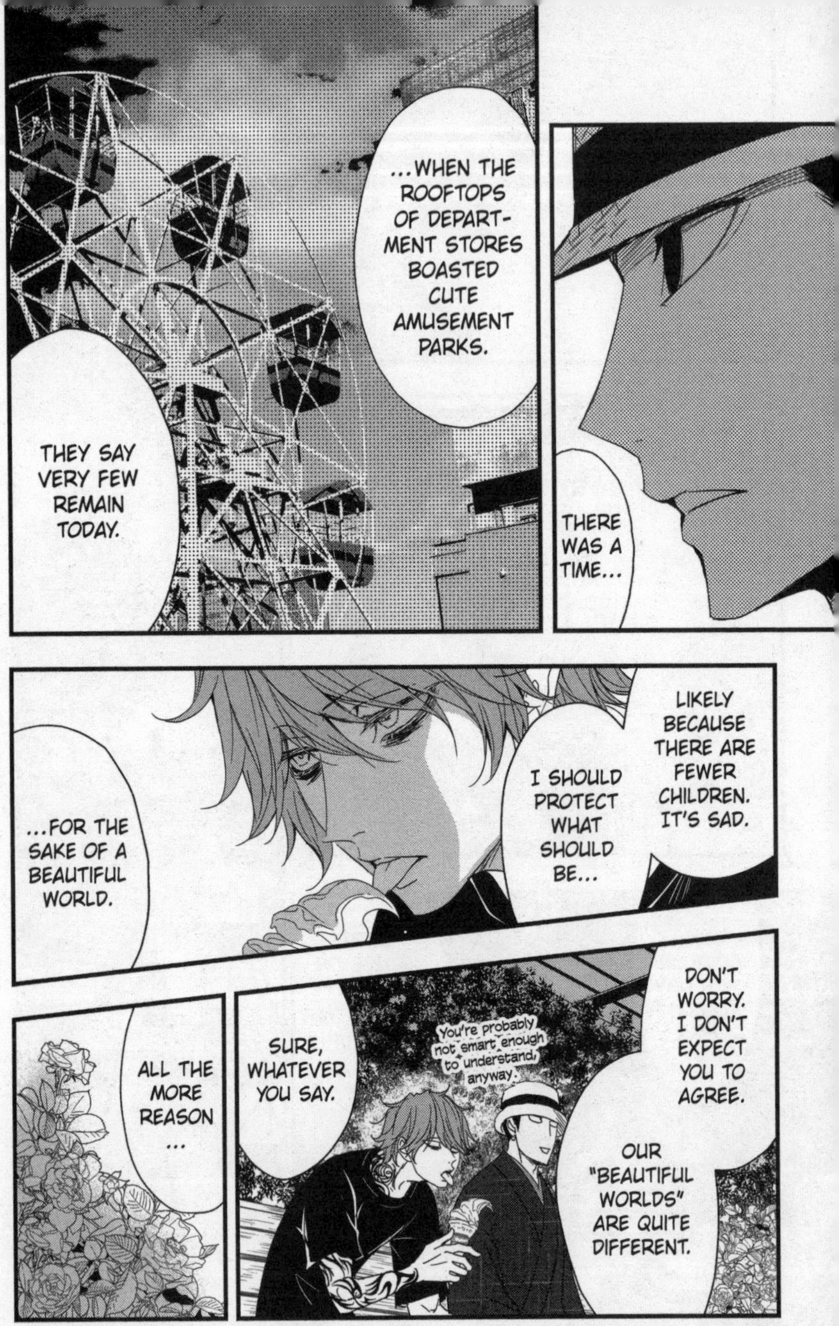
THERE WAS A TIME...
...WHEN THE ROOFTOPS OF DEPARTMENT STORES BOASTED CUTE AMUSEMENT PARKS.
THEY SAY VERY FEW REMAIN TODAY.
LIKELY BECAUSE THERE ARE FEWER CHILDREN. IT'S SAD.
I SHOULD PROTECT WHAT SHOULD BE...
...FOR THE SAKE OF A BEAUTIFUL WORLD.
DON'T WORRY. I DON'T EXPECT YOU TO AGREE.
OUR "BEAUTIFUL WORLDS" ARE QUITE DIFFERENT.
You're probably not smart enough to understand, anyway.
SURE, WHATEVER YOU SAY.
ALL THE MORE REASON ...

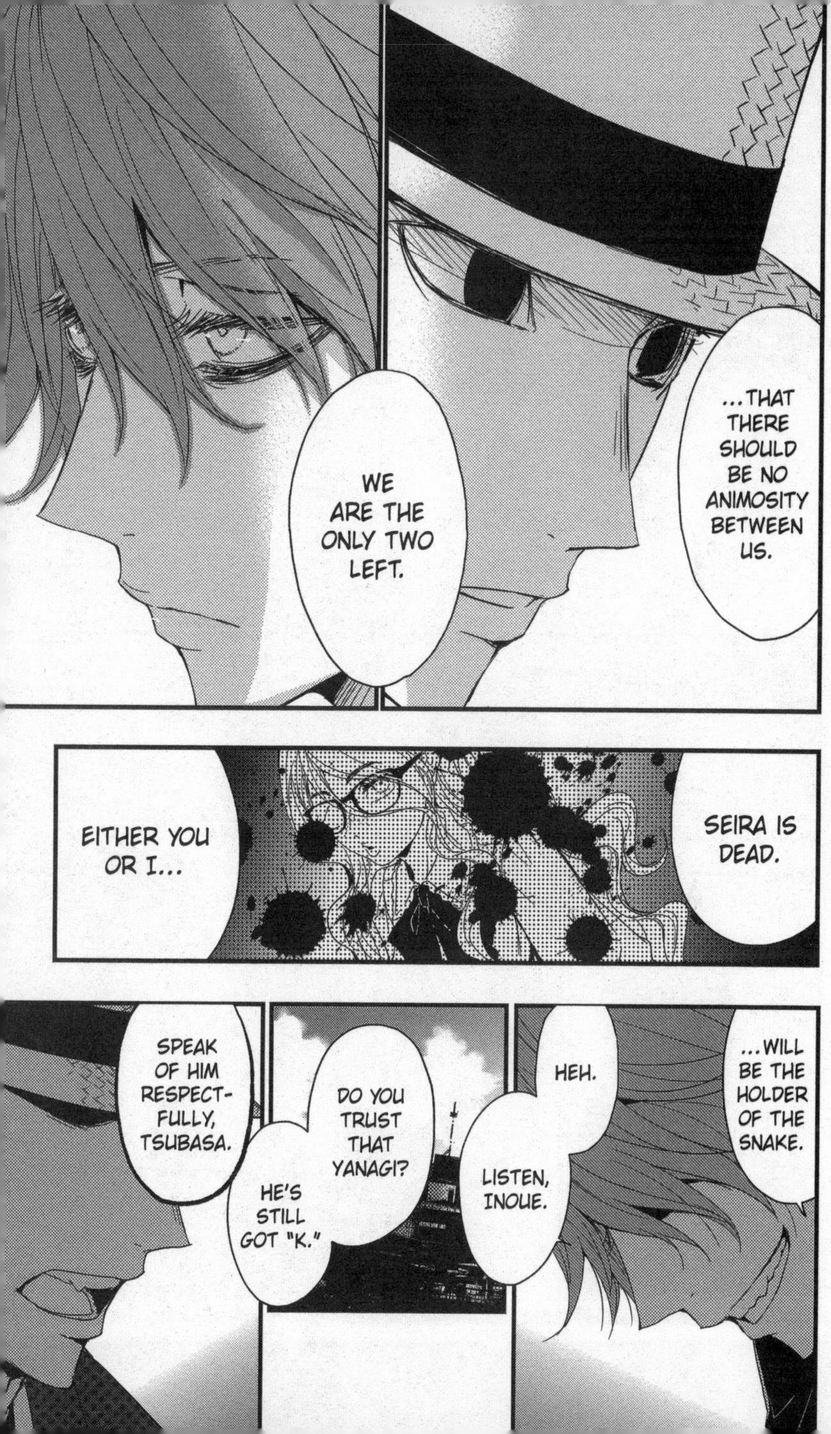
...THAT THERE SHOULD BE NO ANIMOSITY BETWEEN US.
WE ARE THE ONLY TWO LEFT.
SEIRA IS DEAD.
EITHER YOU OR I...
...WILL BE THE HOLDER OF THE SNAKE.
HEH.
LISTEN, INOUE.
DO YOU TRUST THAT YANAGI?
HE'S STILL GOT "K."
SPEAK OF HIM RESPECT-FULLY, TSUBASA.

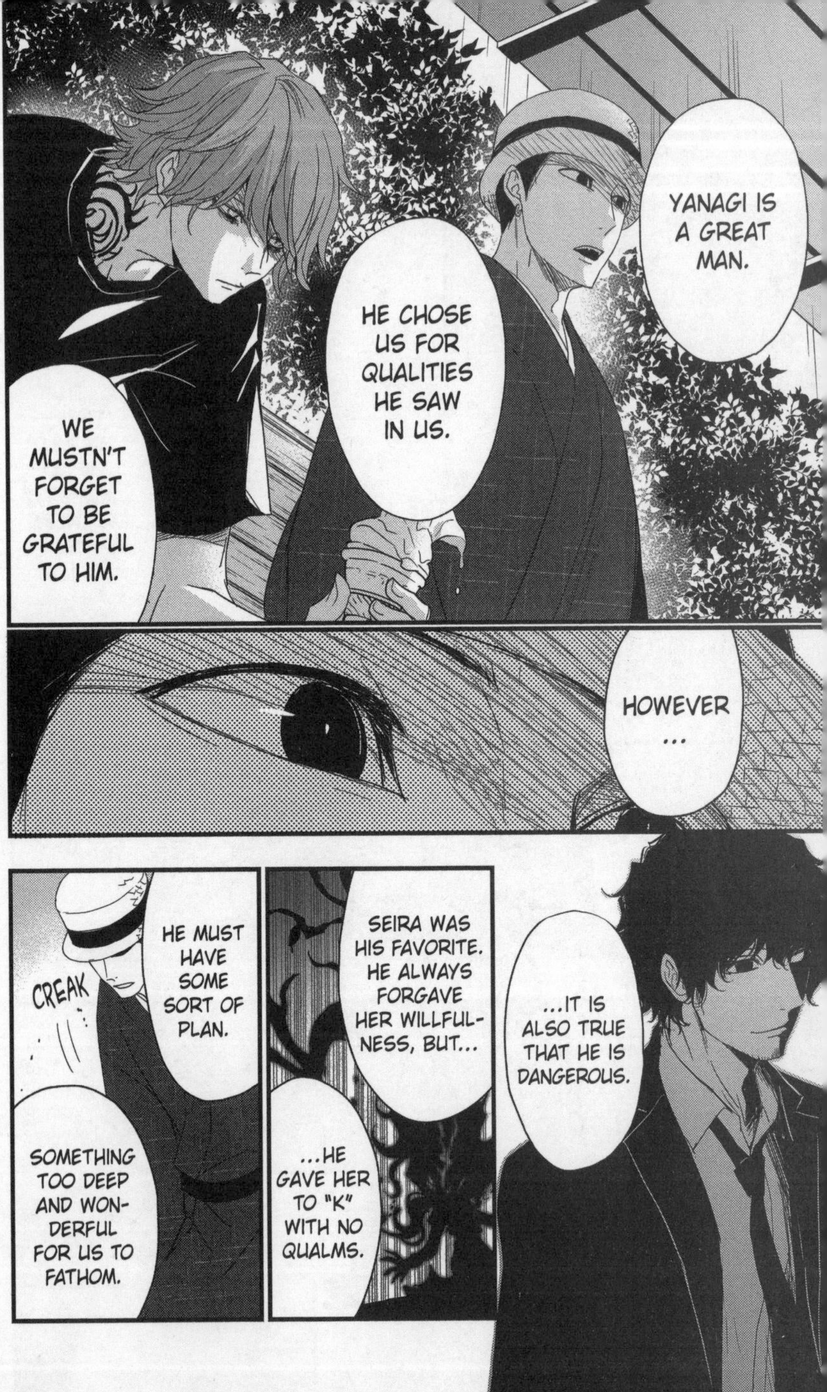
YANAGI IS A GREAT MAN.
HE CHOSE US FOR QUALITIES HE SAW IN US.
WE MUSTN'T FORGET TO BE GRATEFUL TO HIM.
HOWEVER ...
...IT IS ALSO TRUE THAT HE IS DANGEROUS.
SEIRA WAS HIS FAVORITE. HE ALWAYS FORGAVE HER WILLFUL-NESS, BUT...
...HE GAVE HER TO "K" WITH NO QUALMS.
HE MUST HAVE SOME SORT OF PLAN.
CREAK
SOMETHING TOO DEEP AND WON-DERFUL FOR US TO FATHOM.

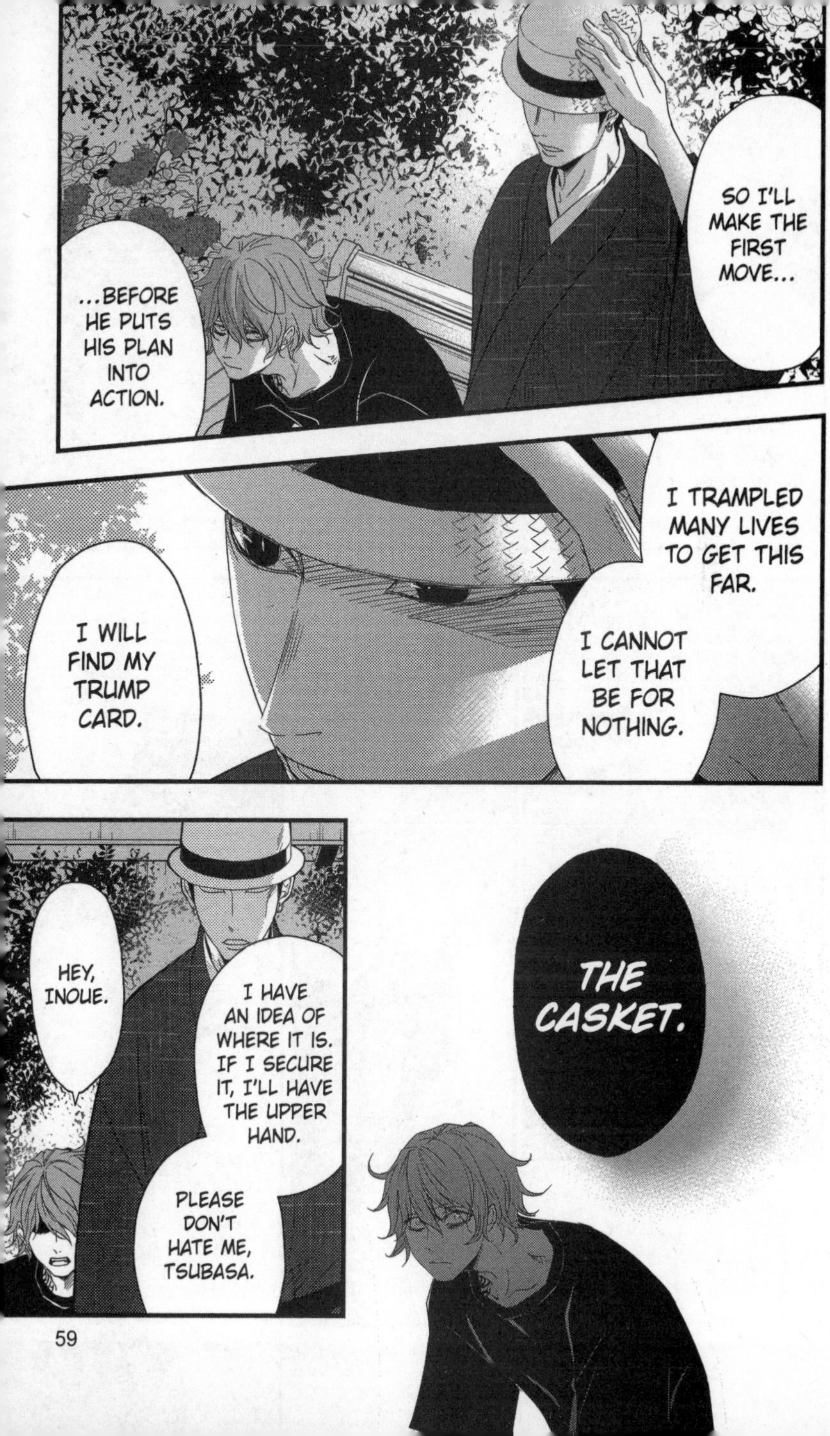
SO I'LL MAKE THE FIRST MOVE...
...BEFORE HE PUTS HIS PLAN INTO ACTION.
I TRAMPLED MANY LIVES TO GET THIS FAR.
I CANNOT LET THAT BE FOR NOTHING.
I WILL FIND MY TRUMP CARD.
THE CASKET.
I HAVE AN IDEA OF WHERE IT IS. IF I SECURE IT, I'LL HAVE THE UPPER HAND.
PLEASE DON'T HATE ME, TSUBASA.
HEY, INOUE.

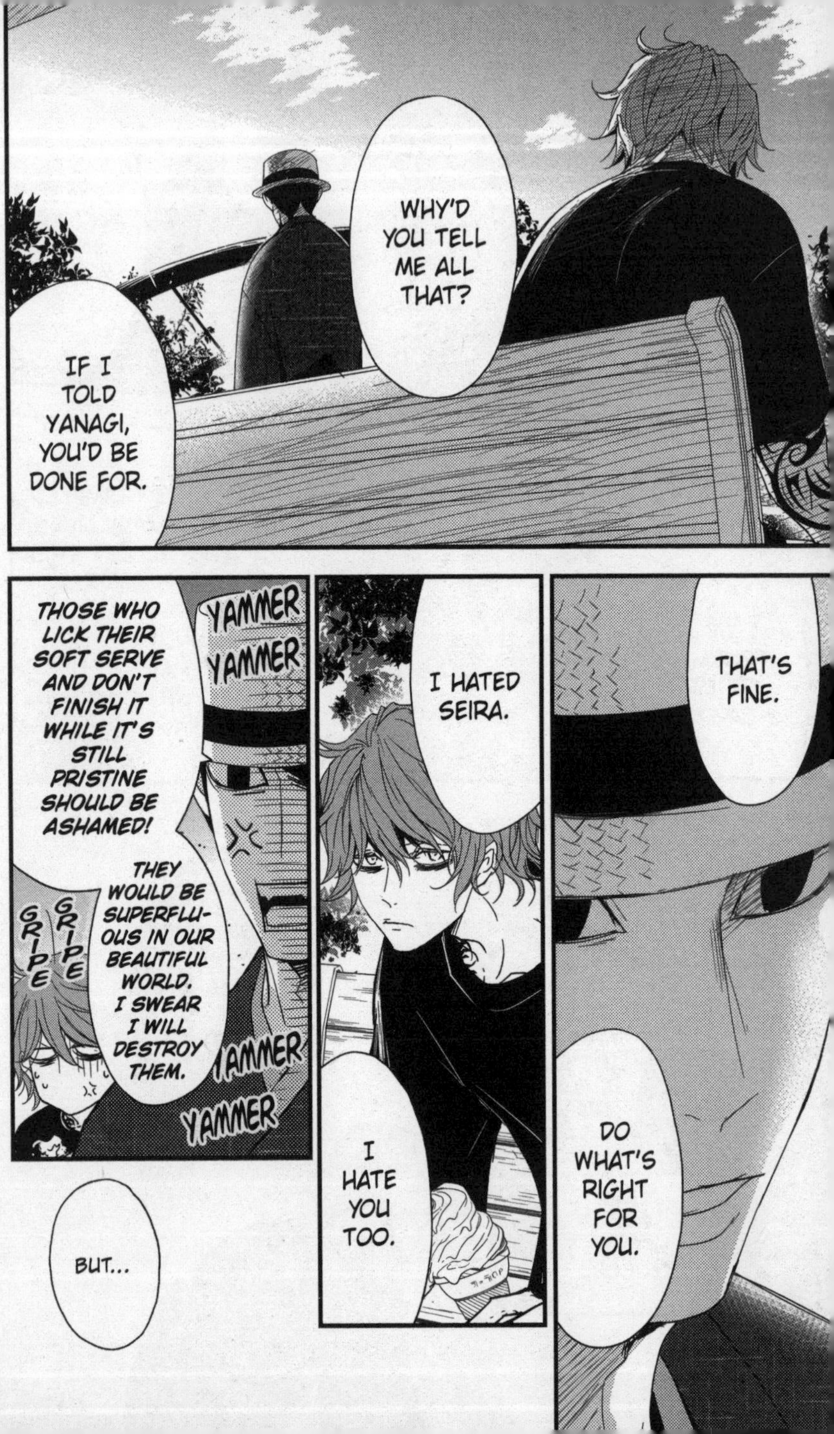
WHY'D YOU TELL ME ALL THAT?
IF I TOLD YANAGI, YOU'D BE DONE FOR.
THAT'S FINE.
DO WHAT'S RIGHT FOR YOU.
I HATED SEIRA.
I HATE YOU TOO.
YAMMER
YAMMER
THOSE WHO LICK THEIR SOFT SERVE AND DON'T FINISH IT WHILE IT'S STILL PRISTINE SHOULD BE ASHAMED!
THEY WOULD BE SUPERFLU-OUS IN OUR BEAUTIFUL WORLD. I SWEAR I WILL DESTROY THEM.
GRIPE
GRIPE
YAMMER
YAMMER
BUT...

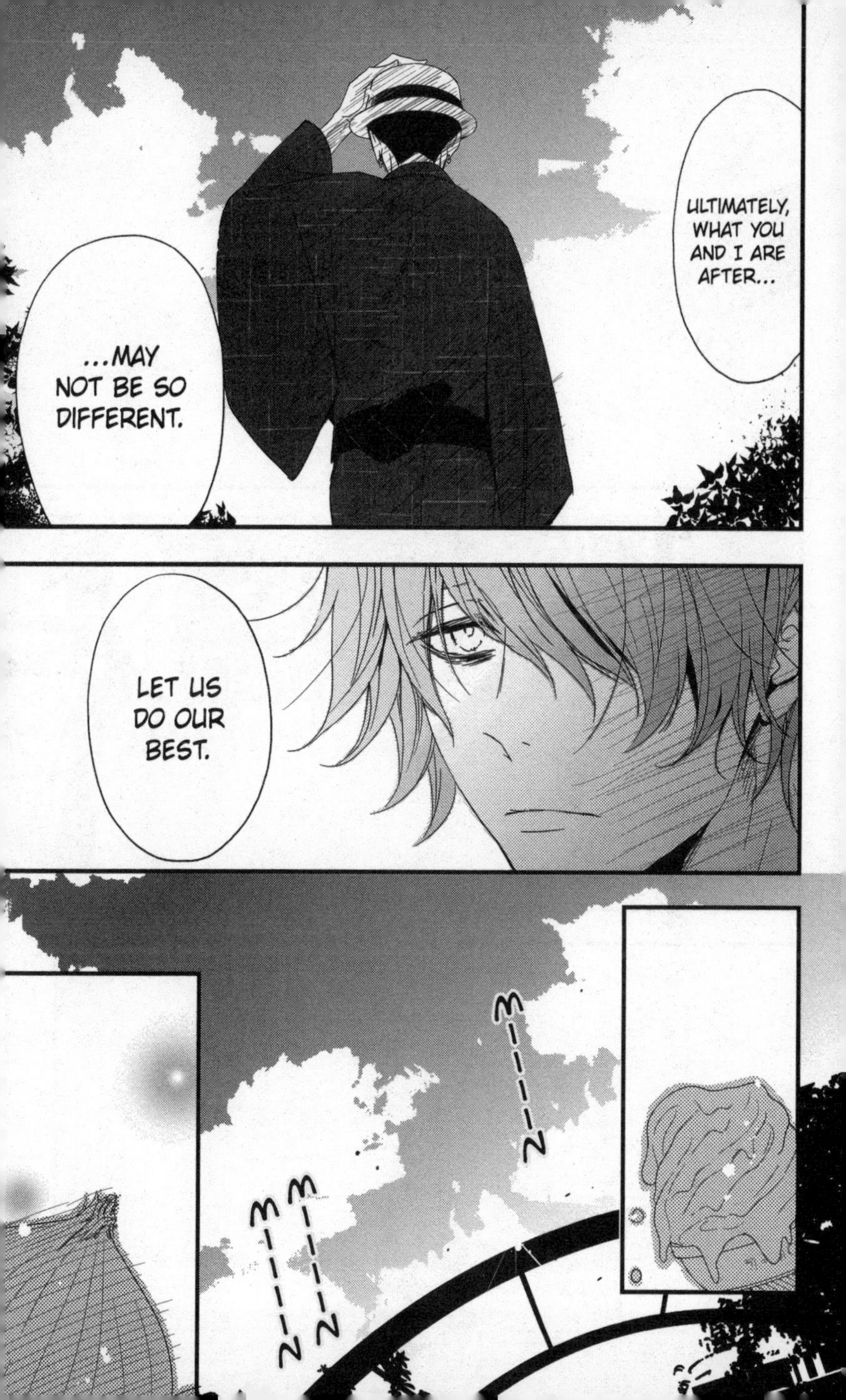
ULTIMATELY, WHAT YOU AND I ARE AFTER...
...MAY NOT BE SO DIFFERENT.
LET US DO OUR BEST.
M-I-I-I-N
M-I-I-I-N
M-I-I-I-N

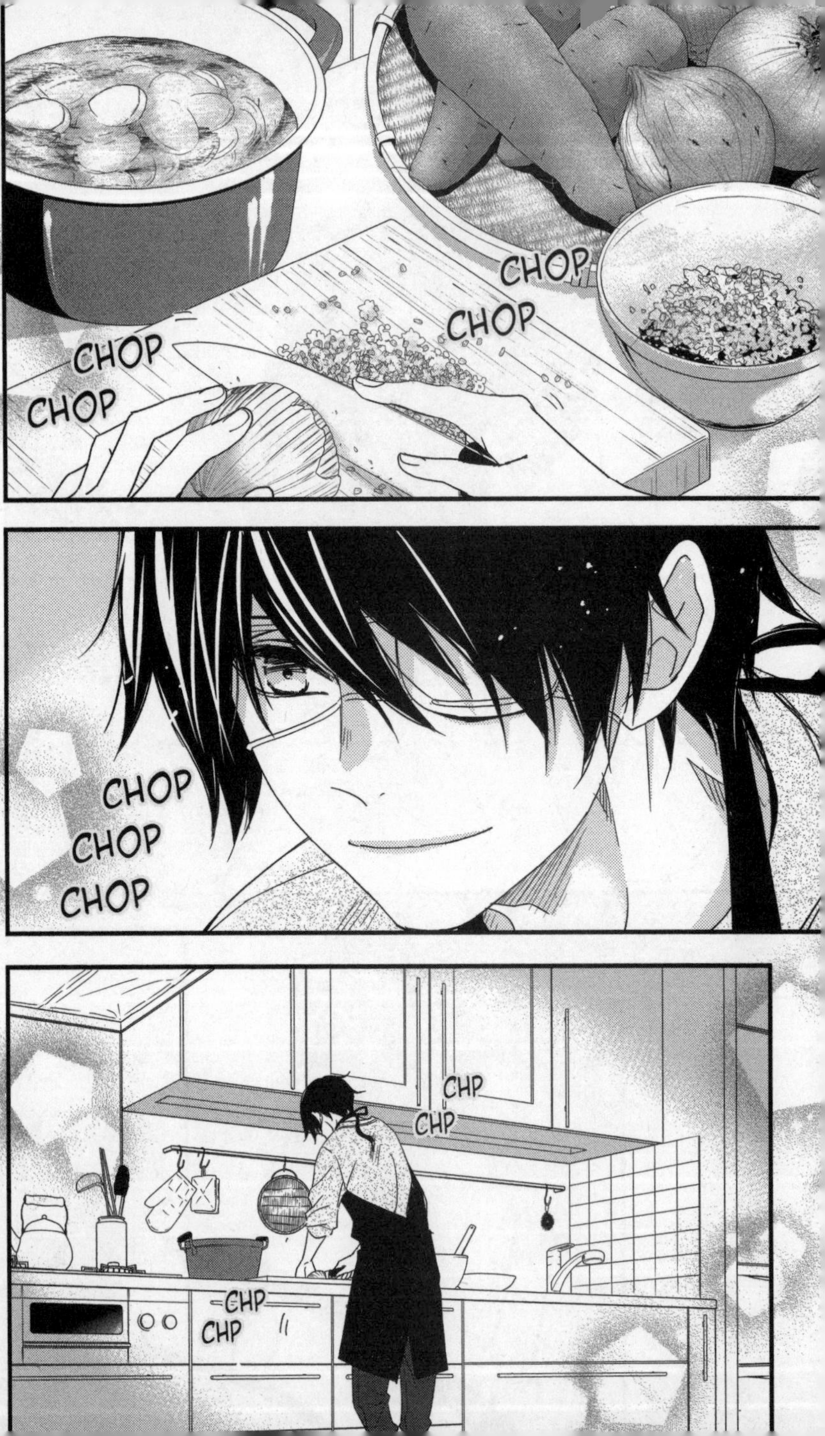
CHOP
CHOP
CHOP
CHOP
CHOP
CHOP
CHOP
CHP
CHP
CHP
CHP

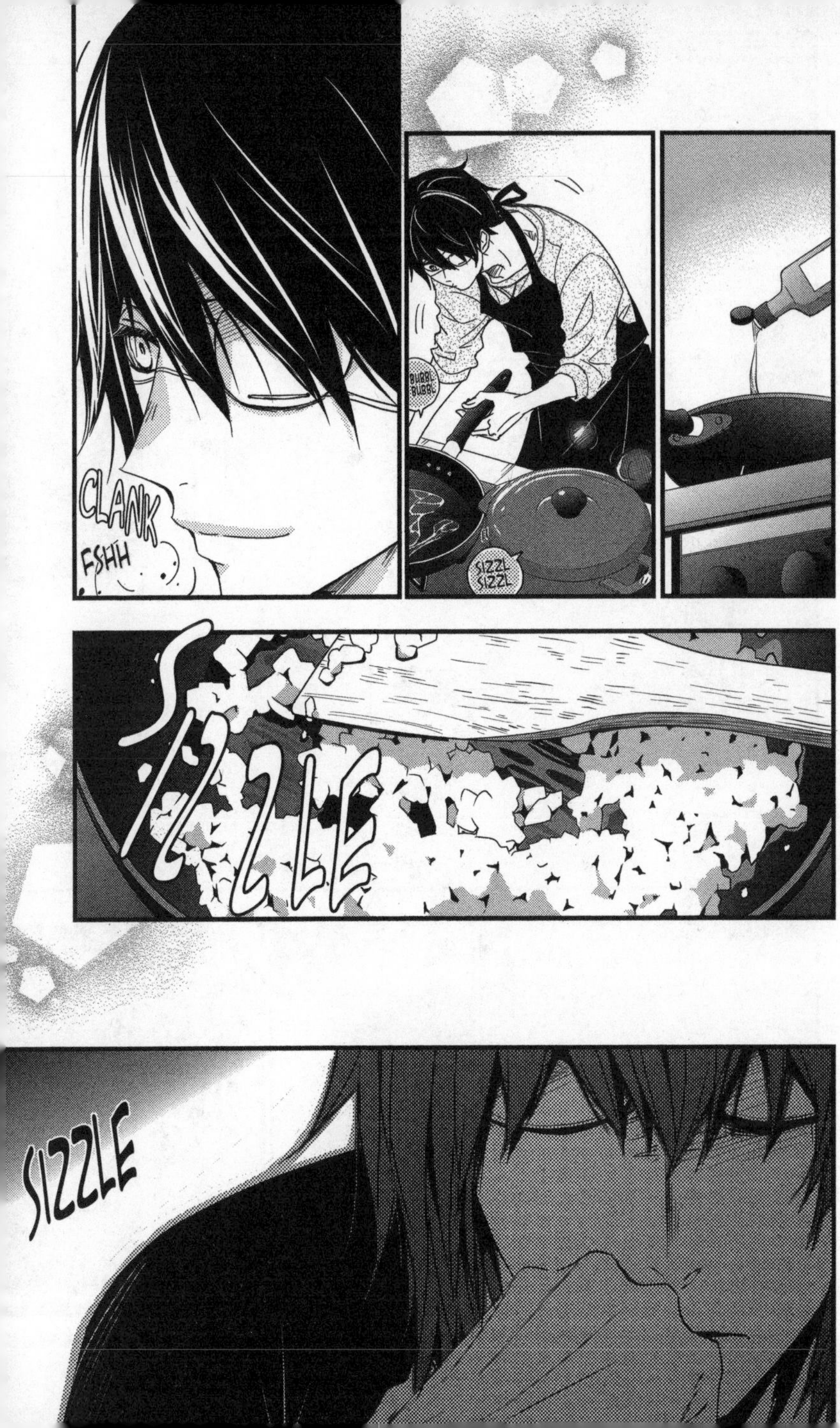
BUBBL BUBBL
SIZZL SIZZL
CLANK
FSHH
SIZZLE
SIZZLE

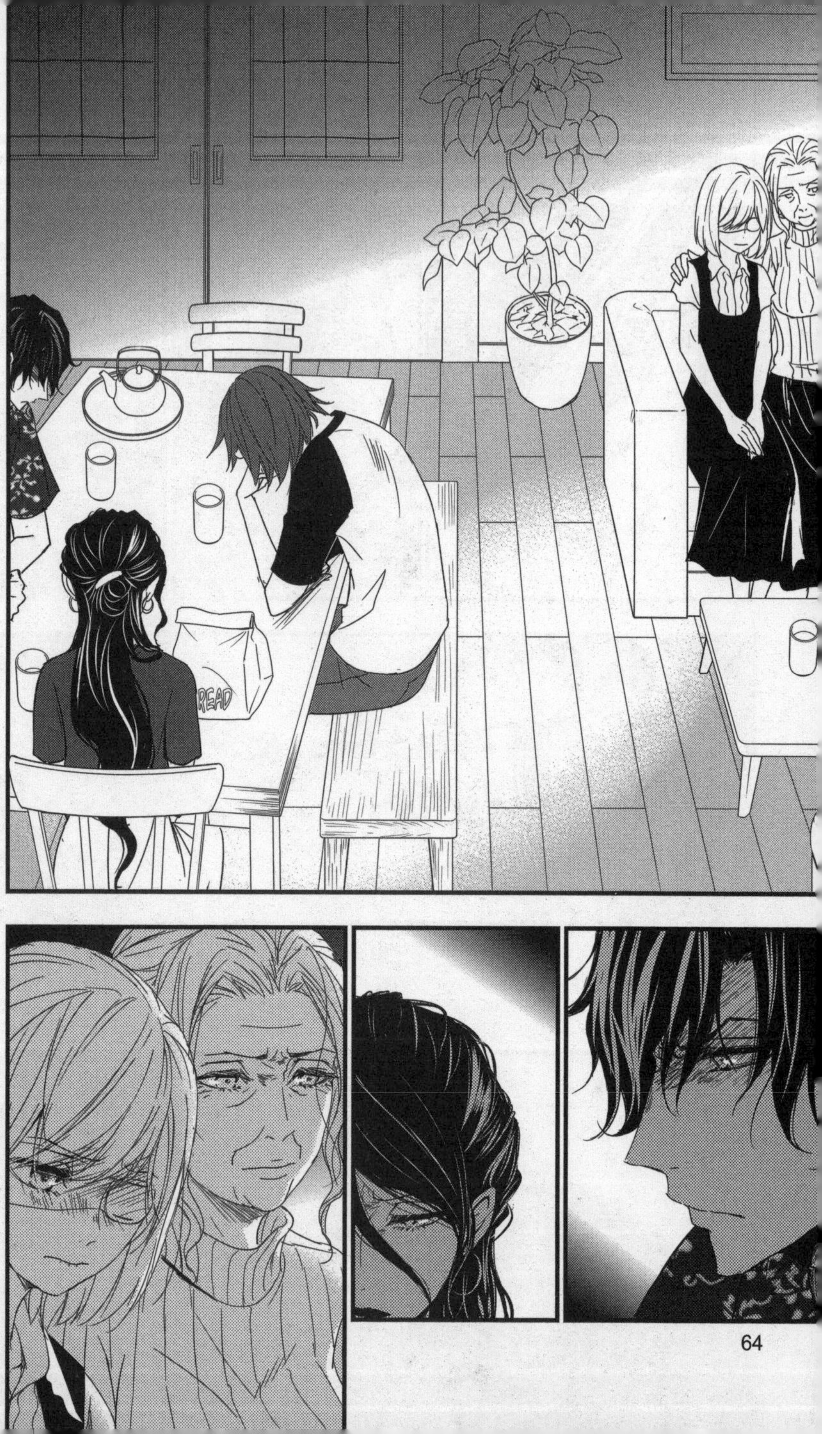

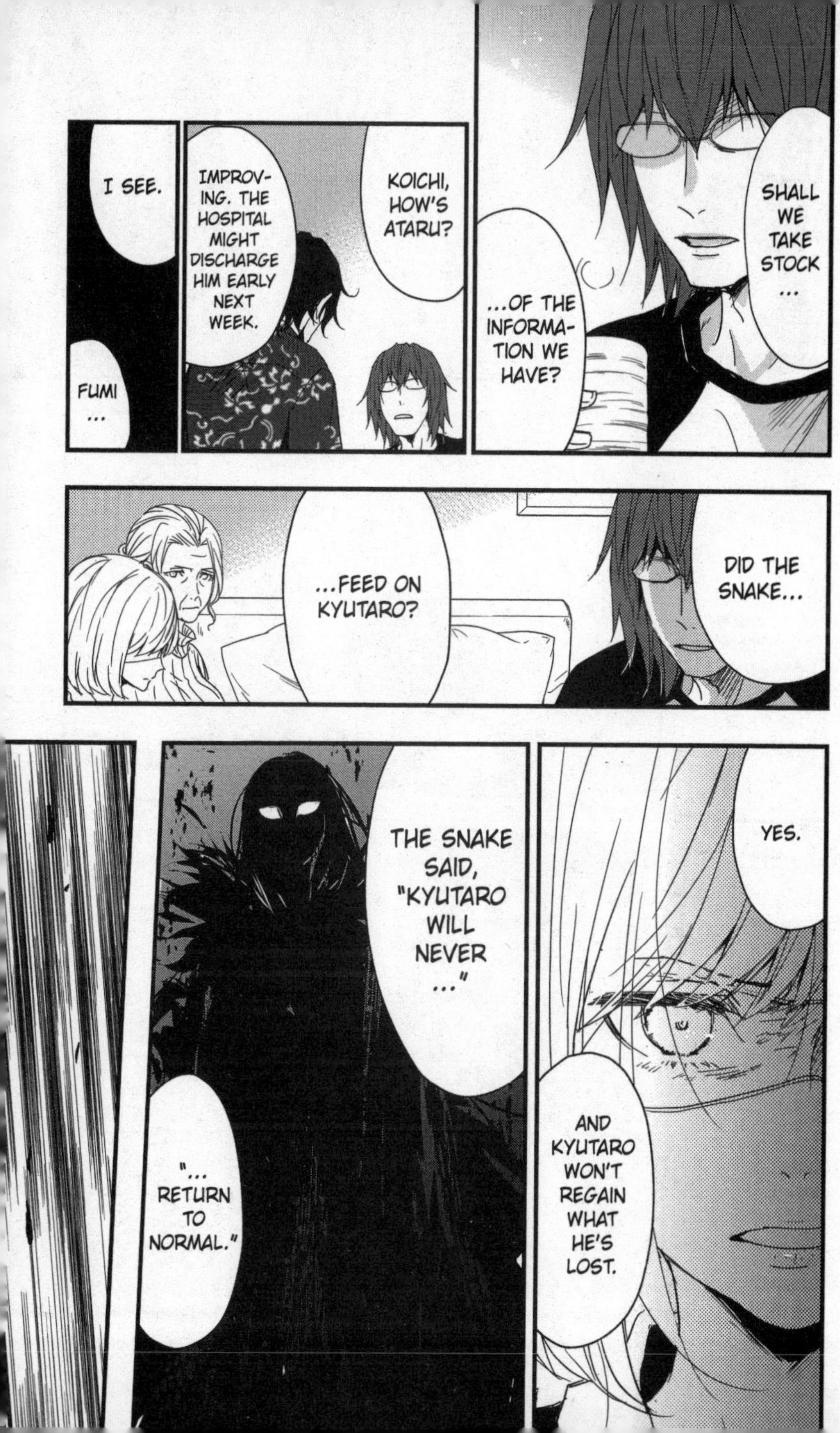
SHALL WE TAKE STOCK ...
...OF THE INFORMATION WE HAVE?
KOICHI, HOW'S ATARU?
IMPROVING. THE HOSPITAL MIGHT DISCHARGE HIM EARLY NEXT WEEK.
I SEE.
FUMI ...
DID THE SNAKE...
...FEED ON KYUTARO?
YES.
AND KYUTARO WON'T REGAIN WHAT HE'S LOST.
THE SNAKE SAID, "KYUTARO WILL NEVER ..."
"... RETURN TO NORMAL."

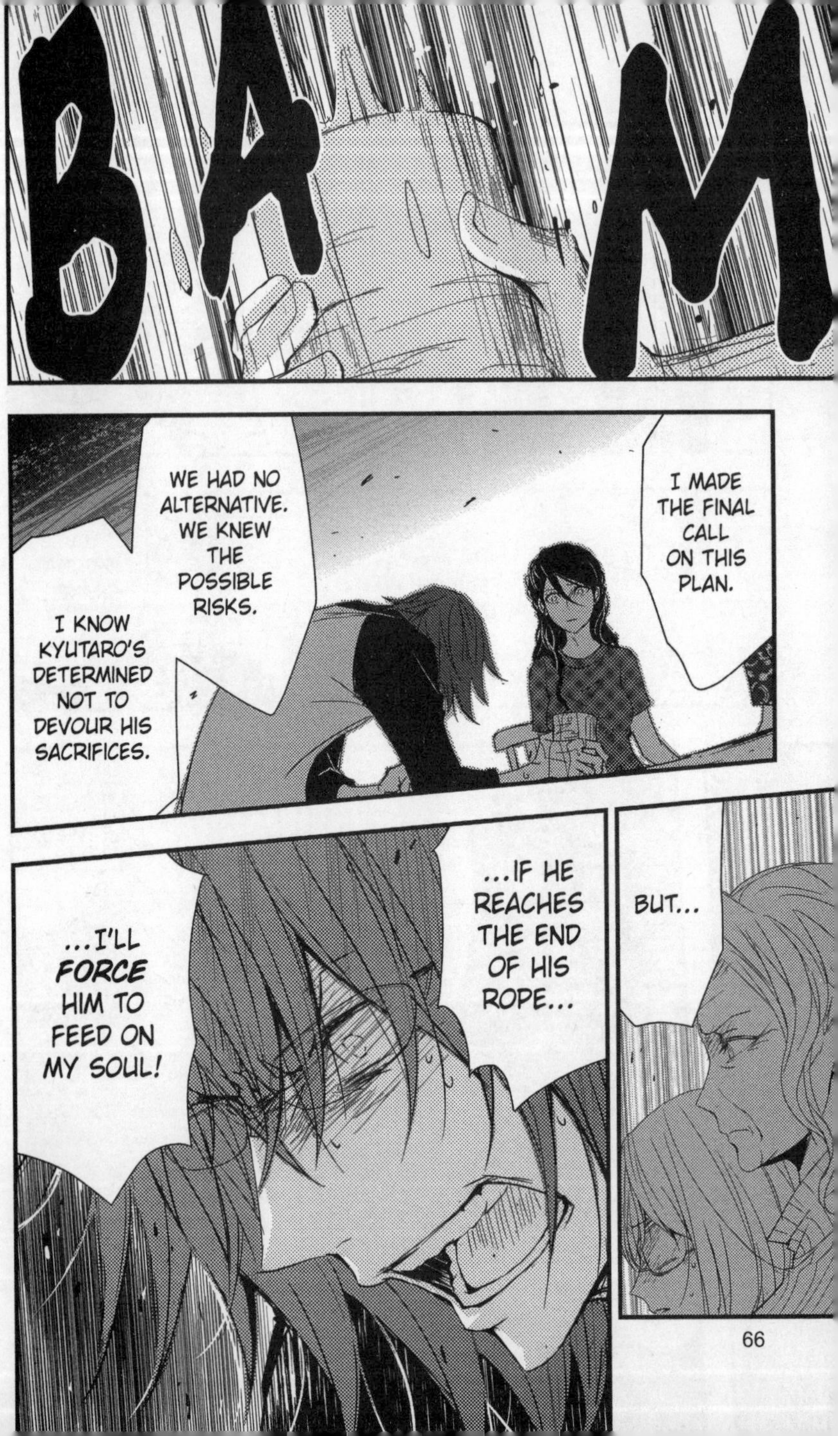
BAM
I MADE THE FINAL CALL ON THIS PLAN.
WE HAD NO ALTERNATIVE. WE KNEW THE POSSIBLE RISKS.
I KNOW KYUTARO'S DETERMINED NOT TO DEVOUR HIS SACRIFICES.
BUT...
...IF HE REACHES THE END OF HIS ROPE...
...I'LL **FORCE** HIM TO FEED ON MY SOUL!

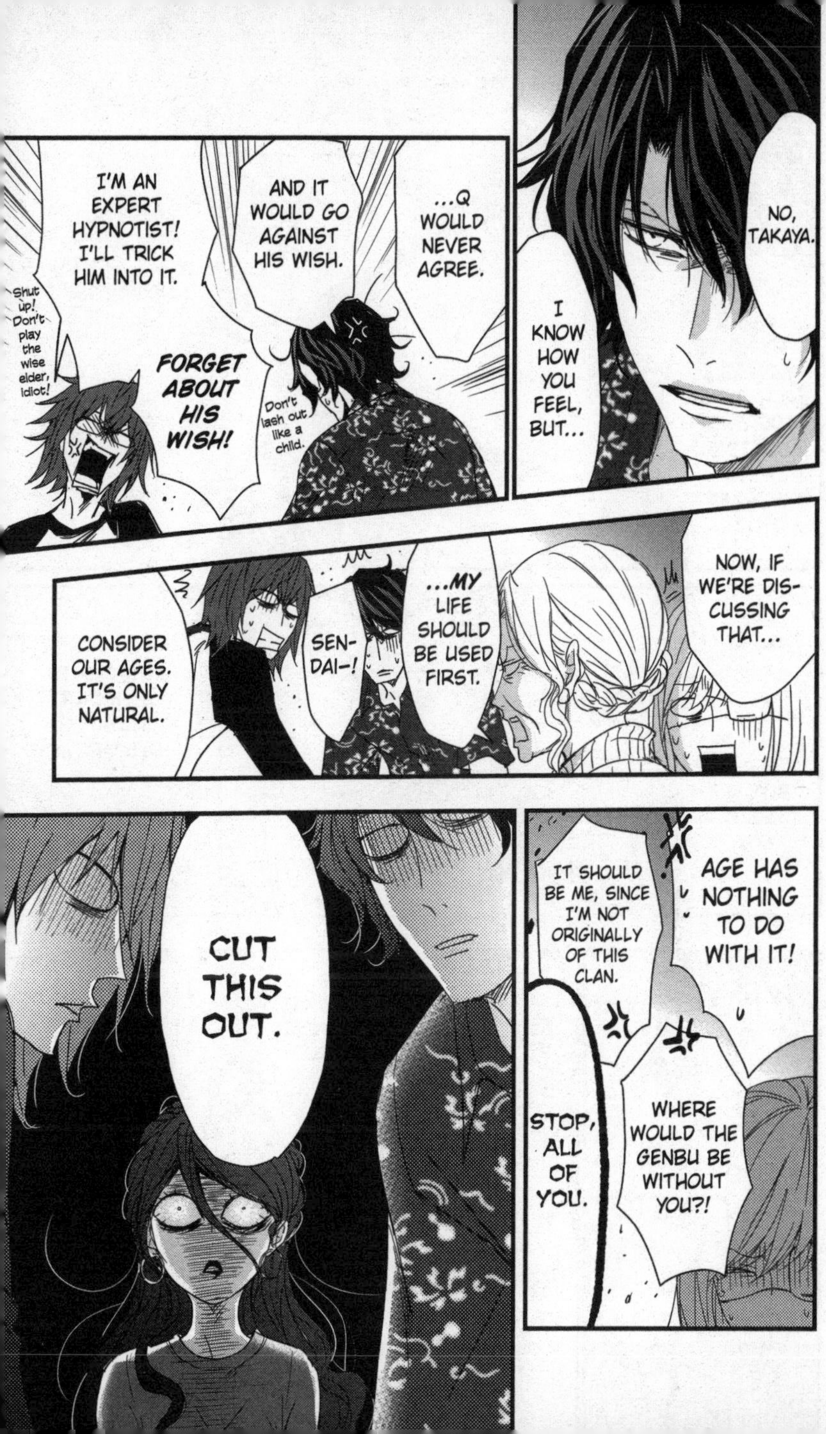
NO, TAKAYA.
I KNOW HOW YOU FEEL, BUT...
...Q WOULD NEVER AGREE.
AND IT WOULD GO AGAINST HIS WISH.
I'M AN EXPERT HYPNOTIST! I'LL TRICK HIM INTO IT.
FORGET ABOUT HIS WISH!
Don't lash out like a child.
Shut up! Don't play the wise elder, idiot!
NOW, IF WE'RE DIS-CUSSING THAT...
...MY LIFE SHOULD BE USED FIRST.
SEN-DAI-!
CONSIDER OUR AGES. IT'S ONLY NATURAL.
AGE HAS NOTHING TO DO WITH IT!
IT SHOULD BE ME, SINCE I'M NOT ORIGINALLY OF THIS CLAN.
WHERE WOULD THE GENBU BE WITHOUT YOU?!
STOP, ALL OF YOU.
CUT THIS OUT.

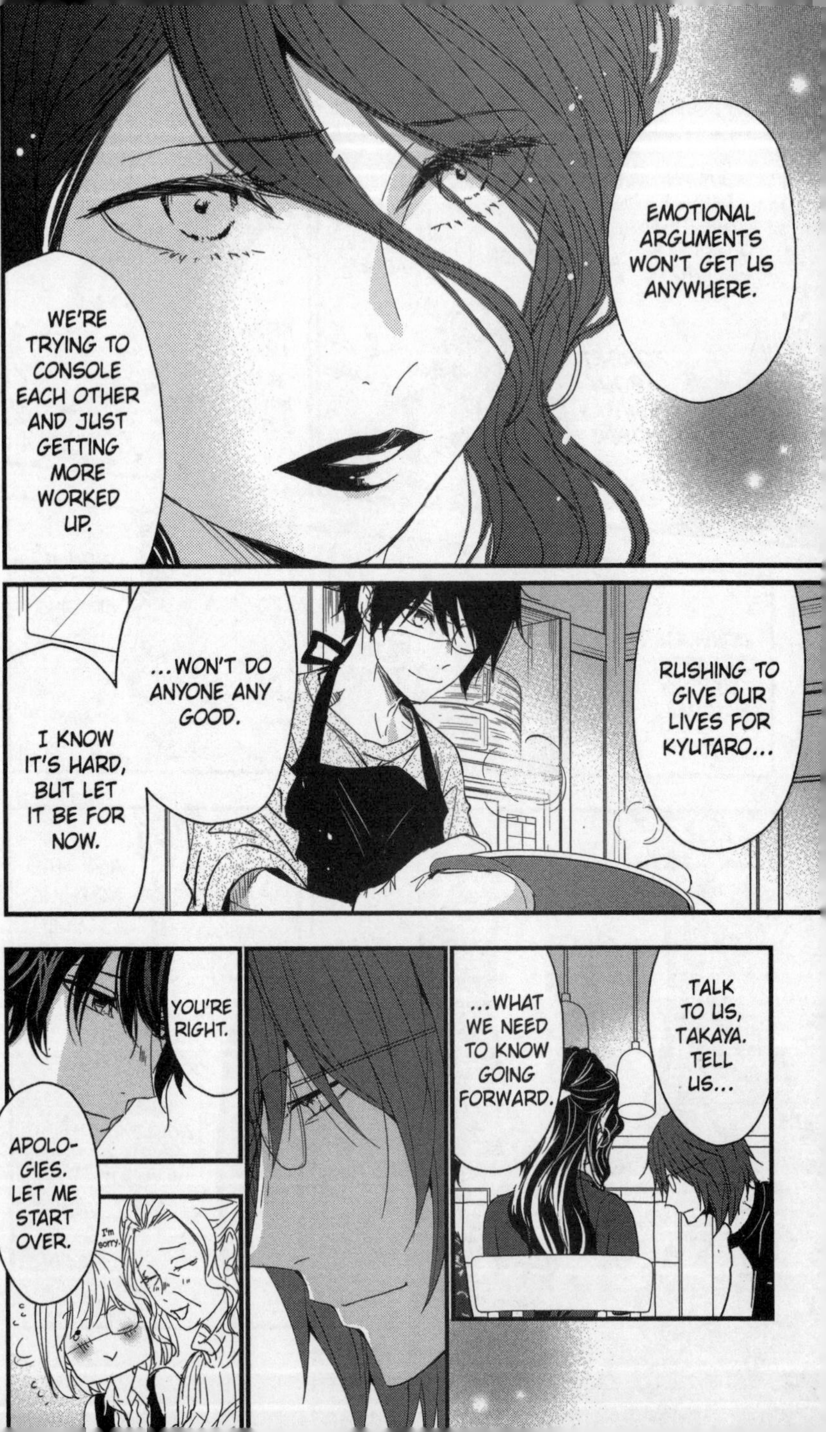
EMOTIONAL ARGUMENTS WON'T GET US ANYWHERE.
WE'RE TRYING TO CONSOLE EACH OTHER AND JUST GETTING MORE WORKED UP.
RUSHING TO GIVE OUR LIVES FOR KYUTARO...
...WON'T DO ANYONE ANY GOOD.
I KNOW IT'S HARD, BUT LET IT BE FOR NOW.
TALK TO US, TAKAYA. TELL US...
...WHAT WE NEED TO KNOW GOING FORWARD.
YOU'RE RIGHT.
APOLOGIES. LET ME START OVER.
I'm sorry.

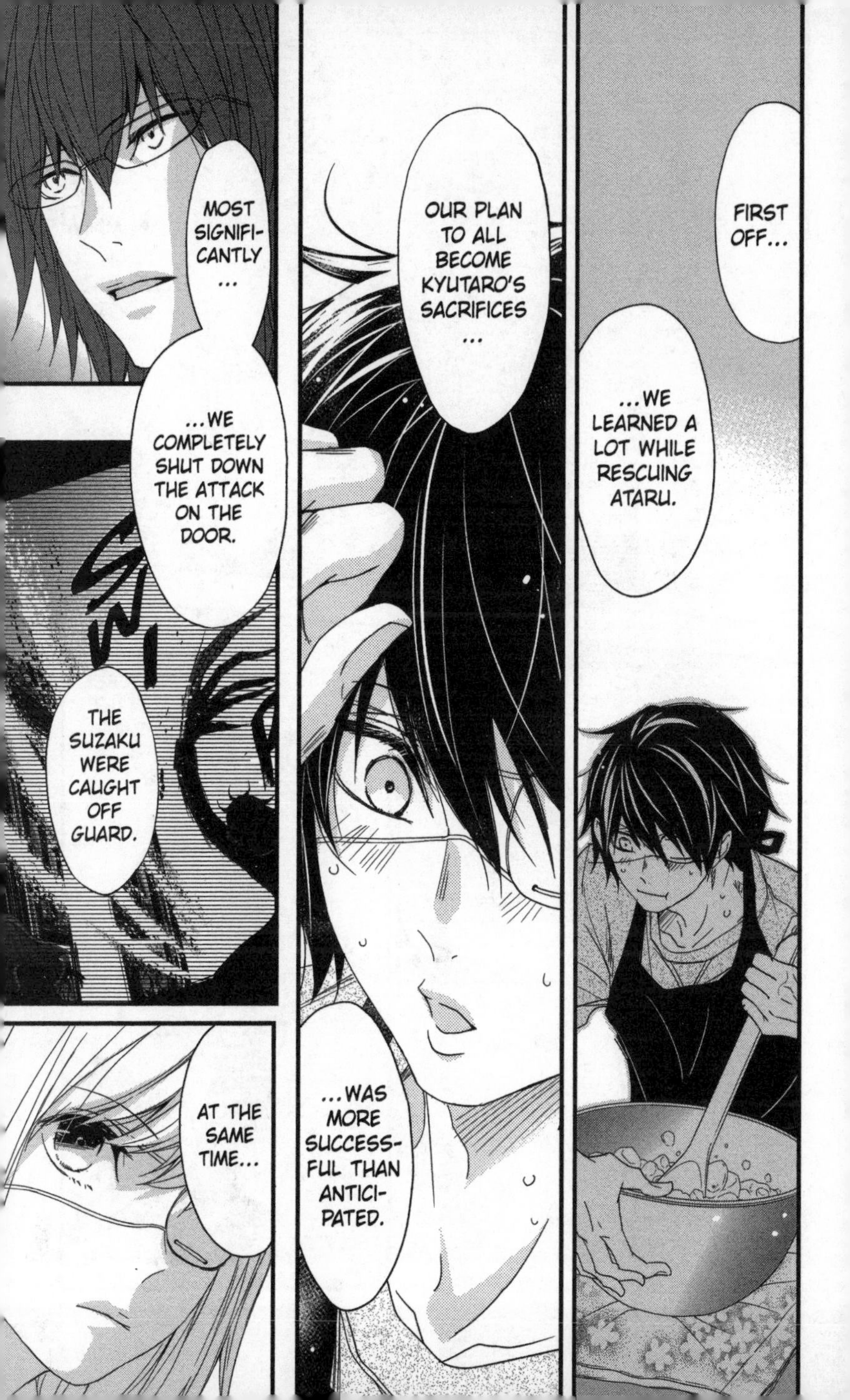
FIRST OFF...
...WE LEARNED A LOT WHILE RESCUING ATARU.
OUR PLAN TO ALL BECOME KYUTARO'S SACRIFICES...
...WAS MORE SUCCESSFUL THAN ANTICIPATED.
MOST SIGNIFICANTLY...
...WE COMPLETELY SHUT DOWN THE ATTACK ON THE DOOR.
THE SUZAKU WERE CAUGHT OFF GUARD.
AT THE SAME TIME...

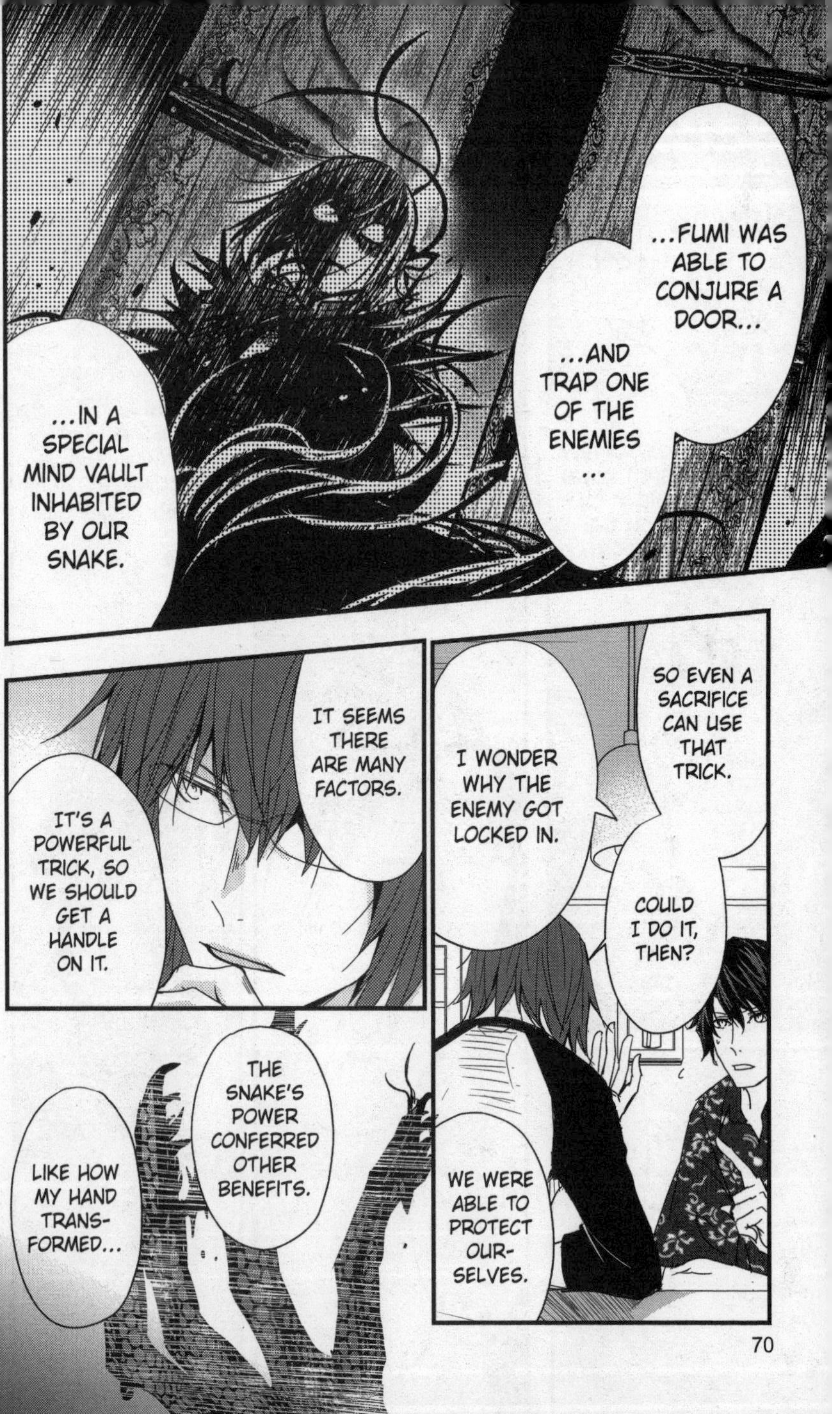
...FUMI WAS ABLE TO CONJURE A DOOR...
...AND TRAP ONE OF THE ENEMIES ...
...IN A SPECIAL MIND VAULT INHABITED BY OUR SNAKE.
SO EVEN A SACRIFICE CAN USE THAT TRICK.
I WONDER WHY THE ENEMY GOT LOCKED IN.
COULD I DO IT, THEN?
WE WERE ABLE TO PROTECT OUR-SELVES.
IT SEEMS THERE ARE MANY FACTORS.
IT'S A POWERFUL TRICK, SO WE SHOULD GET A HANDLE ON IT.
THE SNAKE'S POWER CONFERRED OTHER BENEFITS.
LIKE HOW MY HAND TRANS-FORMED...

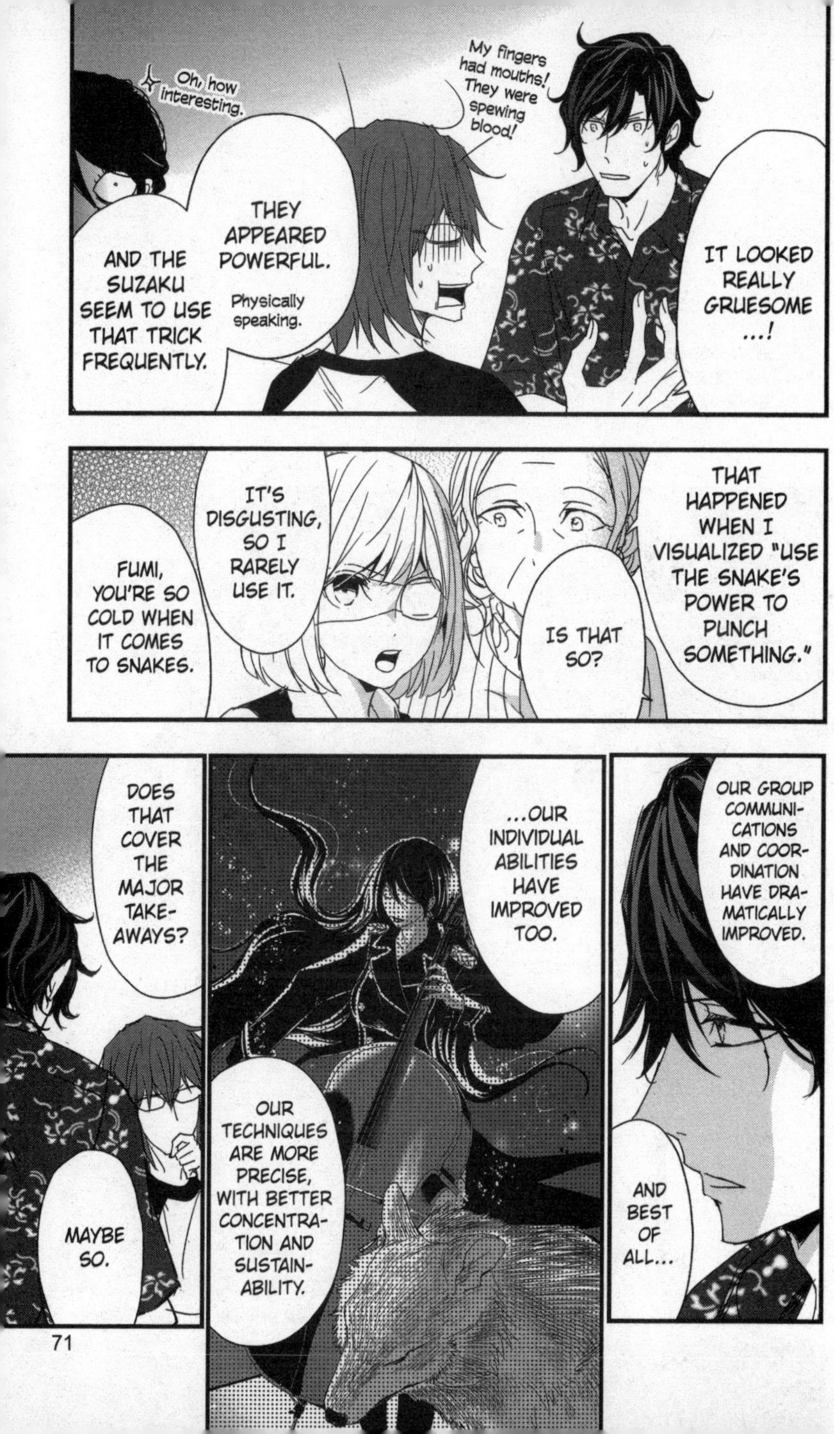

IT LOOKED REALLY GRUESOME ...!
My fingers had mouths! They were spewing blood!
THEY APPEARED POWERFUL.
Physically speaking.
Oh, how interesting.
AND THE SUZAKU SEEM TO USE THAT TRICK FREQUENTLY.
THAT HAPPENED WHEN I VISUALIZED "USE THE SNAKE'S POWER TO PUNCH SOMETHING."
IS THAT SO?
IT'S DISGUSTING, SO I RARELY USE IT.
FUMI, YOU'RE SO COLD WHEN IT COMES TO SNAKES.
OUR GROUP COMMUNI-CATIONS AND COOR-DINATION HAVE DRA-MATICALLY IMPROVED.
AND BEST OF ALL...
...OUR INDIVIDUAL ABILITIES HAVE IMPROVED TOO.
OUR TECHNIQUES ARE MORE PRECISE, WITH BETTER CONCENTRA-TION AND SUSTAIN-ABILITY.
DOES THAT COVER THE MAJOR TAKE-AWAYS?
MAYBE SO.

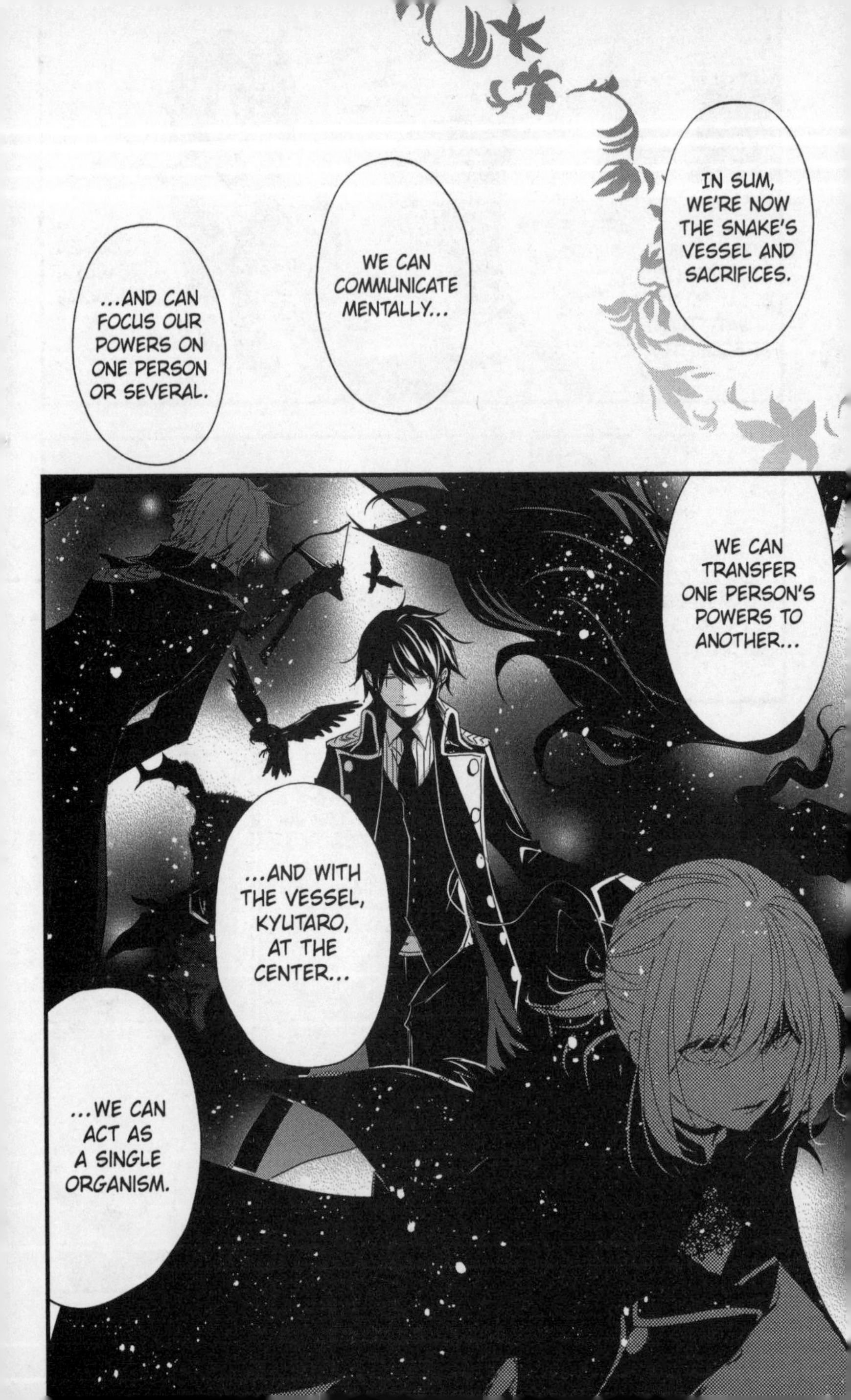
IN SUM, WE'RE NOW THE SNAKE'S VESSEL AND SACRIFICES.
WE CAN COMMUNICATE MENTALLY...
...AND CAN FOCUS OUR POWERS ON ONE PERSON OR SEVERAL.
WE CAN TRANSFER ONE PERSON'S POWERS TO ANOTHER...
...AND WITH THE VESSEL, KYUTARO, AT THE CENTER...
...WE CAN ACT AS A SINGLE ORGANISM.

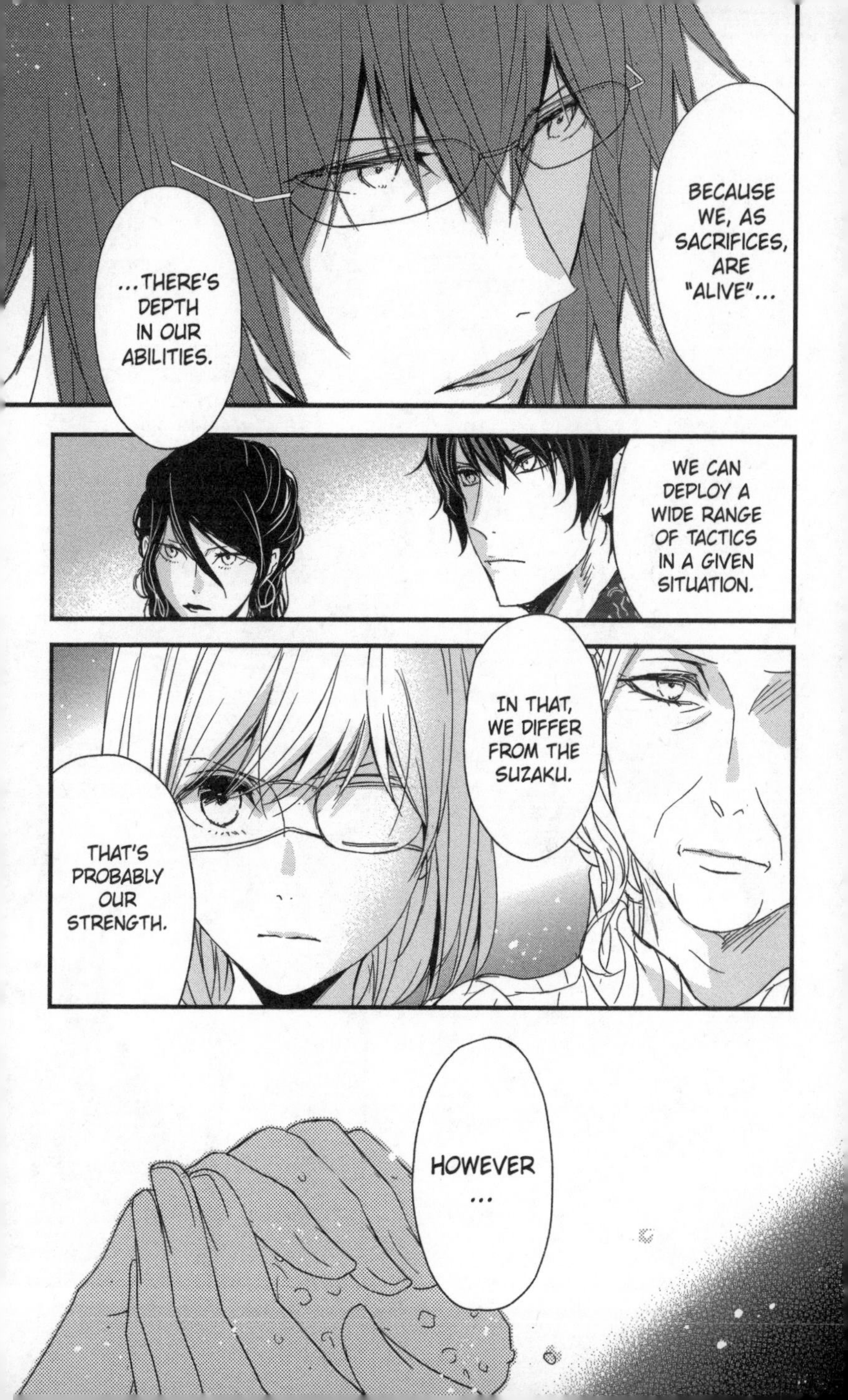
BECAUSE WE, AS SACRIFICES, ARE "ALIVE"...
...THERE'S DEPTH IN OUR ABILITIES.
WE CAN DEPLOY A WIDE RANGE OF TACTICS IN A GIVEN SITUATION.
IN THAT, WE DIFFER FROM THE SUZAKU.
THAT'S PROBABLY OUR STRENGTH.
HOWEVER ...

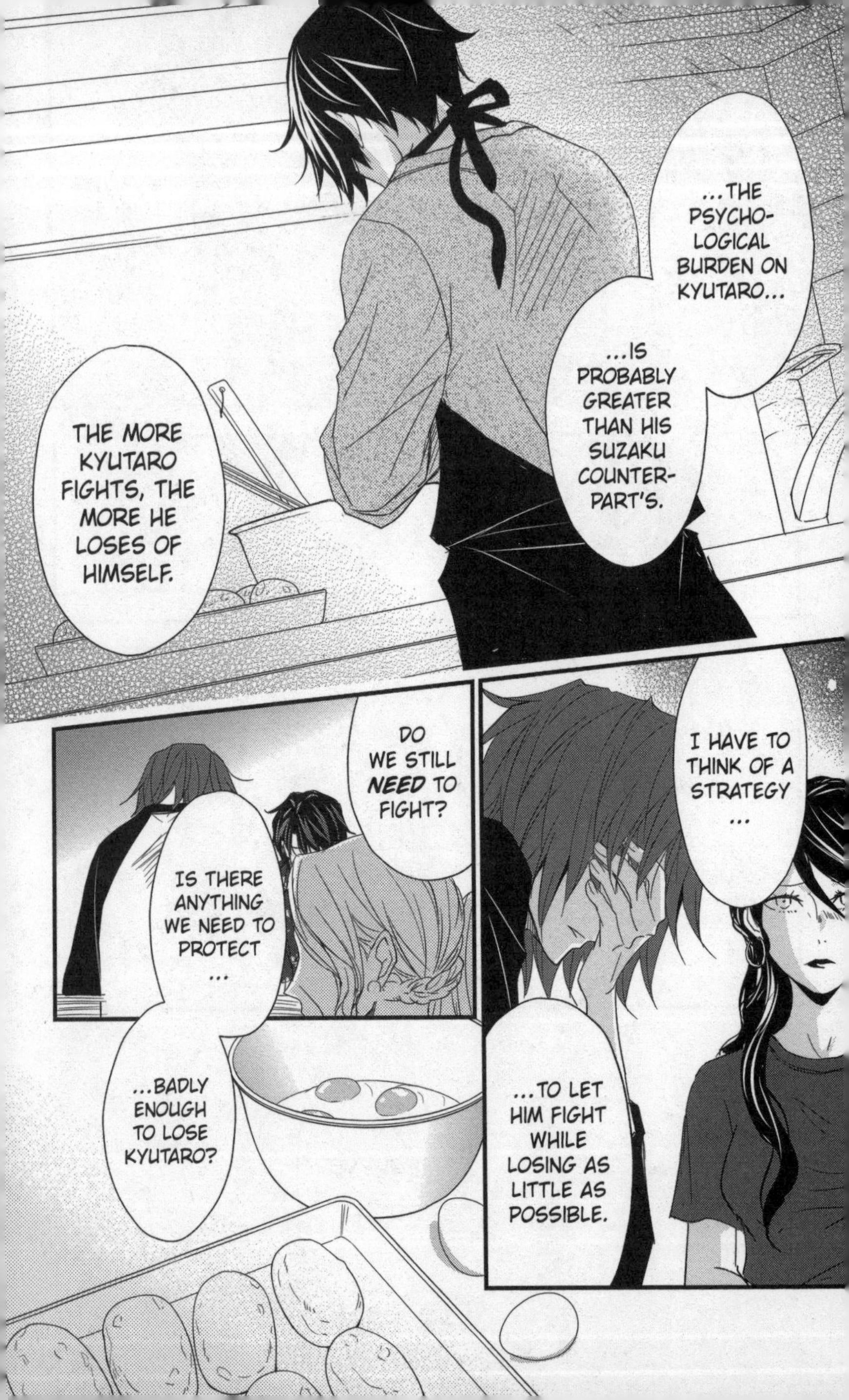
...THE PSYCHOLOGICAL BURDEN ON KYUTARO...
...IS PROBABLY GREATER THAN HIS SUZAKU COUNTERPART'S.
THE MORE KYUTARO FIGHTS, THE MORE HE LOSES OF HIMSELF.
I HAVE TO THINK OF A STRATEGY ...
...TO LET HIM FIGHT WHILE LOSING AS LITTLE AS POSSIBLE.
DO WE STILL *NEED* TO FIGHT?
IS THERE ANYTHING WE NEED TO PROTECT ...
...BADLY ENOUGH TO LOSE KYUTARO?

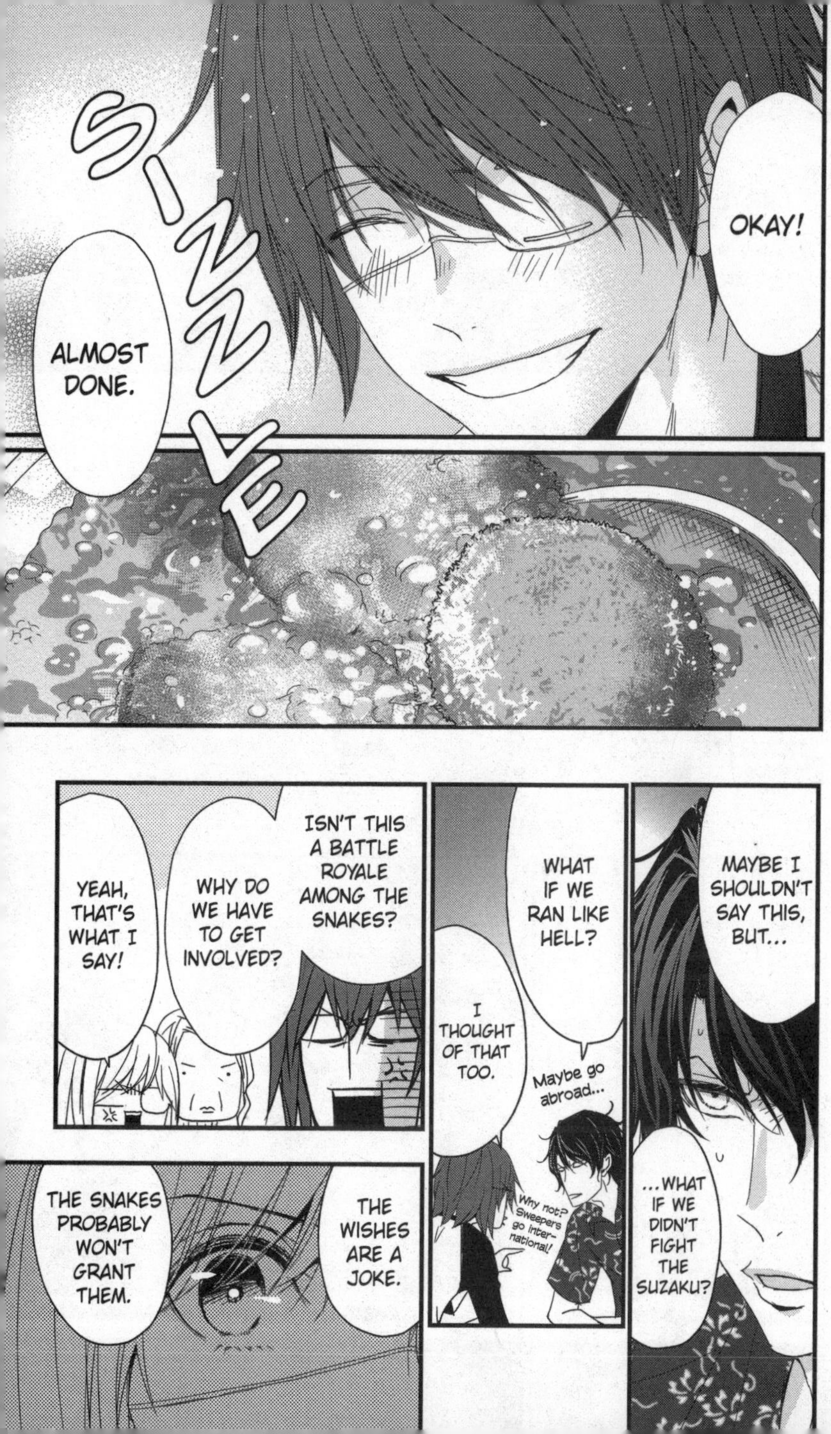
OKAY!
SIZZLE
ALMOST DONE.
MAYBE I SHOULDN'T SAY THIS, BUT...
...WHAT IF WE DIDN'T FIGHT THE SUZAKU?
WHAT IF WE RAN LIKE HELL?
I THOUGHT OF THAT TOO.
Maybe go abroad...
Why not? Sweepers go international!
ISN'T THIS A BATTLE ROYALE AMONG THE SNAKES?
WHY DO WE HAVE TO GET INVOLVED?
YEAH, THAT'S WHAT I SAY!
THE WISHES ARE A JOKE.
THE SNAKES PROBABLY WON'T GRANT THEM.

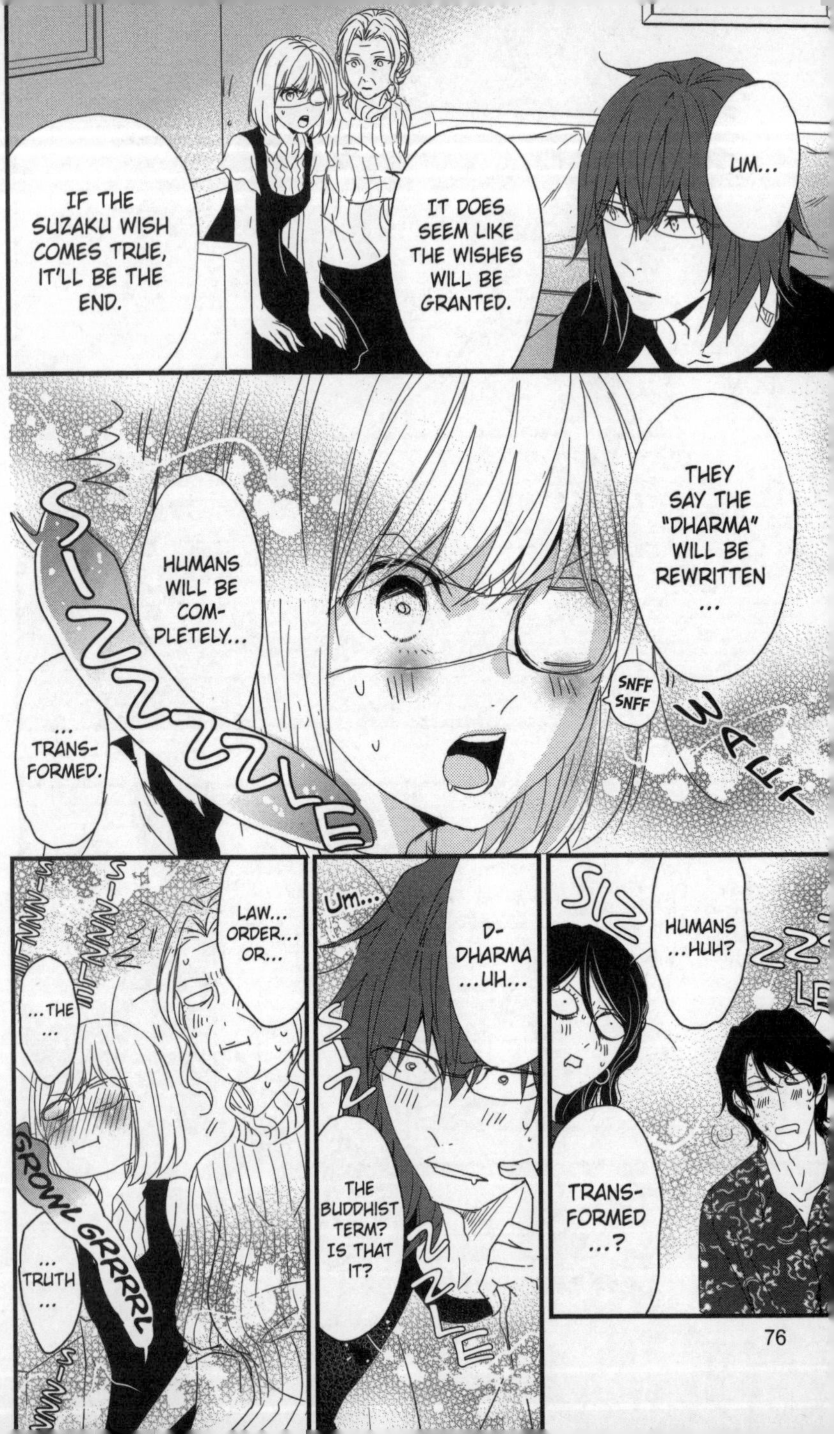
UM...
IT DOES SEEM LIKE THE WISHES WILL BE GRANTED.
IF THE SUZAKU WISH COMES TRUE, IT'LL BE THE END.
THEY SAY THE "DHARMA" WILL BE REWRITTEN ...
WAFT
SNFF SNFF
HUMANS WILL BE COM- PLETELY...
SIZZZZLE
... TRANS- FORMED.
SIZ
ZZZ
LE
HUMANS ...HUH?
TRANS- FORMED ...?
Um...
D- DHARMA ...UH...
THE BUDDHIST TERM? IS THAT IT?
SIZZLE
LAW... ORDER... OR...
...THE ...
... TRUTH ...
GROWL GRRRRL

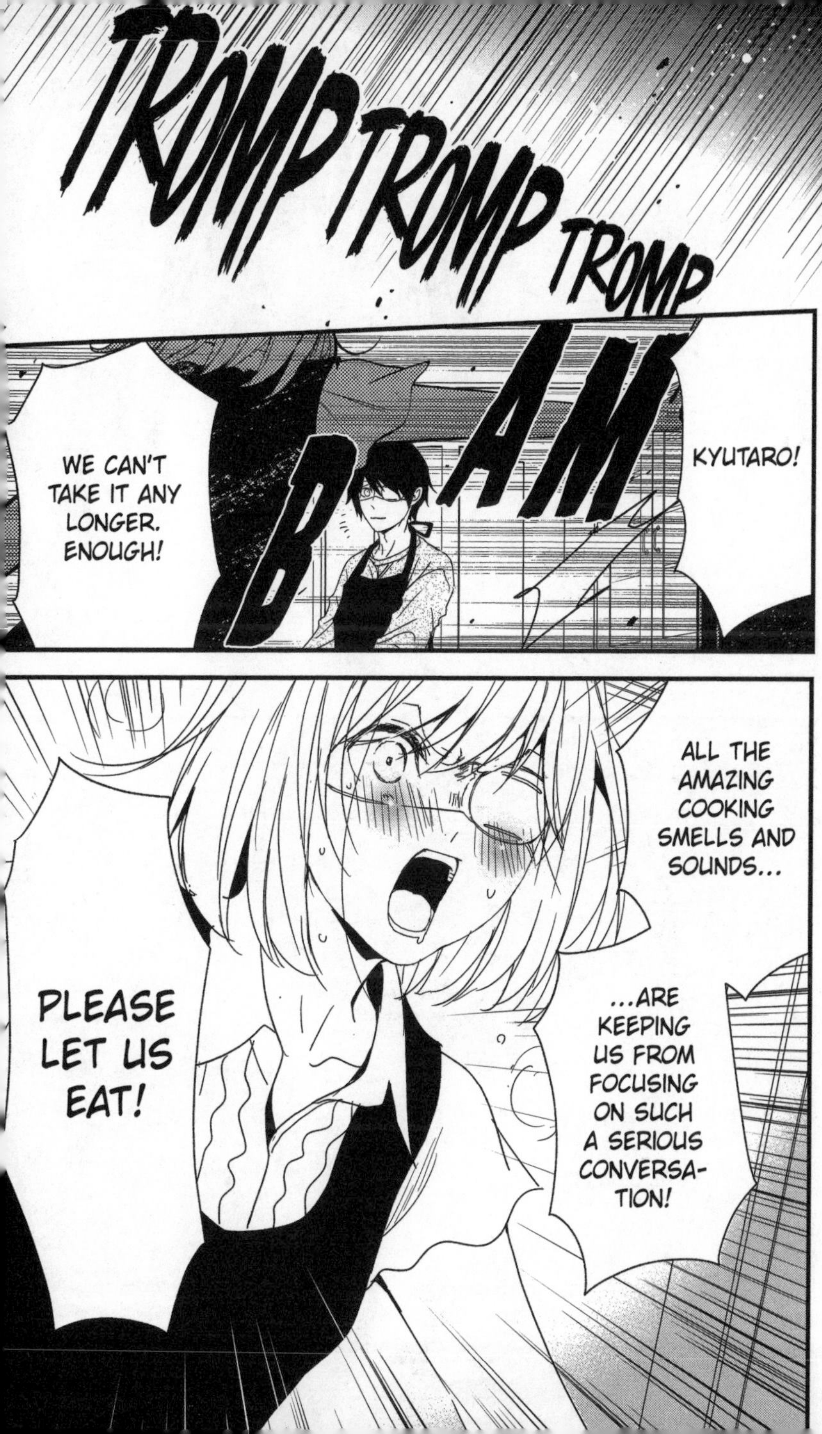
TROMP TROMP TROMP
KYUTARO!
BAM
WE CAN'T TAKE IT ANY LONGER. ENOUGH!
ALL THE AMAZING COOKING SMELLS AND SOUNDS...
...ARE KEEPING US FROM FOCUSING ON SUCH A SERIOUS CONVERSATION!
PLEASE LET US EAT!

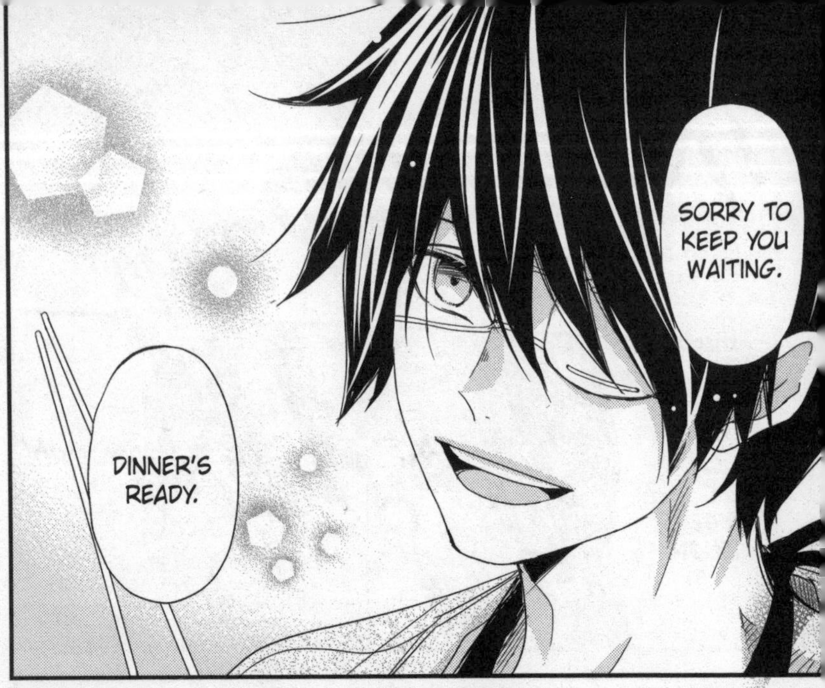
SORRY TO KEEP YOU WAITING.
DINNER'S READY.
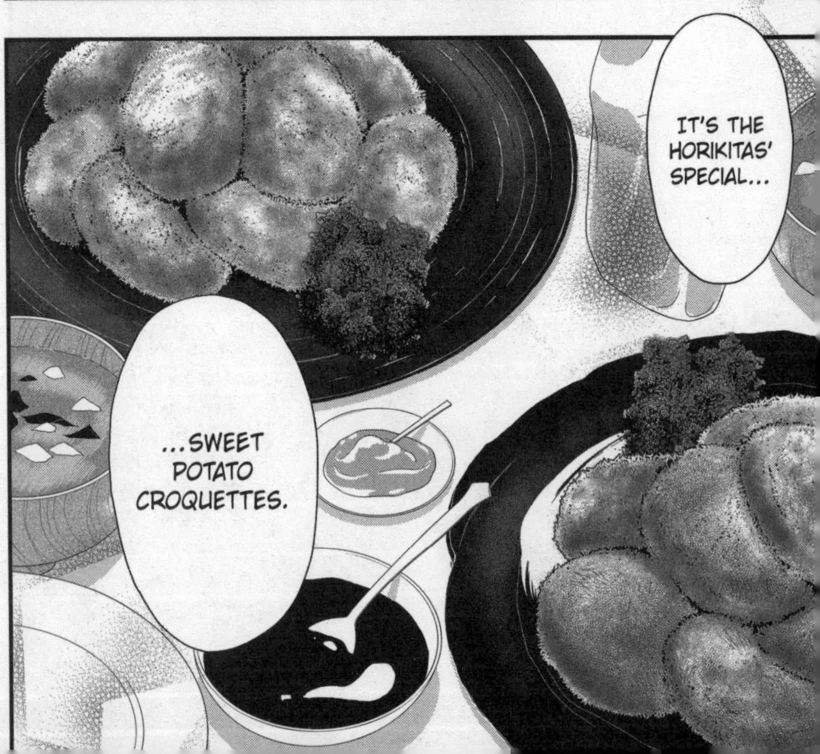
IT'S THE HORIKITAS' SPECIAL...
...SWEET POTATO CROQUETTES.

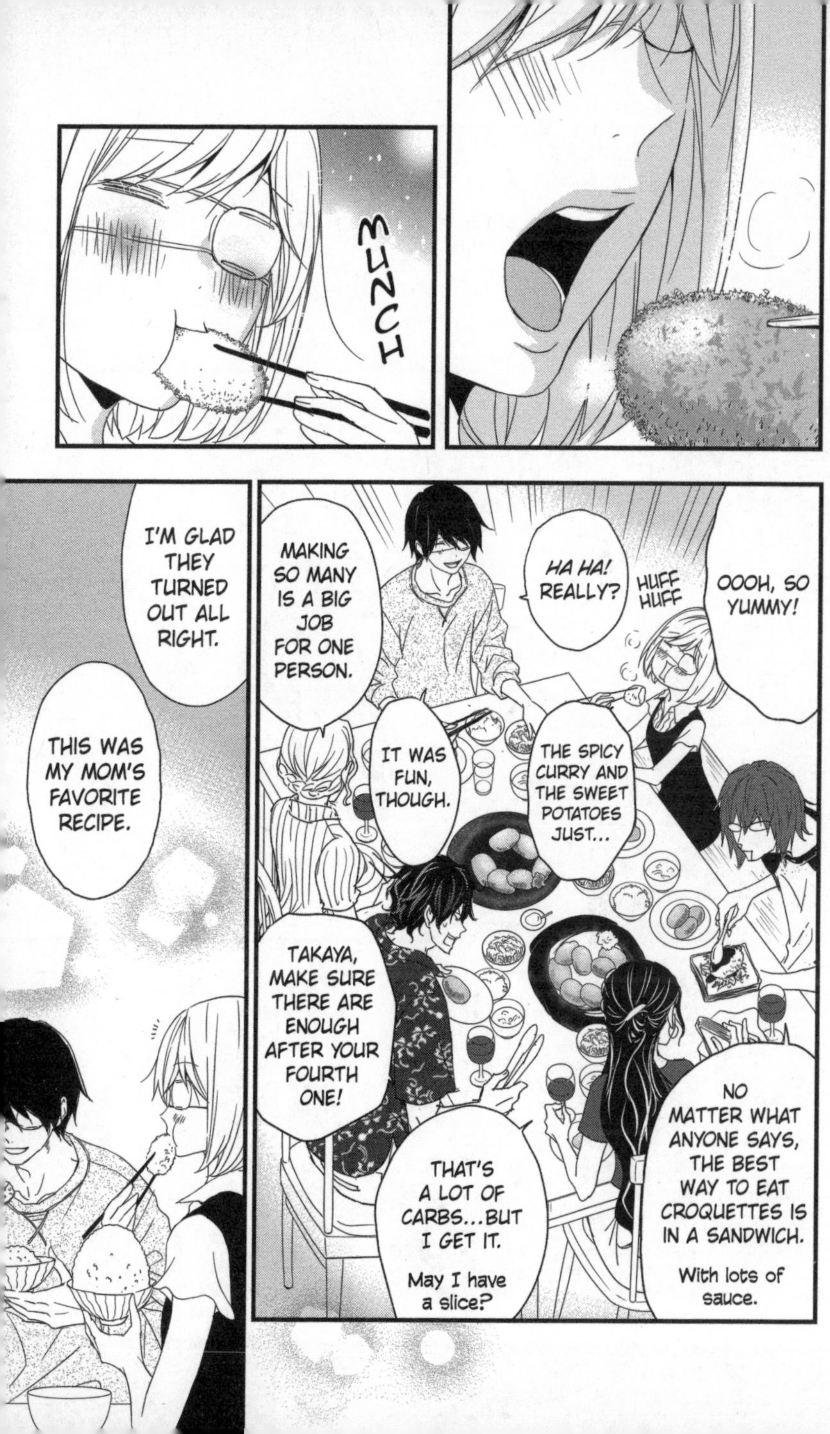
MUNCH
OOOH, SO YUMMY!
HUFF HUFF
HA HA! REALLY?
MAKING SO MANY IS A BIG JOB FOR ONE PERSON.
THE SPICY CURRY AND THE SWEET POTATOES JUST...
IT WAS FUN, THOUGH.
NO MATTER WHAT ANYONE SAYS, THE BEST WAY TO EAT CROQUETTES IS IN A SANDWICH.
With lots of sauce.
TAKAYA, MAKE SURE THERE ARE ENOUGH AFTER YOUR FOURTH ONE!
THAT'S A LOT OF CARBS...BUT I GET IT.
May I have a slice?
I'M GLAD THEY TURNED OUT ALL RIGHT.
THIS WAS MY MOM'S FAVORITE RECIPE.

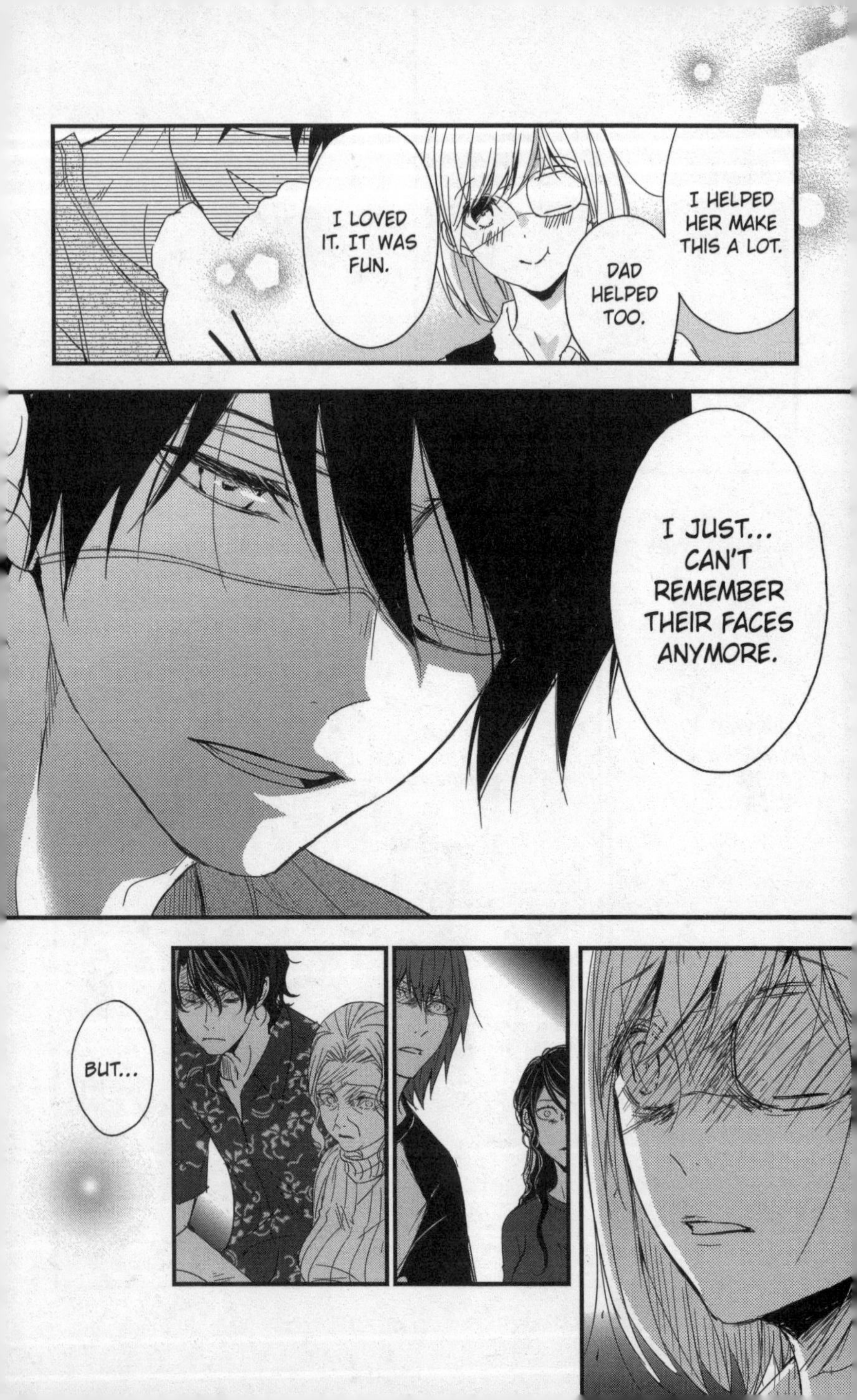
I HELPED HER MAKE THIS A LOT.
DAD HELPED TOO.
I LOVED IT. IT WAS FUN.
I JUST... CAN'T REMEMBER THEIR FACES ANYMORE.
BUT...

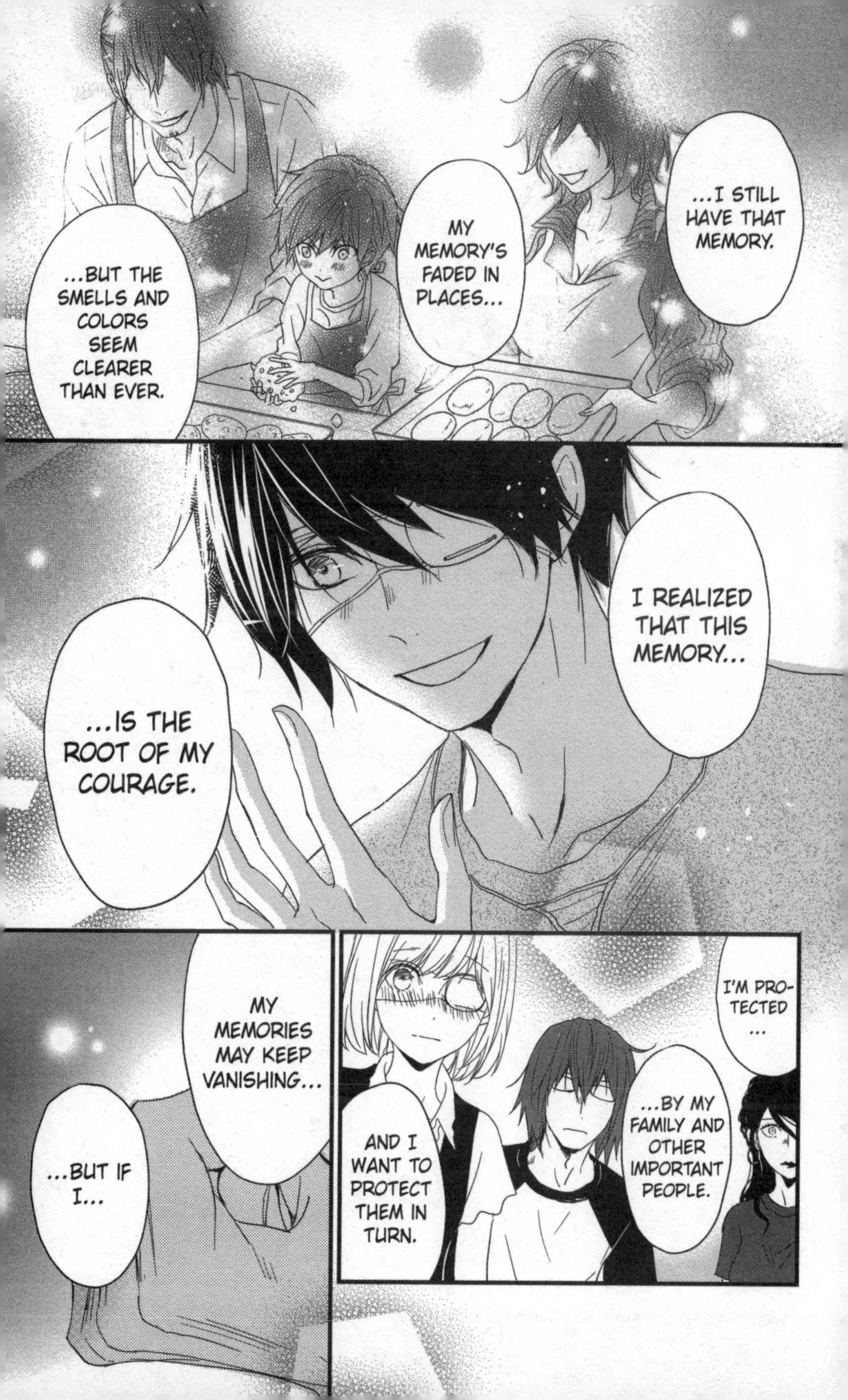
...I STILL HAVE THAT MEMORY.
MY MEMORY'S FADED IN PLACES...
...BUT THE SMELLS AND COLORS SEEM CLEARER THAN EVER.
I REALIZED THAT THIS MEMORY...
...IS THE ROOT OF MY COURAGE.
I'M PROTECTED...
...BY MY FAMILY AND OTHER IMPORTANT PEOPLE.
AND I WANT TO PROTECT THEM IN TURN.
MY MEMORIES MAY KEEP VANISHING...
...BUT IF I...

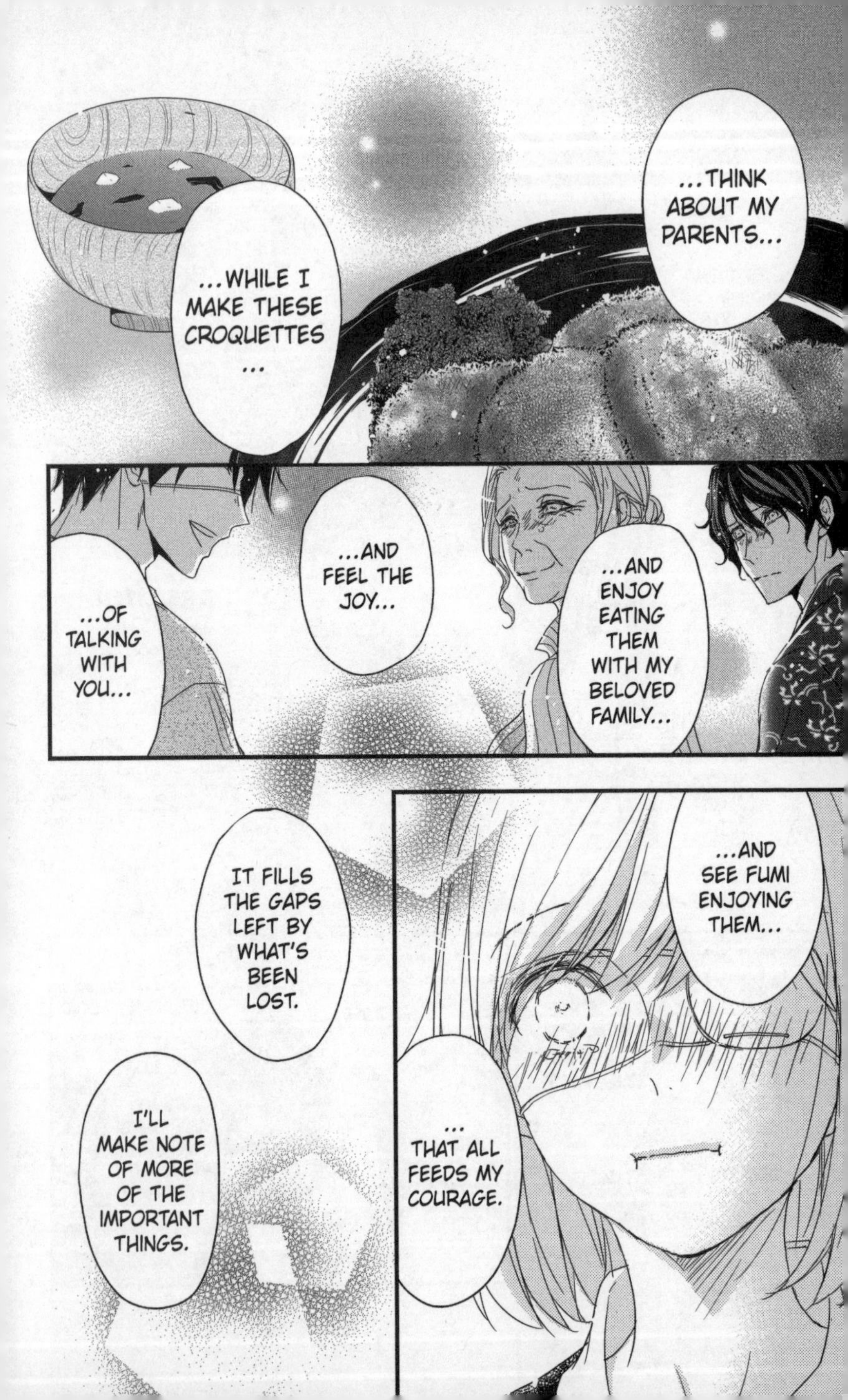
...THINK ABOUT MY PARENTS...
...WHILE I MAKE THESE CROQUETTES...
...AND ENJOY EATING THEM WITH MY BELOVED FAMILY...
...AND FEEL THE JOY...
...OF TALKING WITH YOU...
...AND SEE FUMI ENJOYING THEM...
...THAT ALL FEEDS MY COURAGE.
IT FILLS THE GAPS LEFT BY WHAT'S BEEN LOST.
I'LL MAKE NOTE OF MORE OF THE IMPORTANT THINGS.

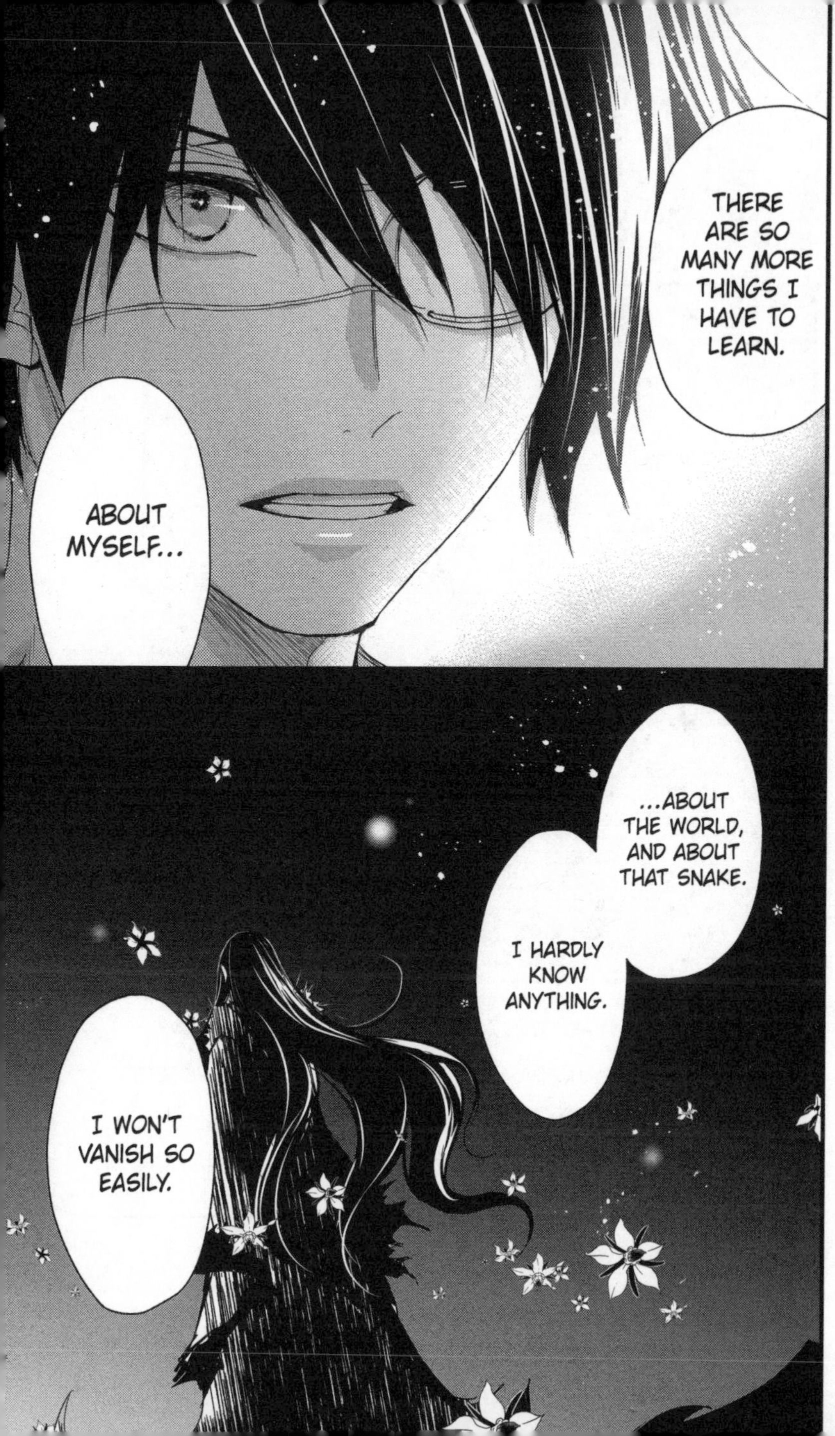
THERE ARE SO MANY MORE THINGS I HAVE TO LEARN.
ABOUT MYSELF...
...ABOUT THE WORLD, AND ABOUT THAT SNAKE.
I HARDLY KNOW ANYTHING.
I WON'T VANISH SO EASILY.

CHAPTER 68

MONTHLY BETSUCOMI SALE DATE NOTICE ON TWITTER AND INSTAGRAM

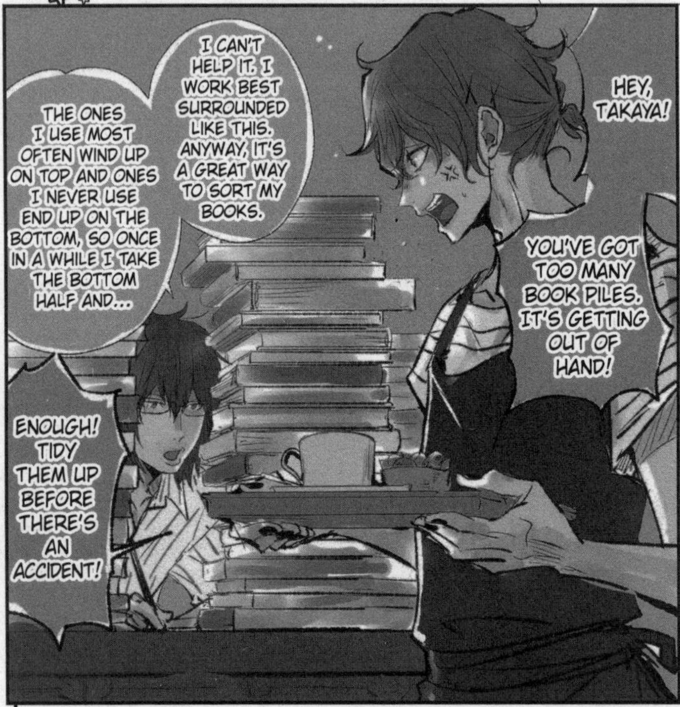
HEY, TAKAYA!
YOU'VE GOT TOO MANY BOOK PILES. IT'S GETTING OUT OF HAND!
I CAN'T HELP IT. I WORK BEST SURROUNDED LIKE THIS. ANYWAY, IT'S A GREAT WAY TO SORT MY BOOKS.
THE ONES I USE MOST OFTEN WIND UP ON TOP AND ONES I NEVER USE END UP ON THE BOTTOM, SO ONCE IN A WHILE I TAKE THE BOTTOM HALF AND...
ENOUGH! TIDY THEM UP BEFORE THERE'S AN ACCIDENT!

LET'S SEE... WHAT'S UP IN *QUEEN'S QUALITY* THIS MONTH?
1) WE SUDDENLY LEARN THAT ATARU AND TAKAYA ARE ROOMING TOGETHER.
2) WHEN THEY GO INTO DARKNESS, THEIR CHESTS GET EXPOSED? (OH DEAR.)
3) THE KIND OF KILLER WHO'LL APPEAR OUT OF NOWHERE BEHIND YOU.

A LOT HAPPENS, BUT THE GIRAFFES ARE ESPECIALLY CUTE IN THIS CHAPTER!

I TWEETED ABOUT IT BEFORE, BUT TAKAYA IS WORKING IN PAJAMAS. HE'S ON A DEADLINE. ATARU HAS HIS HANDS FULL HELPING HIM. SO SORRY. (FOR SOME REASON THE AUTHOR IS APOLOGIZING.)

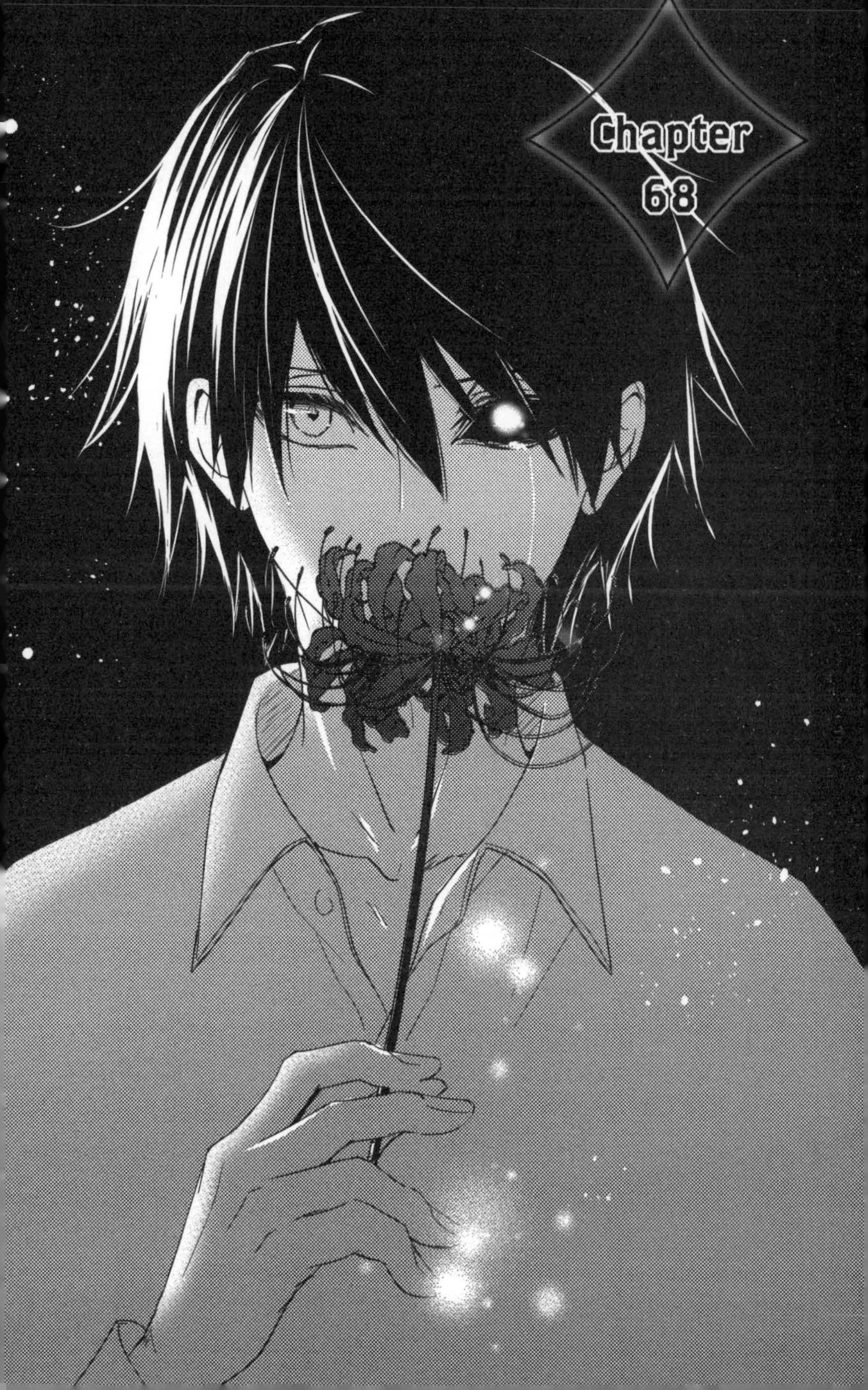
Chapter
68

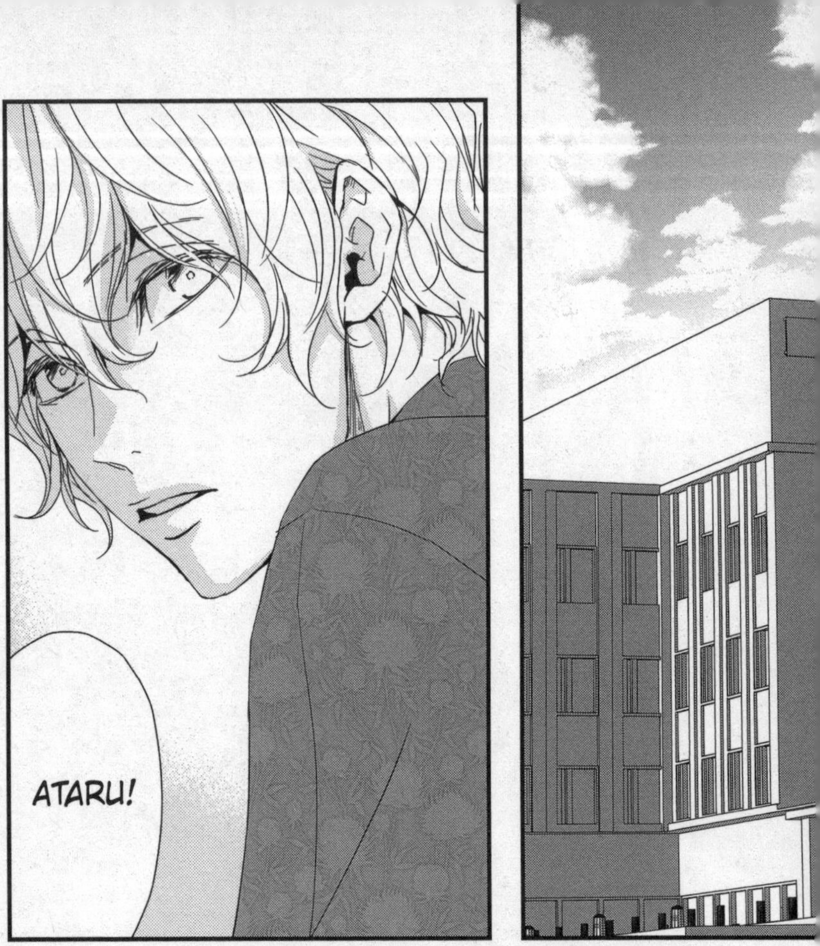
ATARU!

I enjoy reading stories about "Things I'm Glad I Bought" online or in magazines. They're good reference material, and they excite me.

One thing I'm glad I bought recently is a one-liter measuring cup. It's great for when I have to fill a pot for boiling, for watering my plants, for when I want to bleach a towel, or for Kojiro's dishes. I love how the blue lines look on the white background.

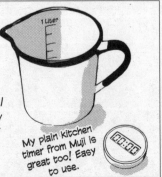

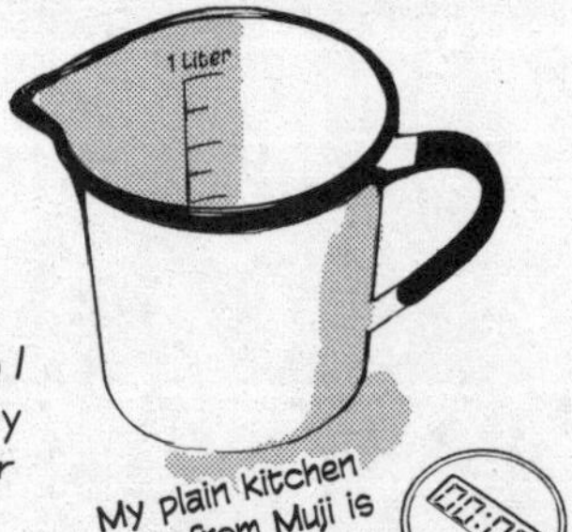
1 Liter
00:00
My plain kitchen timer from Muji is great too! Easy to use.

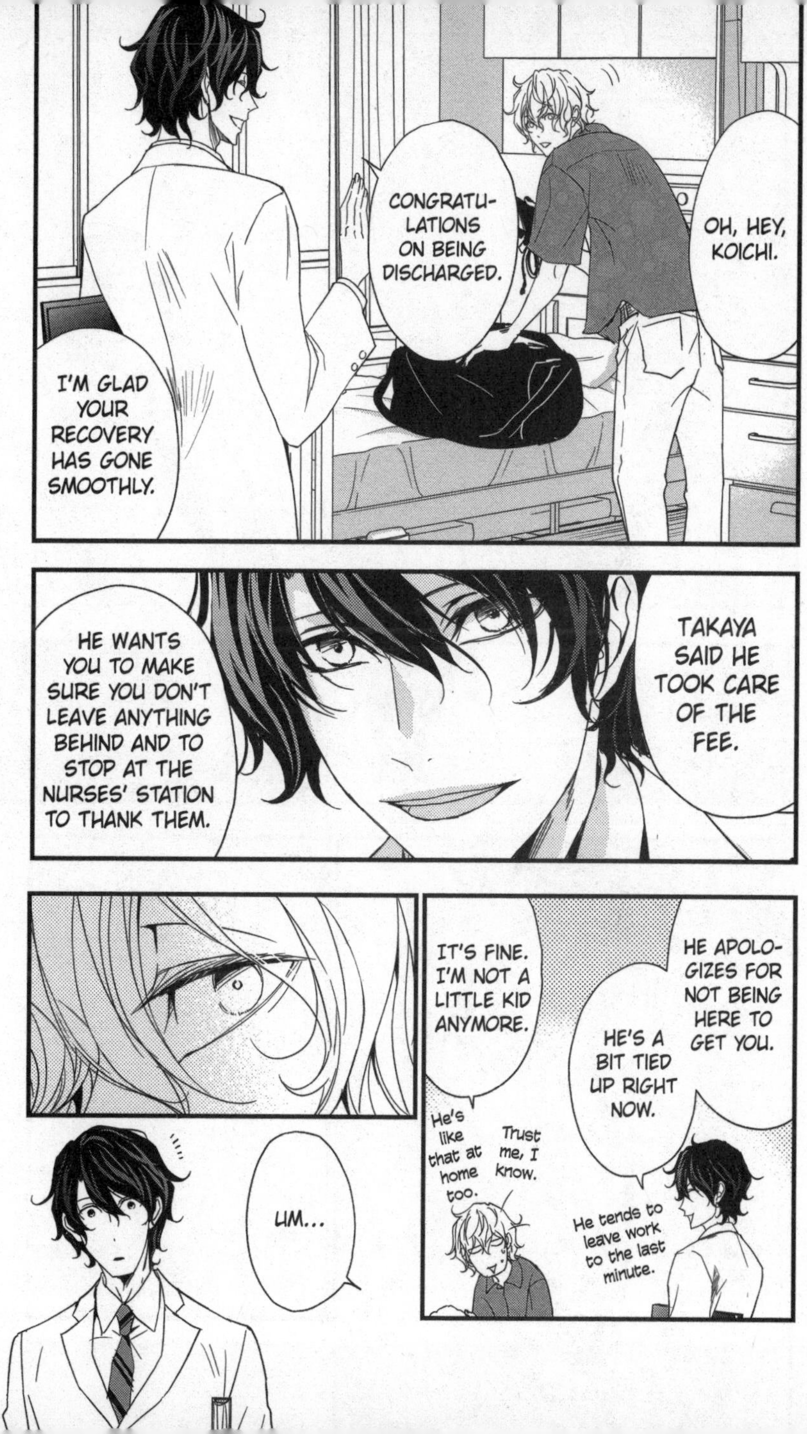
OH, HEY, KOICHI.
CONGRATULATIONS ON BEING DISCHARGED.
I'M GLAD YOUR RECOVERY HAS GONE SMOOTHLY.
TAKAYA SAID HE TOOK CARE OF THE FEE.
HE WANTS YOU TO MAKE SURE YOU DON'T LEAVE ANYTHING BEHIND AND TO STOP AT THE NURSES' STATION TO THANK THEM.
HE APOLOGIZES FOR NOT BEING HERE TO GET YOU.
HE'S A BIT TIED UP RIGHT NOW.
IT'S FINE. I'M NOT A LITTLE KID ANYMORE.
He tends to leave work to the last minute.
Trust me, I know.
He's like that at home too.
UM...

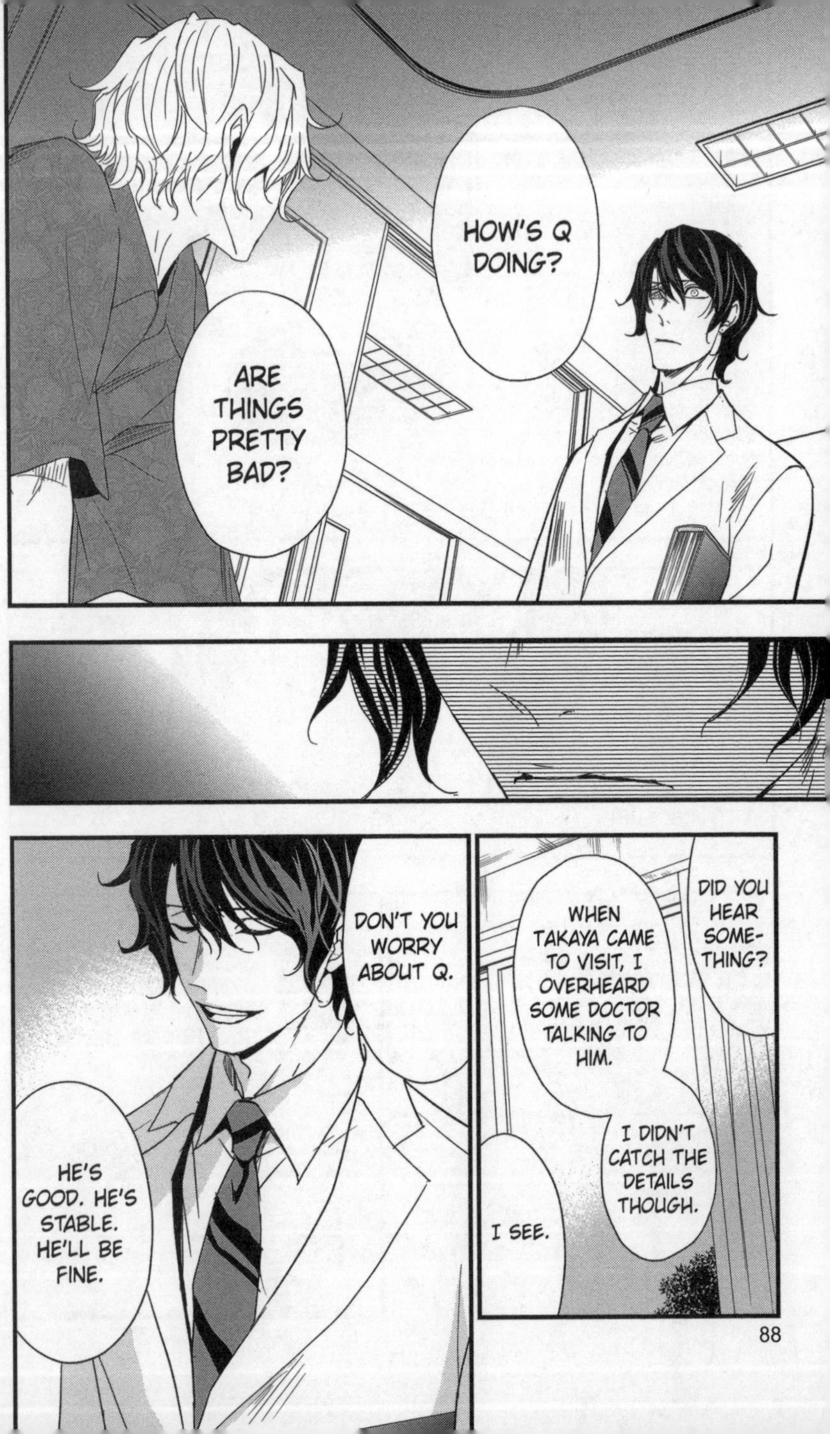
HOW'S Q DOING?
ARE THINGS PRETTY BAD?
DID YOU HEAR SOME-THING?
WHEN TAKAYA CAME TO VISIT, I OVERHEARD SOME DOCTOR TALKING TO HIM.
I DIDN'T CATCH THE DETAILS THOUGH.
I SEE.
DON'T YOU WORRY ABOUT Q.
HE'S GOOD. HE'S STABLE. HE'LL BE FINE.

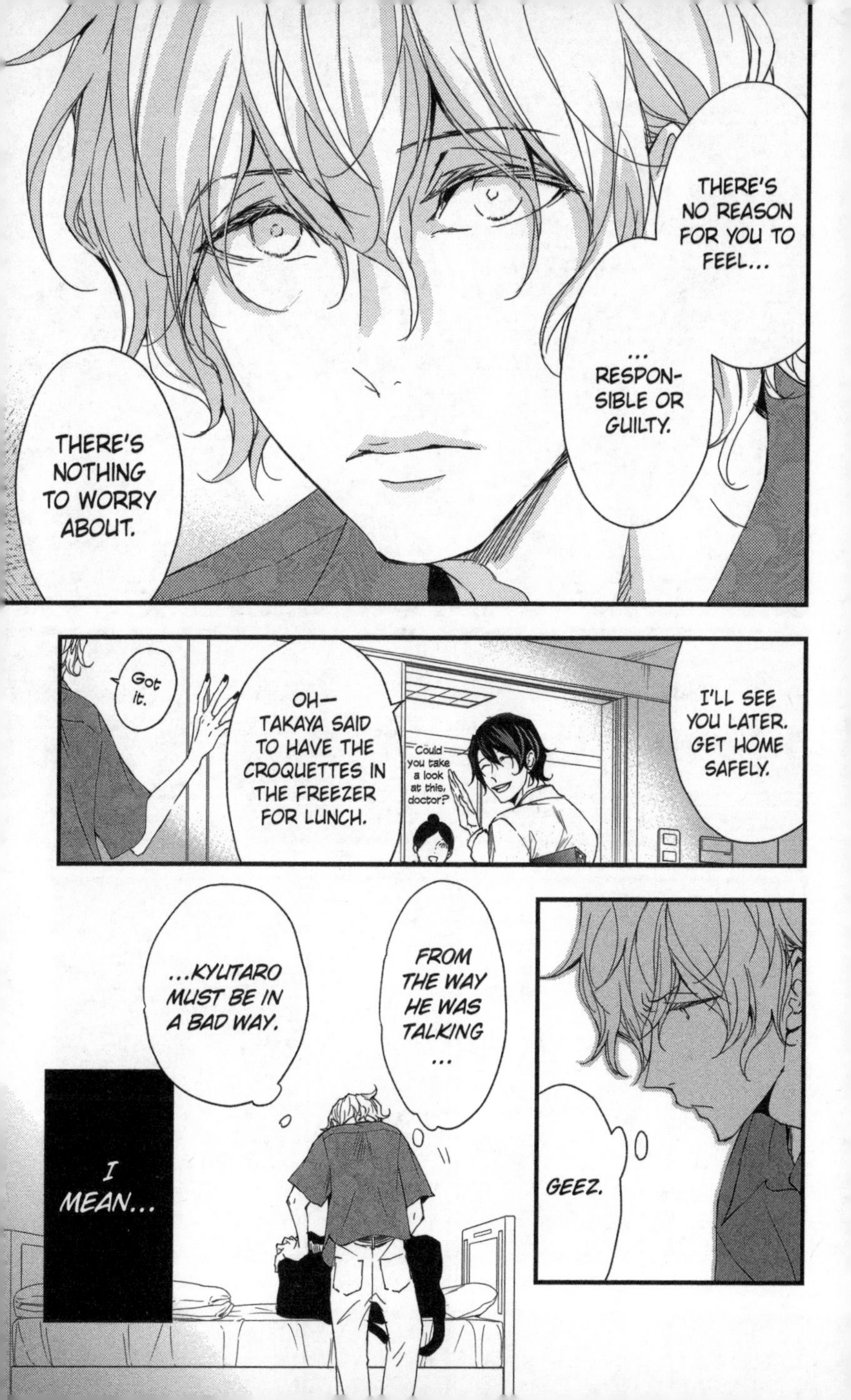
THERE'S NO REASON FOR YOU TO FEEL...
...RESPONSIBLE OR GUILTY.
THERE'S NOTHING TO WORRY ABOUT.
I'LL SEE YOU LATER. GET HOME SAFELY.
Could you take a look at this, doctor?
OH— TAKAYA SAID TO HAVE THE CROQUETTES IN THE FREEZER FOR LUNCH.
Got it.
GEEZ.
FROM THE WAY HE WAS TALKING...
...KYUTARO MUST BE IN A BAD WAY.
I MEAN...

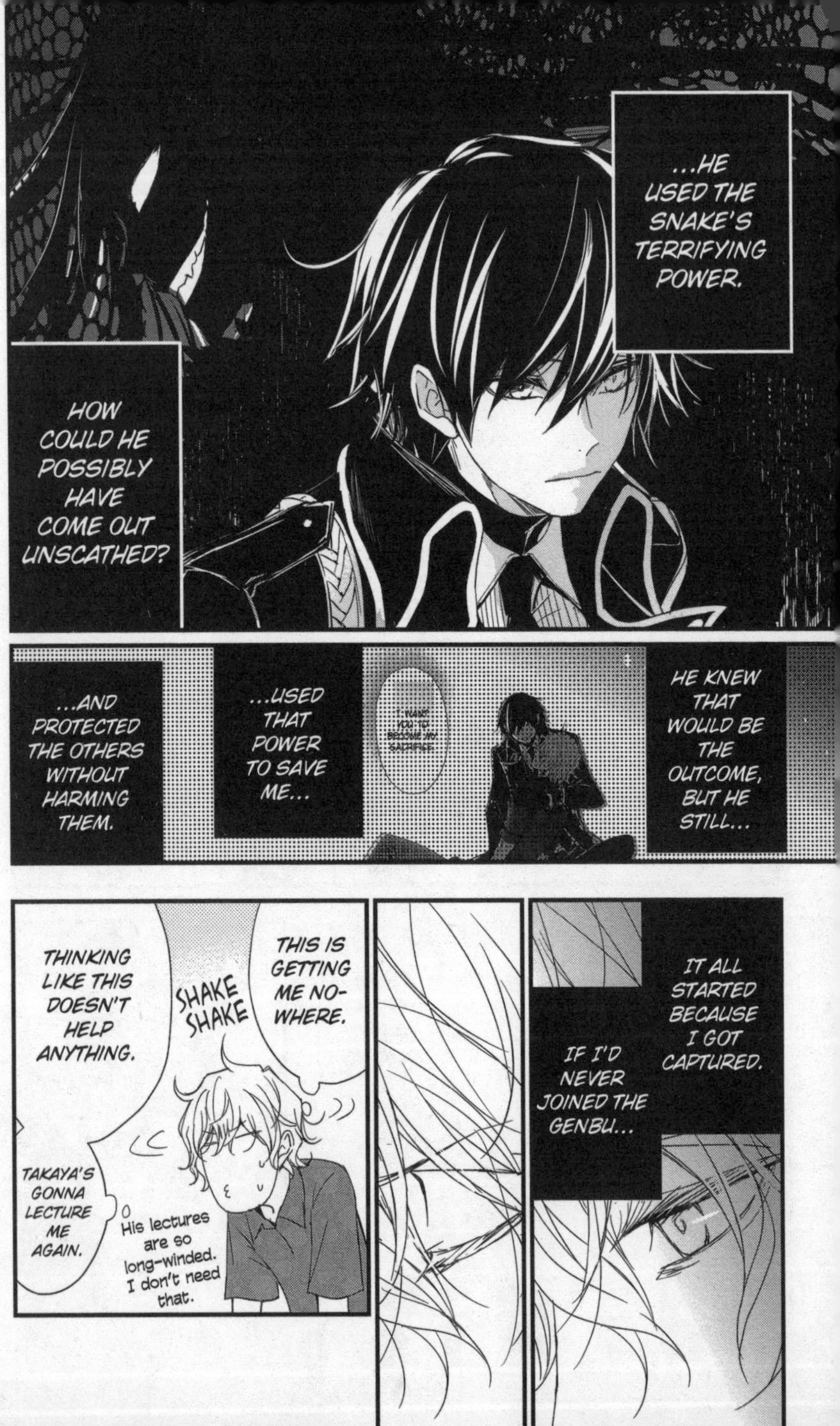
...HE USED THE SNAKE'S TERRIFYING POWER.
HOW COULD HE POSSIBLY HAVE COME OUT UNSCATHED?
HE KNEW THAT WOULD BE THE OUTCOME, BUT HE STILL...
I WANT YOU TO BECOME MY SACRIFICE.
...USED THAT POWER TO SAVE ME...
...AND PROTECTED THE OTHERS WITHOUT HARMING THEM.
IT ALL STARTED BECAUSE I GOT CAPTURED.
IF I'D NEVER JOINED THE GENBU...
THIS IS GETTING ME NO-WHERE.
SHAKE SHAKE
THINKING LIKE THIS DOESN'T HELP ANYTHING.
TAKAYA'S GONNA LECTURE ME AGAIN.
His lectures are so long-winded. I don't need that.

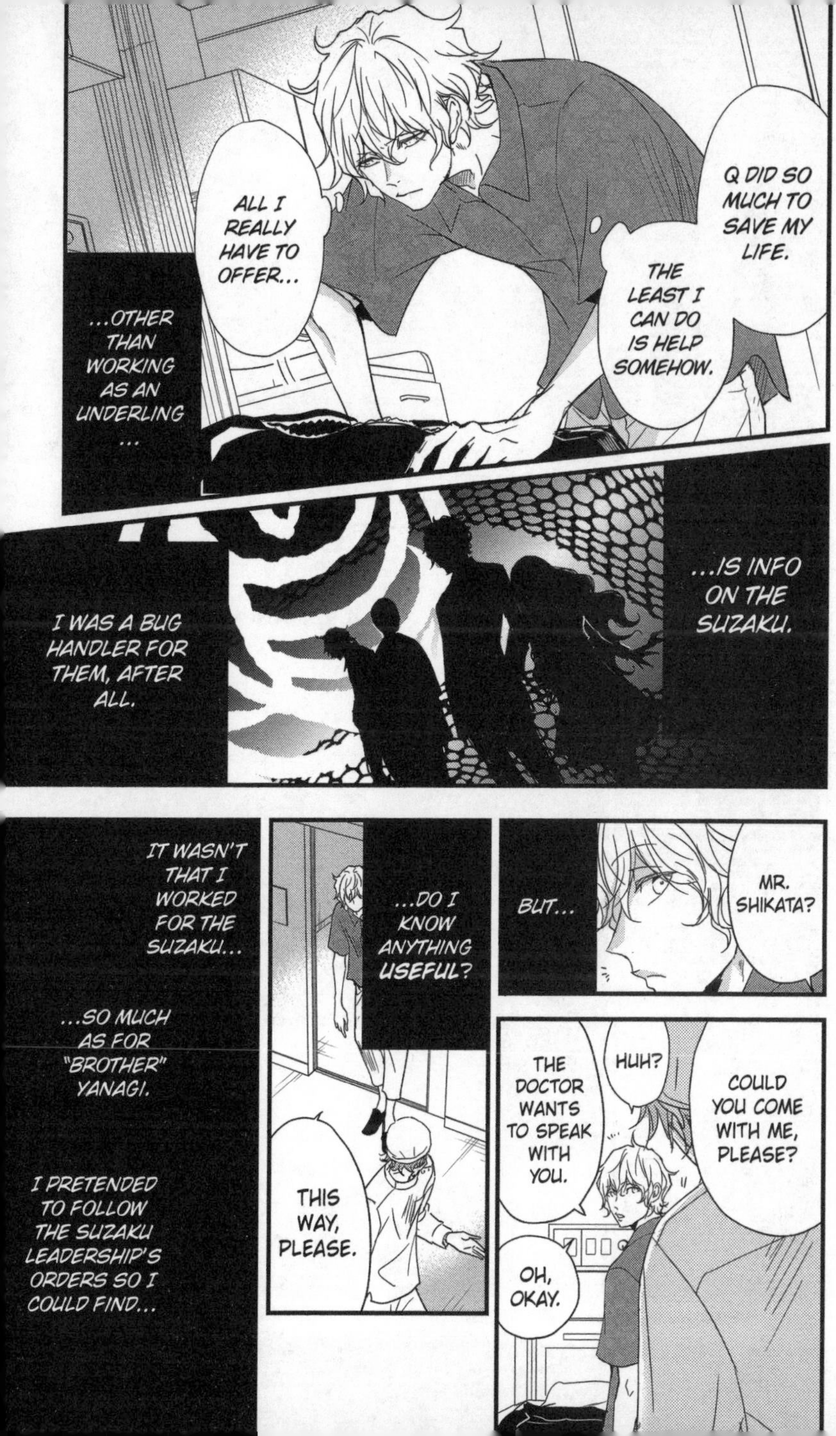
Q DID SO MUCH TO SAVE MY LIFE.
THE LEAST I CAN DO IS HELP SOMEHOW.
ALL I REALLY HAVE TO OFFER...
...OTHER THAN WORKING AS AN UNDERLING...
...IS INFO ON THE SUZAKU.
I WAS A BUG HANDLER FOR THEM, AFTER ALL.
MR. SHIKATA?
BUT...
COULD YOU COME WITH ME, PLEASE?
HUH?
THE DOCTOR WANTS TO SPEAK WITH YOU.
OH, OKAY.
...DO I KNOW ANYTHING USEFUL?
THIS WAY, PLEASE.
IT WASN'T THAT I WORKED FOR THE SUZAKU...
...SO MUCH AS FOR "BROTHER" YANAGI.
I PRETENDED TO FOLLOW THE SUZAKU LEADERSHIP'S ORDERS SO I COULD FIND...

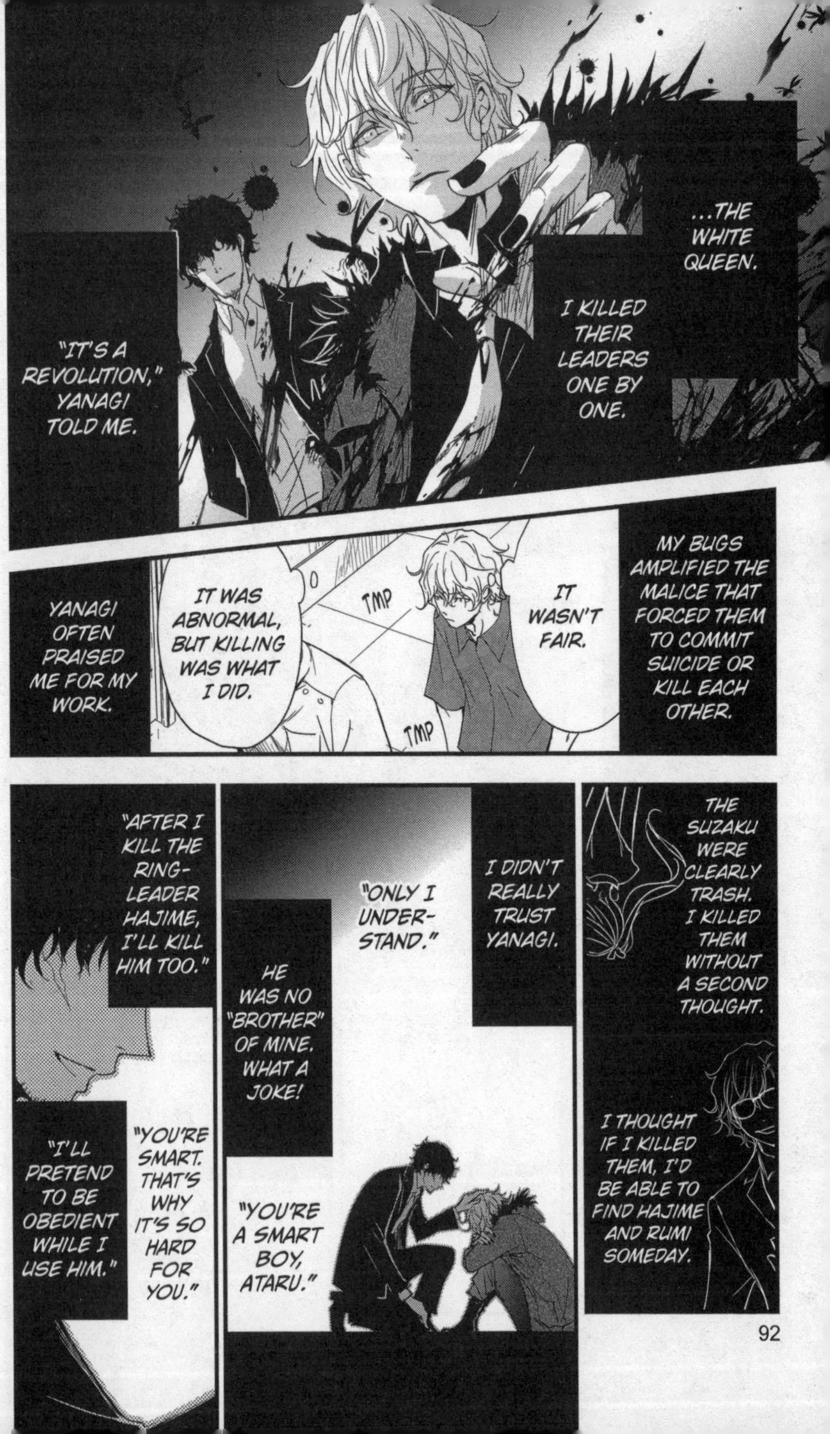
...THE WHITE QUEEN.
I KILLED THEIR LEADERS ONE BY ONE.
"IT'S A REVOLUTION," YANAGI TOLD ME.
MY BUGS AMPLIFIED THE MALICE THAT FORCED THEM TO COMMIT SUICIDE OR KILL EACH OTHER.
IT WASN'T FAIR.
TMP
IT WAS ABNORMAL, BUT KILLING WAS WHAT I DID.
TMP
YANAGI OFTEN PRAISED ME FOR MY WORK.
THE SUZAKU WERE CLEARLY TRASH. I KILLED THEM WITHOUT A SECOND THOUGHT.
I THOUGHT IF I KILLED THEM, I'D BE ABLE TO FIND HAJIME AND RUMI SOMEDAY.
I DIDN'T REALLY TRUST YANAGI.
"ONLY I UNDER-STAND."
HE WAS NO "BROTHER" OF MINE. WHAT A JOKE!
"YOU'RE A SMART BOY, ATARU."
"AFTER I KILL THE RING-LEADER HAJIME, I'LL KILL HIM TOO."
"YOU'RE SMART. THAT'S WHY IT'S SO HARD FOR YOU."
"I'LL PRETEND TO BE OBEDIENT WHILE I USE HIM."

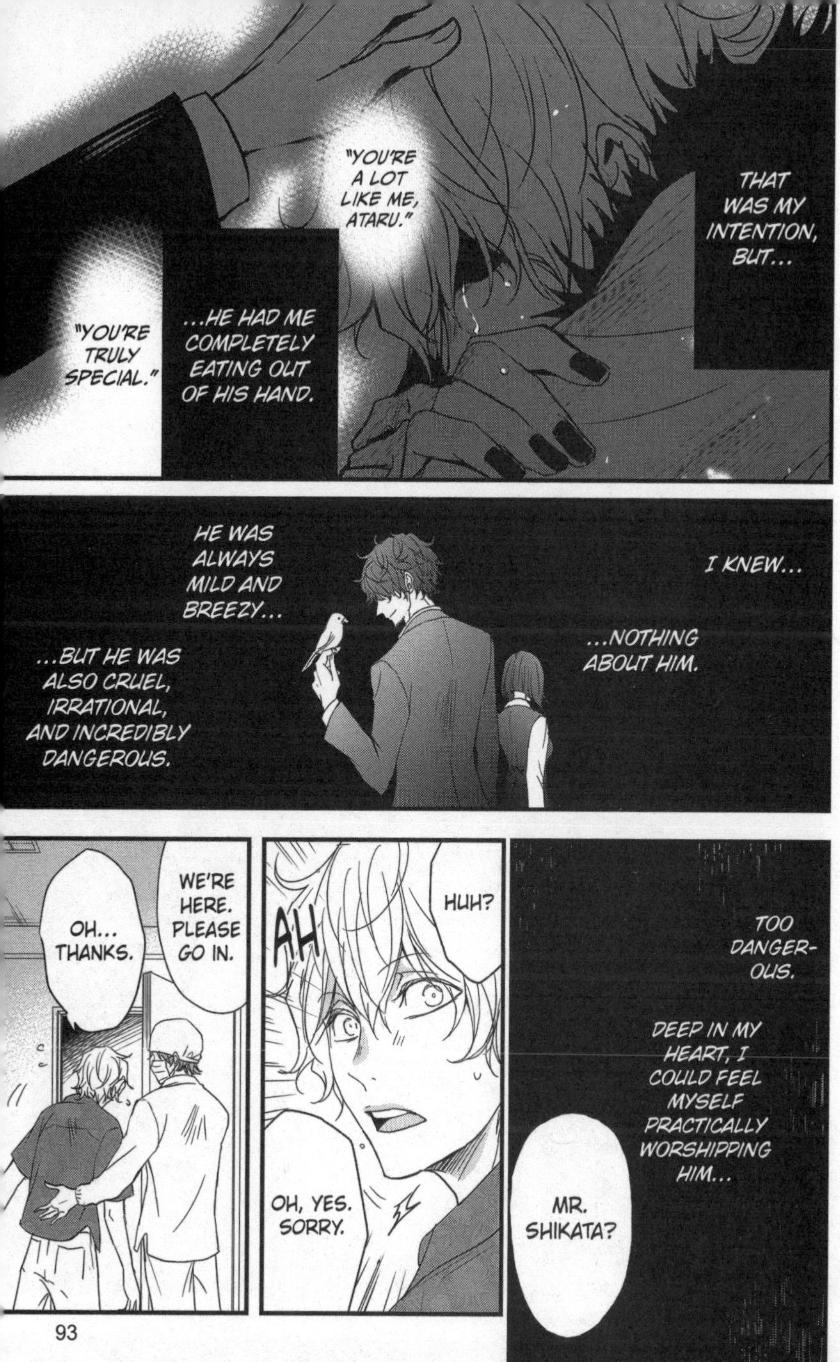
THAT WAS MY INTENTION, BUT...
"YOU'RE A LOT LIKE ME, ATARU."
...HE HAD ME COMPLETELY EATING OUT OF HIS HAND.
"YOU'RE TRULY SPECIAL."
I KNEW...
...NOTHING ABOUT HIM.
HE WAS ALWAYS MILD AND BREEZY...
...BUT HE WAS ALSO CRUEL, IRRATIONAL, AND INCREDIBLY DANGEROUS.
TOO DANGER-OUS.
DEEP IN MY HEART, I COULD FEEL MYSELF PRACTICALLY WORSHIPPING HIM...
MR. SHIKATA?
HUH?
AH
OH, YES. SORRY.
WE'RE HERE. PLEASE GO IN.
OH... THANKS.

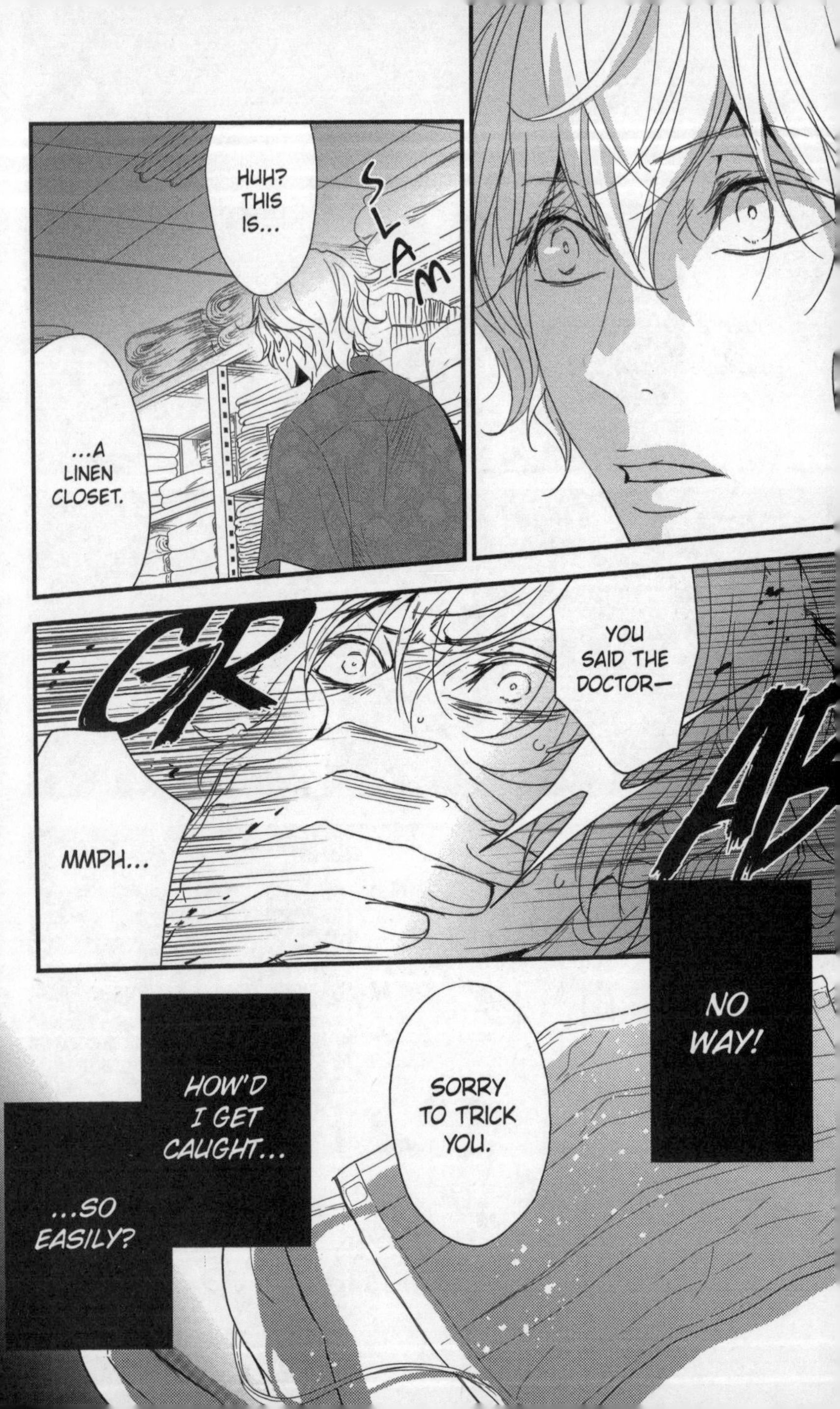
HUH? THIS IS...
SLAM
...A LINEN CLOSET.
YOU SAID THE DOCTOR—
GR
MMPH...
NO WAY!
SORRY TO TRICK YOU.
HOW'D I GET CAUGHT...
...SO EASILY?

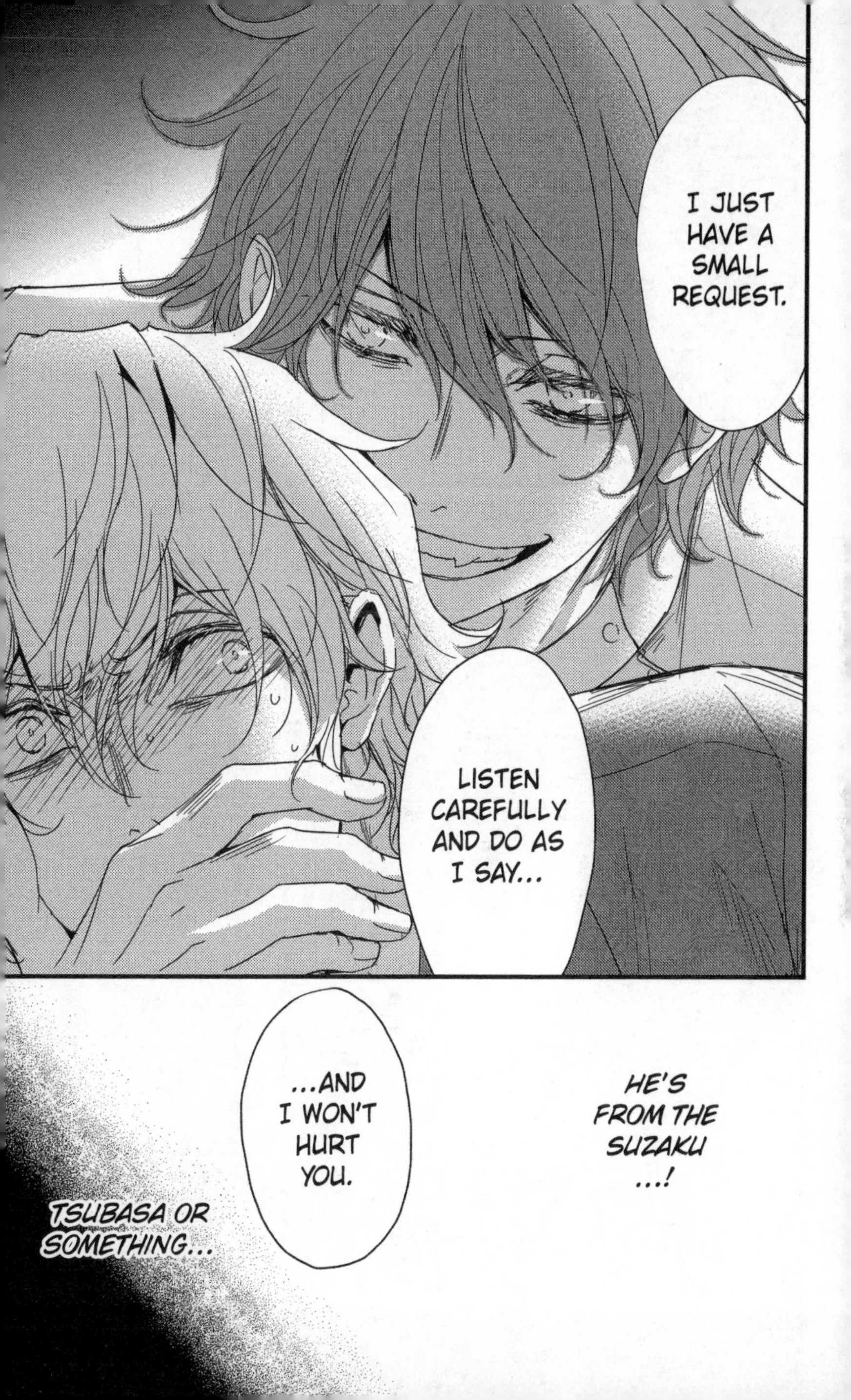
I JUST HAVE A SMALL REQUEST.
LISTEN CAREFULLY AND DO AS I SAY...
HE'S FROM THE SUZAKU ...!
...AND I WON'T HURT YOU.
TSUBASA OR SOMETHING...

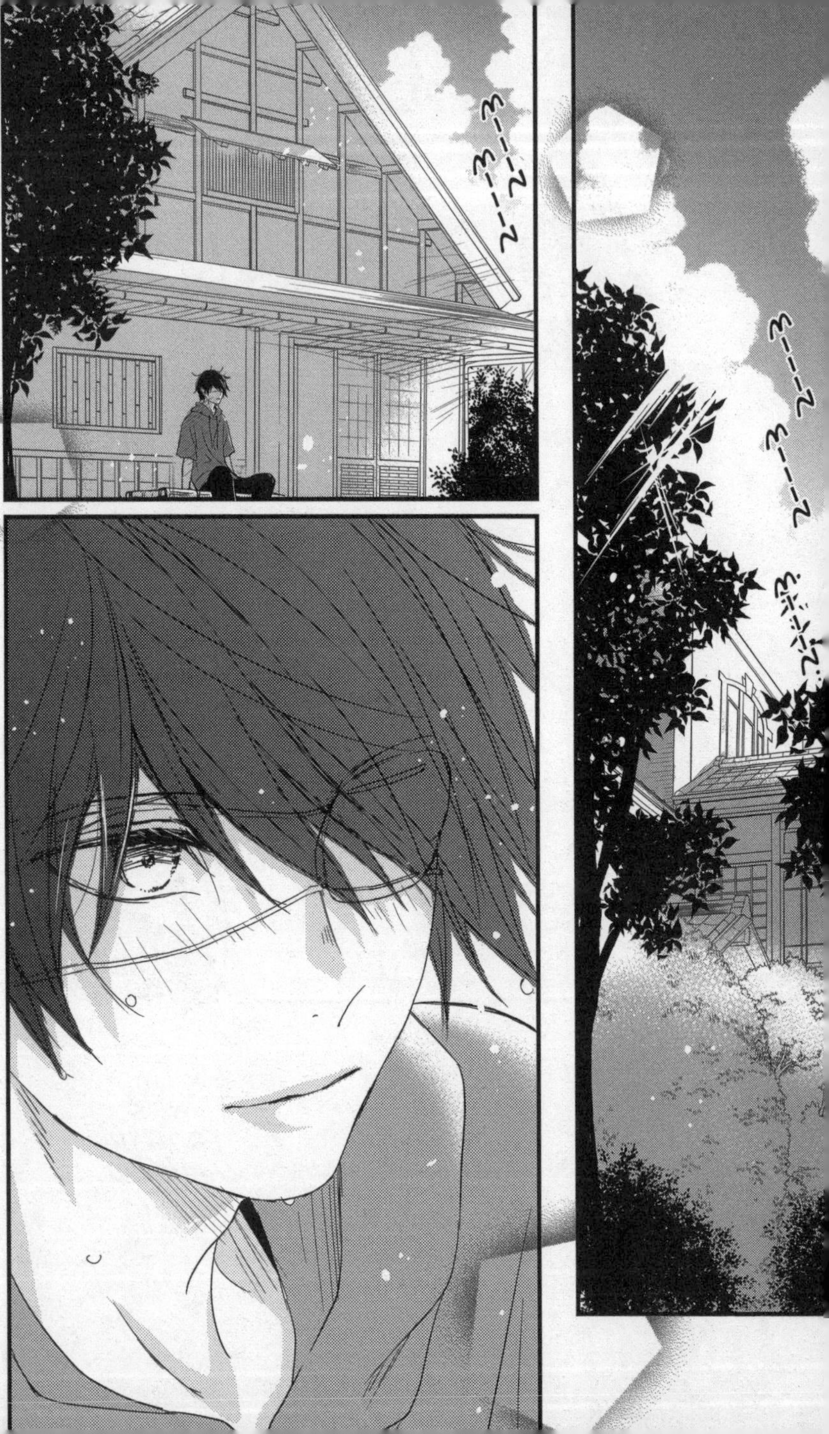
ミーーン
ミーーン
ミ゛ーーン゛…
ミーーン
ミーーン

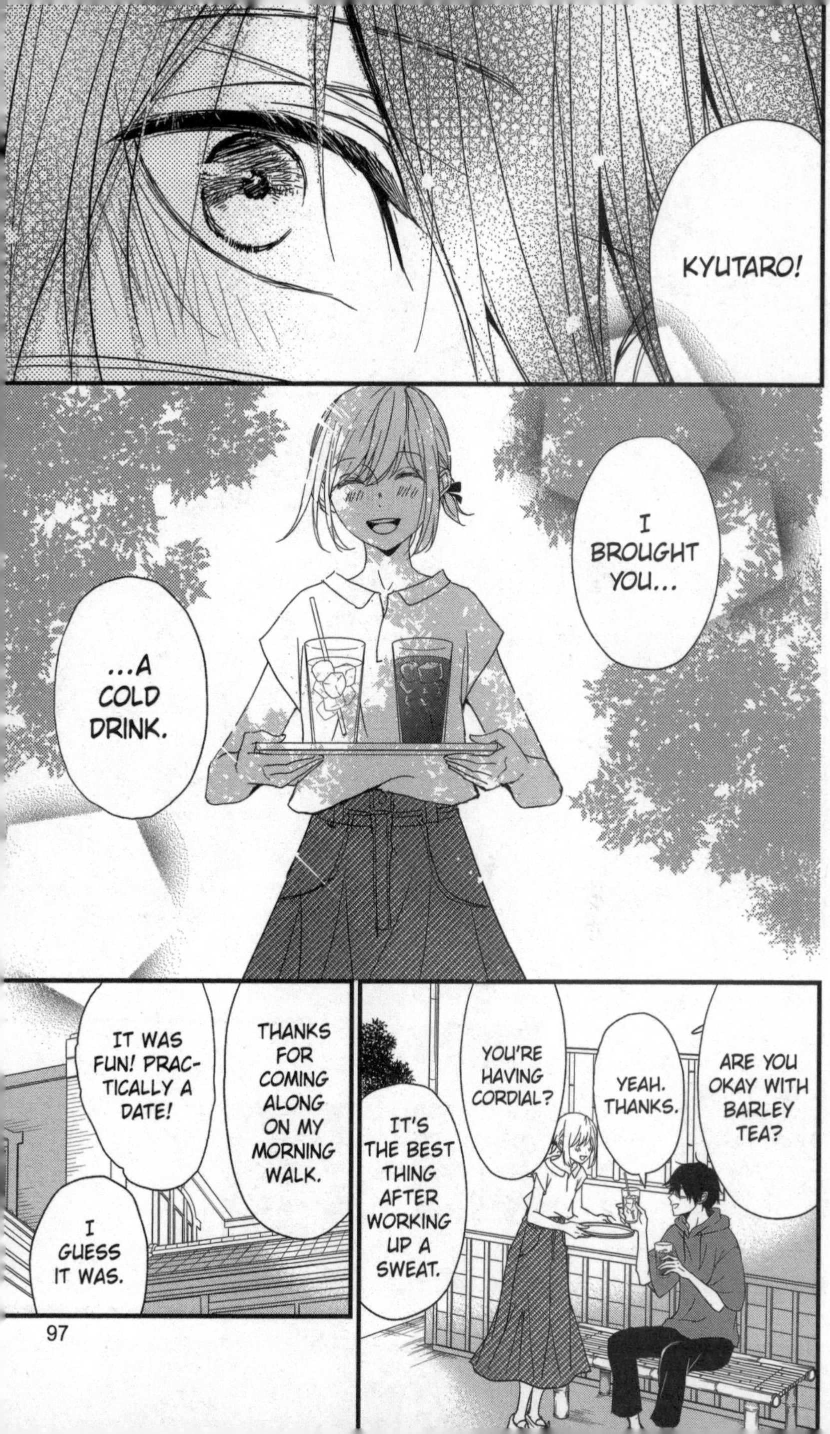
KYUTARO!
I BROUGHT YOU...
...A COLD DRINK.
ARE YOU OKAY WITH BARLEY TEA?
YEAH. THANKS.
YOU'RE HAVING CORDIAL?
IT'S THE BEST THING AFTER WORKING UP A SWEAT.
THANKS FOR COMING ALONG ON MY MORNING WALK.
IT WAS FUN! PRAC-TICALLY A DATE!
I GUESS IT WAS.

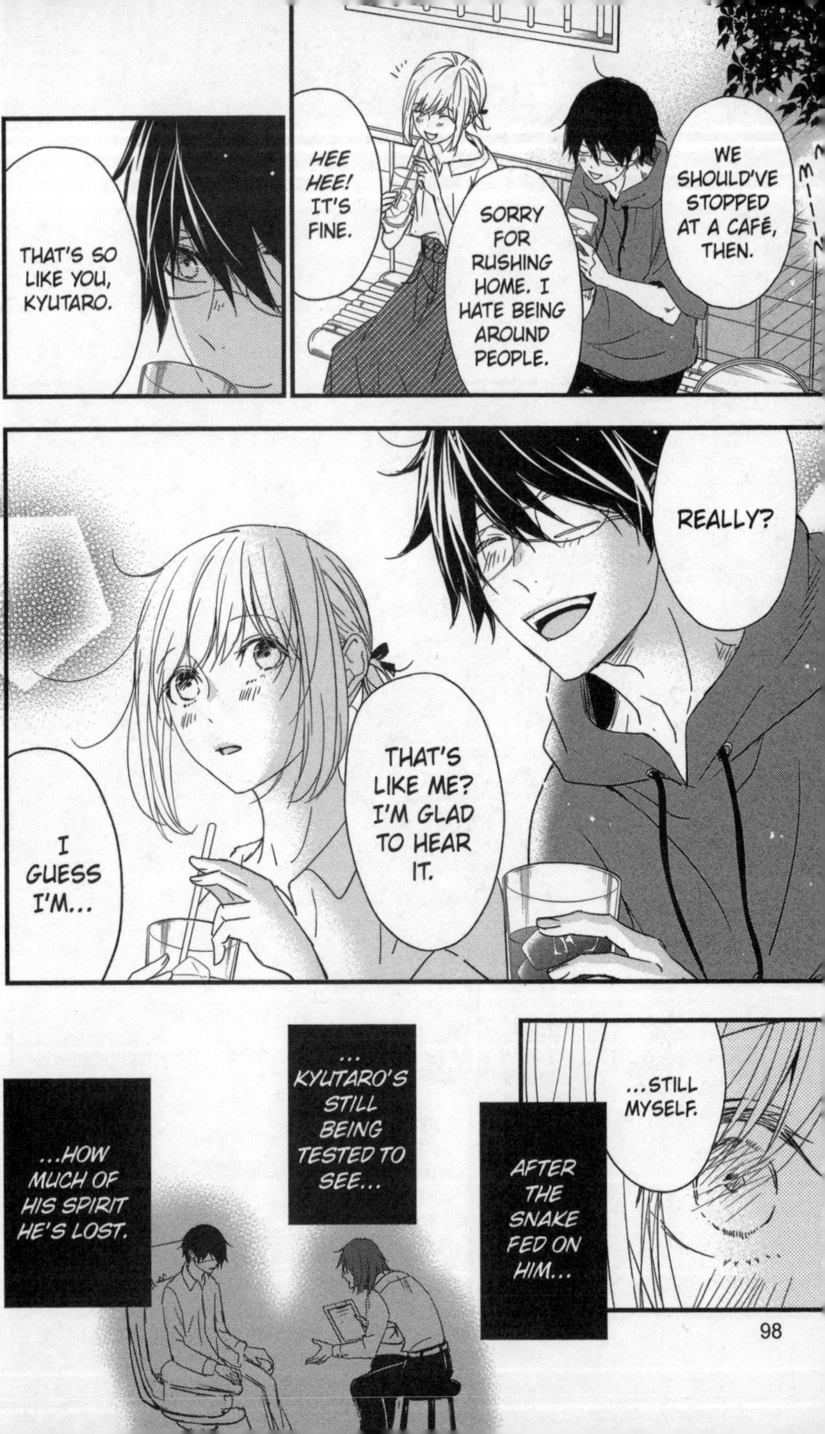
WE SHOULD'VE STOPPED AT A CAFÉ, THEN.
SORRY FOR RUSHING HOME. I HATE BEING AROUND PEOPLE.
HEE HEE! IT'S FINE.
THAT'S SO LIKE YOU, KYUTARO.
REALLY?
THAT'S LIKE ME? I'M GLAD TO HEAR IT.
I GUESS I'M...
...STILL MYSELF.
AFTER THE SNAKE FED ON HIM...
...KYUTARO'S STILL BEING TESTED TO SEE...
...HOW MUCH OF HIS SPIRIT HE'S LOST.

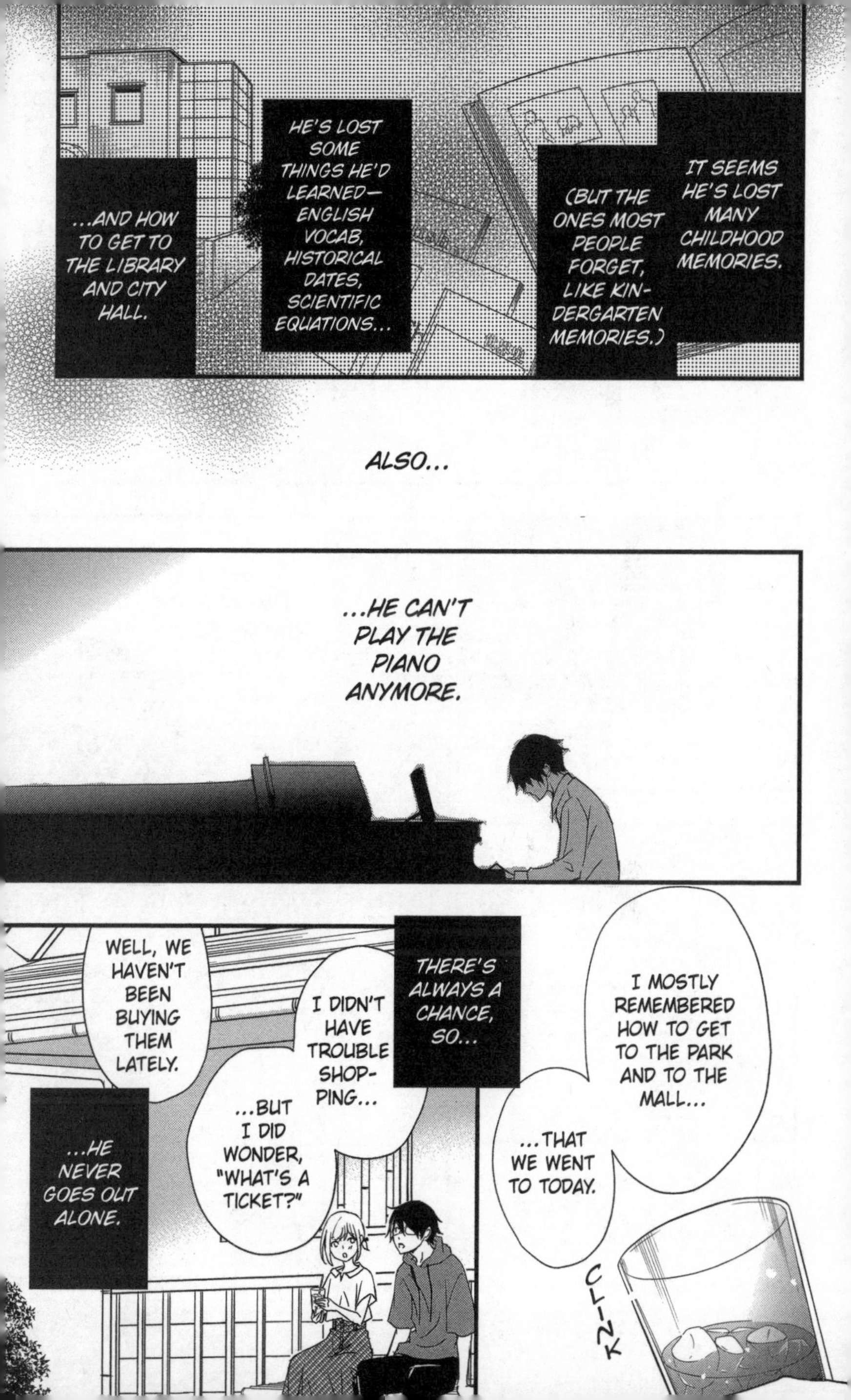
IT SEEMS HE'S LOST MANY CHILDHOOD MEMORIES.
(BUT THE ONES MOST PEOPLE FORGET, LIKE KIN-DERGARTEN MEMORIES.)
HE'S LOST SOME THINGS HE'D LEARNED—ENGLISH VOCAB, HISTORICAL DATES, SCIENTIFIC EQUATIONS...
...AND HOW TO GET TO THE LIBRARY AND CITY HALL.
ALSO...
...HE CAN'T PLAY THE PIANO ANYMORE.
I MOSTLY REMEMBERED HOW TO GET TO THE PARK AND TO THE MALL...
...THAT WE WENT TO TODAY.
CLINK
THERE'S ALWAYS A CHANCE, SO...
I DIDN'T HAVE TROUBLE SHOP-PING...
...BUT I DID WONDER, "WHAT'S A TICKET?"
WELL, WE HAVEN'T BEEN BUYING THEM LATELY.
...HE NEVER GOES OUT ALONE.

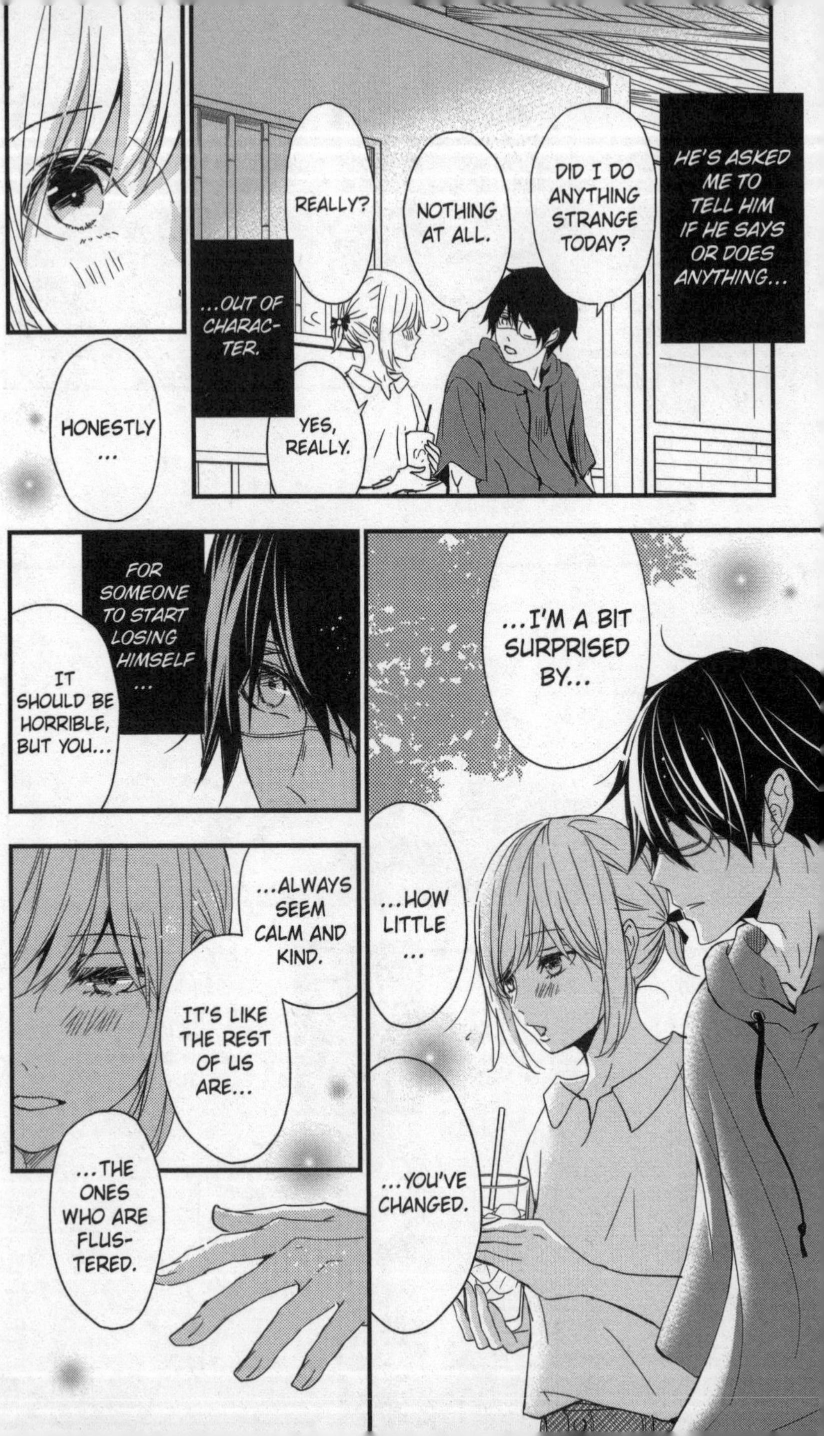

HE'S ASKED ME TO TELL HIM IF HE SAYS OR DOES ANYTHING...
DID I DO ANYTHING STRANGE TODAY?
NOTHING AT ALL.
REALLY?
...OUT OF CHARACTER.
YES, REALLY.
HONESTLY...
...I'M A BIT SURPRISED BY...
...HOW LITTLE...
...YOU'VE CHANGED.
FOR SOMEONE TO START LOSING HIMSELF...
IT SHOULD BE HORRIBLE, BUT YOU...
...ALWAYS SEEM CALM AND KIND.
IT'S LIKE THE REST OF US ARE...
...THE ONES WHO ARE FLUS-TERED.

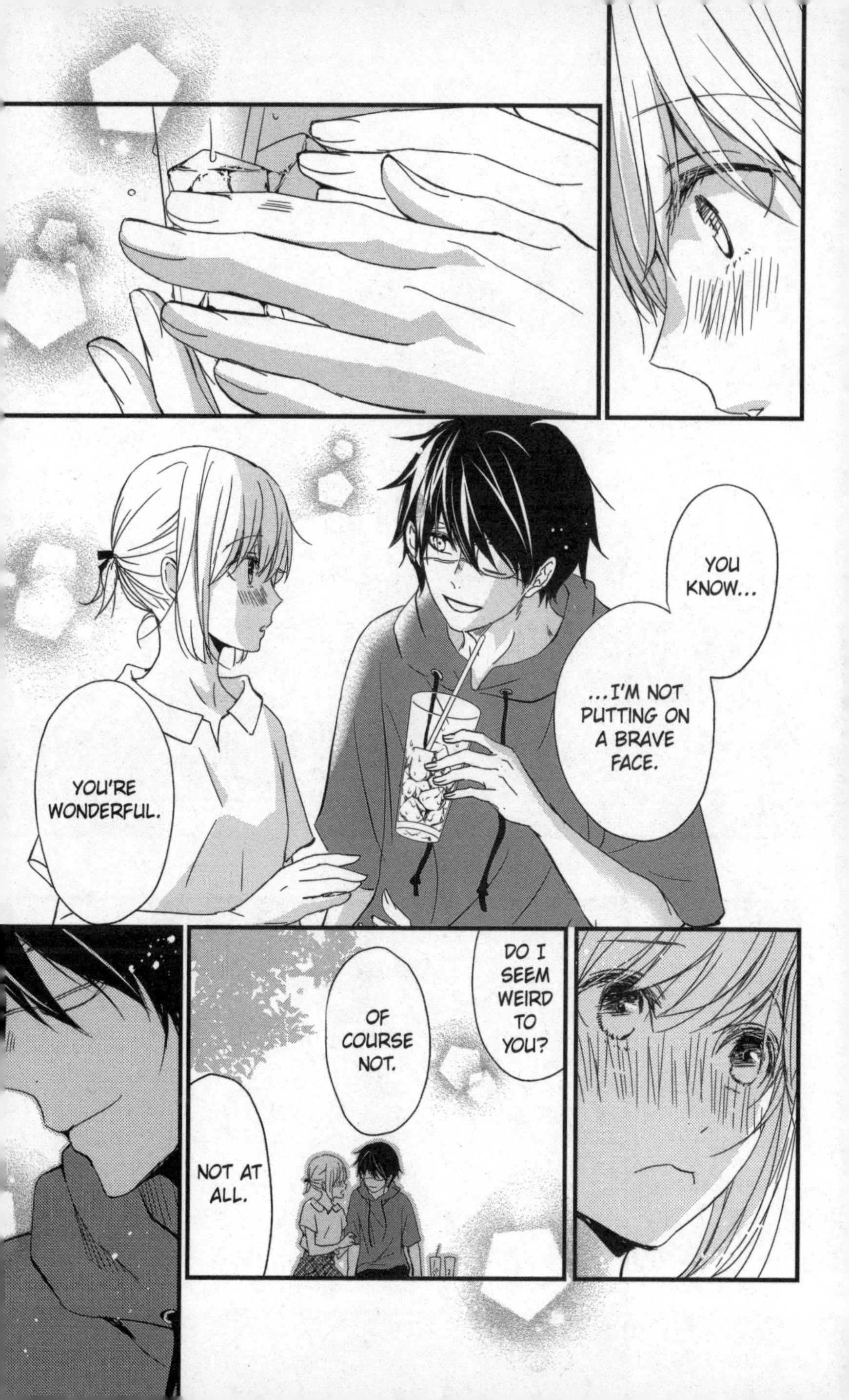
YOU KNOW...
...I'M NOT PUTTING ON A BRAVE FACE.
YOU'RE WONDERFUL.
DO I SEEM WEIRD TO YOU?
OF COURSE NOT.
NOT AT ALL.

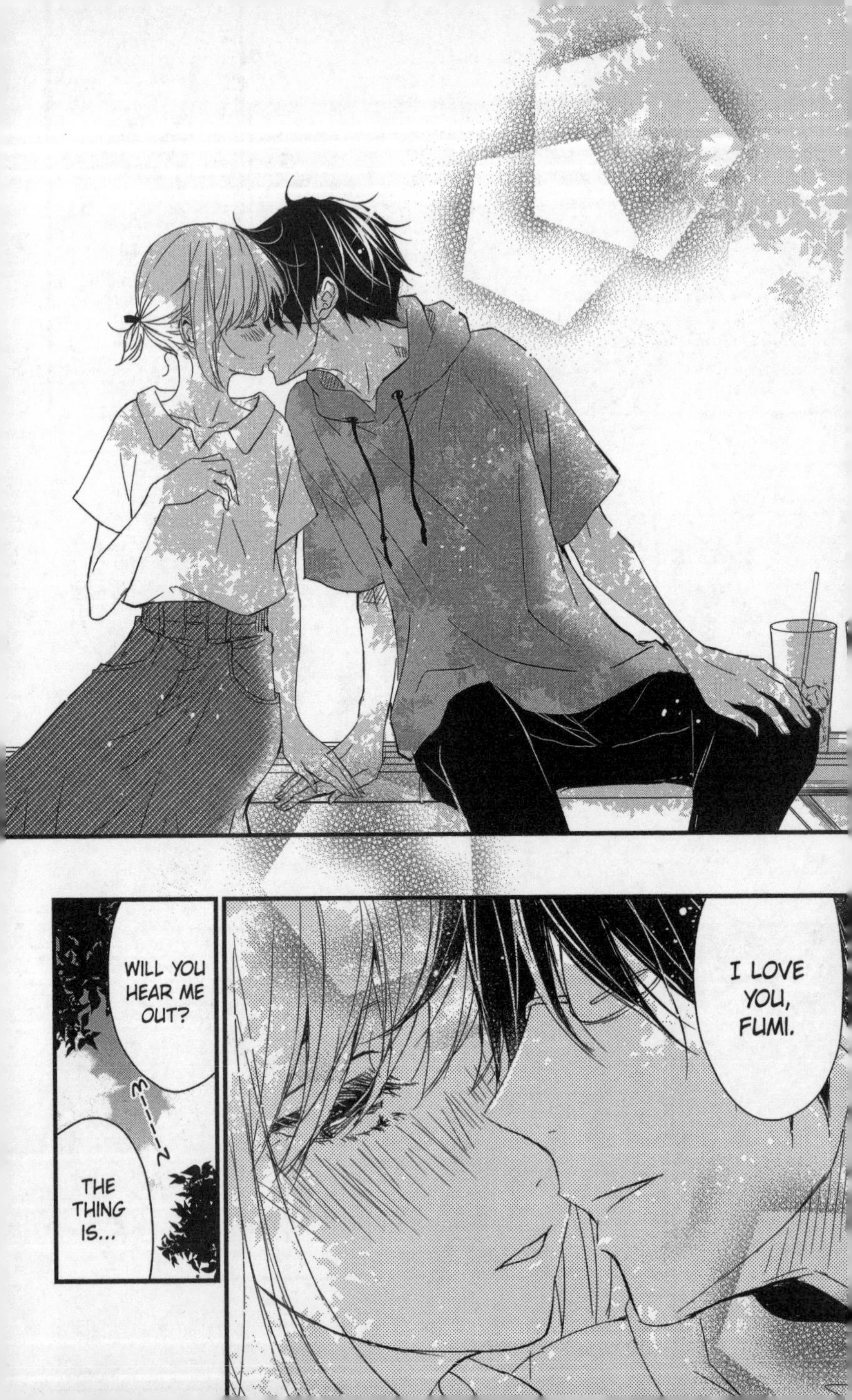
I LOVE YOU, FUMI.
WILL YOU HEAR ME OUT?
THE THING IS...

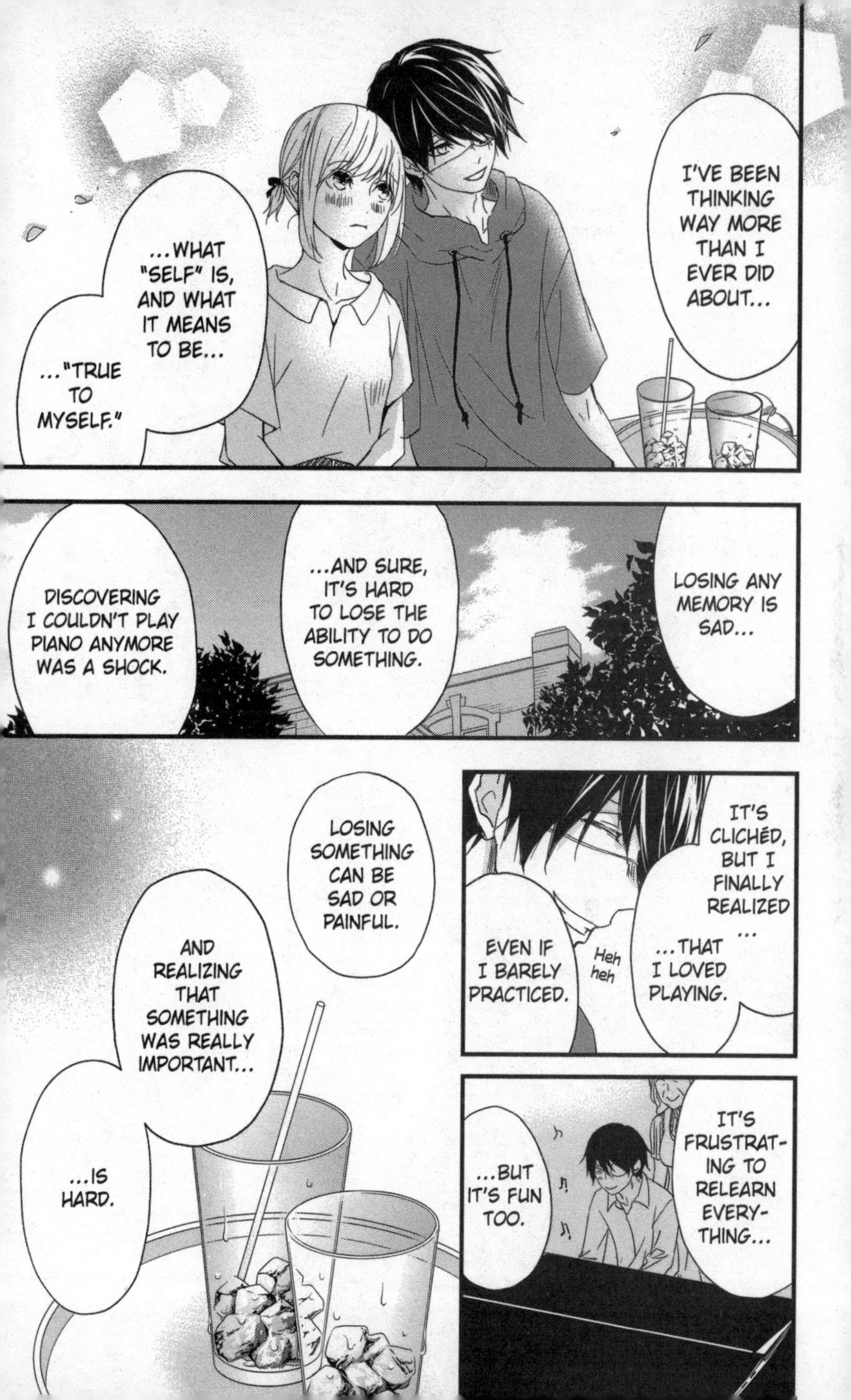
I'VE BEEN THINKING WAY MORE THAN I EVER DID ABOUT...
...WHAT "SELF" IS, AND WHAT IT MEANS TO BE...
..."TRUE TO MYSELF."
LOSING ANY MEMORY IS SAD...
...AND SURE, IT'S HARD TO LOSE THE ABILITY TO DO SOMETHING.
DISCOVERING I COULDN'T PLAY PIANO ANYMORE WAS A SHOCK.
IT'S CLICHÉD, BUT I FINALLY REALIZED...
...THAT I LOVED PLAYING.
Heh heh
EVEN IF I BARELY PRACTICED.
IT'S FRUSTRATING TO RELEARN EVERYTHING...
...BUT IT'S FUN TOO.
LOSING SOMETHING CAN BE SAD OR PAINFUL.
AND REALIZING THAT SOMETHING WAS REALLY IMPORTANT...
...IS HARD.

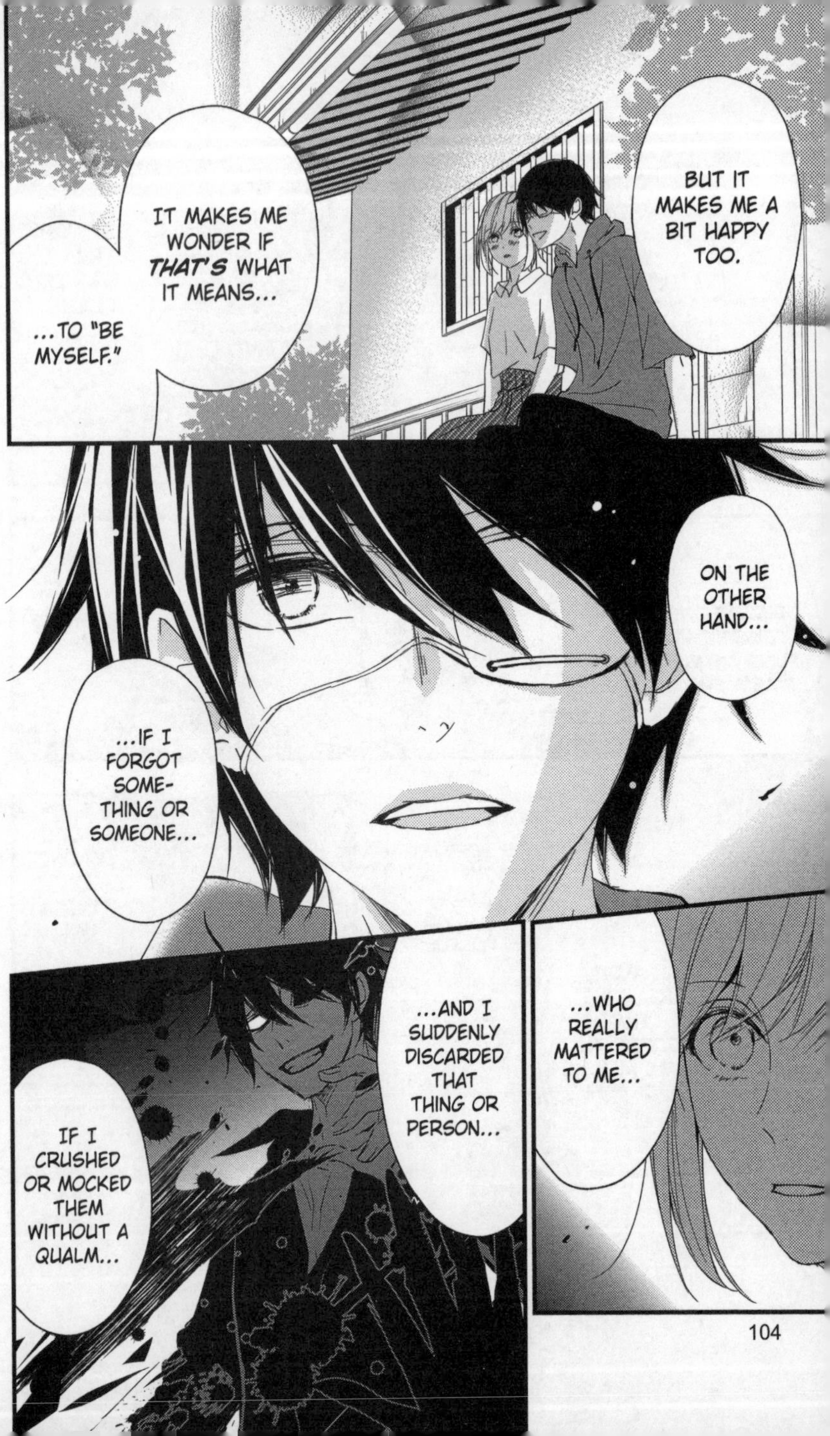
BUT IT MAKES ME A BIT HAPPY TOO.
IT MAKES ME WONDER IF *THAT'S* WHAT IT MEANS...
...TO "BE MYSELF."
ON THE OTHER HAND...
...IF I FORGOT SOME-THING OR SOMEONE...
...WHO REALLY MATTERED TO ME...
...AND I SUDDENLY DISCARDED THAT THING OR PERSON...
IF I CRUSHED OR MOCKED THEM WITHOUT A QUALM...

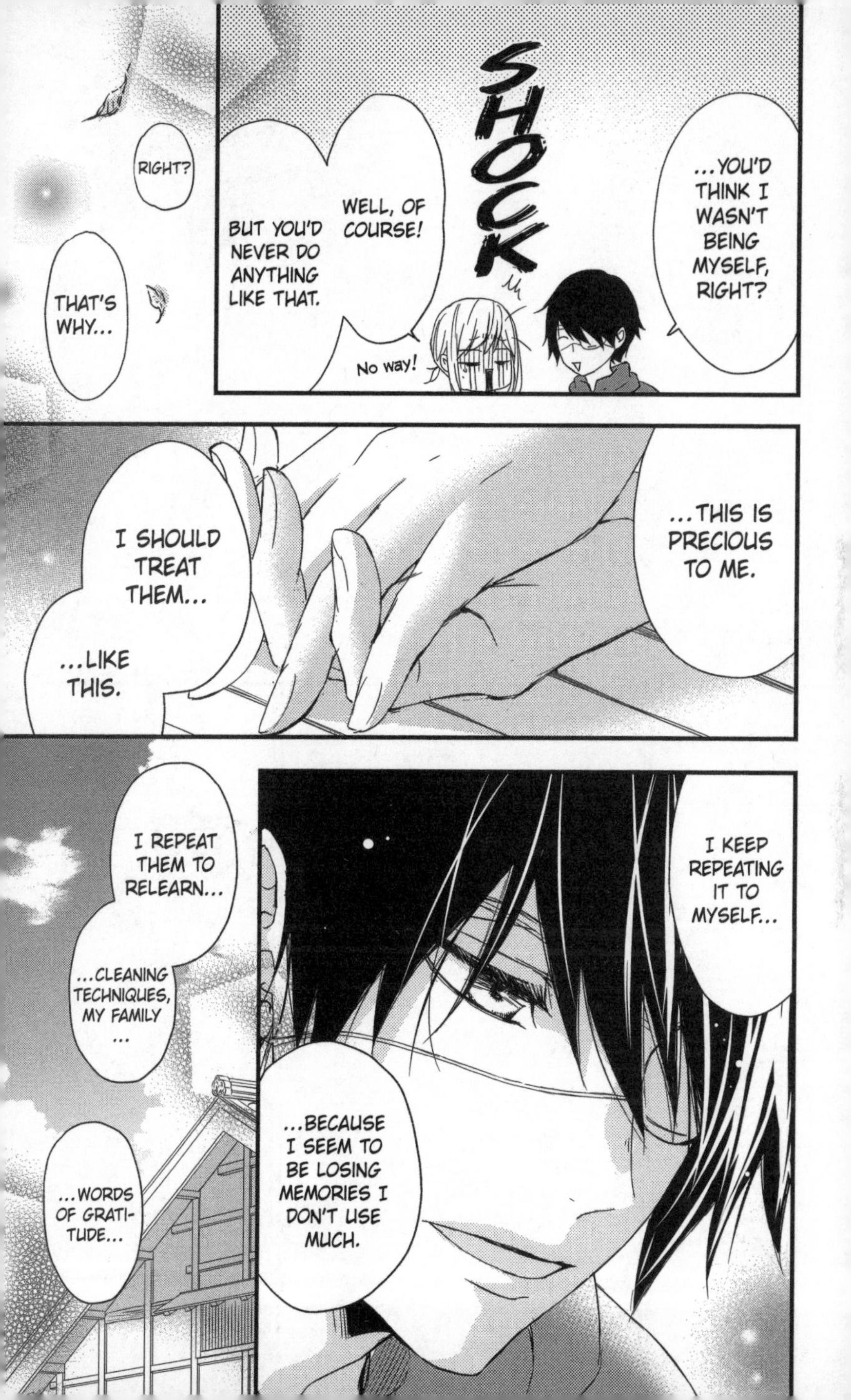
...YOU'D THINK I WASN'T BEING MYSELF, RIGHT?
SHOCK
WELL, OF COURSE!
BUT YOU'D NEVER DO ANYTHING LIKE THAT.
No way!
RIGHT?
THAT'S WHY...
...THIS IS PRECIOUS TO ME.
I SHOULD TREAT THEM...
...LIKE THIS.
I KEEP REPEATING IT TO MYSELF...
...BECAUSE I SEEM TO BE LOSING MEMORIES I DON'T USE MUCH.
I REPEAT THEM TO RELEARN...
...CLEANING TECHNIQUES, MY FAMILY ...
...WORDS OF GRATI-TUDE...

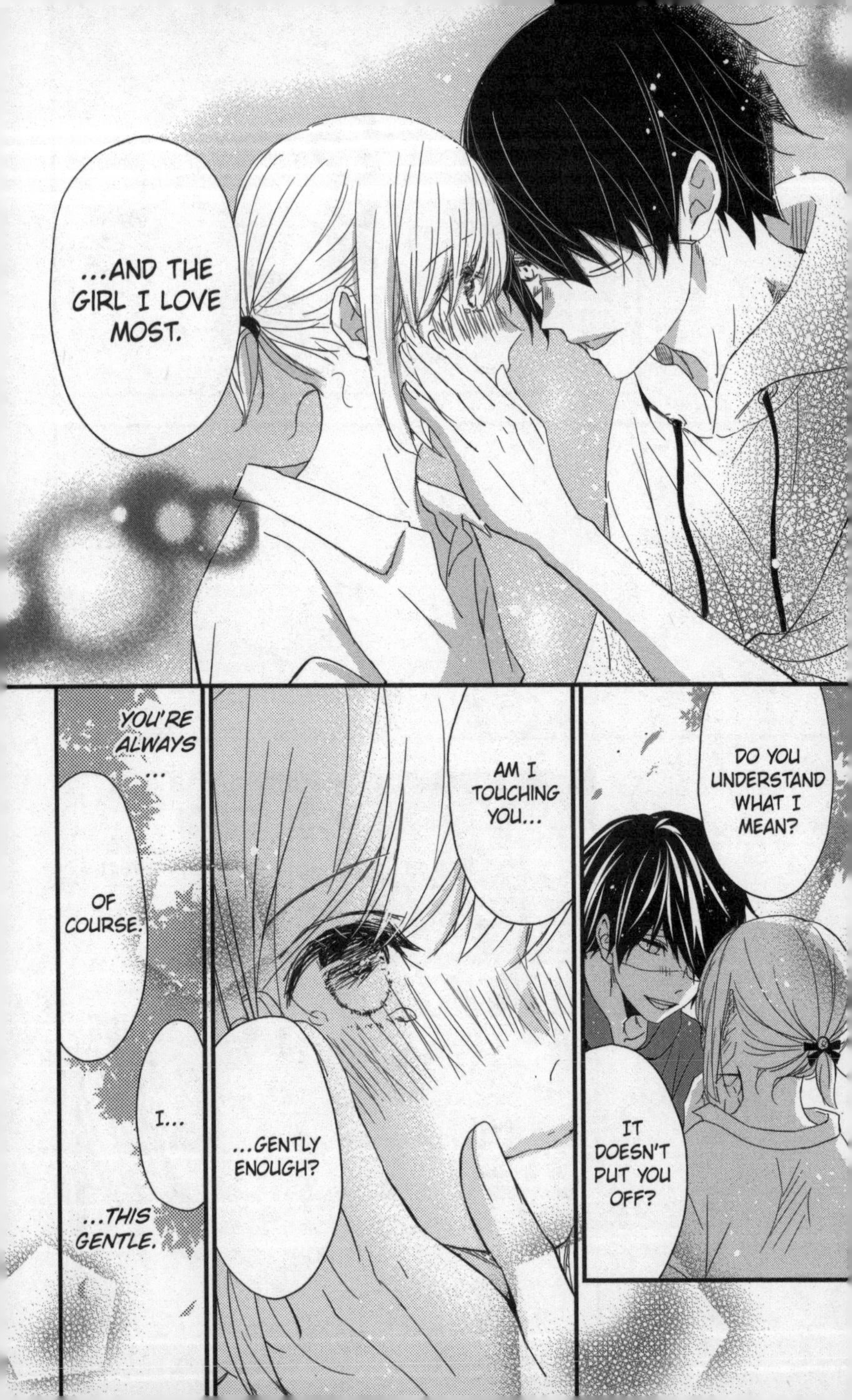
...AND THE GIRL I LOVE MOST.
DO YOU UNDERSTAND WHAT I MEAN?
IT DOESN'T PUT YOU OFF?
AM I TOUCHING YOU...
...GENTLY ENOUGH?
YOU'RE ALWAYS ...
OF COURSE.
I...
...THIS GENTLE.

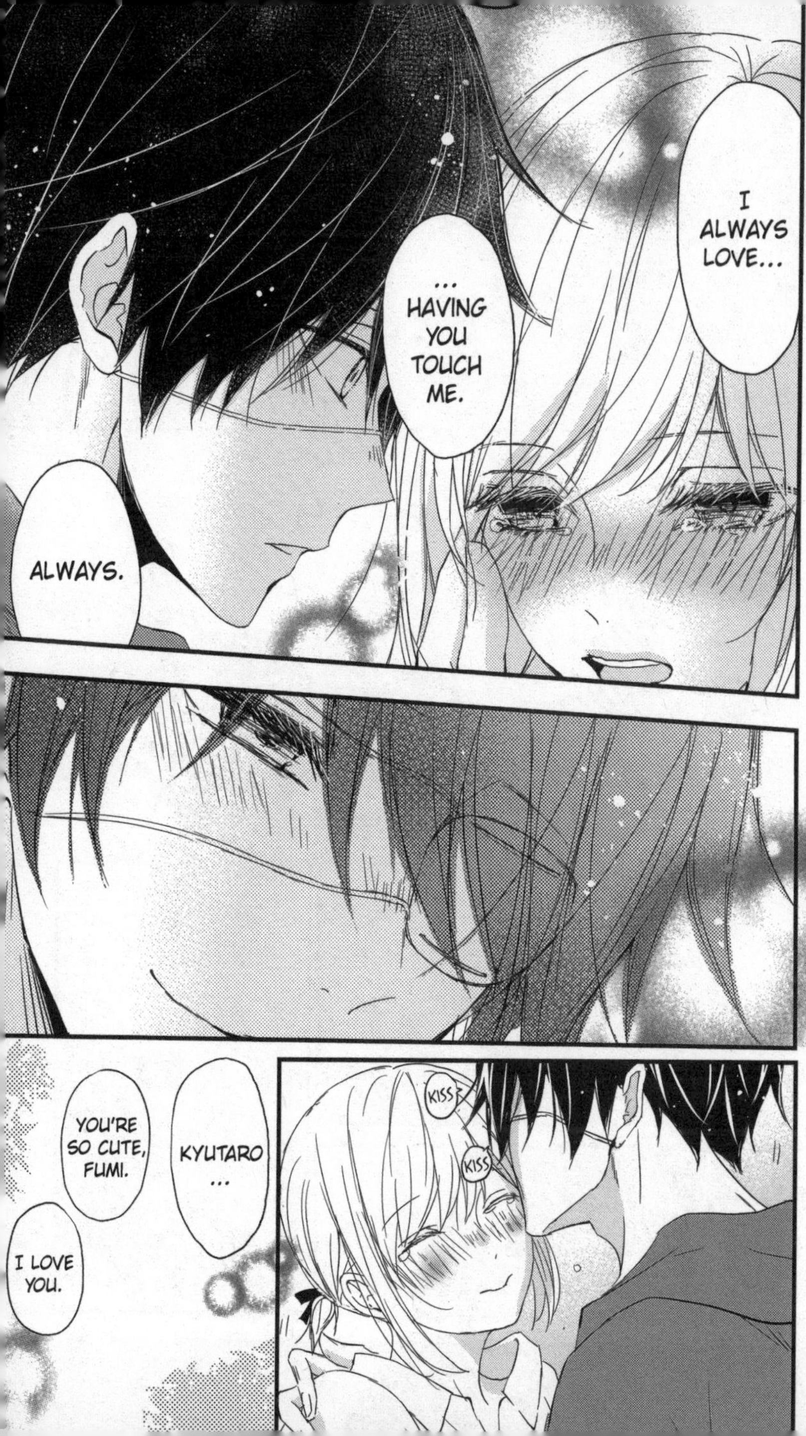
I ALWAYS LOVE...
...HAVING YOU TOUCH ME.
ALWAYS.
KISS
KISS
KYUTARO...
YOU'RE SO CUTE, FUMI.
I LOVE YOU.

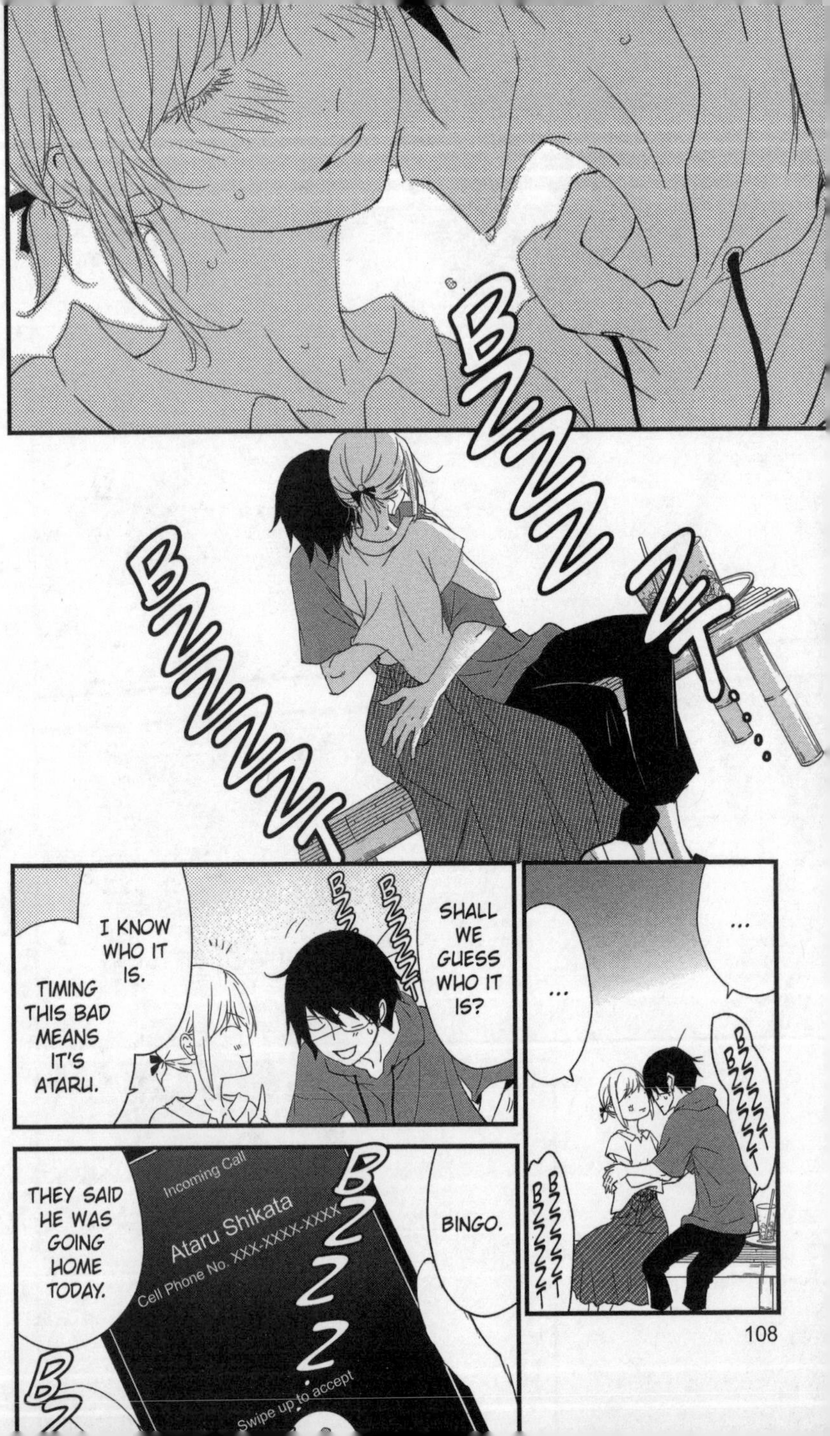

BZZZZNK...
BZZZZZNK
...
...
BZZZZZT
BZZZZZT
BZZZZZT
BZZZZZT
SHALL WE GUESS WHO IT IS?
BZZZT
BZZZT
I KNOW WHO IT IS.
TIMING THIS BAD MEANS IT'S ATARU.
BINGO.
BZZZ
Incoming Call
Ataru Shikata
Cell Phone No. XXX-XXXX-XXXX
Swipe up to accept
THEY SAID HE WAS GOING HOME TODAY.

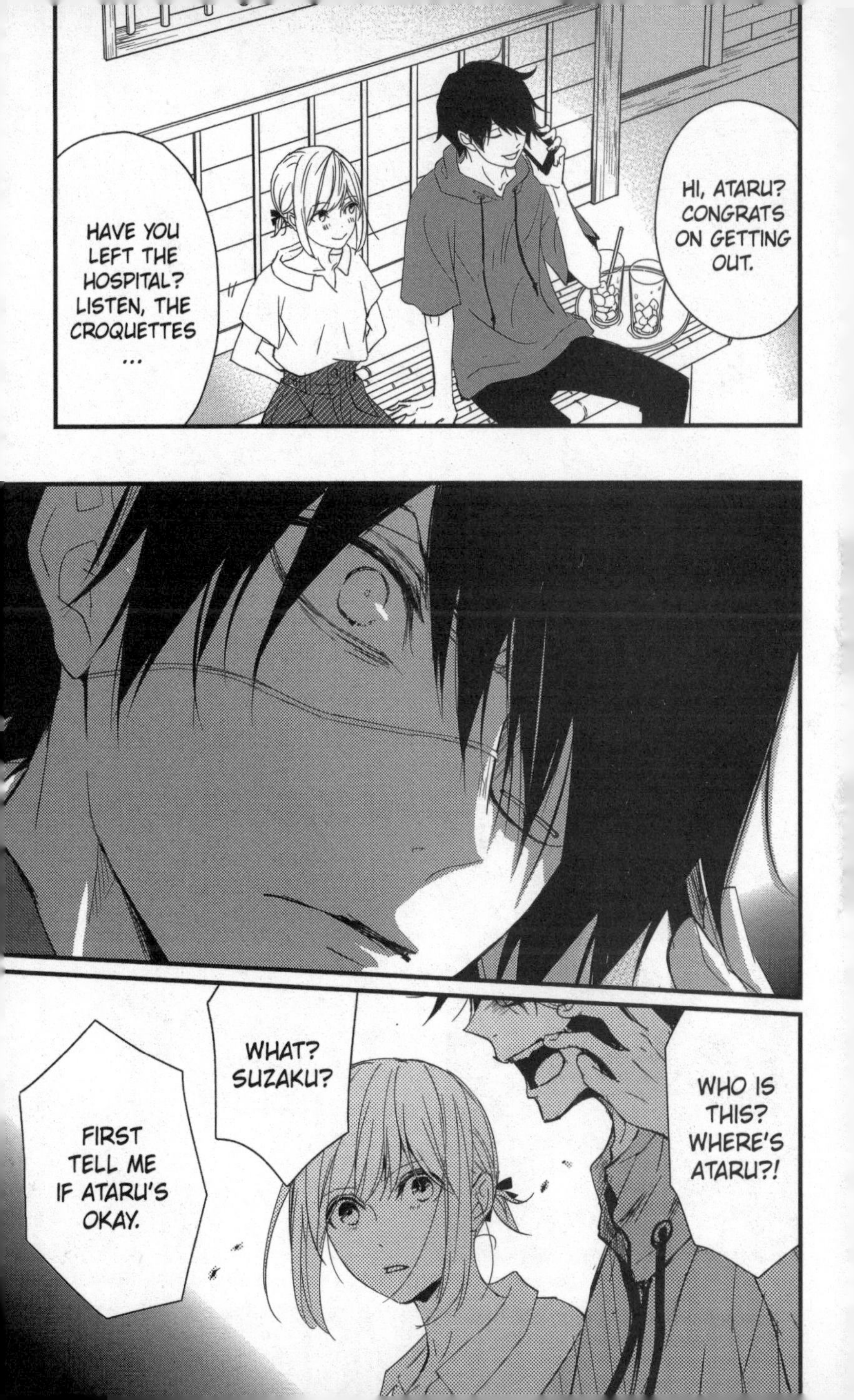
HI, ATARU? CONGRATS ON GETTING OUT.
HAVE YOU LEFT THE HOSPITAL? LISTEN, THE CROQUETTES ...
WHO IS THIS? WHERE'S ATARU?!
WHAT? SUZAKU?
FIRST TELL ME IF ATARU'S OKAY.

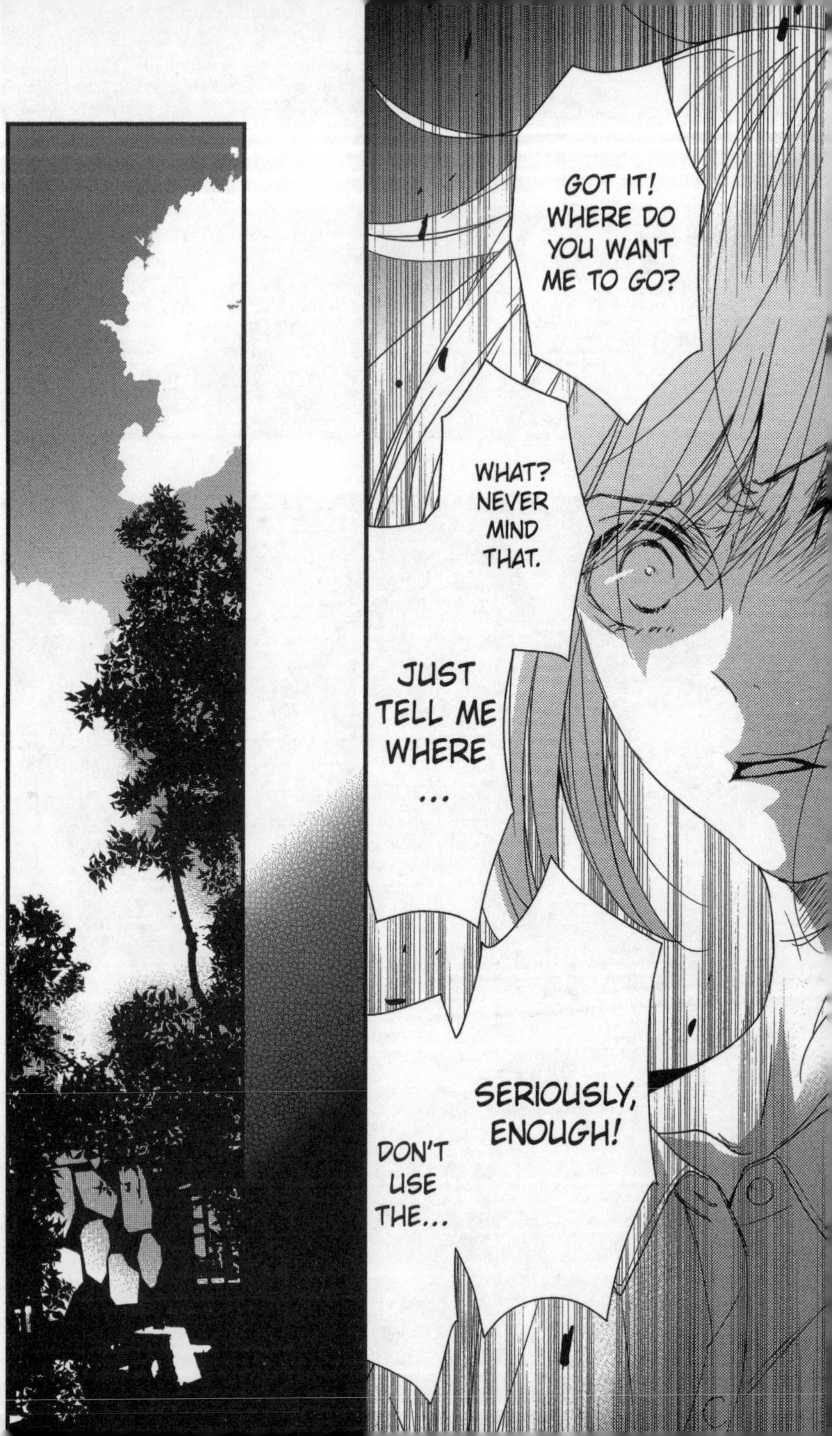
GOT IT! WHERE DO YOU WANT ME TO GO?
WHAT? NEVER MIND THAT.
JUST TELL ME WHERE ...
SERIOUSLY, ENOUGH!
DON'T USE THE...

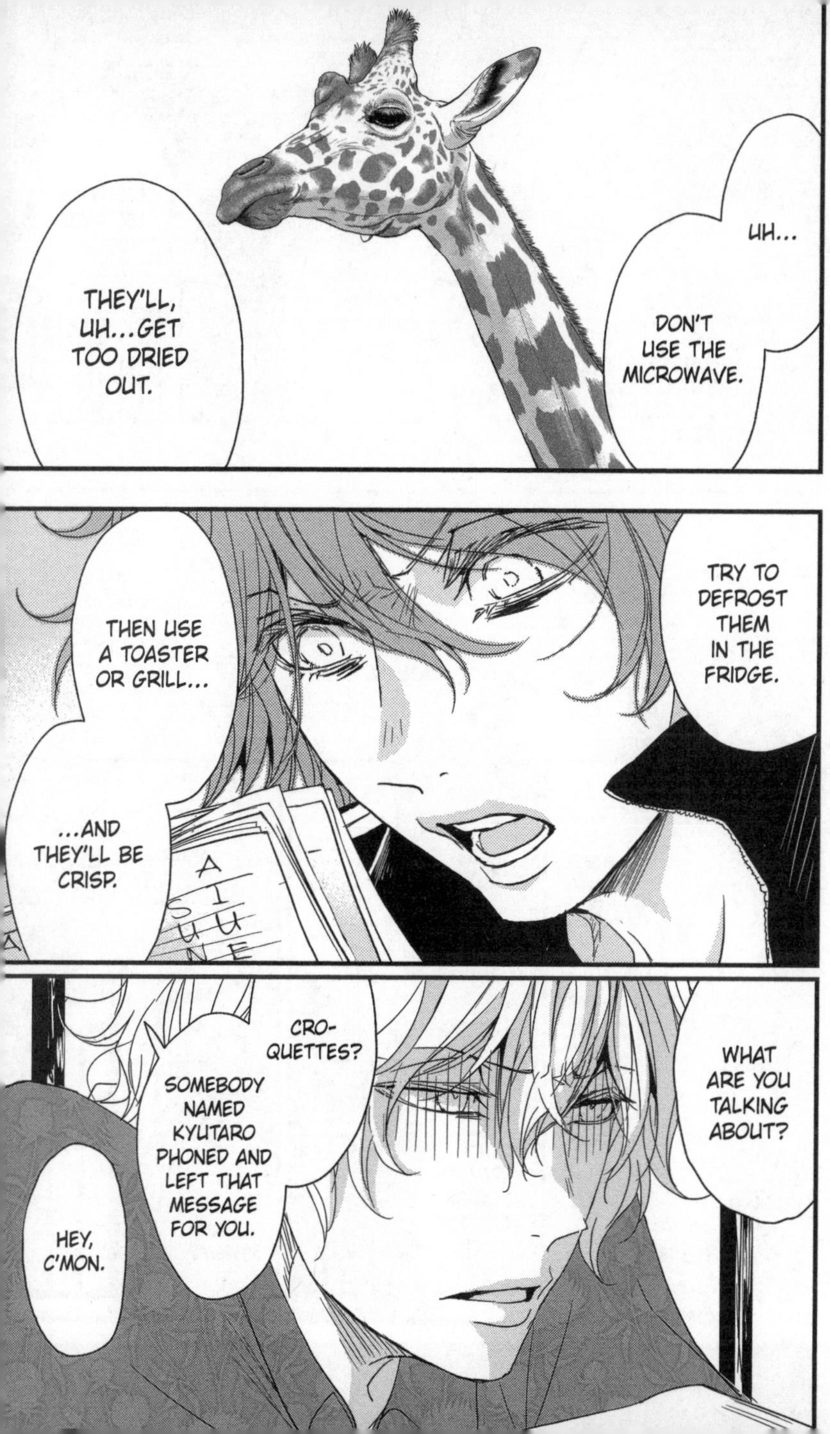
UH...
DON'T USE THE MICROWAVE.
THEY'LL, UH...GET TOO DRIED OUT.
TRY TO DEFROST THEM IN THE FRIDGE.
THEN USE A TOASTER OR GRILL...
...AND THEY'LL BE CRISP.
WHAT ARE YOU TALKING ABOUT?
CRO-QUETTES?
SOMEBODY NAMED KYUTARO PHONED AND LEFT THAT MESSAGE FOR YOU.
HEY, C'MON.

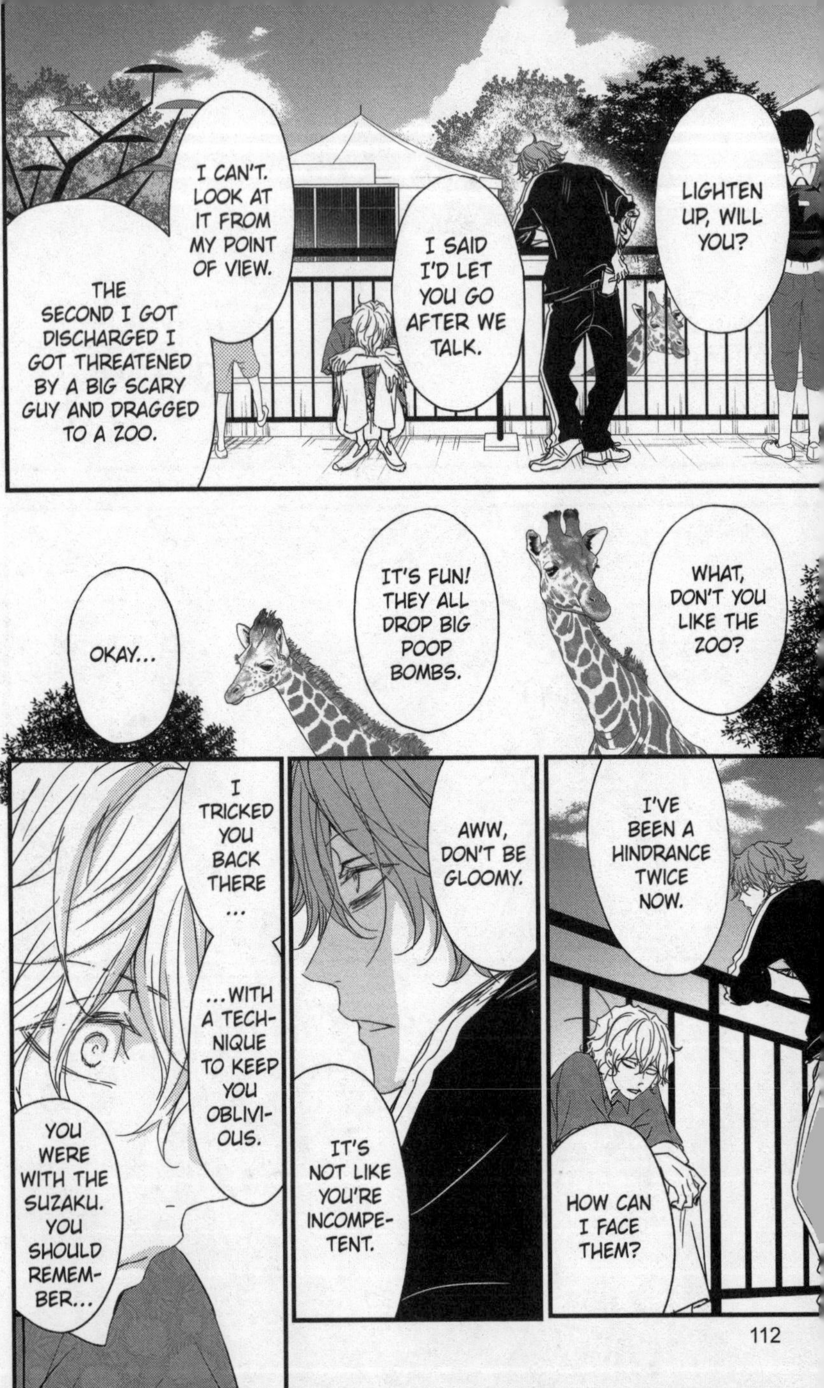
LIGHTEN UP, WILL YOU?
I SAID I'D LET YOU GO AFTER WE TALK.
I CAN'T. LOOK AT IT FROM MY POINT OF VIEW.
THE SECOND I GOT DISCHARGED I GOT THREATENED BY A BIG SCARY GUY AND DRAGGED TO A ZOO.
WHAT, DON'T YOU LIKE THE ZOO?
IT'S FUN! THEY ALL DROP BIG POOP BOMBS.
OKAY...
I'VE BEEN A HINDRANCE TWICE NOW.
HOW CAN I FACE THEM?
AWW, DON'T BE GLOOMY.
IT'S NOT LIKE YOU'RE INCOMPETENT.
I TRICKED YOU BACK THERE ...
...WITH A TECHNIQUE TO KEEP YOU OBLIVIOUS.
YOU WERE WITH THE SUZAKU. YOU SHOULD REMEMBER...

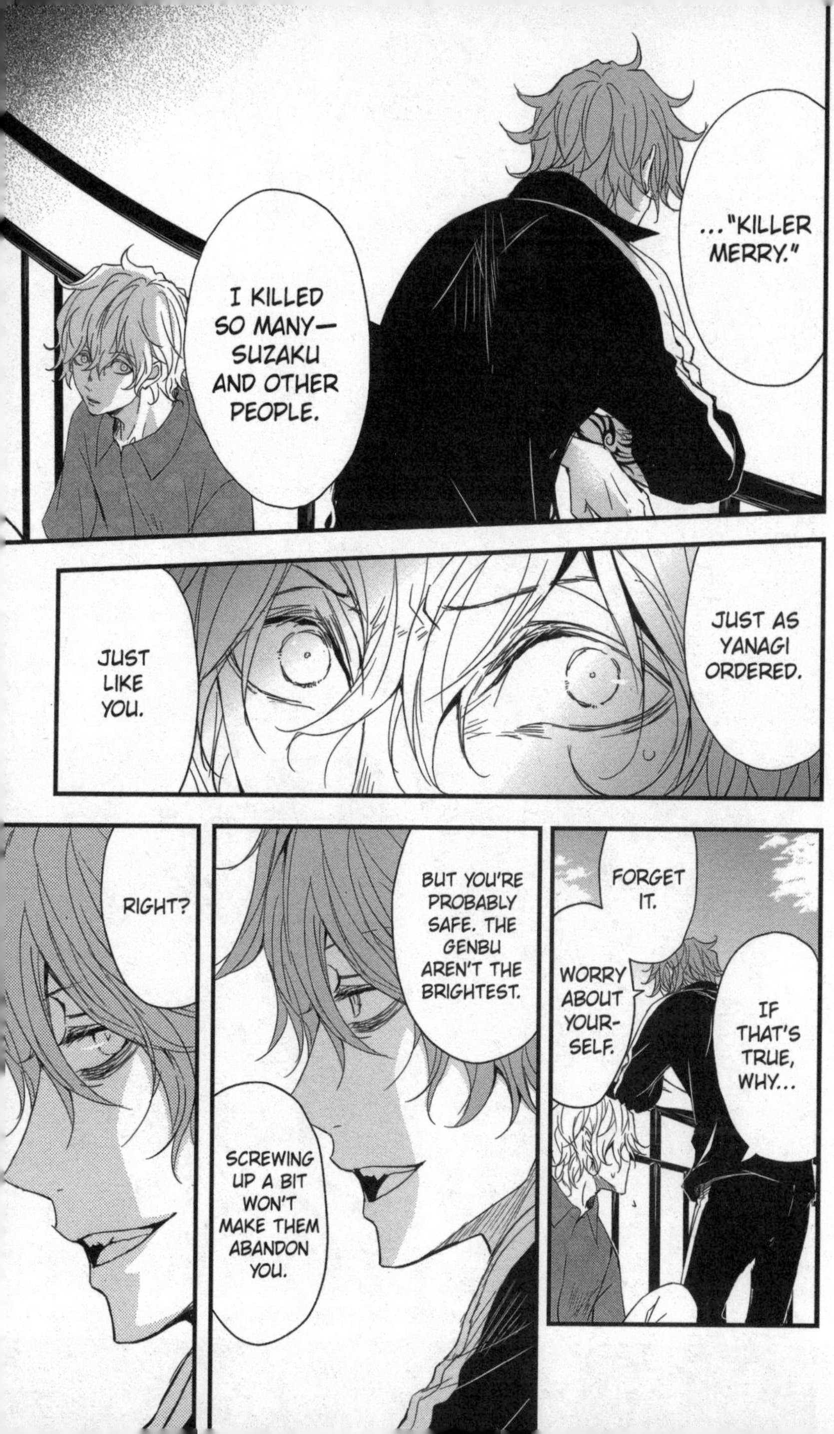
..."KILLER MERRY."
I KILLED SO MANY— SUZAKU AND OTHER PEOPLE.
JUST AS YANAGI ORDERED.
JUST LIKE YOU.
IF THAT'S TRUE, WHY...
FORGET IT.
WORRY ABOUT YOUR-SELF.
BUT YOU'RE PROBABLY SAFE. THE GENBU AREN'T THE BRIGHTEST.
SCREWING UP A BIT WON'T MAKE THEM ABANDON YOU.
RIGHT?

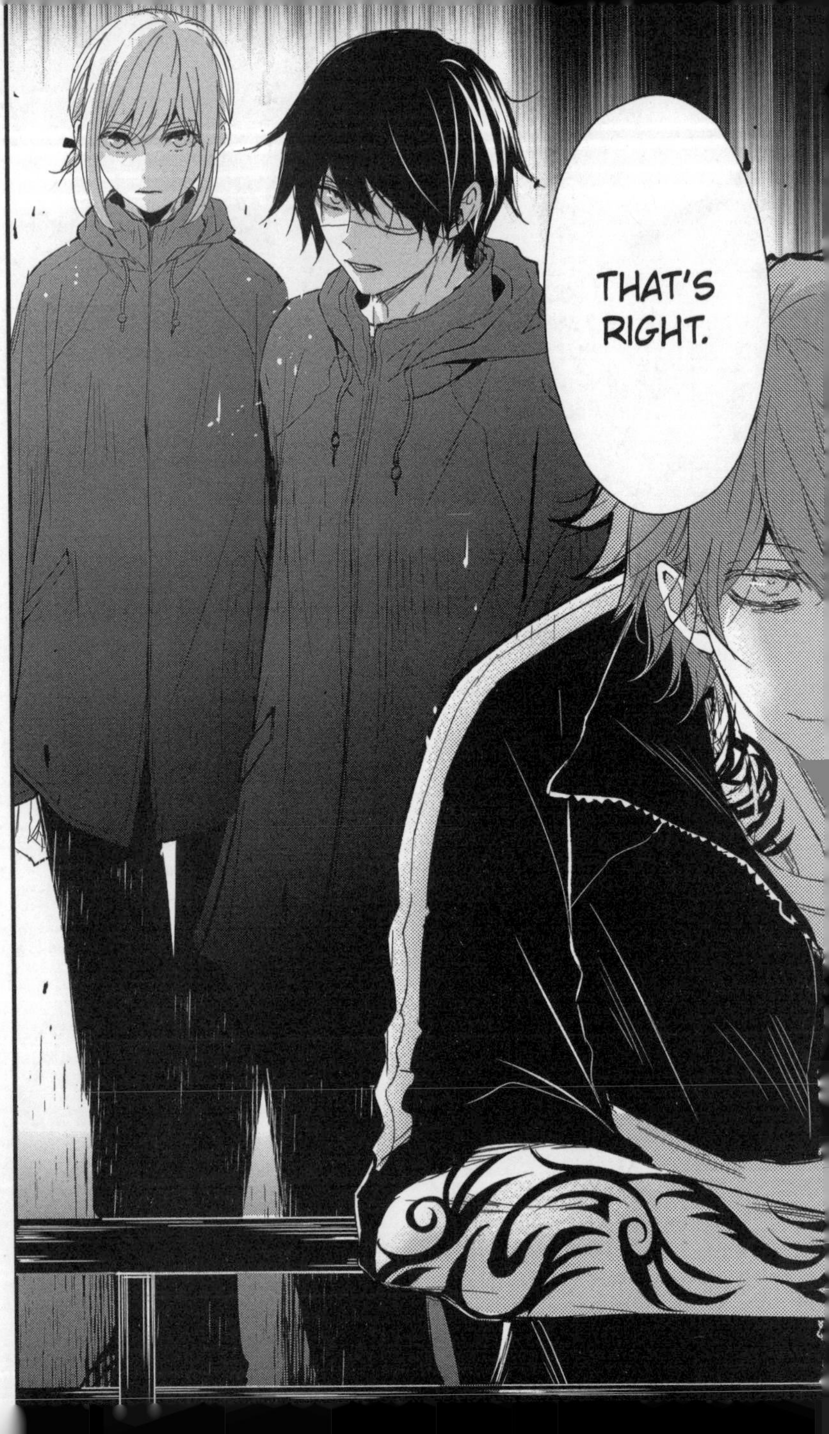
THAT'S RIGHT.

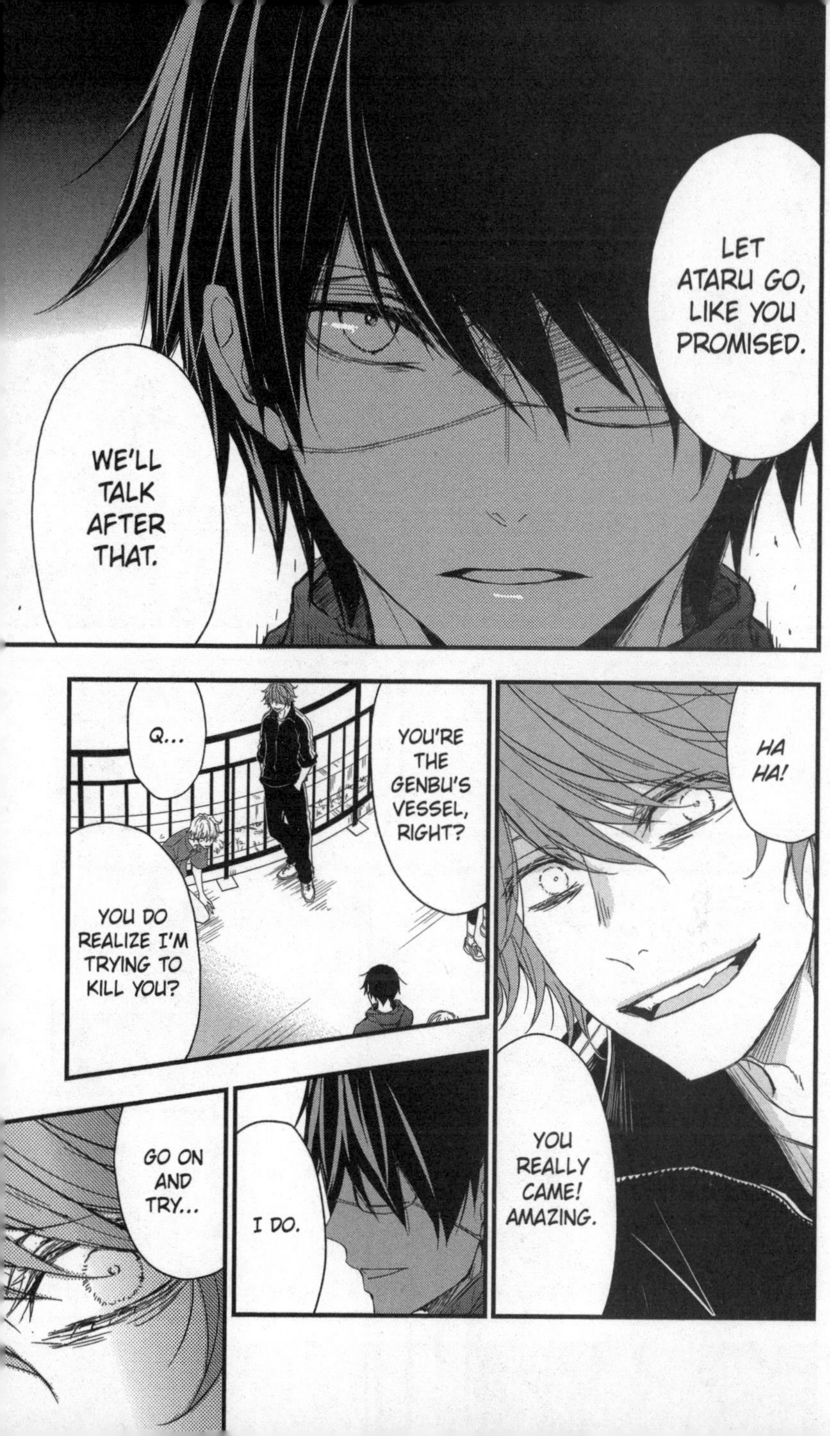
LET ATARU GO, LIKE YOU PROMISED.
WE'LL TALK AFTER THAT.
HA HA!
YOU REALLY CAME! AMAZING.
YOU'RE THE GENBU'S VESSEL, RIGHT?
Q...
YOU DO REALIZE I'M TRYING TO KILL YOU?
I DO.
GO ON AND TRY...

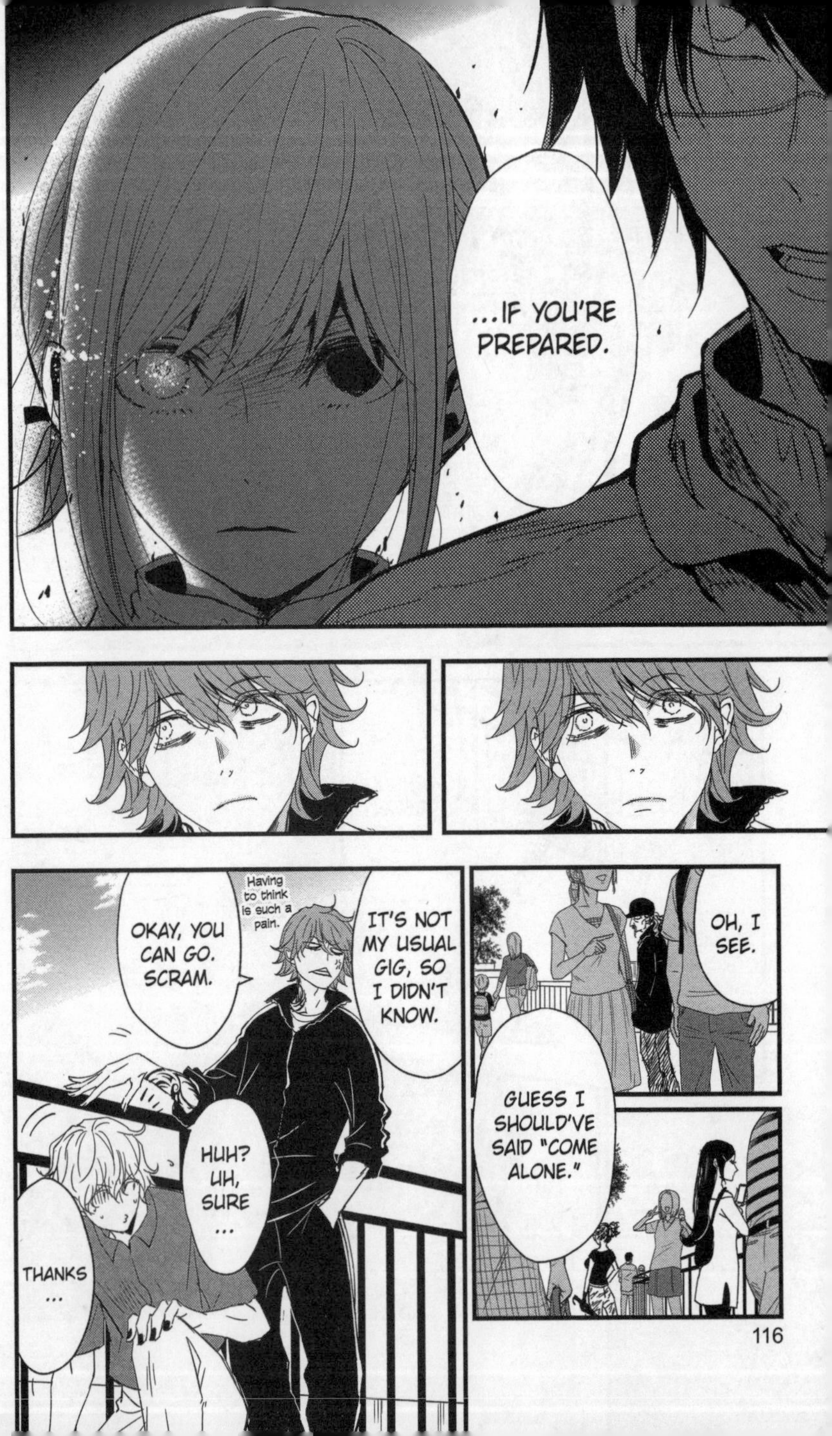
...IF YOU'RE PREPARED.
OH, I SEE.
GUESS I SHOULD'VE SAID "COME ALONE."
IT'S NOT MY USUAL GIG, SO I DIDN'T KNOW.
Having to think is such a pain.
OKAY, YOU CAN GO. SCRAM.
HUH? UH, SURE ...
THANKS ...

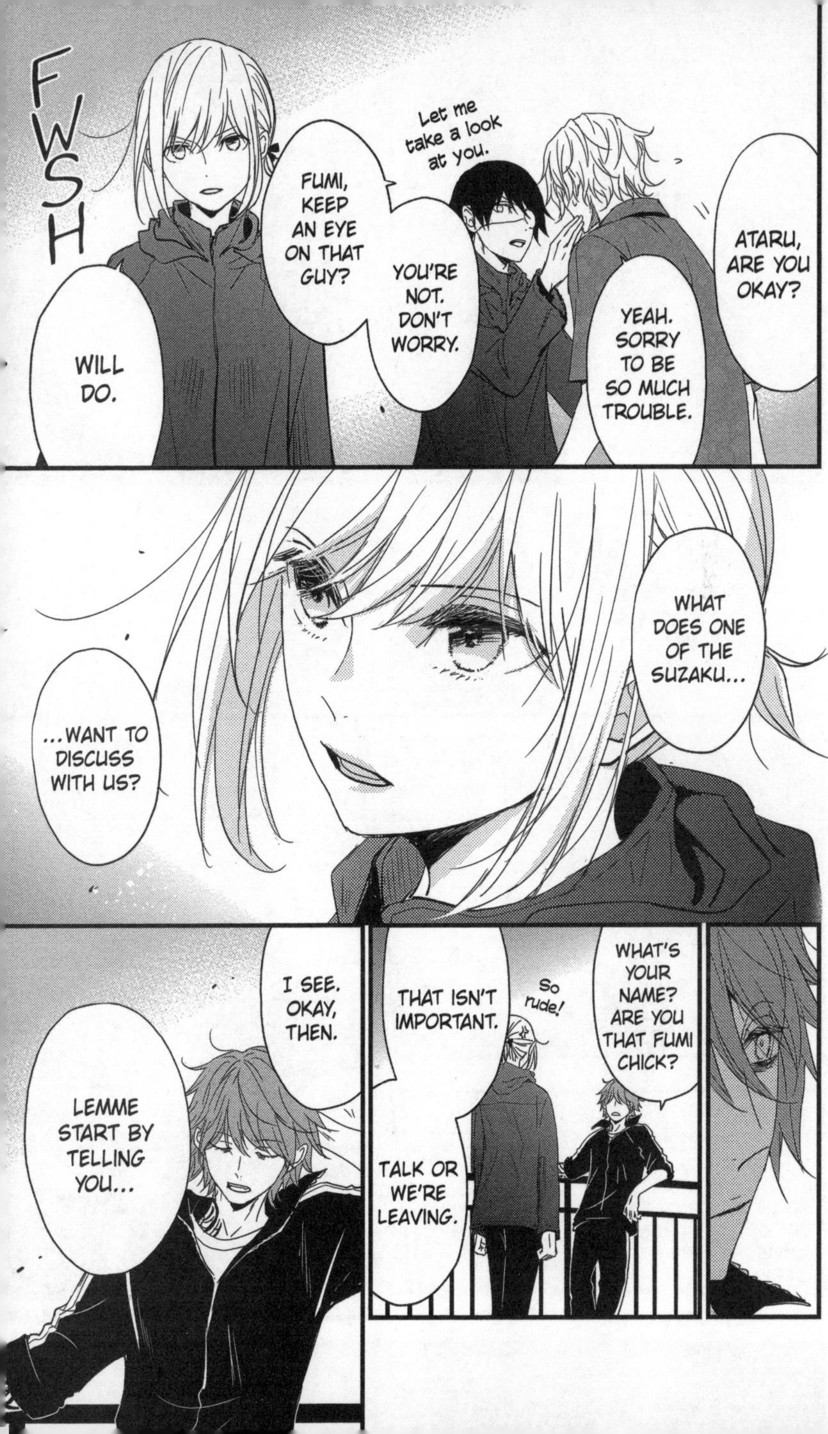
ATARU, ARE YOU OKAY?
YEAH. SORRY TO BE SO MUCH TROUBLE.
Let me take a look at you.
YOU'RE NOT. DON'T WORRY.
FUMI, KEEP AN EYE ON THAT GUY?
WILL DO.
FWSH
WHAT DOES ONE OF THE SUZAKU...
...WANT TO DISCUSS WITH US?
WHAT'S YOUR NAME? ARE YOU THAT FUMI CHICK?
So rude!
THAT ISN'T IMPORTANT.
TALK OR WE'RE LEAVING.
I SEE. OKAY, THEN.
LEMME START BY TELLING YOU...

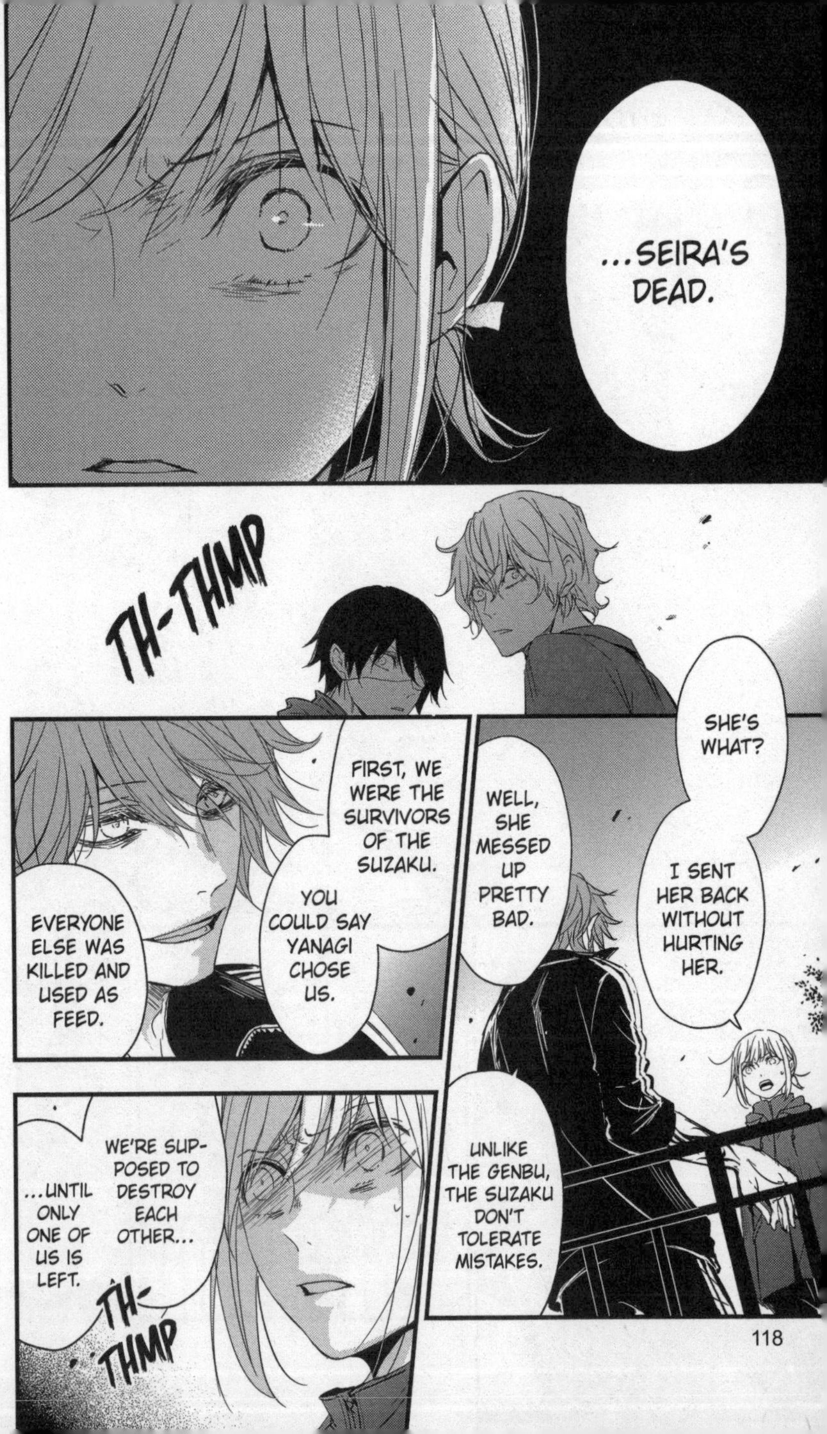
...SEIRA'S DEAD.
TH-THMP
SHE'S WHAT?
I SENT HER BACK WITHOUT HURTING HER.
WELL, SHE MESSED UP PRETTY BAD.
UNLIKE THE GENBU, THE SUZAKU DON'T TOLERATE MISTAKES.
FIRST, WE WERE THE SURVIVORS OF THE SUZAKU.
YOU COULD SAY YANAGI CHOSE US.
EVERYONE ELSE WAS KILLED AND USED AS FEED.
WE'RE SUP-POSED TO DESTROY EACH OTHER...
...UNTIL ONLY ONE OF US IS LEFT.
TH-THMP

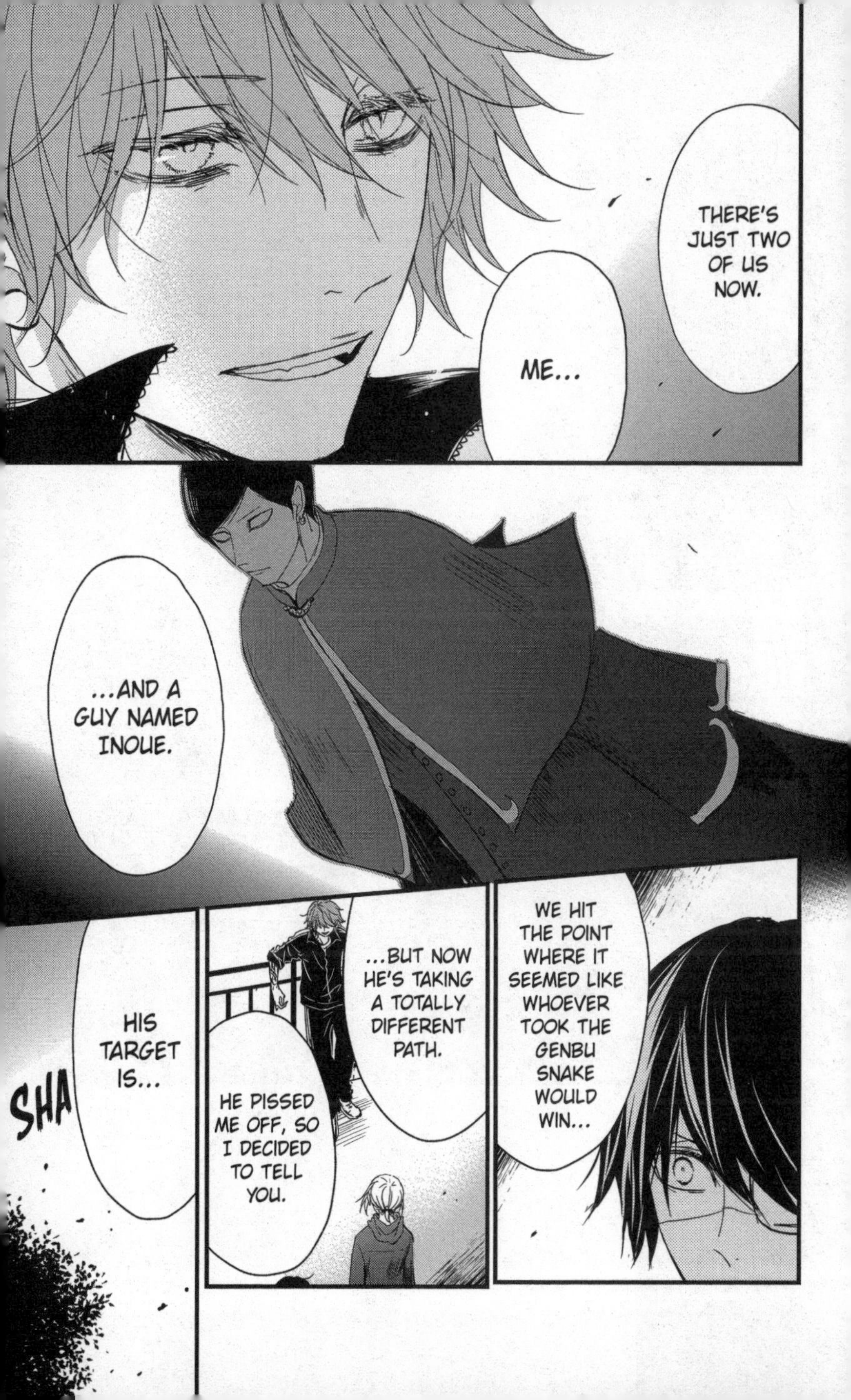
THERE'S JUST TWO OF US NOW.
ME...
...AND A GUY NAMED INOUE.
WE HIT THE POINT WHERE IT SEEMED LIKE WHOEVER TOOK THE GENBU SNAKE WOULD WIN...
...BUT NOW HE'S TAKING A TOTALLY DIFFERENT PATH.
HE PISSED ME OFF, SO I DECIDED TO TELL YOU.
HIS TARGET IS...
SHA

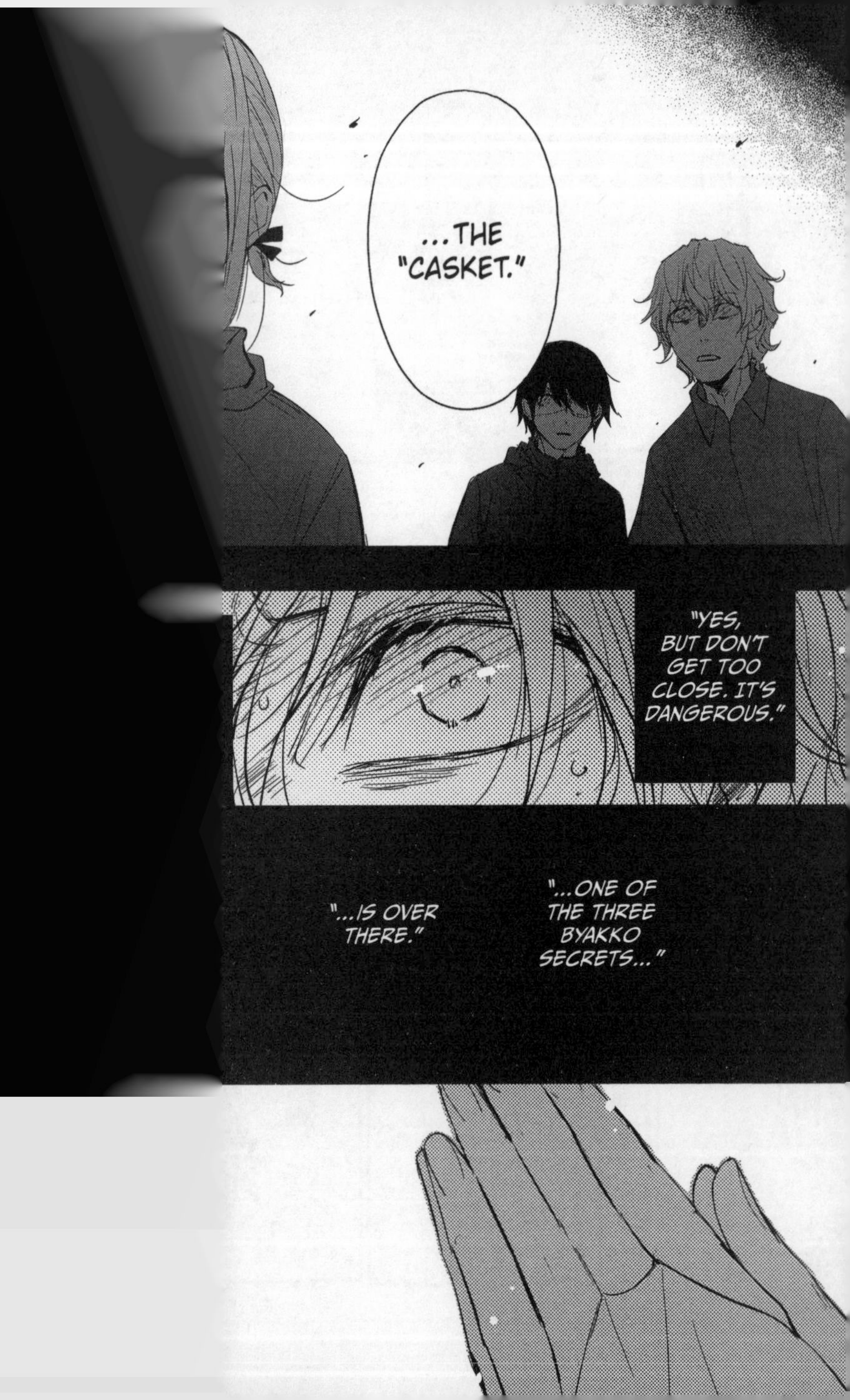

..."THE "CASKET."
"YES, BUT DON'T GET TOO CLOSE. IT'S DANGEROUS."
"...ONE OF THE THREE BYAKKO SECRETS..."
"...IS OVER THERE."

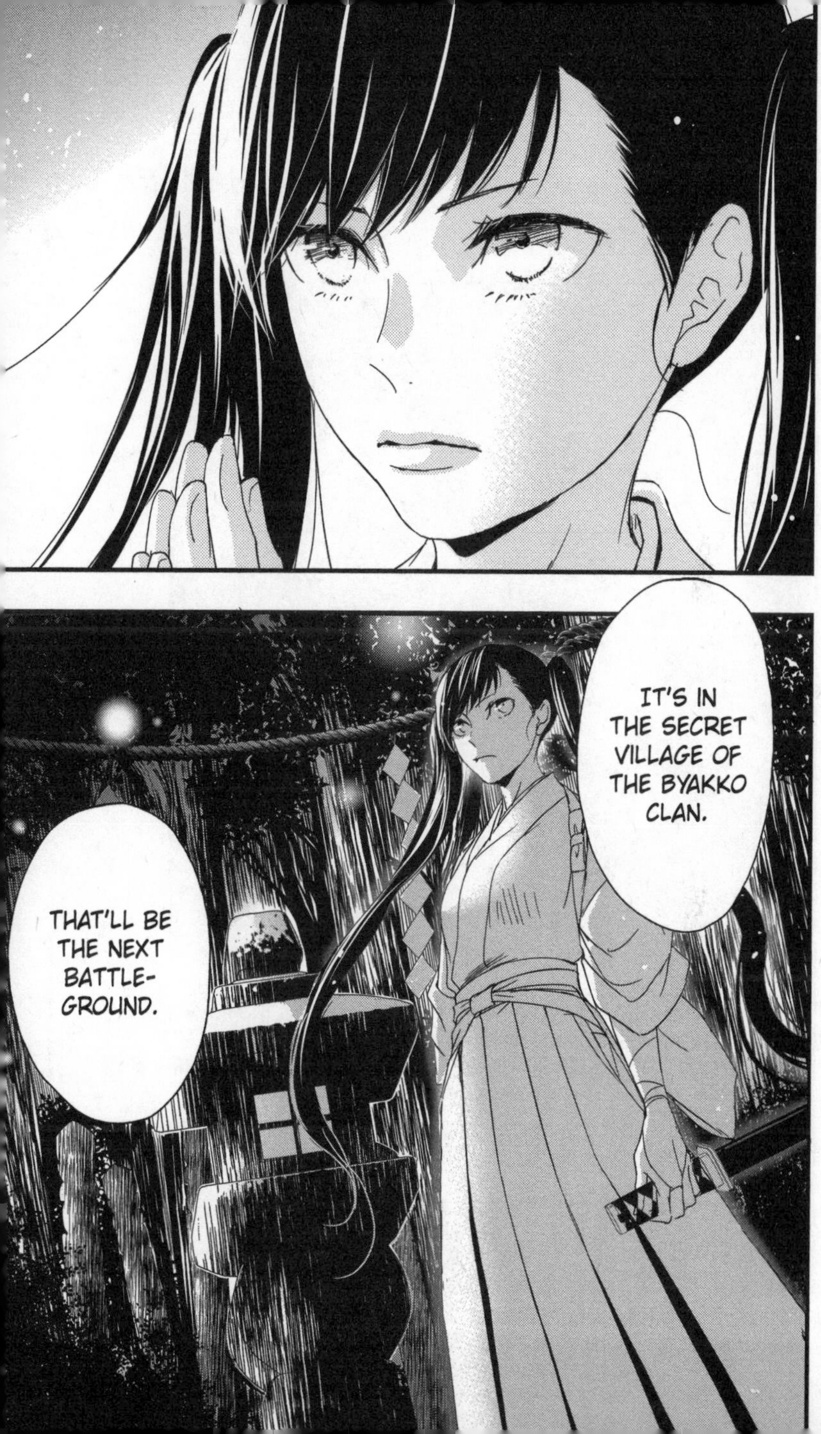
IT'S IN THE SECRET VILLAGE OF THE BYAKKO CLAN.
THAT'LL BE THE NEXT BATTLE-GROUND.

CHAPTER 69

MONTHLY BETSUCOMI SALE DATE NOTICE ON TWITTER AND INSTAGRAM

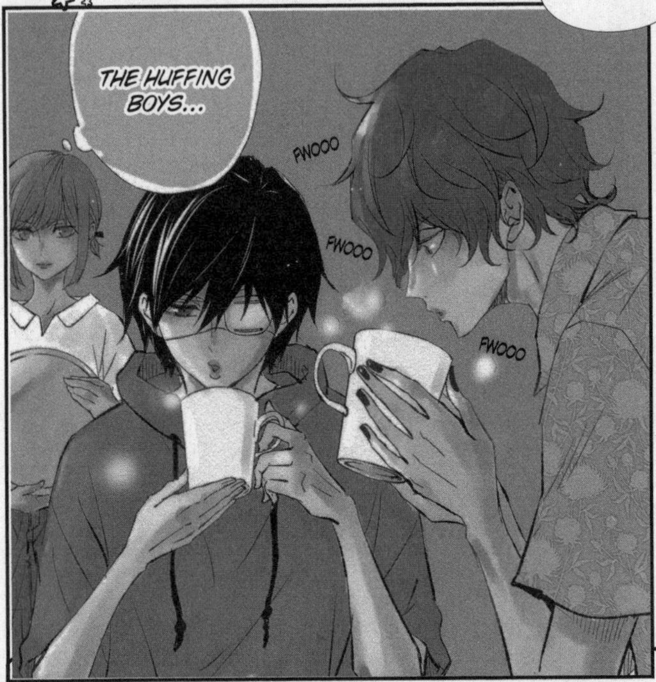
THE HUFFING BOYS...
FWOOO
FWOOO
FWOOO

LET'S SEE... WHAT'S UP IN *QUEEN'S QUALITY* THIS MONTH?
1) I'M SURPRISED TSUBASA REMEMBERED THE WORD "MANIFEST."
2) ATARU CAN'T TAKE HOT DRINKS EITHER.
3) LOOK AT THE PEOPLE DOING THE CHOO-CHOO TRAIN DANCE IN THE BACKGROUND. THAT TAKES ME BACK.

THE SUBTLE SUBPLOT FROM WAY BACK WHEN HAS RESURFACED! WE SEE THE BYAKKO CLAN AGAIN IN THIS CHAPTER!

ONE OF THE BYAKKO CLAN STORY LINES WILL BE PICKED BACK UP HERE, BUT THERE'S ANOTHER ONE (NO, MAYBE IT CAN'T BE CONSIDERED A SUBPLOT, BUT...) COMING BACK IN CHAPTER 71 (IN THE NEXT VOLUME). PERHAPS THAT'S SOMETHING TO LOOK FORWARD TO SOMEWHAT.

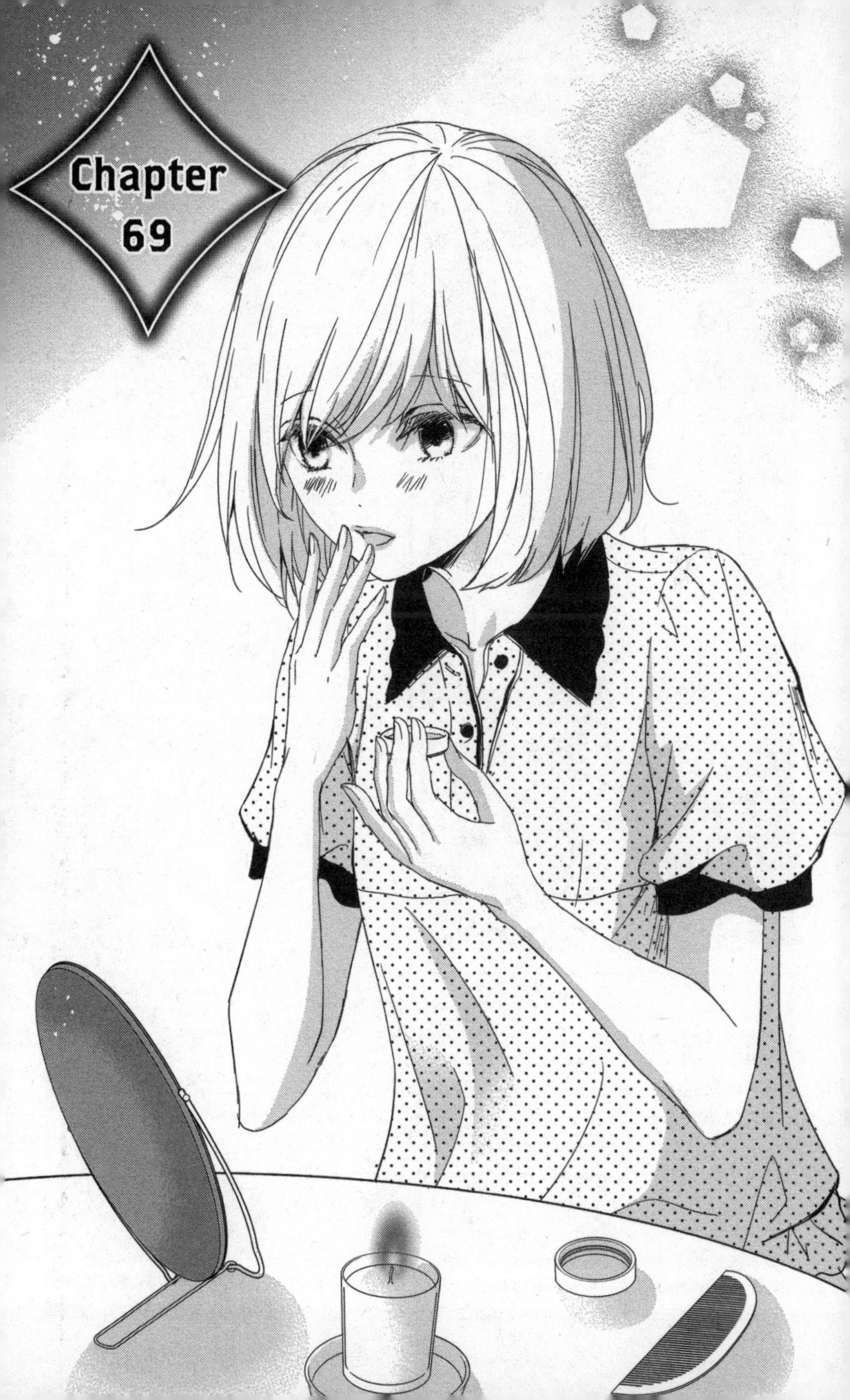
Chapter 69

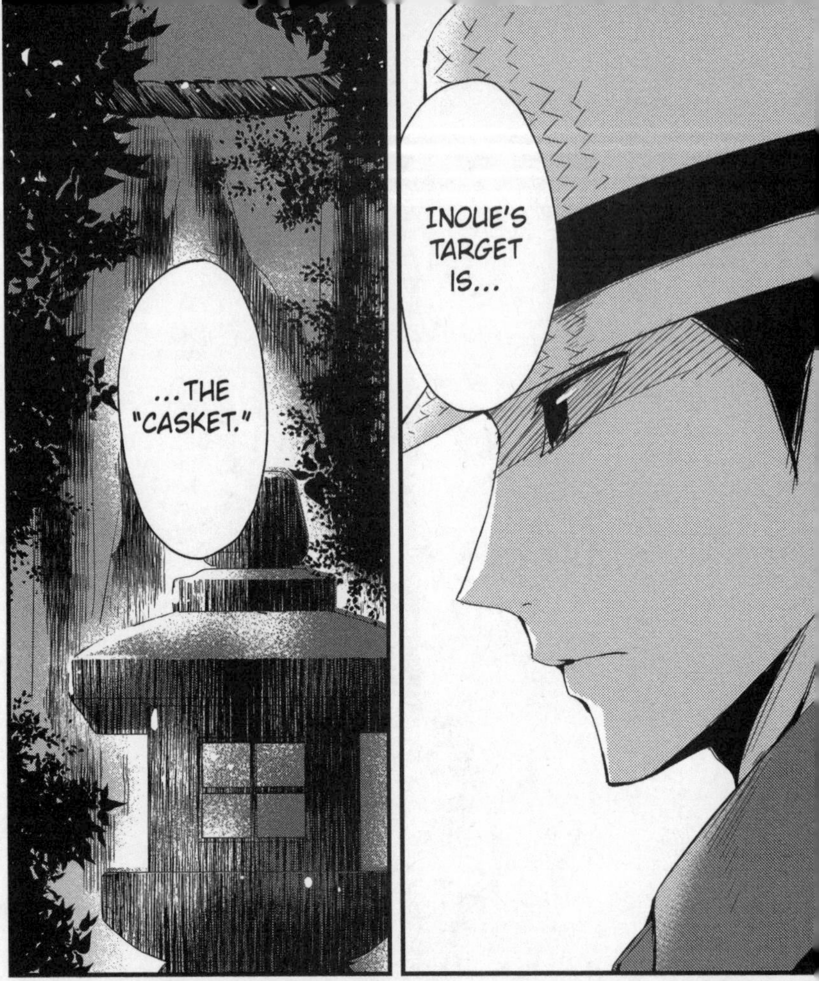
INOUE'S TARGET IS...
...THE "CASKET."

I've been playing the Final Fantasy XIV game for about two years now. I play a little bit during breaks from work. I recently got caught up to the present. (I don't do any of the difficult stuff; I only play for the fun of it.) The fields are beautiful and walking around makes me feel like I'm traveling the world. I have made more friends. I may cry or pout when it isn't going well for me, but that won't help my game, so I've learned to keep a cool head. This game has been great for both my work and my life.

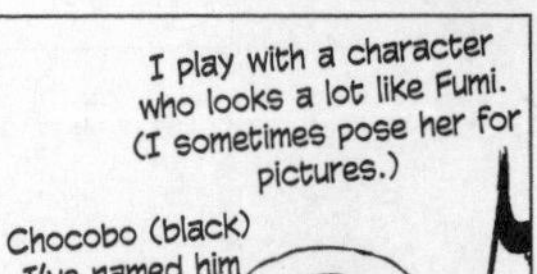
I play with a character who looks a lot like Fumi. (I sometimes pose her for pictures.)
Chocobo (black) I've named him Kyutaro.

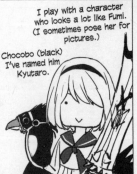

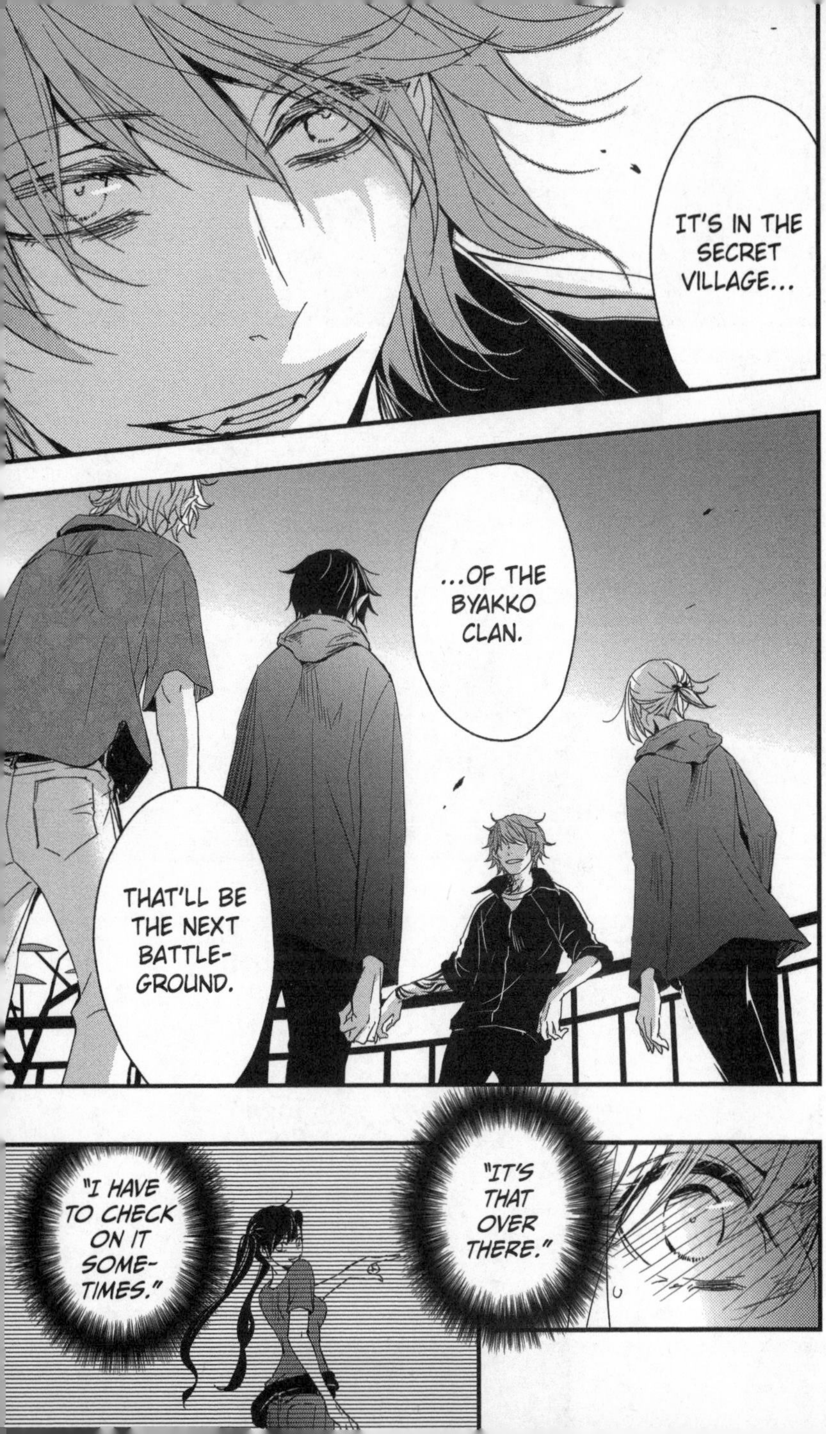
IT'S IN THE SECRET VILLAGE...
...OF THE BYAKKO CLAN.
THAT'LL BE THE NEXT BATTLE-GROUND.
"IT'S THAT OVER THERE."
"I HAVE TO CHECK ON IT SOME-TIMES."

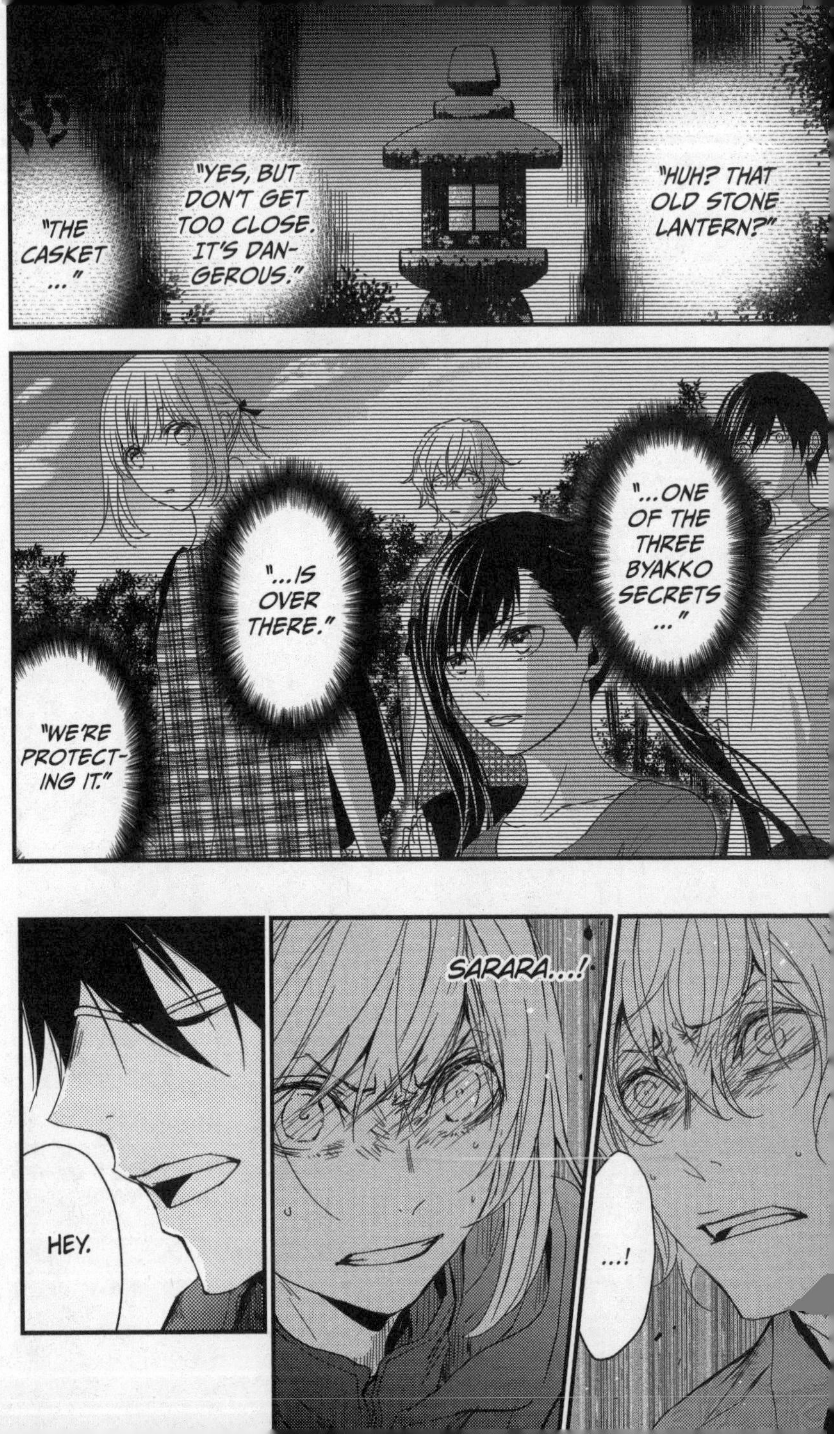
"HUH? THAT OLD STONE LANTERN?"
"YES, BUT DON'T GET TOO CLOSE. IT'S DAN-GEROUS."
"THE CASKET ..."
"...ONE OF THE THREE BYAKKO SECRETS ..."
"...IS OVER THERE."
"WE'RE PROTECT-ING IT."
...!
SARARA...!
HEY.

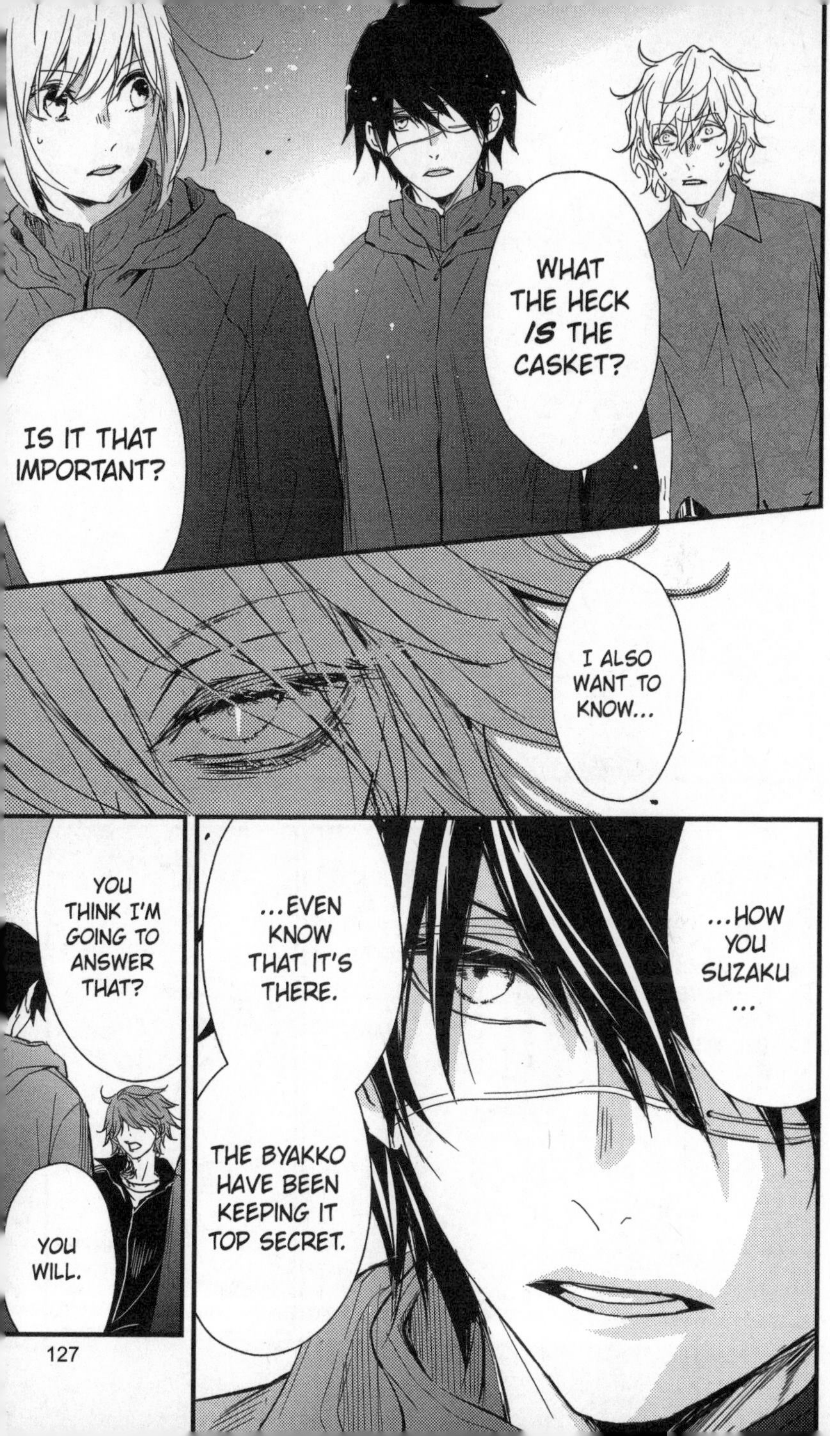
WHAT THE HECK *IS* THE CASKET?
IS IT THAT IMPORTANT?
I ALSO WANT TO KNOW...
...HOW YOU SUZAKU ...
...EVEN KNOW THAT IT'S THERE.
THE BYAKKO HAVE BEEN KEEPING IT TOP SECRET.
YOU THINK I'M GOING TO ANSWER THAT?
YOU WILL.

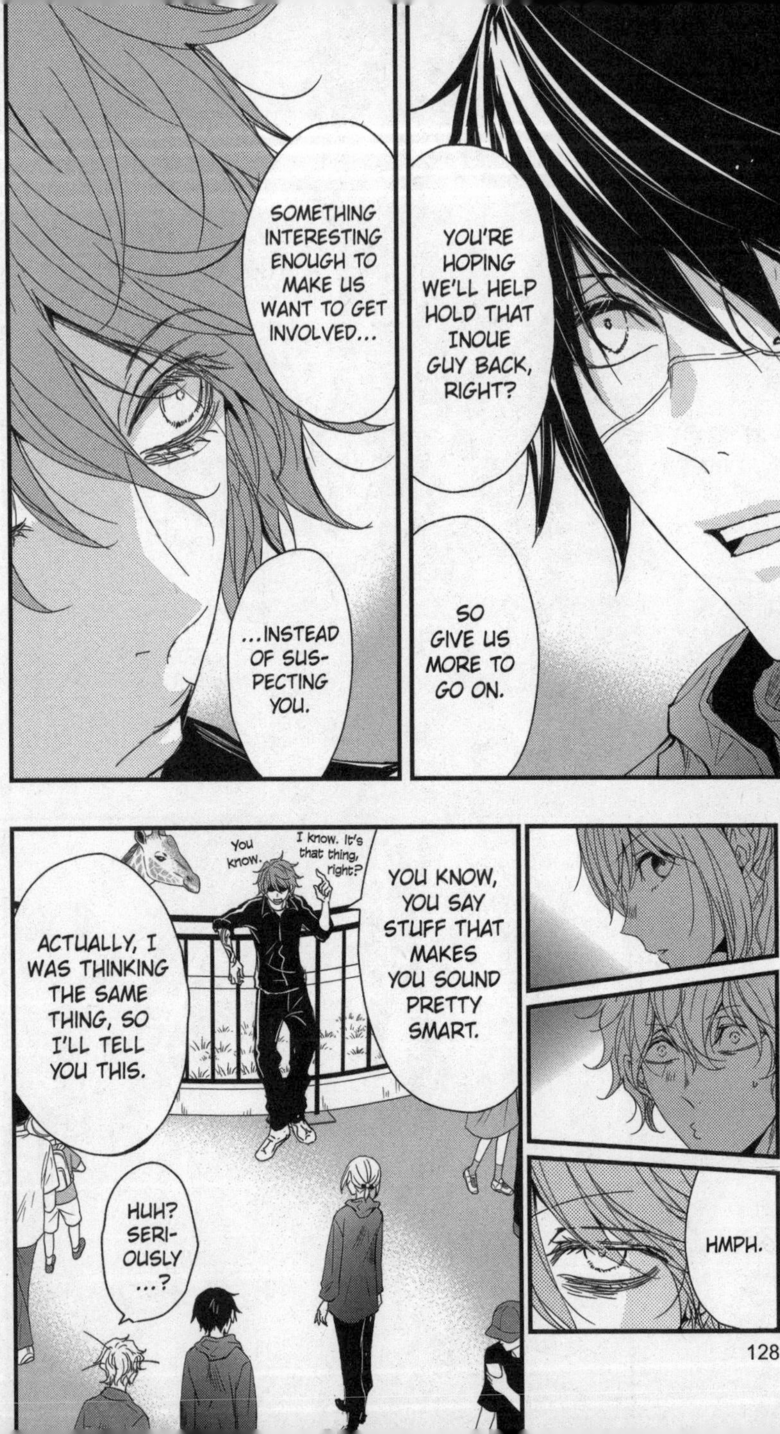
YOU'RE HOPING WE'LL HELP HOLD THAT INOUE GUY BACK, RIGHT?
SO GIVE US MORE TO GO ON.
SOMETHING INTERESTING ENOUGH TO MAKE US WANT TO GET INVOLVED...
...INSTEAD OF SUS-PECTING YOU.
HMPH.
YOU KNOW, YOU SAY STUFF THAT MAKES YOU SOUND PRETTY SMART.
I know. It's that thing, right?
You know.
ACTUALLY, I WAS THINKING THE SAME THING, SO I'LL TELL YOU THIS.
HUH? SERI-OUSLY ...?

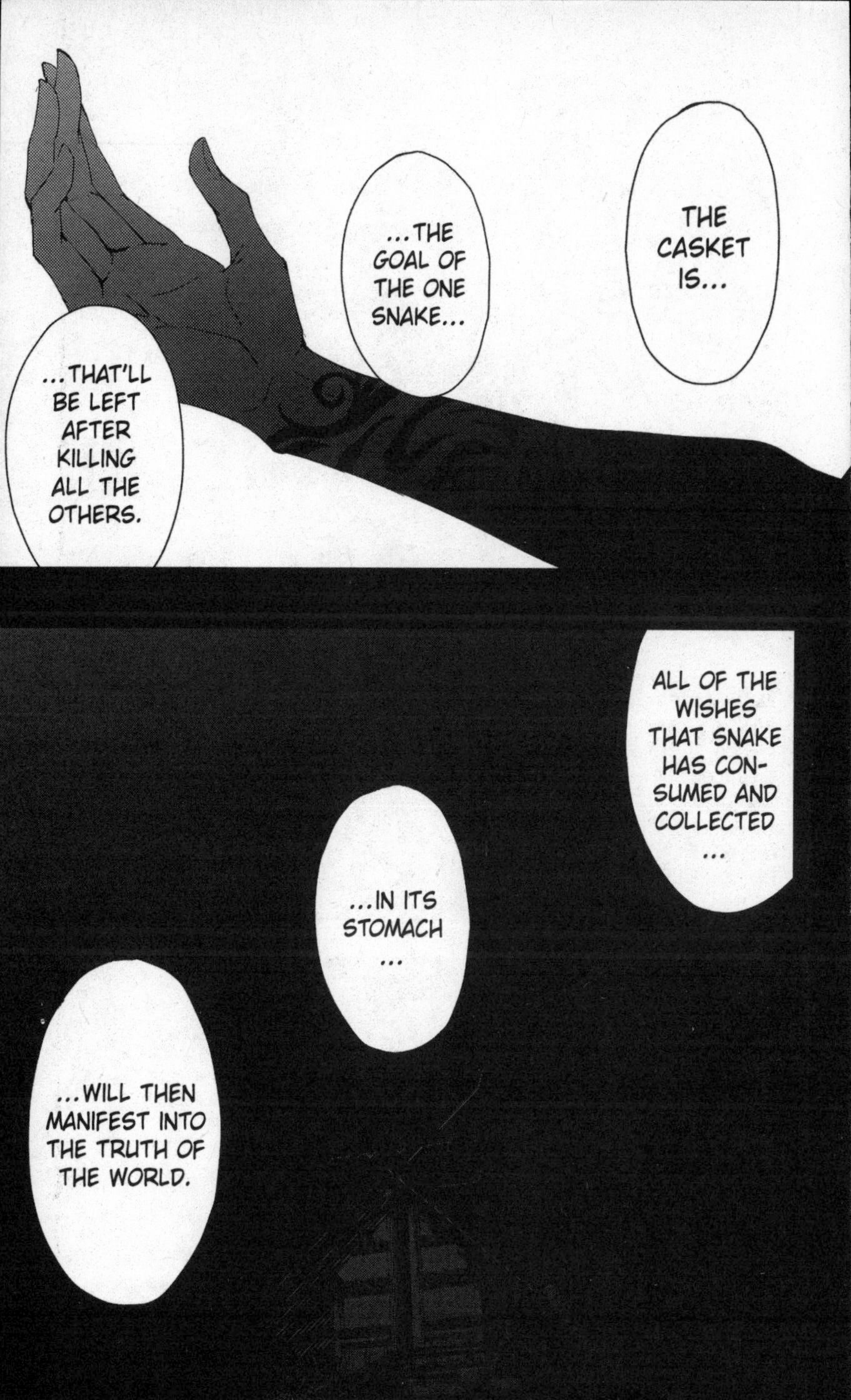
THE CASKET IS...
...THE GOAL OF THE ONE SNAKE...
...THAT'LL BE LEFT AFTER KILLING ALL THE OTHERS.
ALL OF THE WISHES THAT SNAKE HAS CON-SUMED AND COLLECTED ...
...IN ITS STOMACH ...
...WILL THEN MANIFEST INTO THE TRUTH OF THE WORLD.

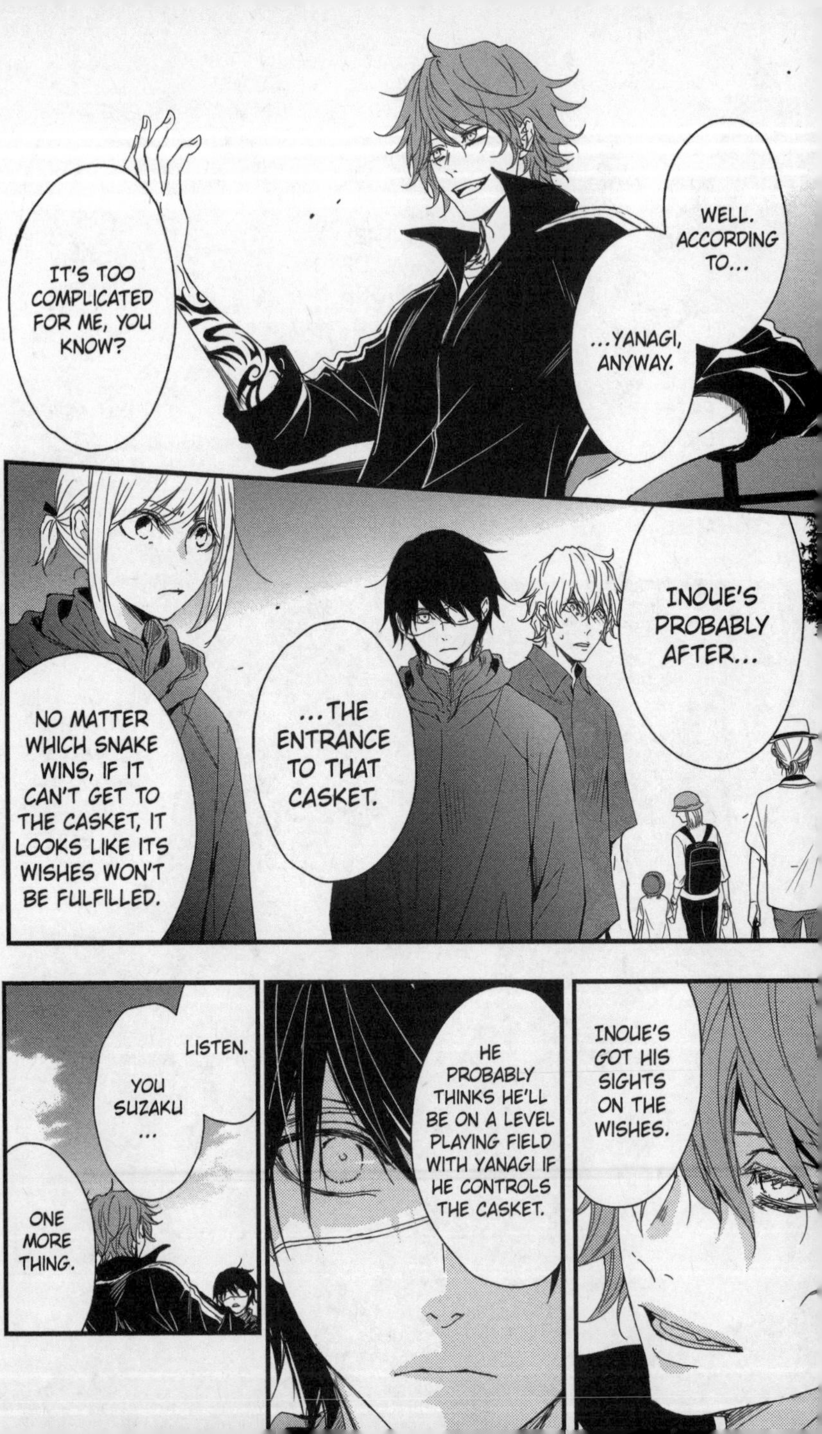
WELL. ACCORDING TO...
...YANAGI, ANYWAY.
IT'S TOO COMPLICATED FOR ME, YOU KNOW?
INOUE'S PROBABLY AFTER...
...THE ENTRANCE TO THAT CASKET.
NO MATTER WHICH SNAKE WINS, IF IT CAN'T GET TO THE CASKET, IT LOOKS LIKE ITS WISHES WON'T BE FULFILLED.
INOUE'S GOT HIS SIGHTS ON THE WISHES.
HE PROBABLY THINKS HE'LL BE ON A LEVEL PLAYING FIELD WITH YANAGI IF HE CONTROLS THE CASKET.
LISTEN.
YOU SUZAKU ...
ONE MORE THING.

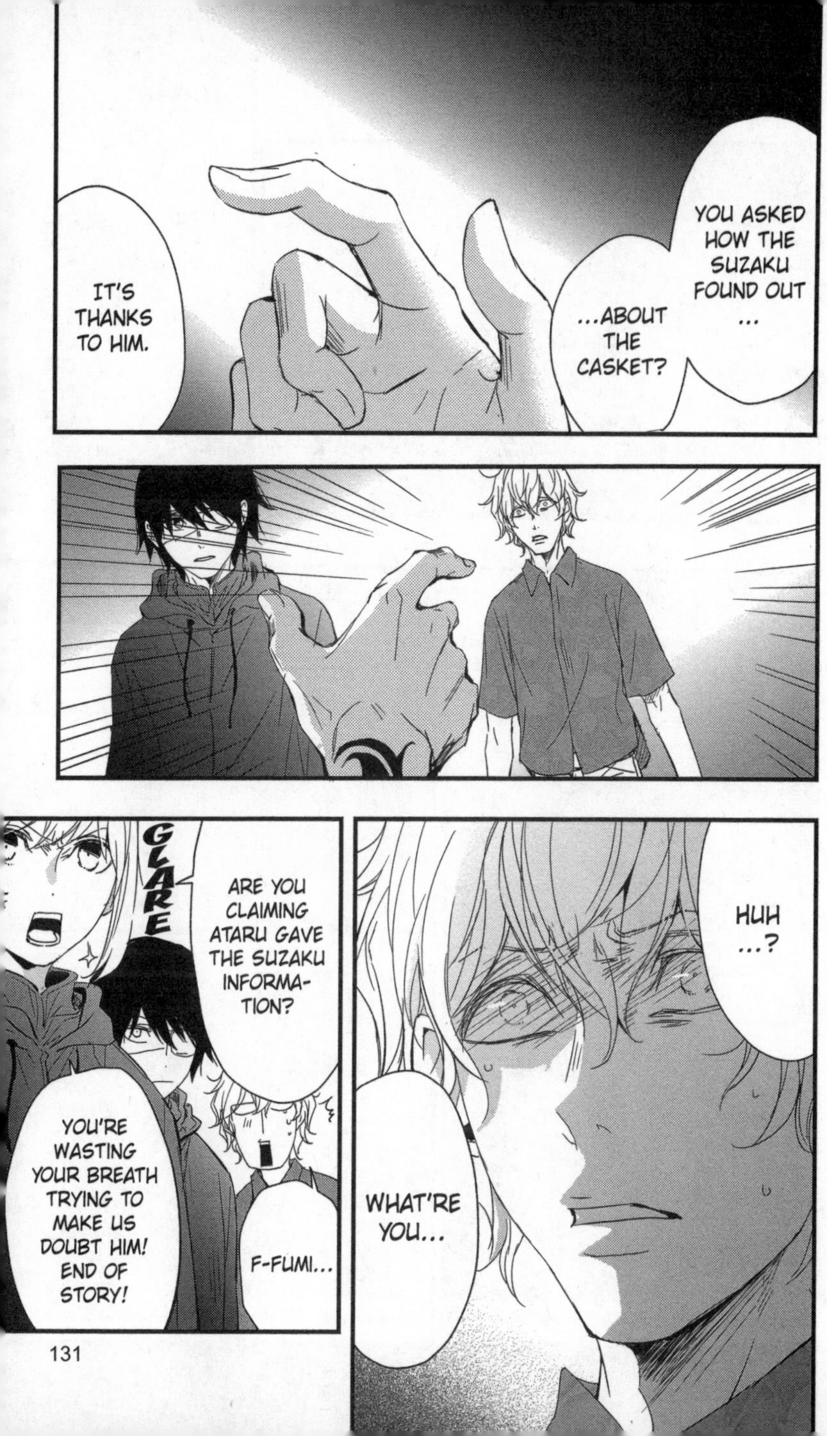
YOU ASKED HOW THE SUZAKU FOUND OUT ...
...ABOUT THE CASKET?
IT'S THANKS TO HIM.
HUH ...?
WHAT'RE YOU...
GLARE
ARE YOU CLAIMING ATARU GAVE THE SUZAKU INFORMATION?
YOU'RE WASTING YOUR BREATH TRYING TO MAKE US DOUBT HIM! END OF STORY!
F-FUMI...

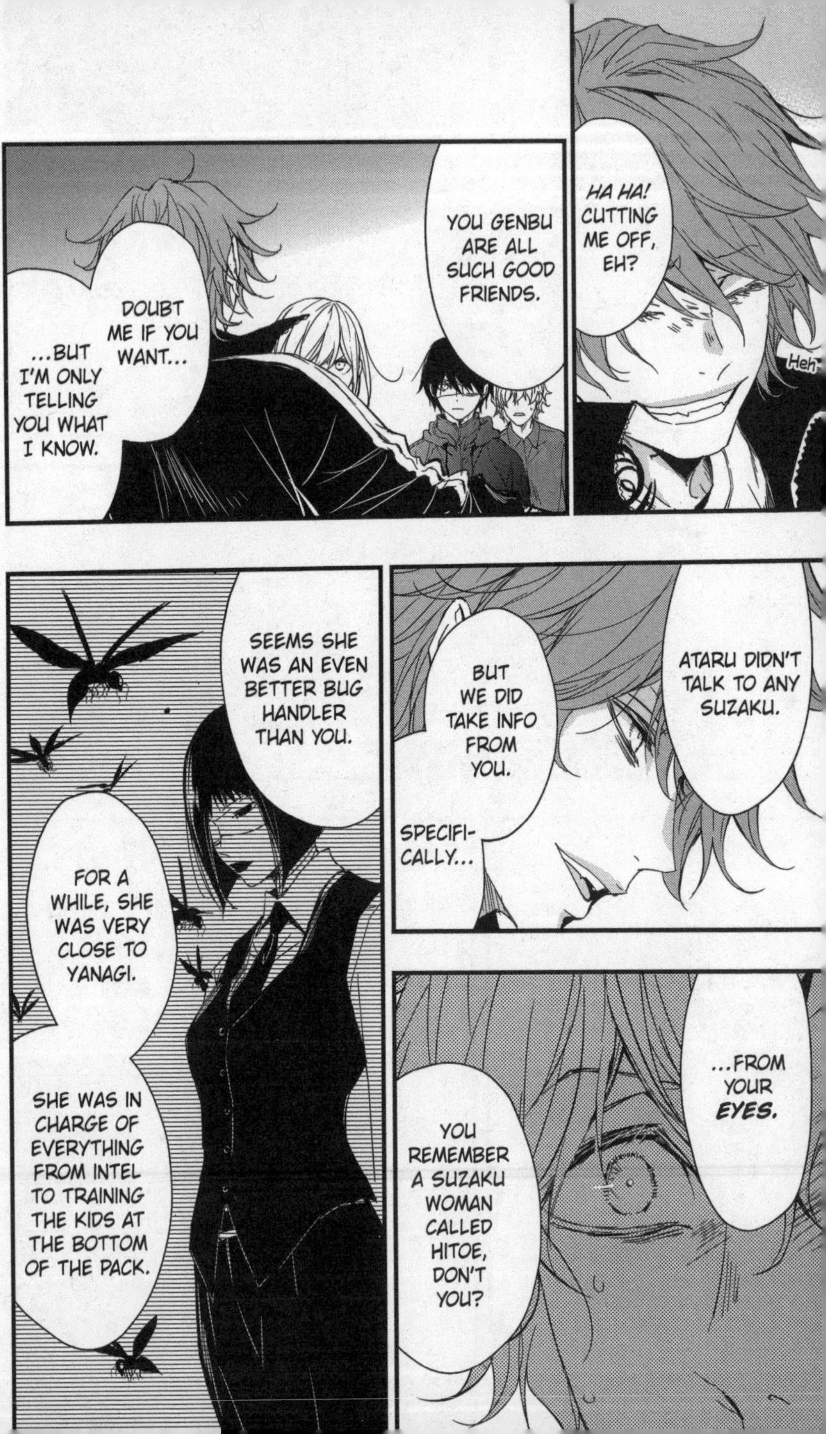
HA HA! CUTTING ME OFF, EH?
Heh
YOU GENBU ARE ALL SUCH GOOD FRIENDS.
DOUBT ME IF YOU WANT...
...BUT I'M ONLY TELLING YOU WHAT I KNOW.
ATARU DIDN'T TALK TO ANY SUZAKU.
BUT WE DID TAKE INFO FROM YOU.
SPECIFI-CALLY...
...FROM YOUR *EYES.*
YOU REMEMBER A SUZAKU WOMAN CALLED HITOE, DON'T YOU?
SEEMS SHE WAS AN EVEN BETTER BUG HANDLER THAN YOU.
FOR A WHILE, SHE WAS VERY CLOSE TO YANAGI.
SHE WAS IN CHARGE OF EVERYTHING FROM INTEL TO TRAINING THE KIDS AT THE BOTTOM OF THE PACK.

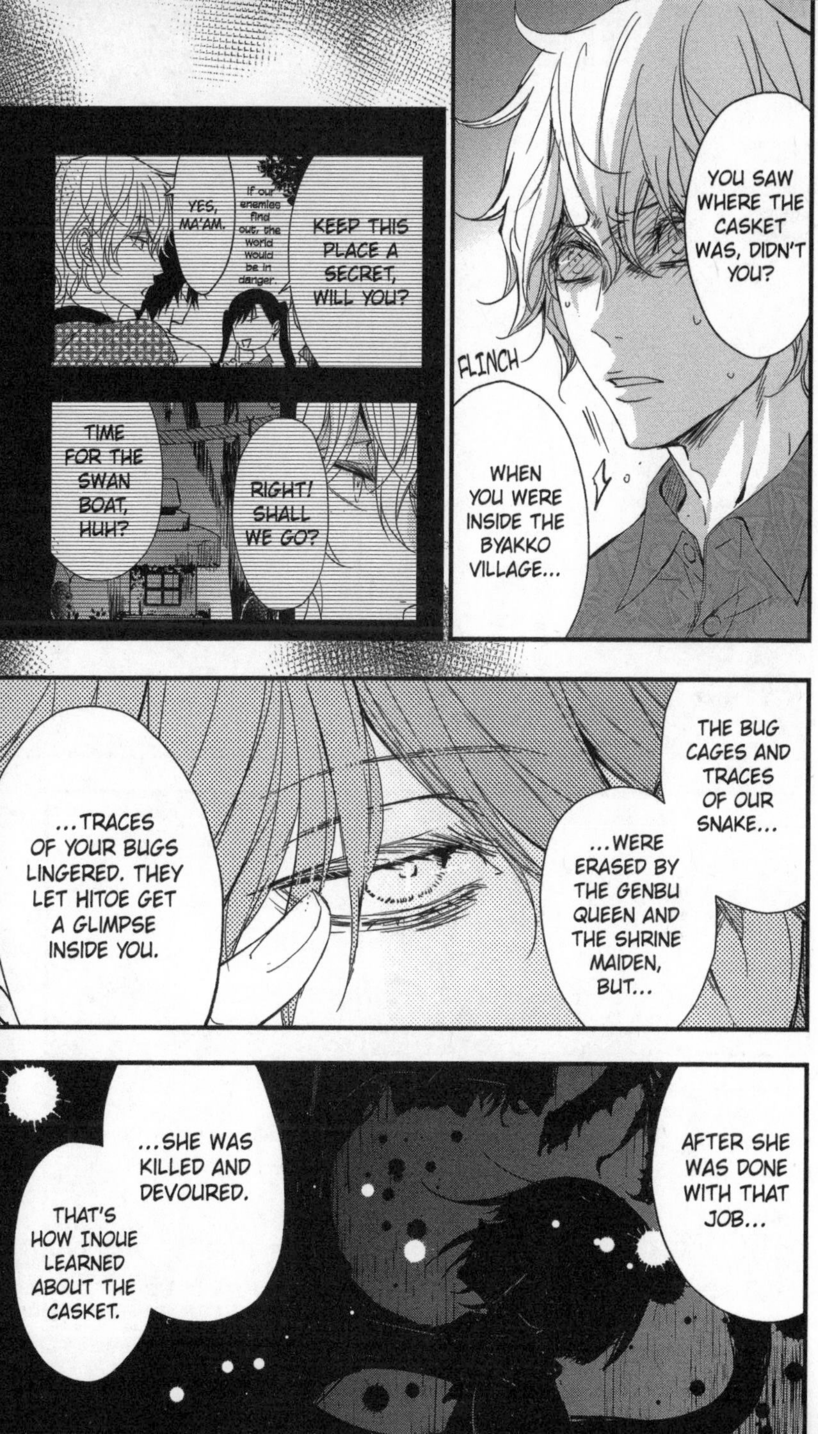
YOU SAW WHERE THE CASKET WAS, DIDN'T YOU?
FLINCH
WHEN YOU WERE INSIDE THE BYAKKO VILLAGE...
KEEP THIS PLACE A SECRET, WILL YOU?
If our enemies find out, the world would be in danger.
YES, MA'AM.
RIGHT! SHALL WE GO?
TIME FOR THE SWAN BOAT, HUH?
THE BUG CAGES AND TRACES OF OUR SNAKE...
...WERE ERASED BY THE GENBU QUEEN AND THE SHRINE MAIDEN, BUT...
...TRACES OF YOUR BUGS LINGERED. THEY LET HITOE GET A GLIMPSE INSIDE YOU.
AFTER SHE WAS DONE WITH THAT JOB...
...SHE WAS KILLED AND DEVOURED.
THAT'S HOW INOUE LEARNED ABOUT THE CASKET.

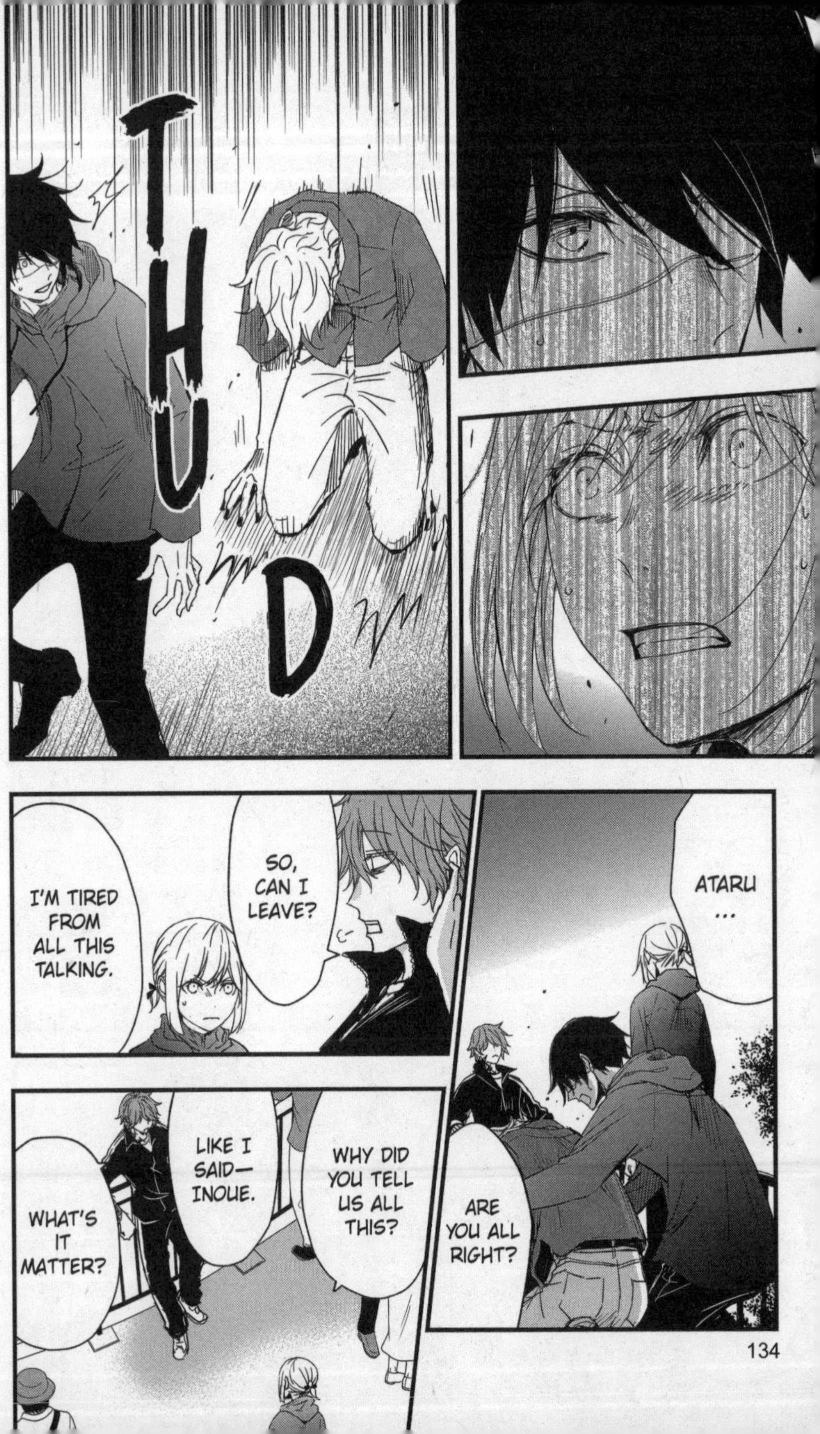
THUD
ATARU ...
ARE YOU ALL RIGHT?
SO, CAN I LEAVE?
I'M TIRED FROM ALL THIS TALKING.
WHY DID YOU TELL US ALL THIS?
LIKE I SAID— INOUE.
WHAT'S IT MATTER?

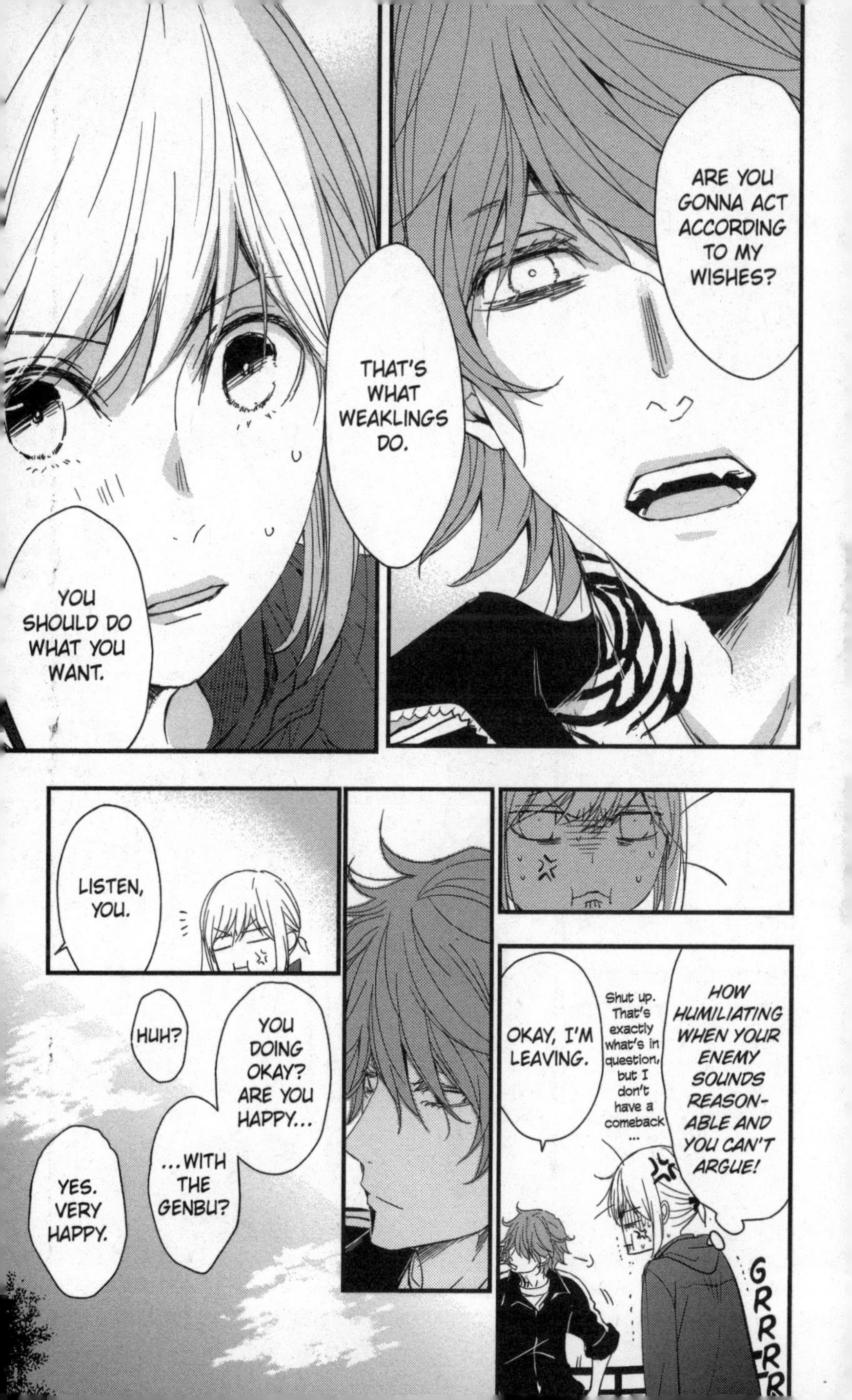
ARE YOU GONNA ACT ACCORDING TO MY WISHES?
THAT'S WHAT WEAKLINGS DO.
YOU SHOULD DO WHAT YOU WANT.
LISTEN, YOU.
HUH?
YOU DOING OKAY? ARE YOU HAPPY...
...WITH THE GENBU?
YES. VERY HAPPY.
OKAY, I'M LEAVING.
HOW HUMILIATING WHEN YOUR ENEMY SOUNDS REASON-ABLE AND YOU CAN'T ARGUE!
Shut up. That's exactly what's in question, but I don't have a comeback...
GRRRRR

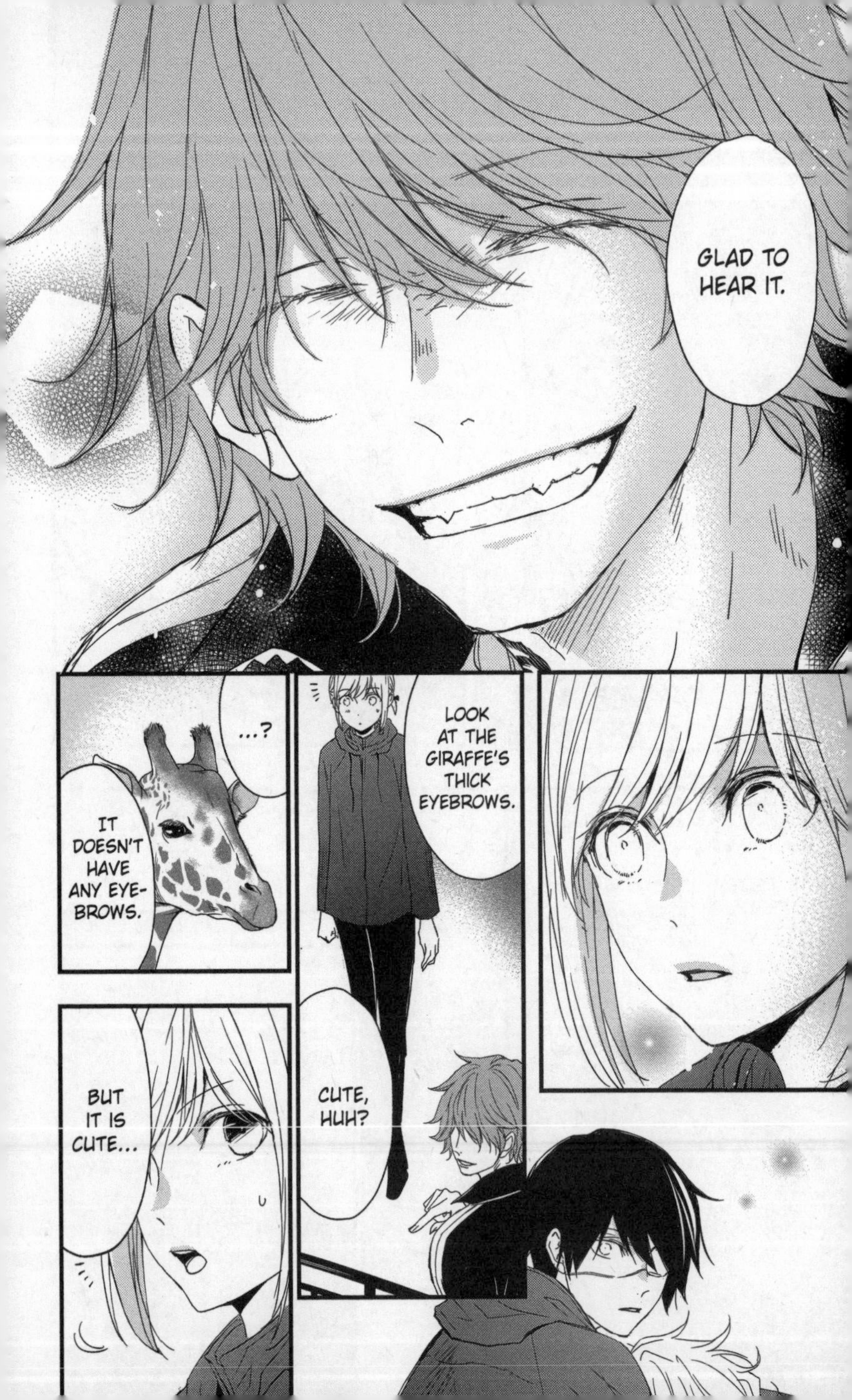
GLAD TO HEAR IT.
LOOK AT THE GIRAFFE'S THICK EYEBROWS.
...?
IT DOESN'T HAVE ANY EYE-BROWS.
CUTE, HUH?
BUT IT IS CUTE...

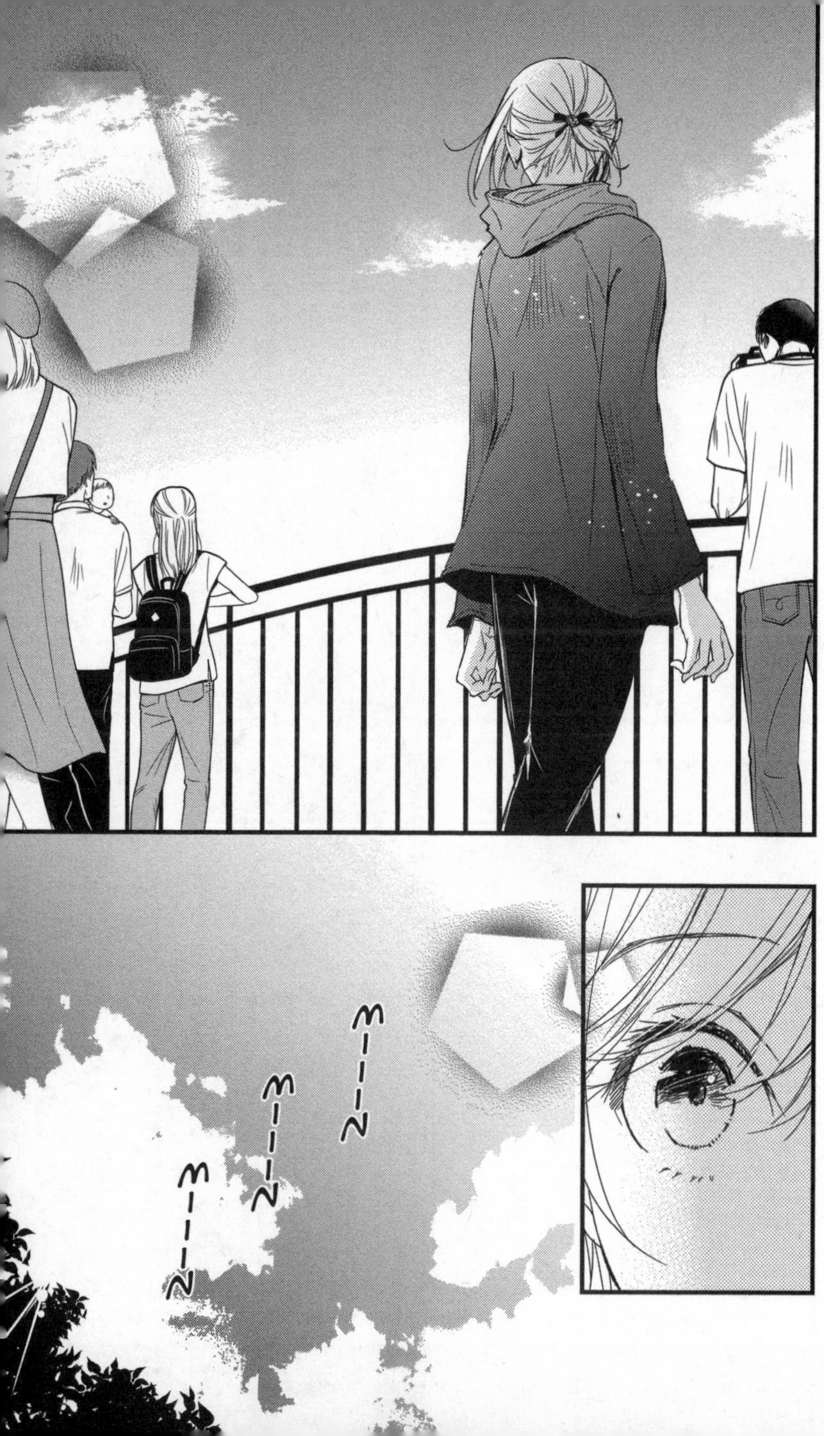

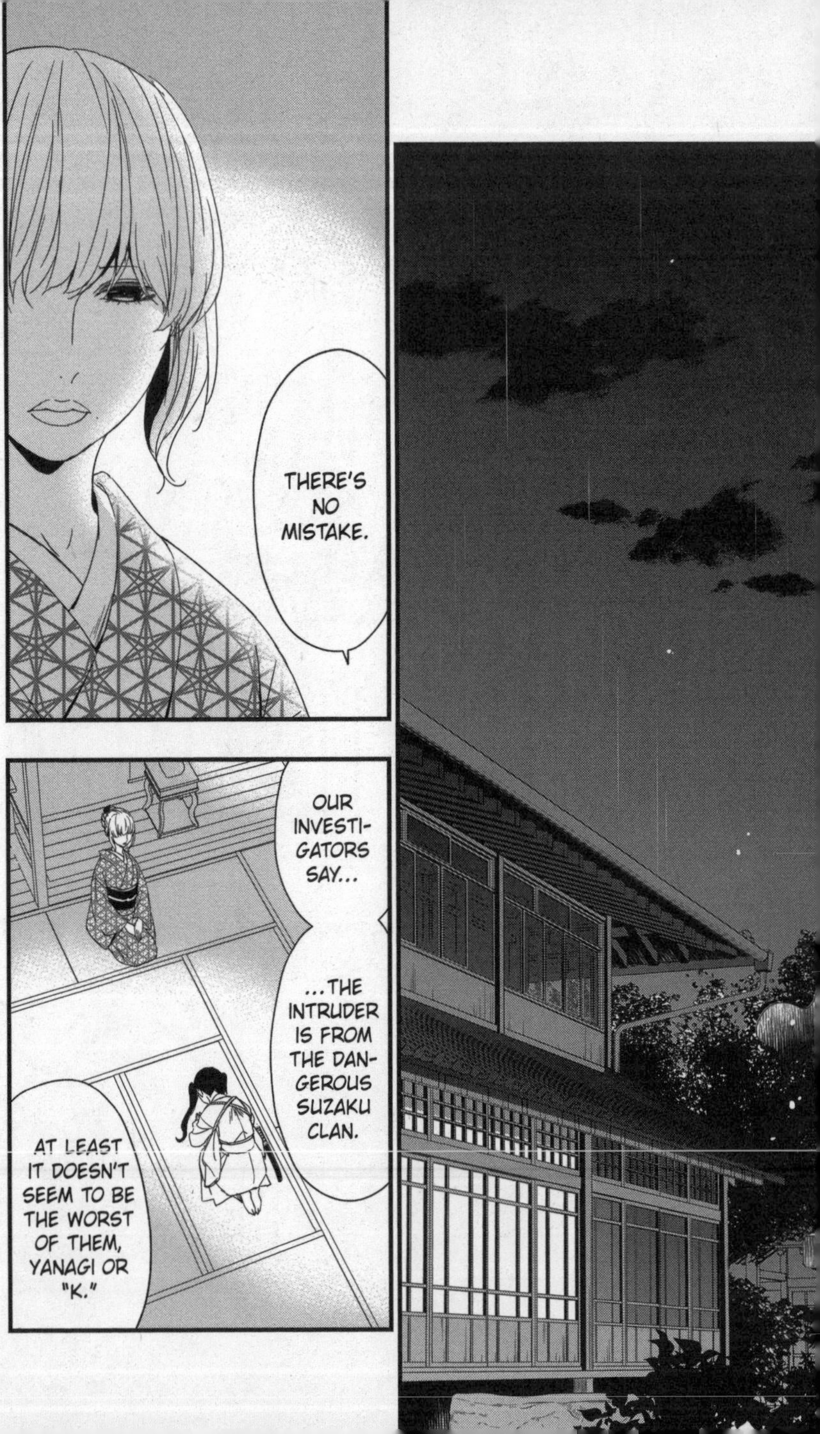
THERE'S NO MISTAKE.
OUR INVESTIGATORS SAY...
...THE INTRUDER IS FROM THE DANGEROUS SUZAKU CLAN.
AT LEAST IT DOESN'T SEEM TO BE THE WORST OF THEM, YANAGI OR "K."

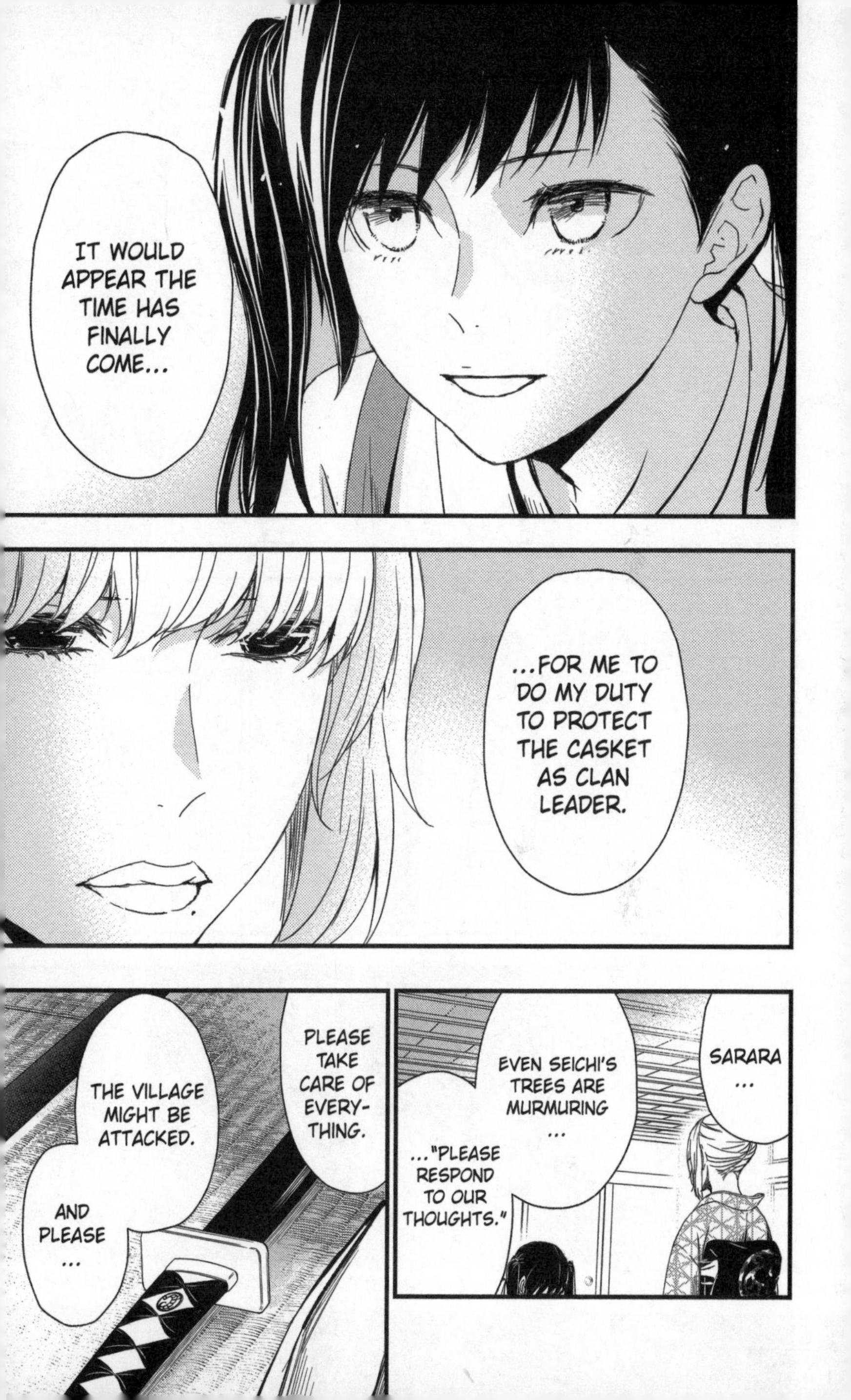
IT WOULD APPEAR THE TIME HAS FINALLY COME...
...FOR ME TO DO MY DUTY TO PROTECT THE CASKET AS CLAN LEADER.
SARARA...
EVEN SEICHI'S TREES ARE MURMURING...
..."PLEASE RESPOND TO OUR THOUGHTS."
PLEASE TAKE CARE OF EVERY-THING.
THE VILLAGE MIGHT BE ATTACKED.
AND PLEASE...

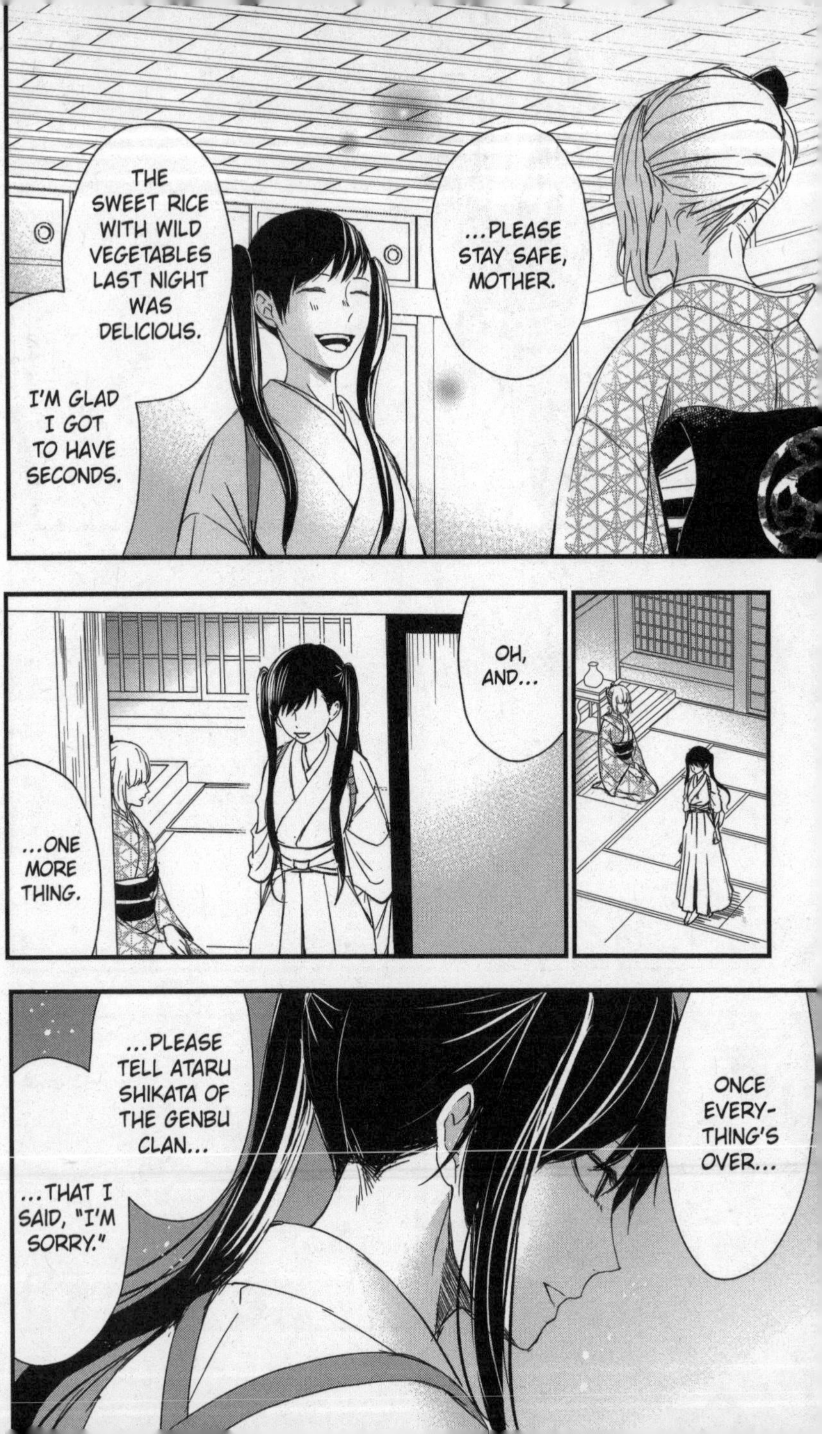
...PLEASE STAY SAFE, MOTHER.
THE SWEET RICE WITH WILD VEGETABLES LAST NIGHT WAS DELICIOUS.
I'M GLAD I GOT TO HAVE SECONDS.
OH, AND...
...ONE MORE THING.
ONCE EVERY-THING'S OVER...
...PLEASE TELL ATARU SHIKATA OF THE GENBU CLAN...
...THAT I SAID, "I'M SORRY."

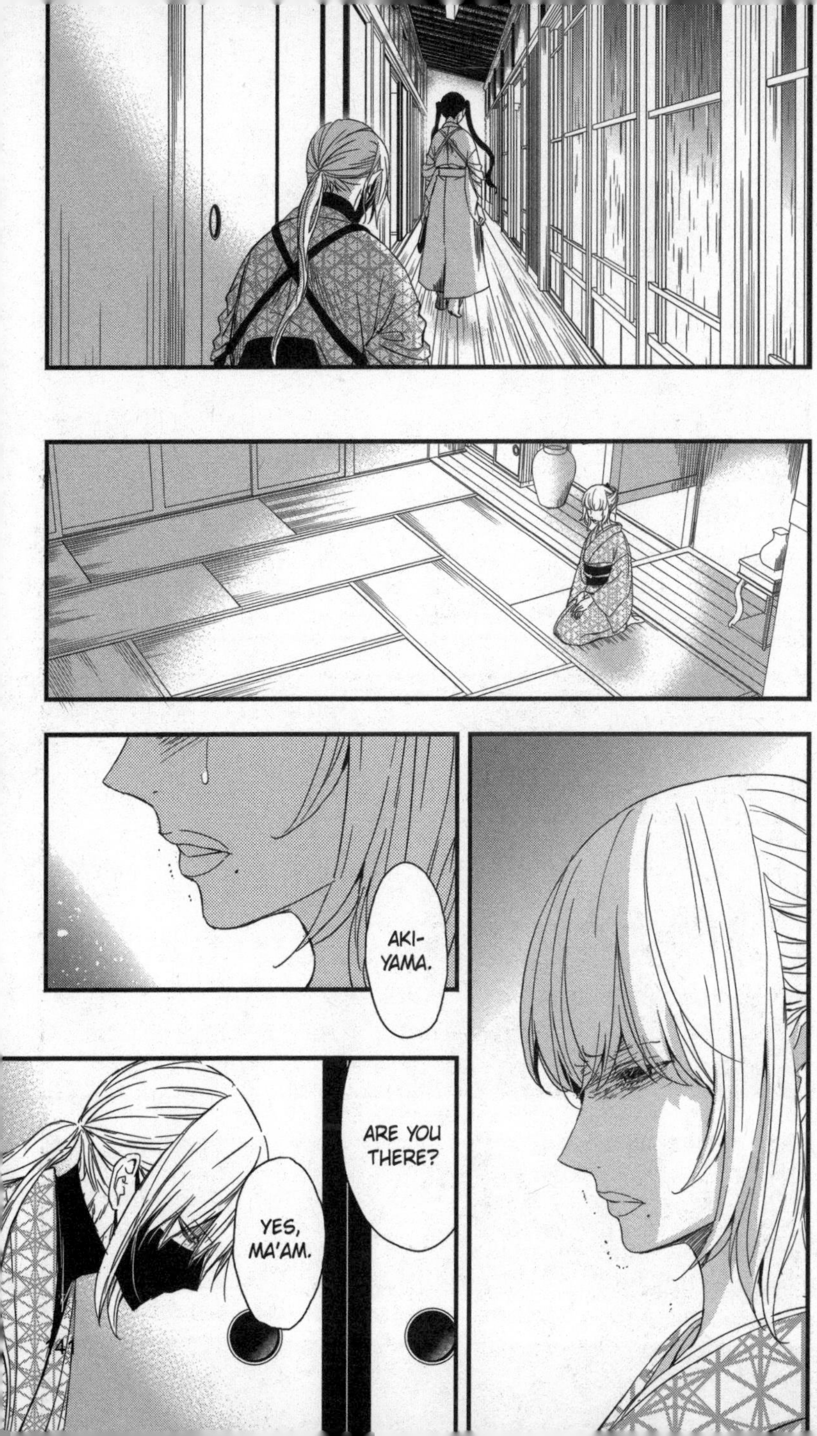
AKI-YAMA.
ARE YOU THERE?
YES, MA'AM.

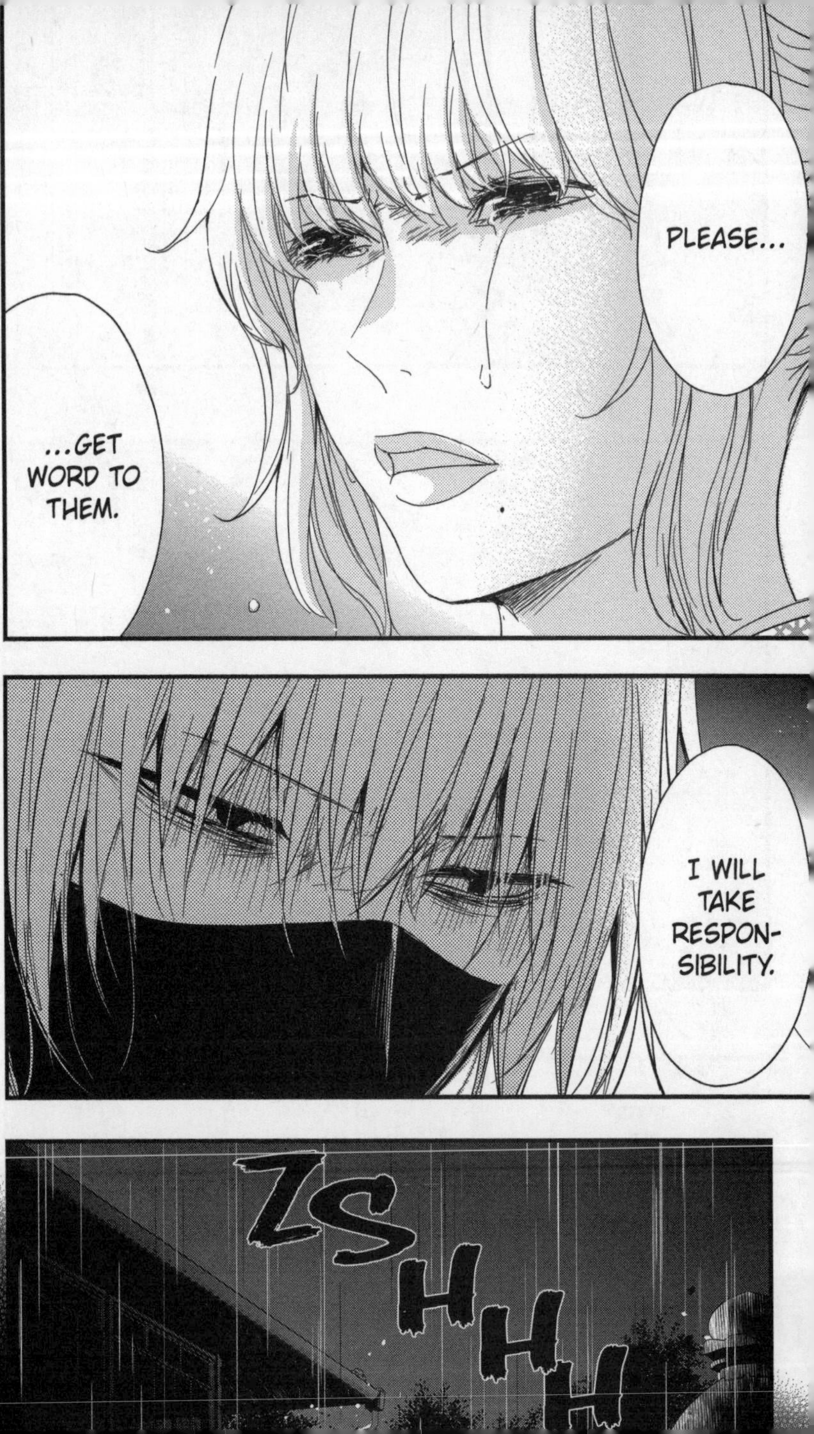
PLEASE...
...GET WORD TO THEM.
I WILL TAKE RESPONSIBILITY.
ZSHHH

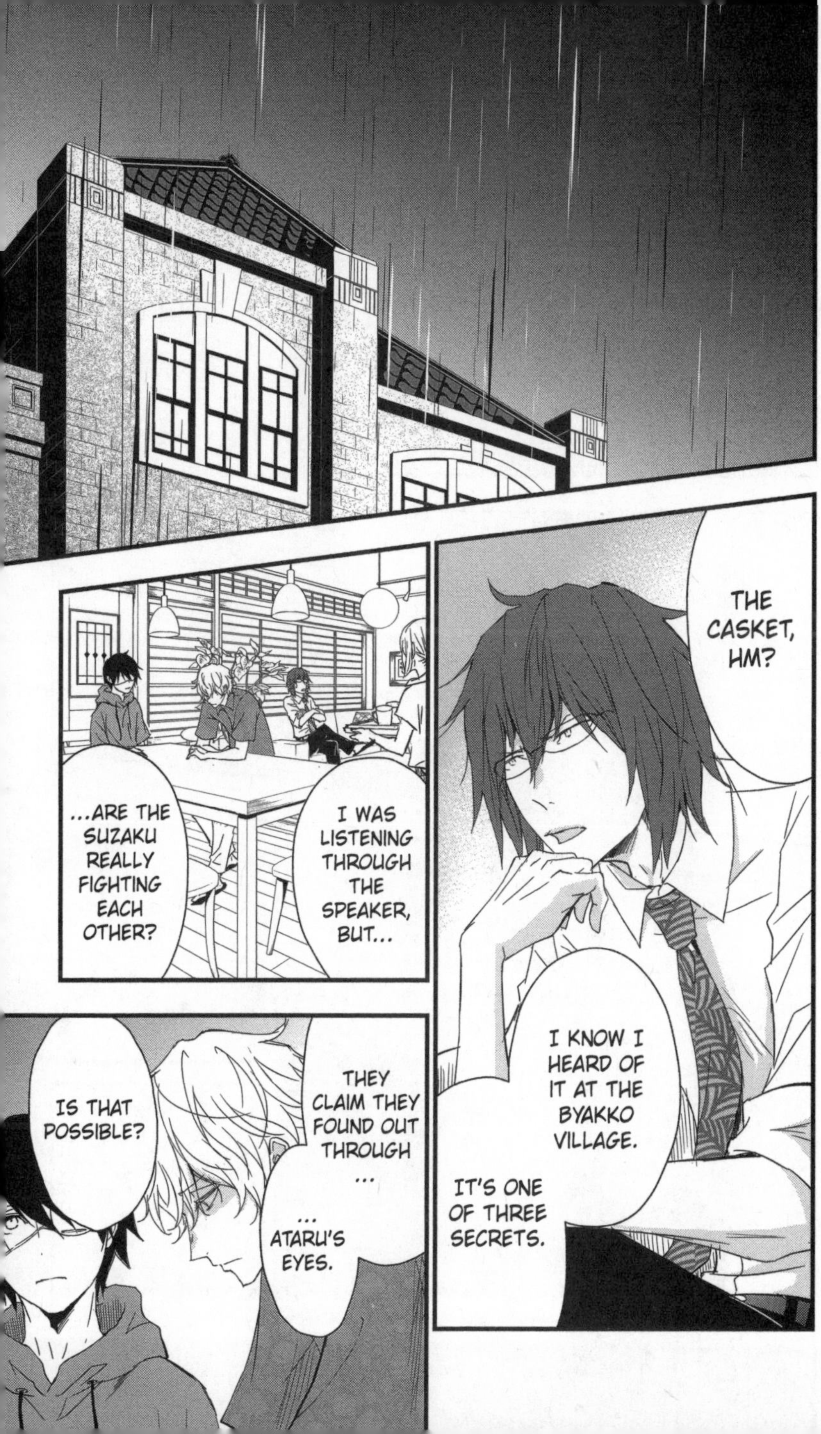
THE CASKET, HM?
I KNOW I HEARD OF IT AT THE BYAKKO VILLAGE.
IT'S ONE OF THREE SECRETS.
I WAS LISTENING THROUGH THE SPEAKER, BUT...
...ARE THE SUZAKU REALLY FIGHTING EACH OTHER?
THEY CLAIM THEY FOUND OUT THROUGH ...
... ATARU'S EYES.
IS THAT POSSIBLE?

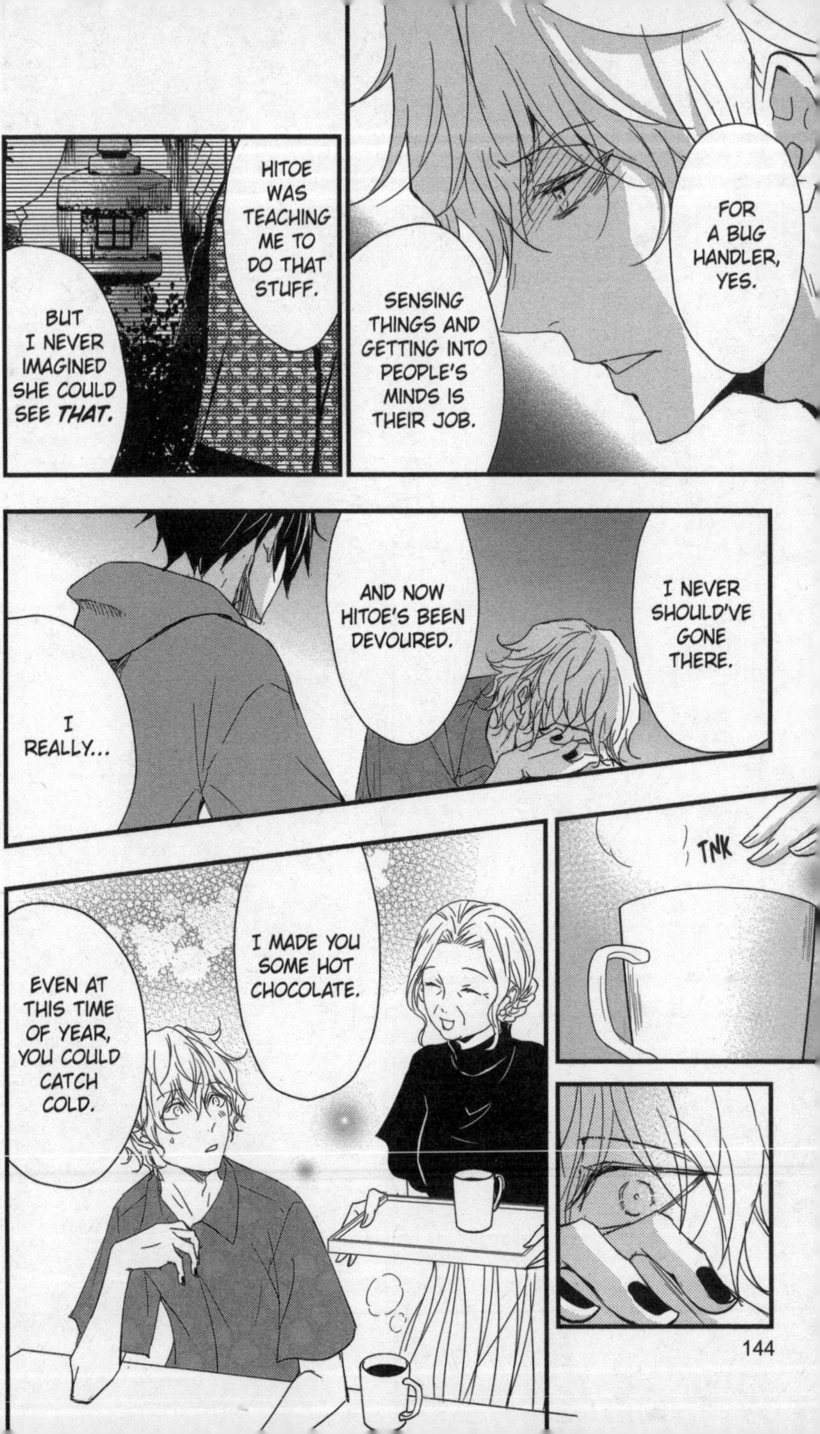
FOR A BUG HANDLER, YES.
SENSING THINGS AND GETTING INTO PEOPLE'S MINDS IS THEIR JOB.
HITOE WAS TEACHING ME TO DO THAT STUFF.
BUT I NEVER IMAGINED SHE COULD SEE *THAT*.
I NEVER SHOULD'VE GONE THERE.
AND NOW HITOE'S BEEN DEVOURED.
I REALLY...
TNK
I MADE YOU SOME HOT CHOCOLATE.
EVEN AT THIS TIME OF YEAR, YOU COULD CATCH COLD.

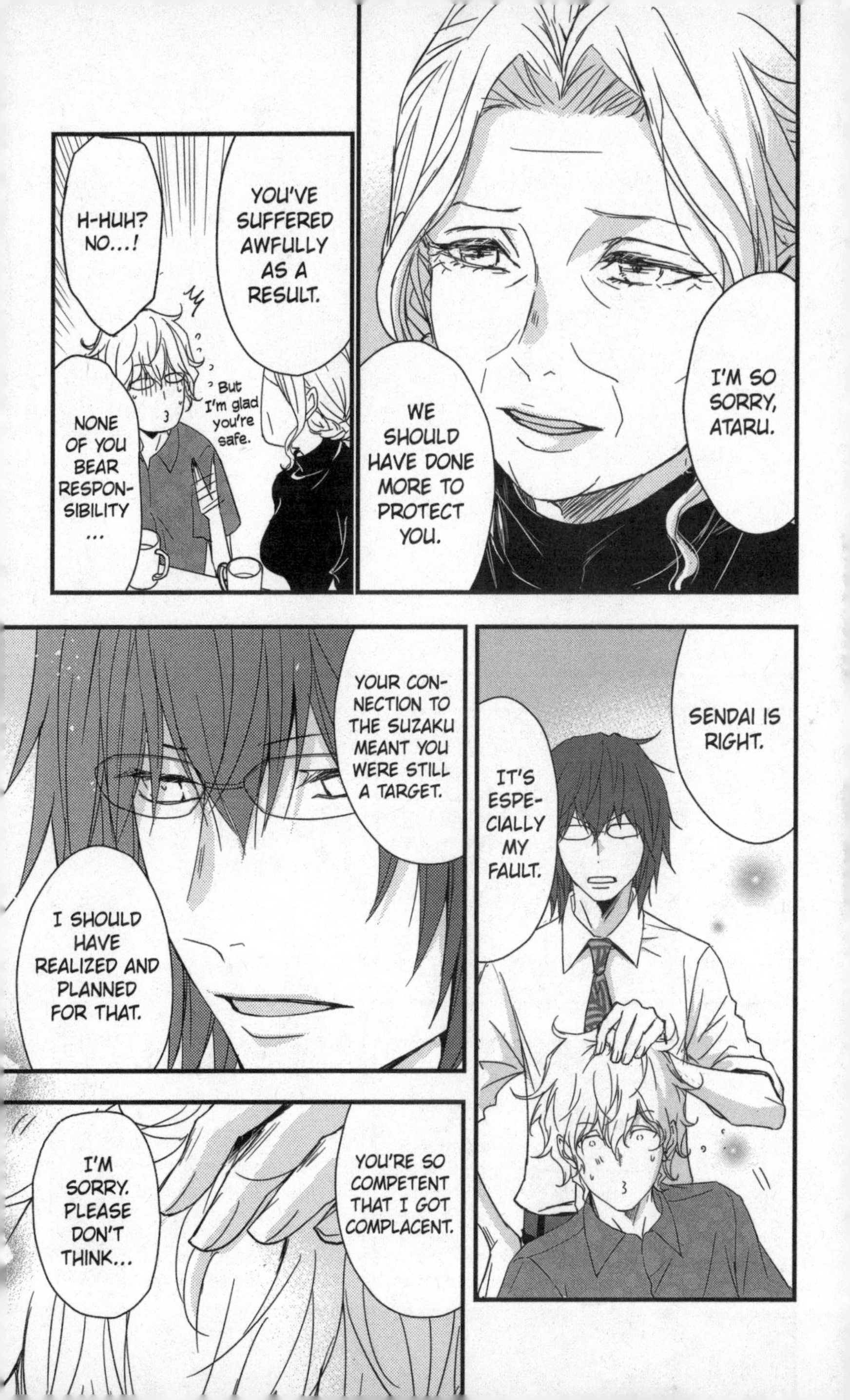
I'M SO SORRY, ATARU.
WE SHOULD HAVE DONE MORE TO PROTECT YOU.
YOU'VE SUFFERED AWFULLY AS A RESULT.
H-HUH? NO...!
But I'm glad you're safe.
NONE OF YOU BEAR RESPONSIBILITY...
SENDAI IS RIGHT.
IT'S ESPECIALLY MY FAULT.
YOUR CONNECTION TO THE SUZAKU MEANT YOU WERE STILL A TARGET.
I SHOULD HAVE REALIZED AND PLANNED FOR THAT.
YOU'RE SO COMPETENT THAT I GOT COMPLACENT.
I'M SORRY. PLEASE DON'T THINK...

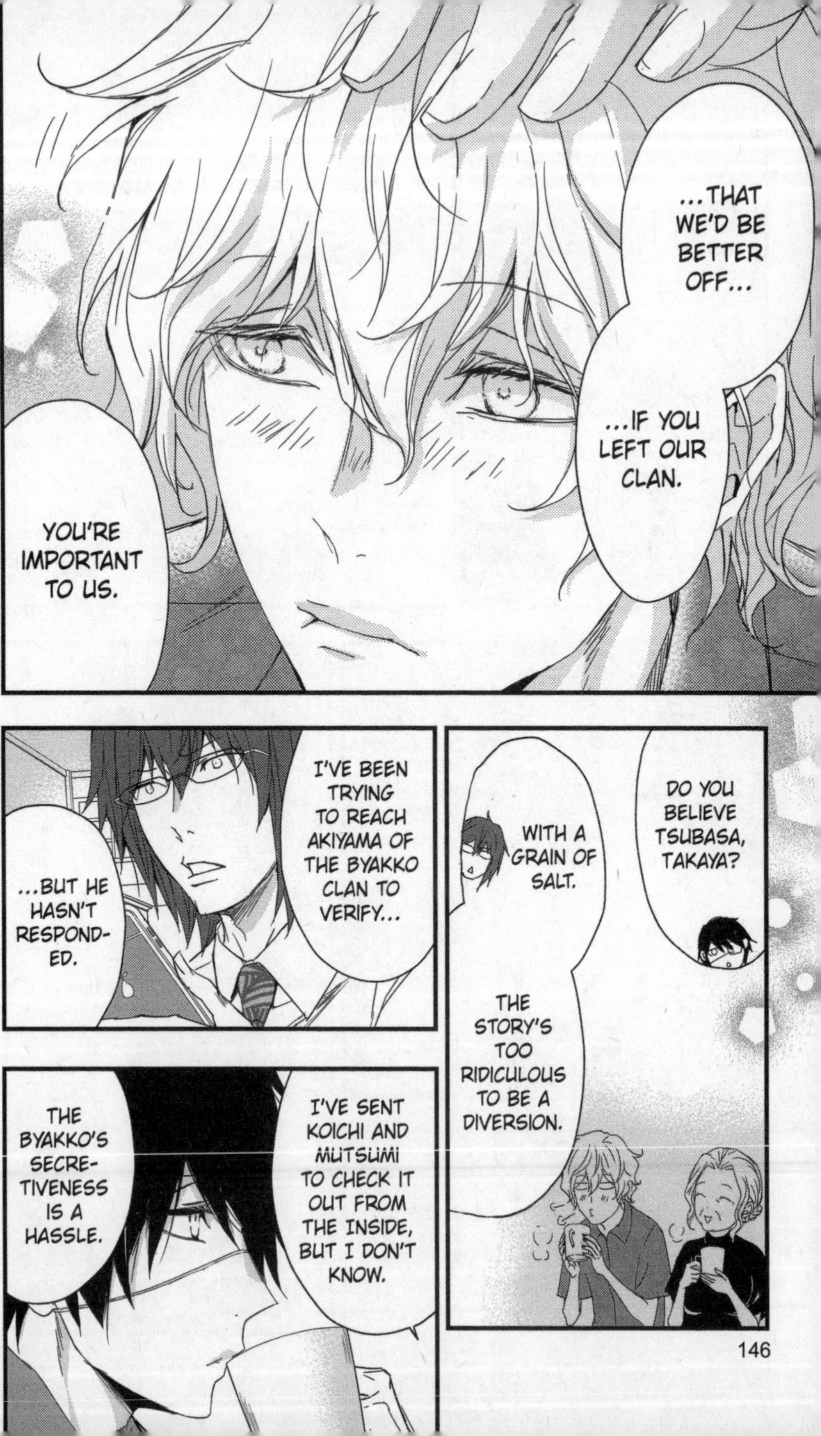
...THAT WE'D BE BETTER OFF...
...IF YOU LEFT OUR CLAN.
YOU'RE IMPORTANT TO US.
DO YOU BELIEVE TSUBASA, TAKAYA?
WITH A GRAIN OF SALT.
THE STORY'S TOO RIDICULOUS TO BE A DIVERSION.
I'VE BEEN TRYING TO REACH AKIYAMA OF THE BYAKKO CLAN TO VERIFY...
...BUT HE HASN'T RESPOND-ED.
I'VE SENT KOICHI AND MUTSUMI TO CHECK IT OUT FROM THE INSIDE, BUT I DON'T KNOW.
THE BYAKKO'S SECRE-TIVENESS IS A HASSLE.

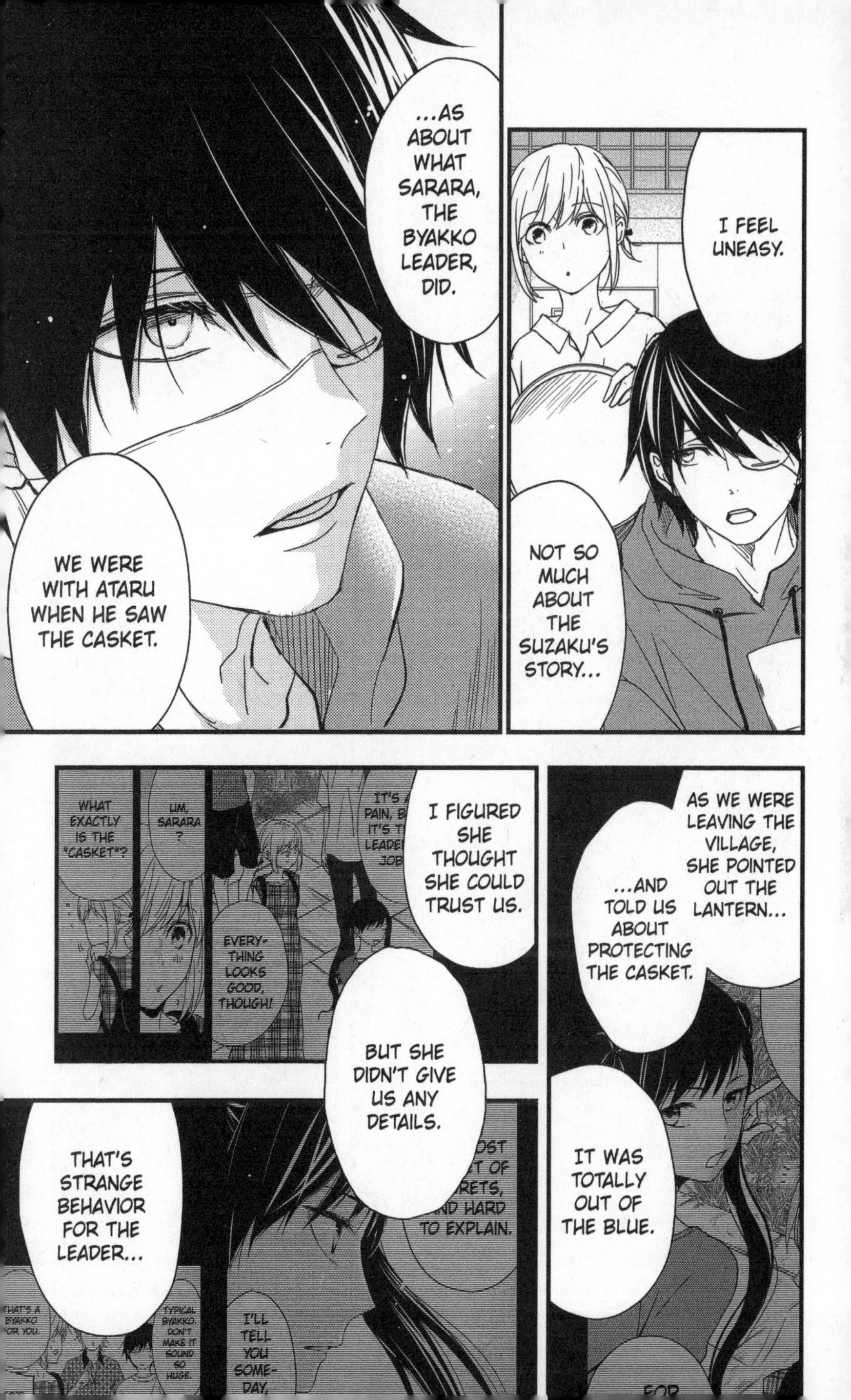
I FEEL UNEASY.
NOT SO MUCH ABOUT THE SUZAKU'S STORY...
...AS ABOUT WHAT SARARA, THE BYAKKO LEADER, DID.
WE WERE WITH ATARU WHEN HE SAW THE CASKET.
AS WE WERE LEAVING THE VILLAGE, SHE POINTED OUT THE LANTERN...
...AND TOLD US ABOUT PROTECTING THE CASKET.
IT WAS TOTALLY OUT OF THE BLUE.
I FIGURED SHE THOUGHT SHE COULD TRUST US.
UM, SARARA?
WHAT EXACTLY IS THE "CASKET"?
EVERY-THING LOOKS GOOD, THOUGH!
BUT SHE DIDN'T GIVE US ANY DETAILS.
AND HARD TO EXPLAIN.
THAT'S STRANGE BEHAVIOR FOR THE LEADER...
I'LL TELL YOU SOME-DAY.
TYPICAL BYAKKO. DON'T MAKE IT SOUND SO HUGE.
THAT'S A BYAKKO FOR YOU.

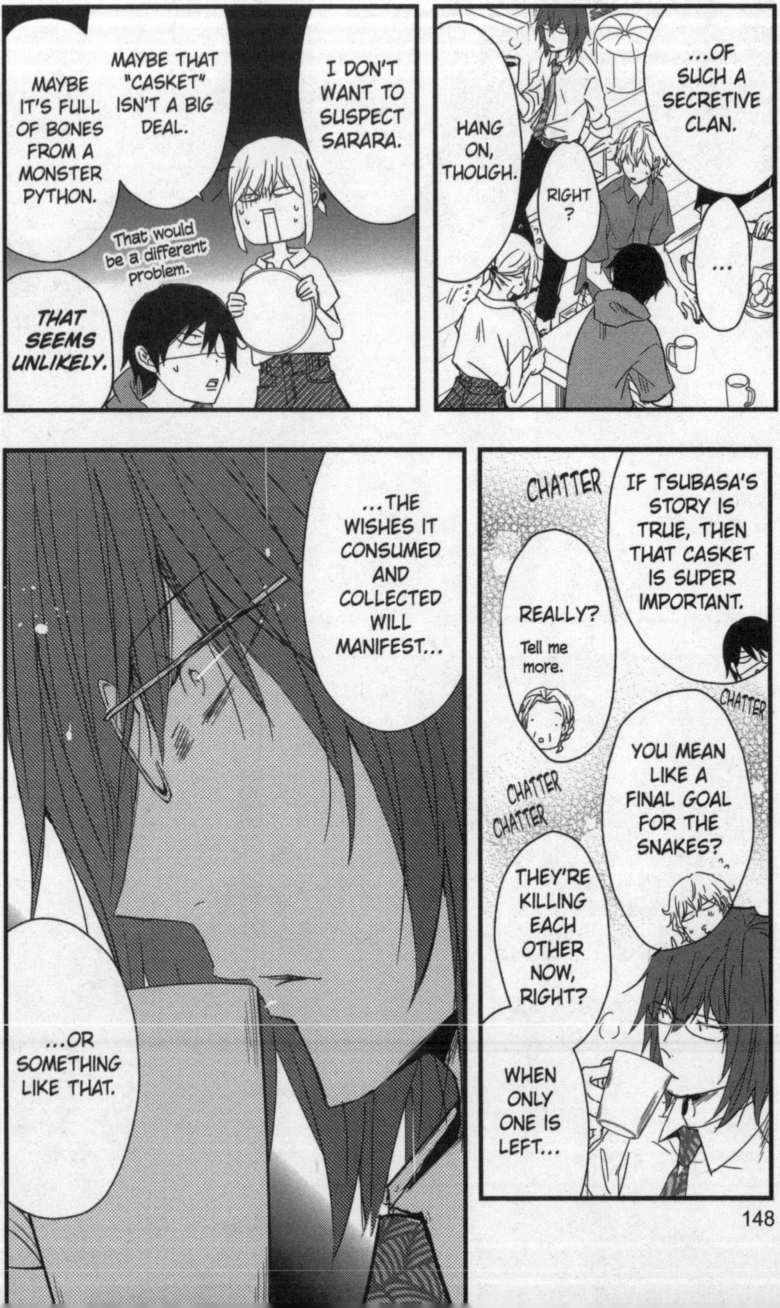
...OF SUCH A SECRETIVE CLAN.
HANG ON, THOUGH.
RIGHT?
...
I DON'T WANT TO SUSPECT SARARA.
MAYBE THAT "CASKET" ISN'T A BIG DEAL.
MAYBE IT'S FULL OF BONES FROM A MONSTER PYTHON.
That would be a different problem.
THAT SEEMS UNLIKELY.
CHATTER
IF TSUBASA'S STORY IS TRUE, THEN THAT CASKET IS SUPER IMPORTANT.
REALLY?
Tell me more.
CHATTER
YOU MEAN LIKE A FINAL GOAL FOR THE SNAKES?
CHATTER
CHATTER
THEY'RE KILLING EACH OTHER NOW, RIGHT?
WHEN ONLY ONE IS LEFT...
...THE WISHES IT CONSUMED AND COLLECTED WILL MANIFEST...
...OR SOMETHING LIKE THAT.

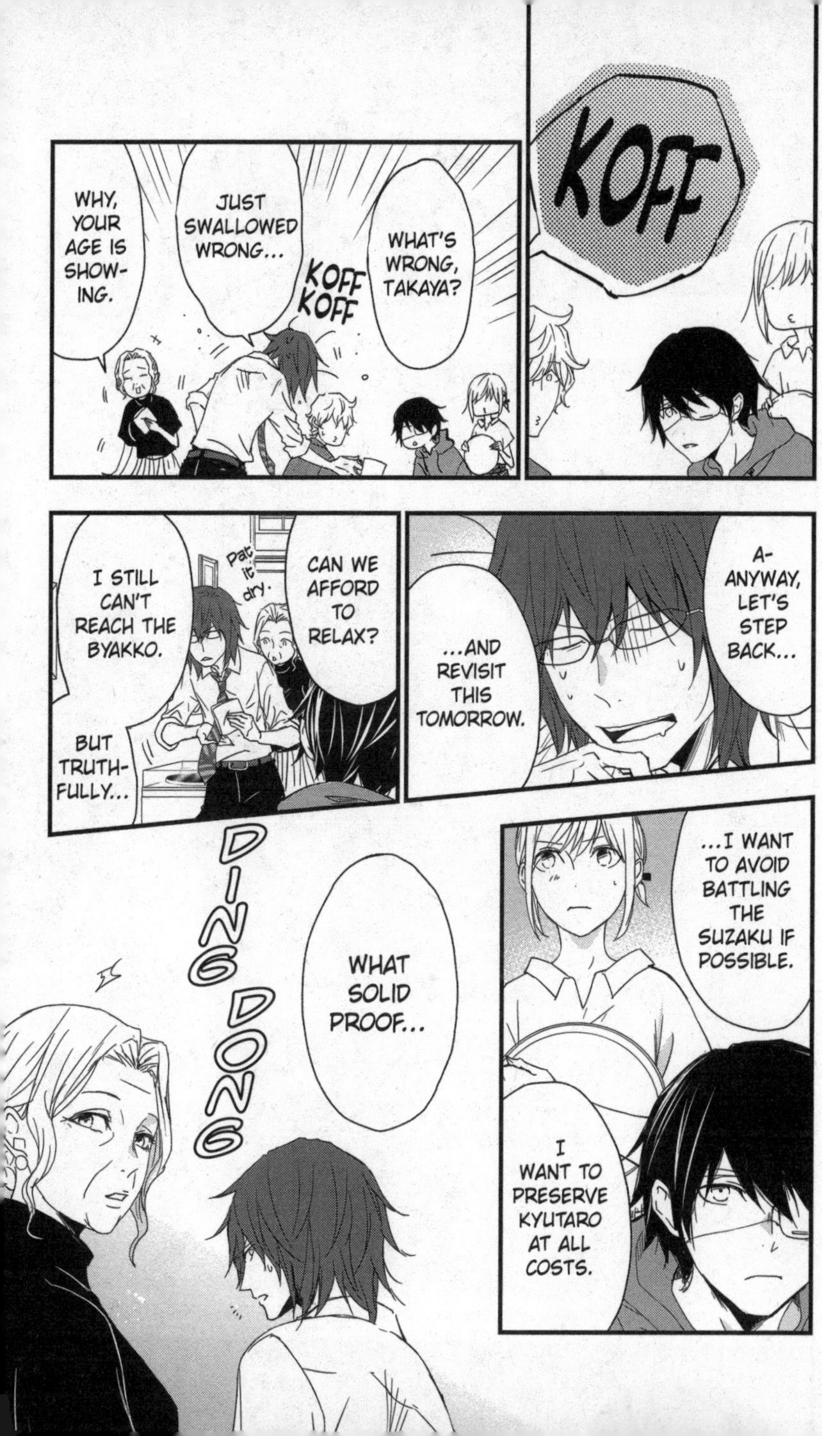
KOFF
WHAT'S WRONG, TAKAYA?
KOFF KOFF
JUST SWALLOWED WRONG...
WHY, YOUR AGE IS SHOW-ING.
A- ANYWAY, LET'S STEP BACK...
...AND REVISIT THIS TOMORROW.
CAN WE AFFORD TO RELAX?
Pat it dry.
I STILL CAN'T REACH THE BYAKKO.
BUT TRUTH-FULLY...
...I WANT TO AVOID BATTLING THE SUZAKU IF POSSIBLE.
I WANT TO PRESERVE KYUTARO AT ALL COSTS.
WHAT SOLID PROOF...
DING DONG

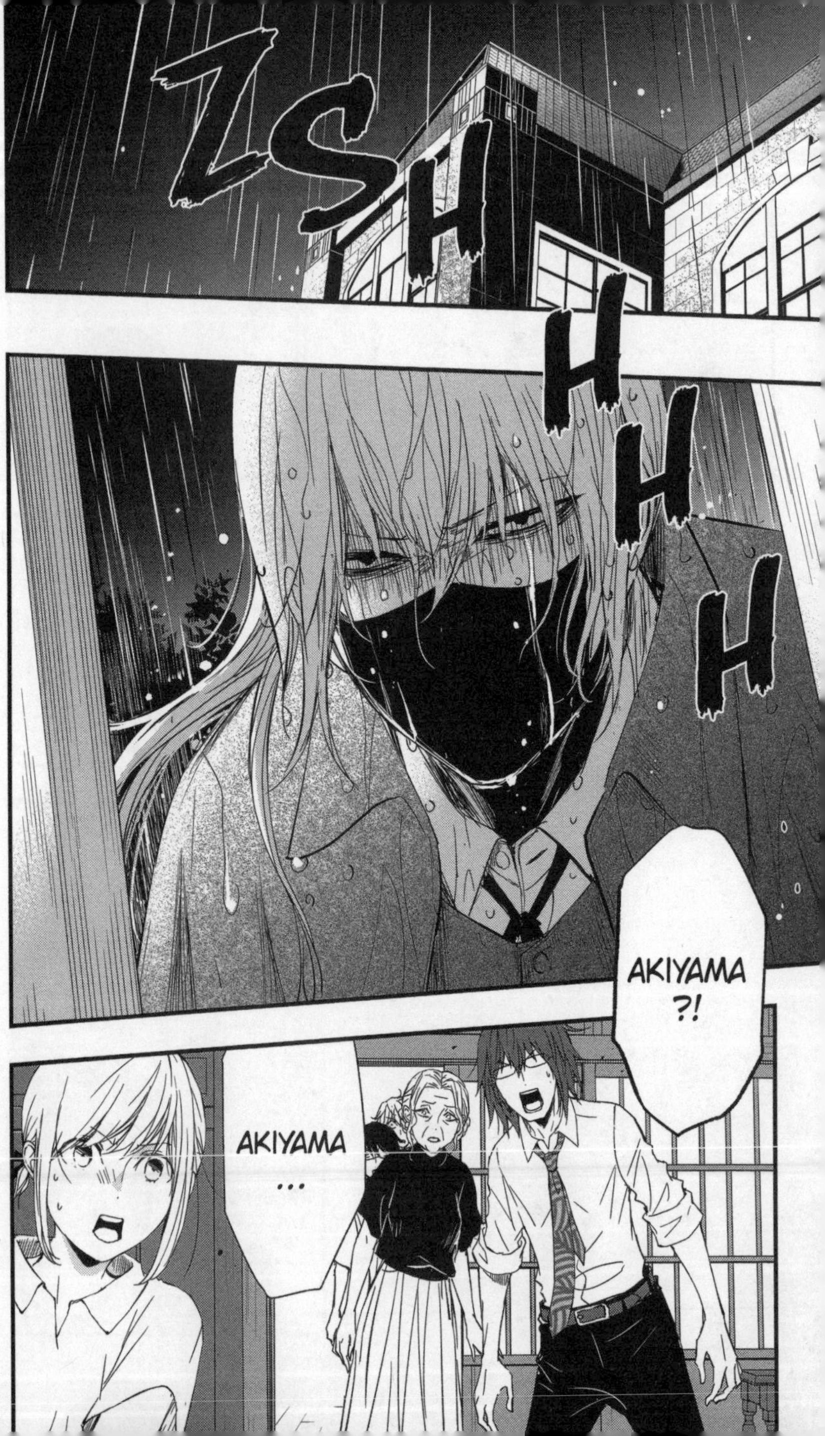
ZSHHHH
AKIYAMA ?!
AKIYAMA ...

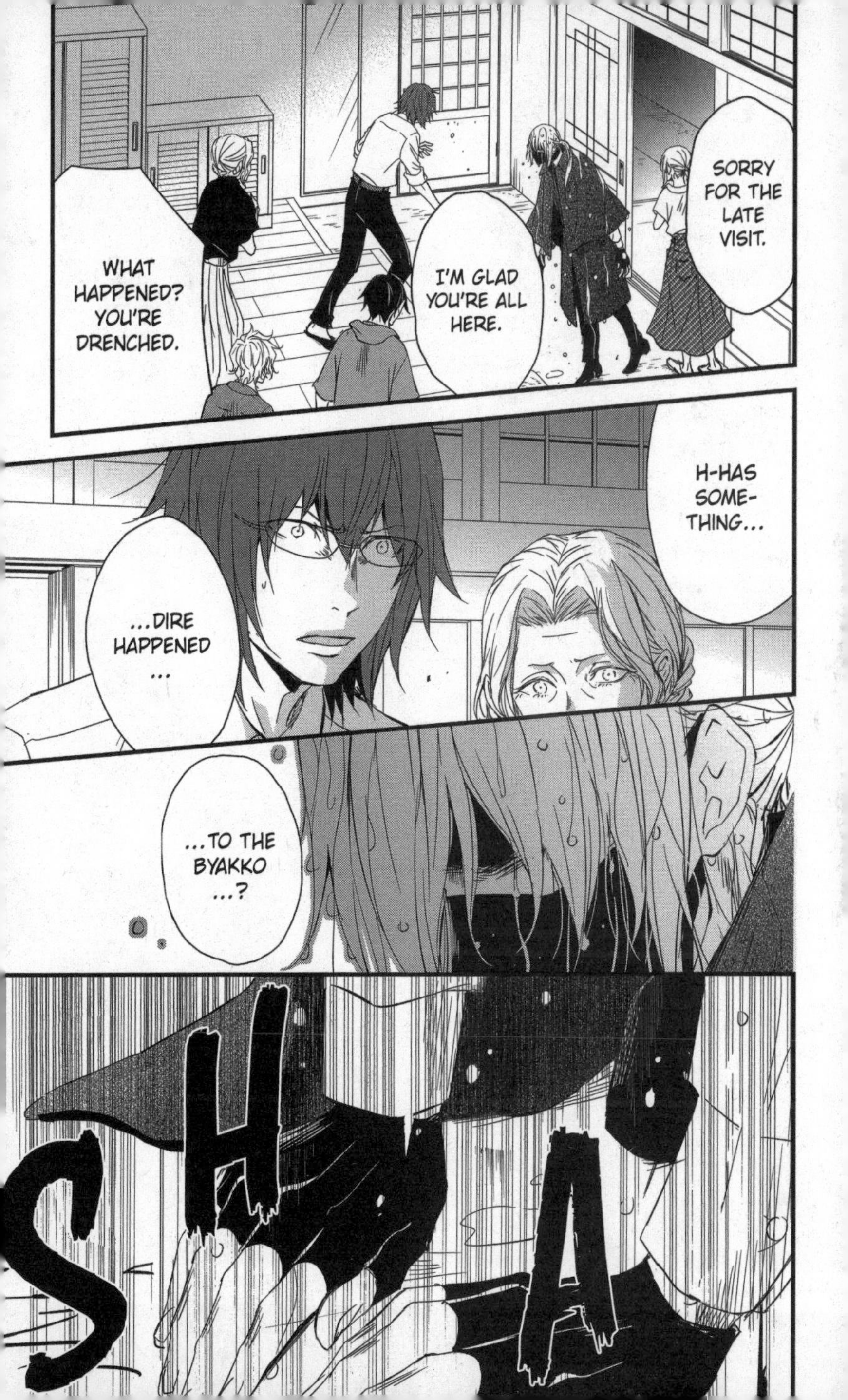
SORRY FOR THE LATE VISIT.
I'M GLAD YOU'RE ALL HERE.
WHAT HAPPENED? YOU'RE DRENCHED.
H-HAS SOME-THING...
...DIRE HAPPENED...
...TO THE BYAKKO...?
SHA

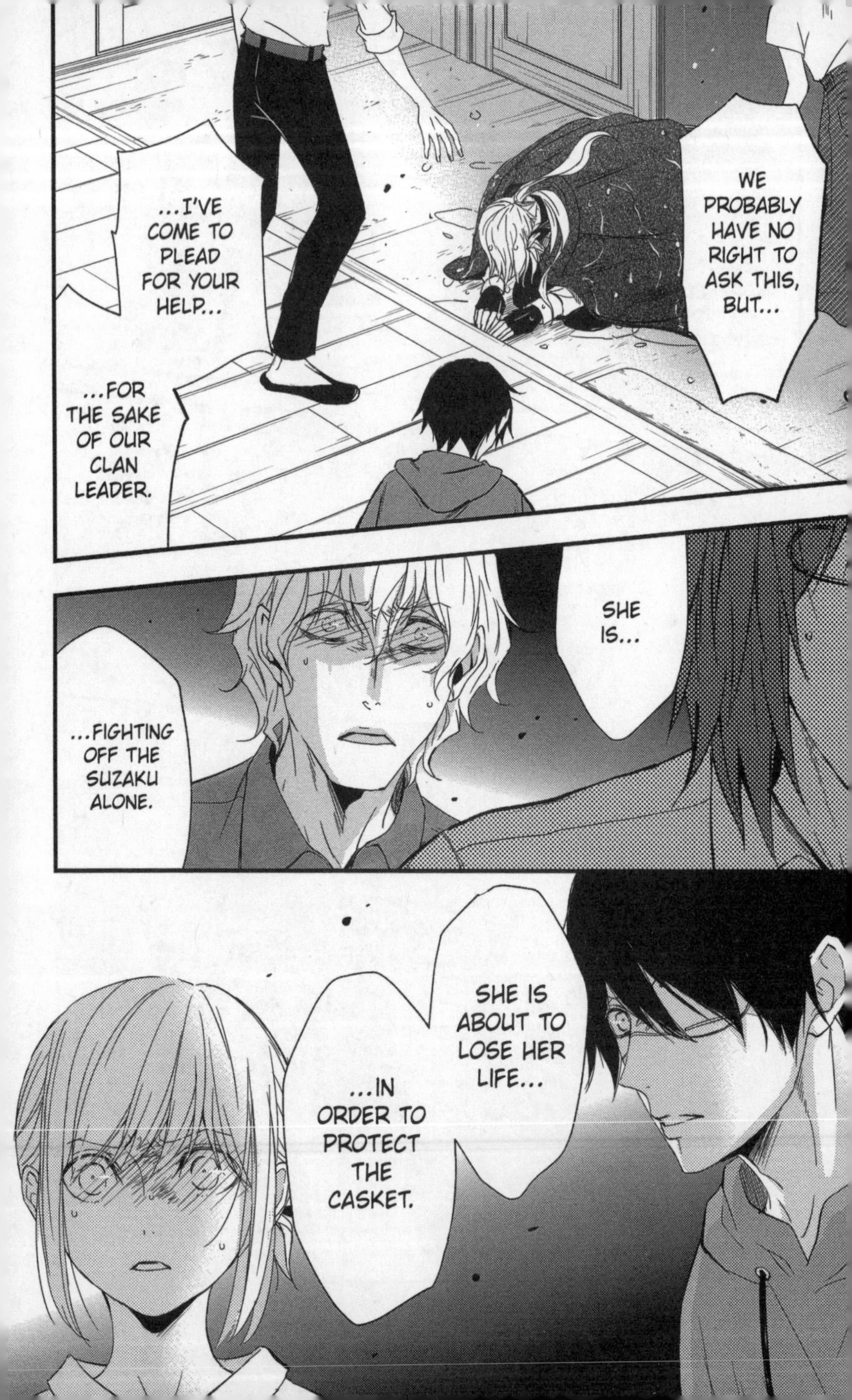
WE PROBABLY HAVE NO RIGHT TO ASK THIS, BUT...
...I'VE COME TO PLEAD FOR YOUR HELP...
...FOR THE SAKE OF OUR CLAN LEADER.
SHE IS...
...FIGHTING OFF THE SUZAKU ALONE.
SHE IS ABOUT TO LOSE HER LIFE...
...IN ORDER TO PROTECT THE CASKET.

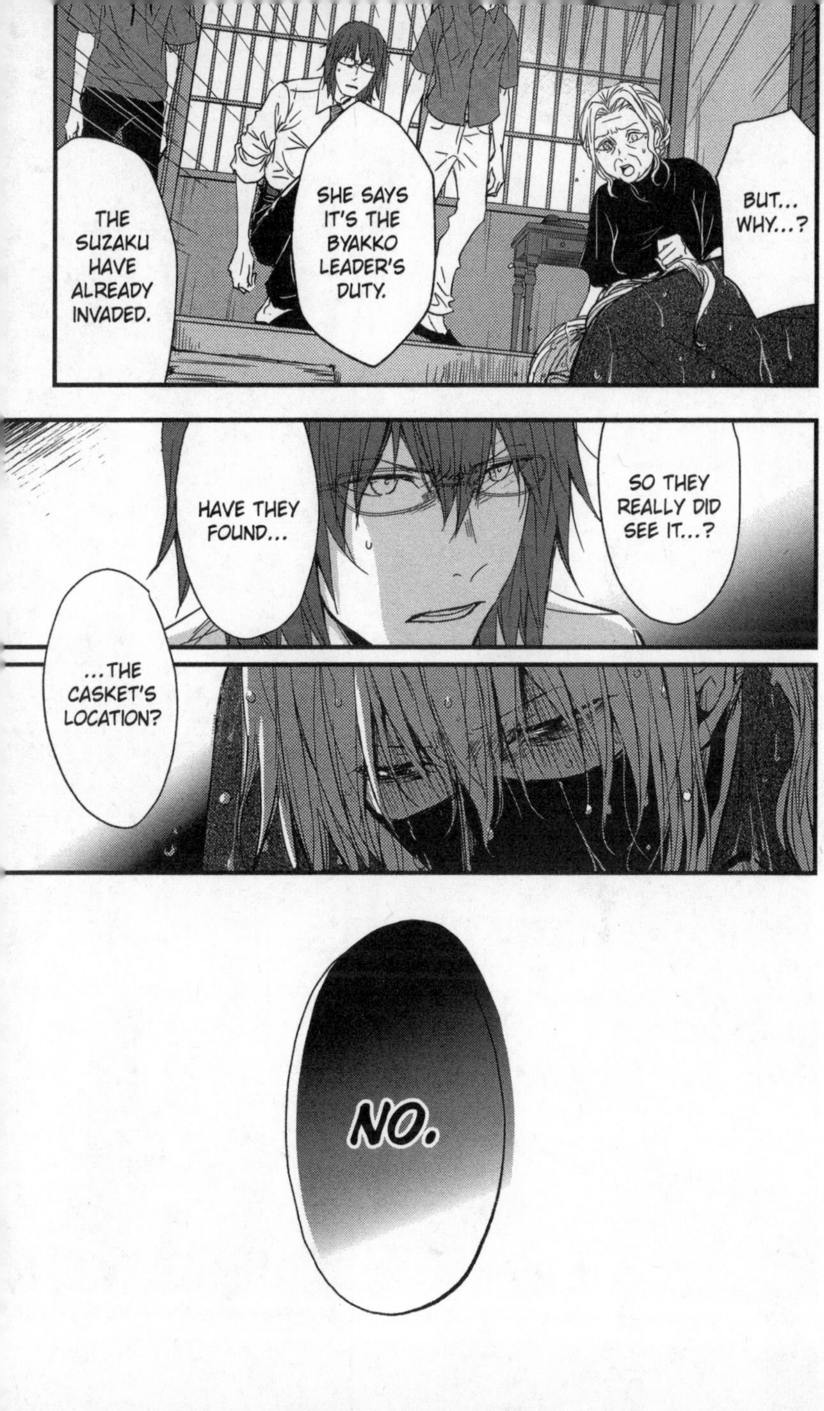
BUT... WHY...?
SHE SAYS IT'S THE BYAKKO LEADER'S DUTY.
THE SUZAKU HAVE ALREADY INVADED.
SO THEY REALLY DID SEE IT...?
HAVE THEY FOUND...
...THE CASKET'S LOCATION?
NO.

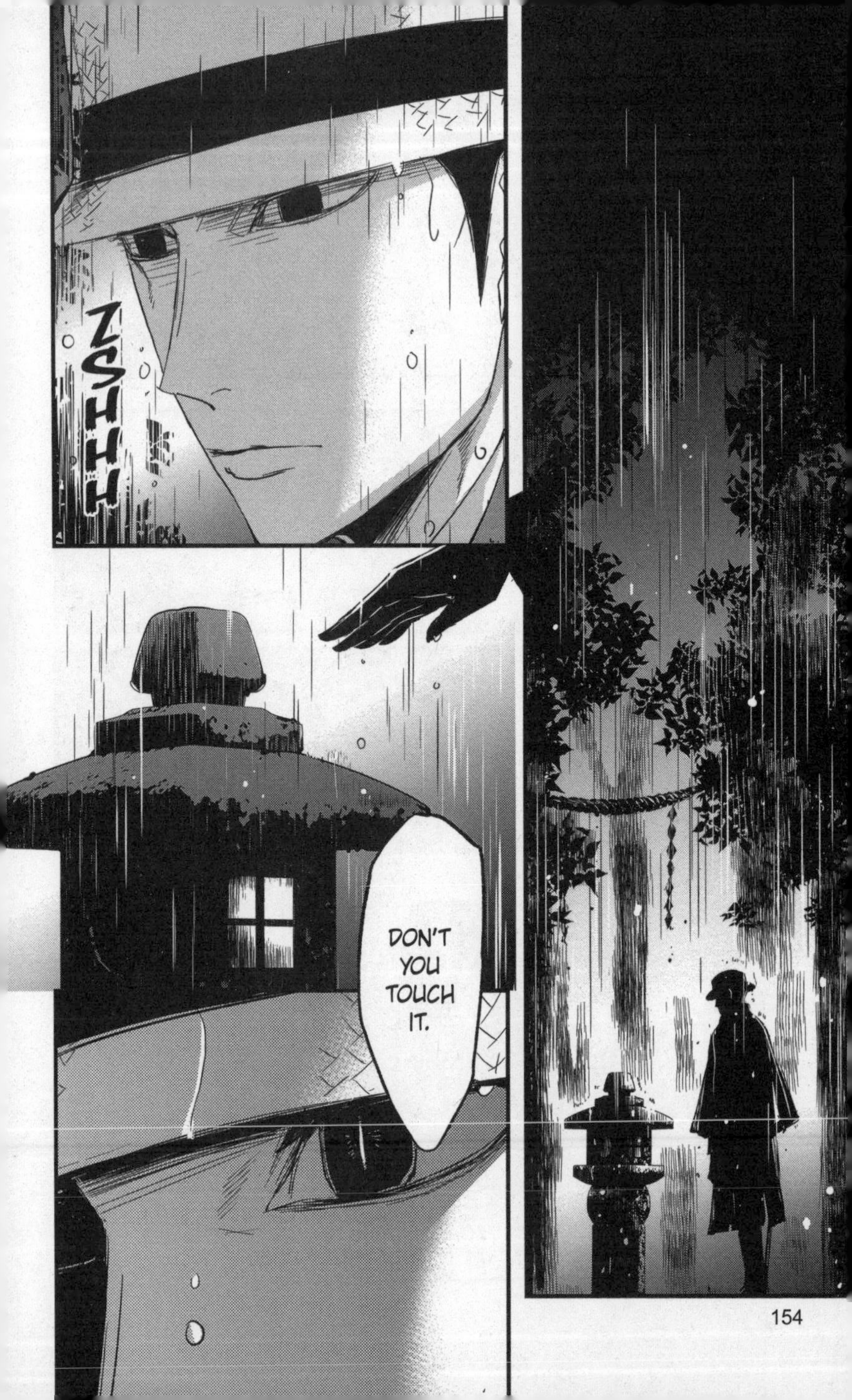
ZSHHH
DON'T YOU TOUCH IT.

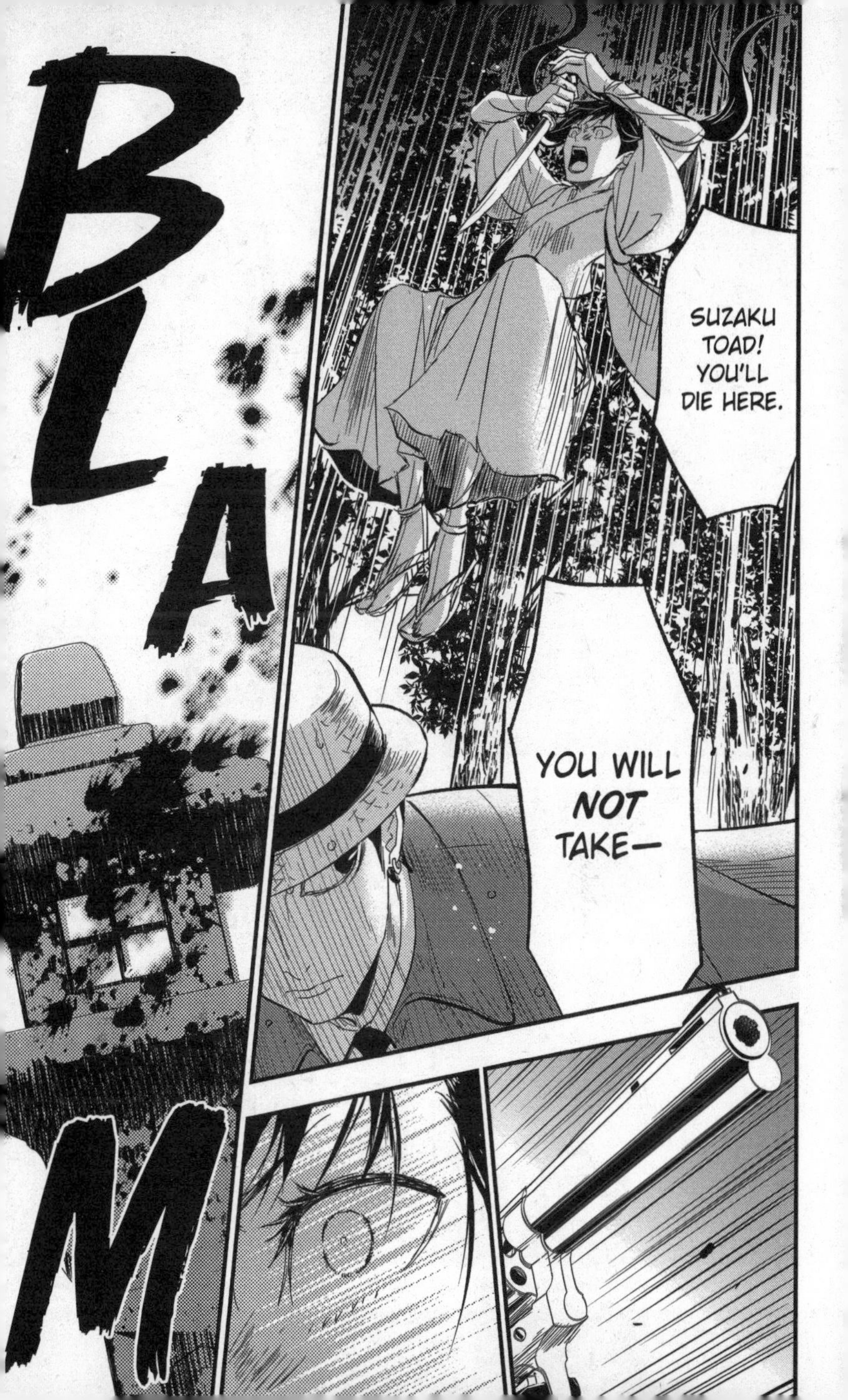
SUZAKU TOAD! YOU'LL DIE HERE.
YOU WILL *NOT* TAKE—
BLAM

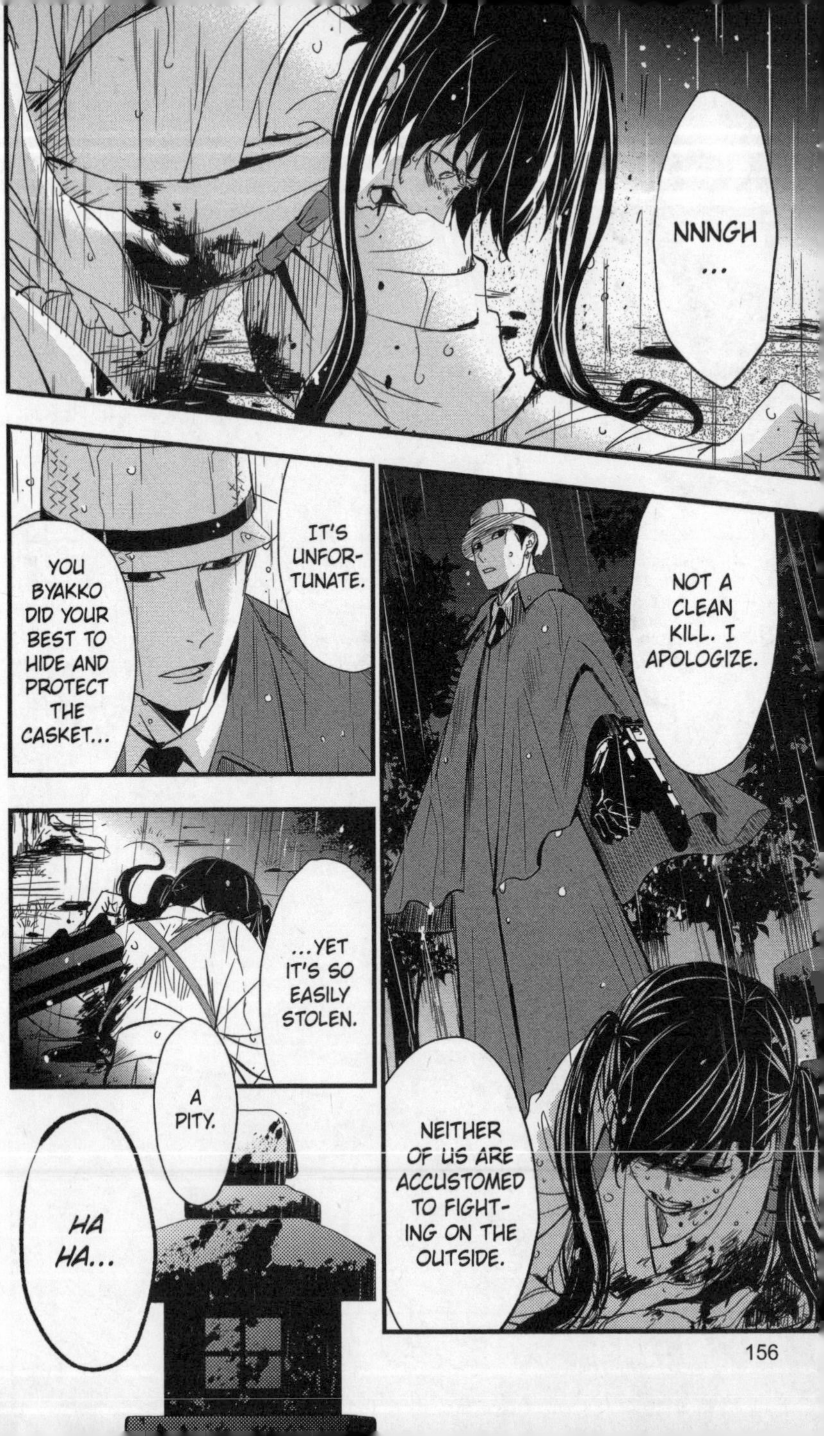
NNNGH ...
NOT A CLEAN KILL. I APOLOGIZE.
NEITHER OF US ARE ACCUSTOMED TO FIGHT-ING ON THE OUTSIDE.
IT'S UNFOR-TUNATE.
YOU BYAKKO DID YOUR BEST TO HIDE AND PROTECT THE CASKET...
...YET IT'S SO EASILY STOLEN.
A PITY.
HA HA...

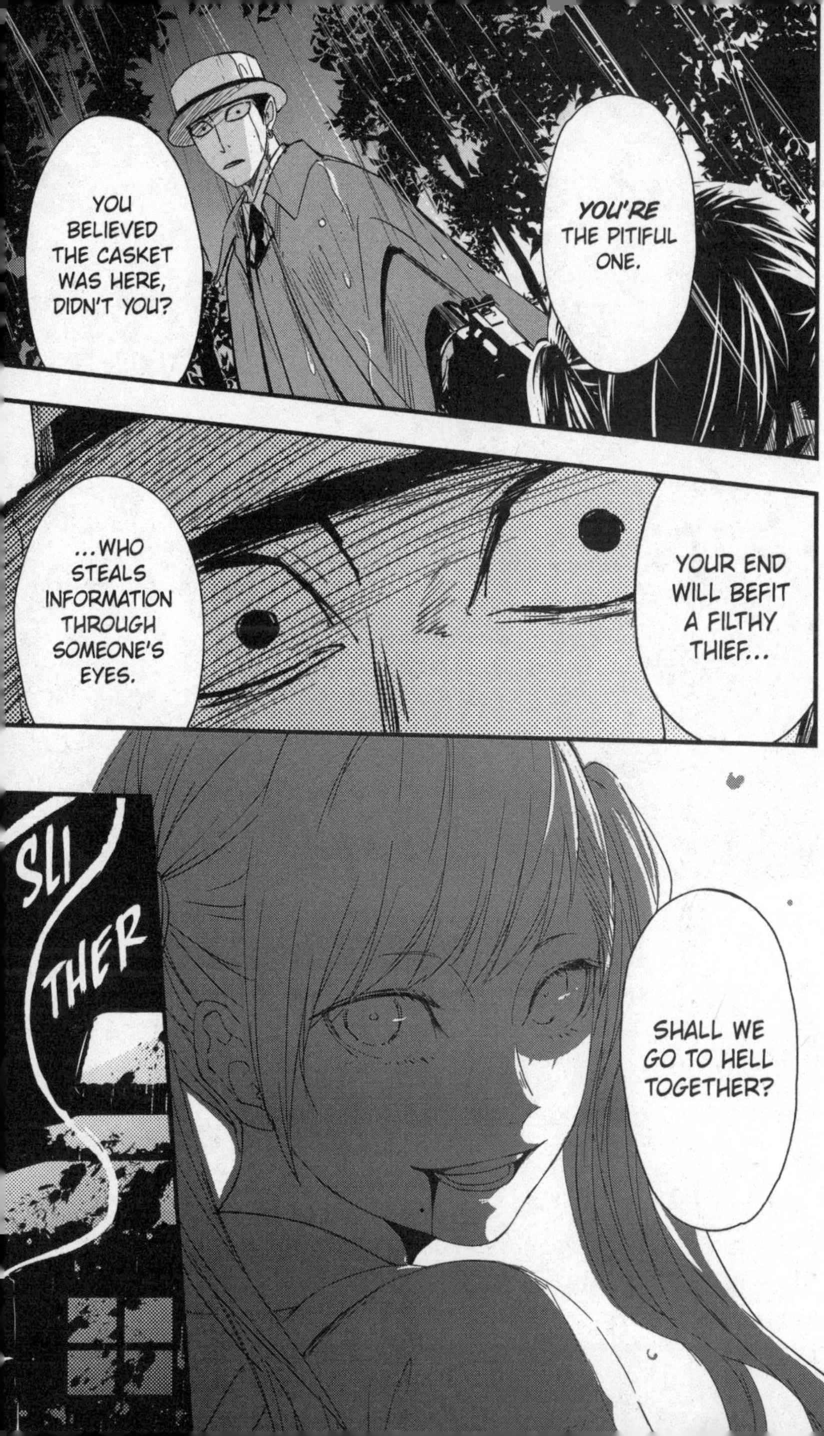
YOU'RE THE PITIFUL ONE.
YOU BELIEVED THE CASKET WAS HERE, DIDN'T YOU?
YOUR END WILL BEFIT A FILTHY THIEF...
...WHO STEALS INFORMATION THROUGH SOMEONE'S EYES.
SHALL WE GO TO HELL TOGETHER?
SLI THER

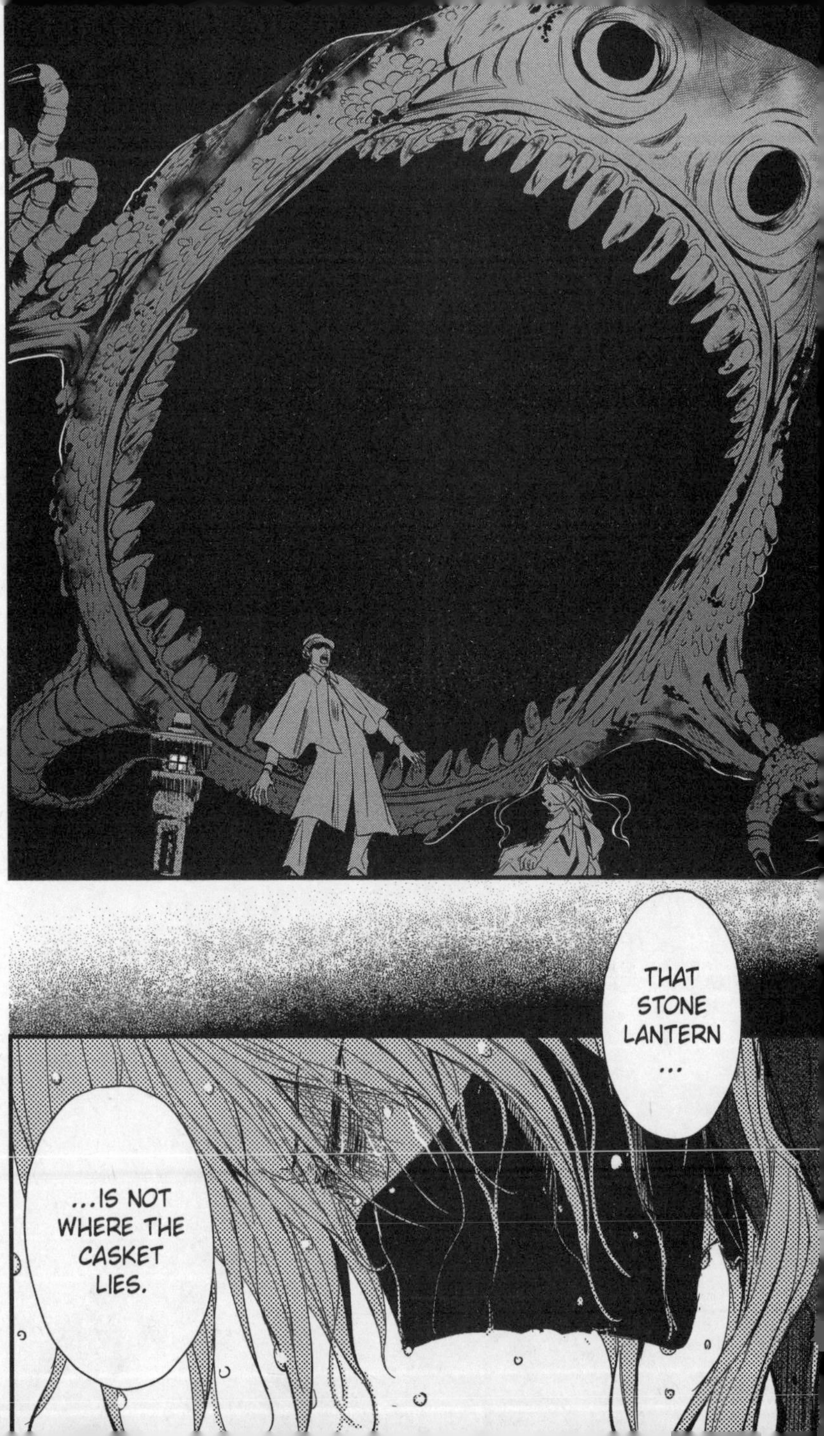
THAT STONE LANTERN ...
...IS NOT WHERE THE CASKET LIES.

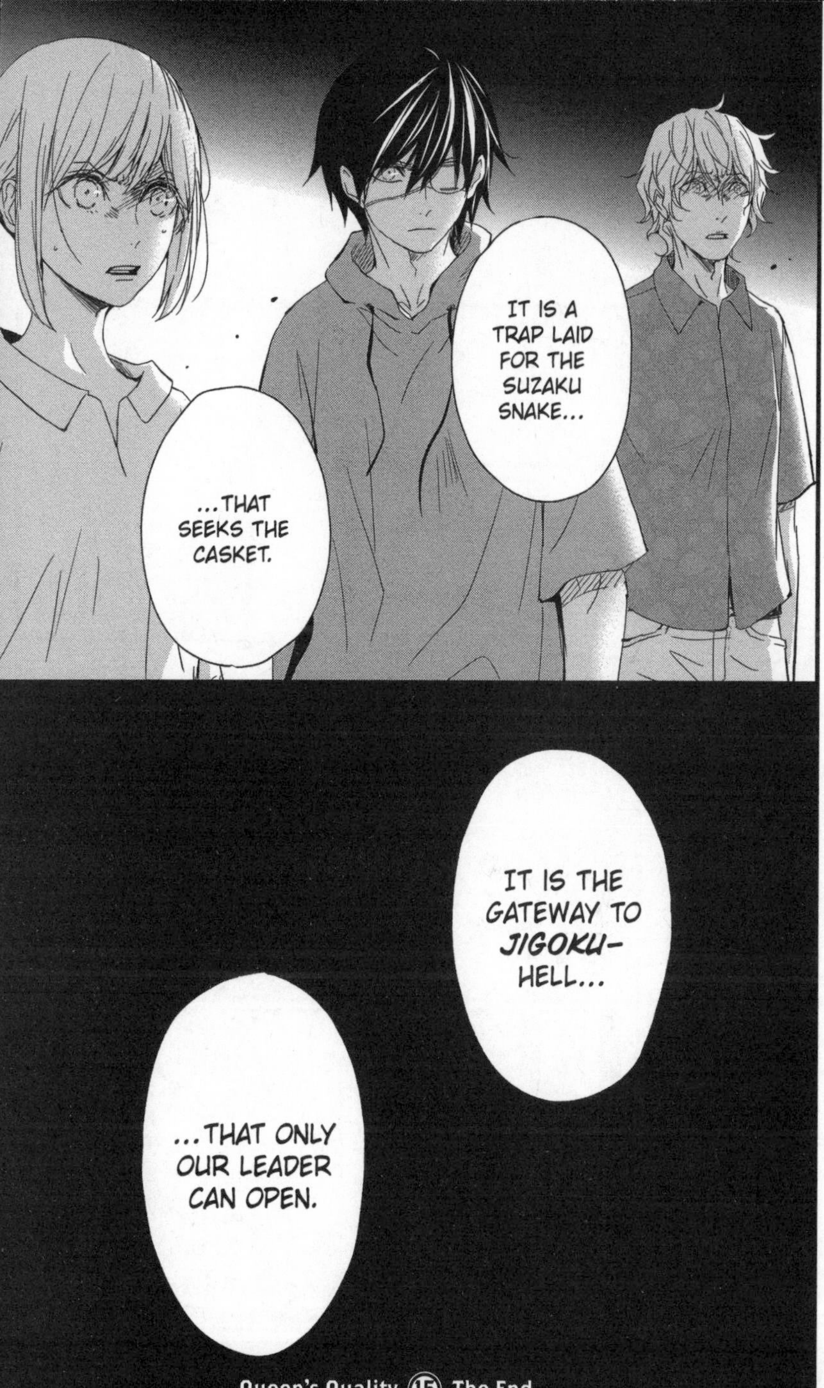
IT IS A TRAP LAID FOR THE SUZAKU SNAKE...
...THAT SEEKS THE CASKET.
IT IS THE GATEWAY TO *JIGOKU*-HELL...
...THAT ONLY OUR LEADER CAN OPEN.

Queen's Quality ⑮ The End

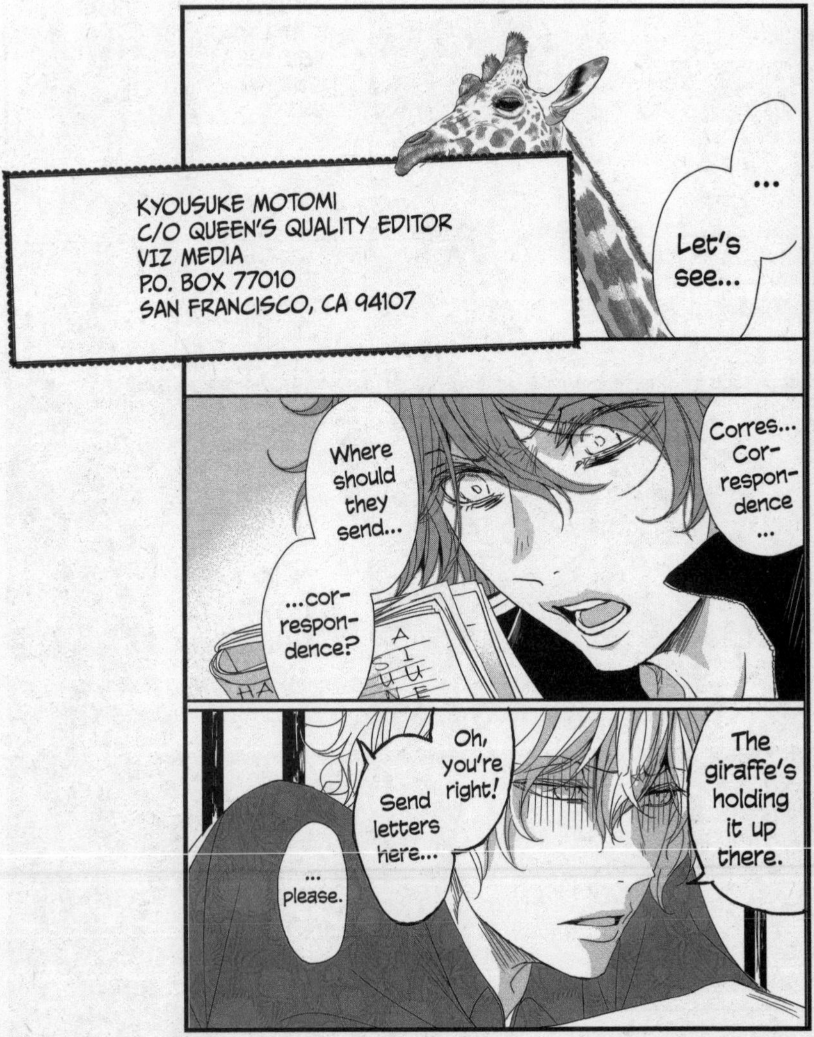
...
Let's see...
KYOUSUKE MOTOMI
C/O QUEEN'S QUALITY EDITOR
VIZ MEDIA
P.O. BOX 77010
SAN FRANCISCO, CA 94107
Corres... Cor-respon-dence...
Where should they send...
...cor-respon-dence?
The giraffe's holding it up there.
Oh, you're right!
Send letters here...
...please.

We are still being advised to self-isolate [in Japan]. Both Kojiro and I are very good at isolating ourselves, so we're both fine.

—Kyousuke Motomi

Author Bio

Born on August 1, Kyousuke Motomi debuted in *Deluxe Betsucomi* with *Hetakuso Kyupiddo* (No Good Cupid) in 2002. She is the creator of *Dengeki Daisy*, *Beast Master*, and *QQ Sweeper*, all available in North America from VIZ Media. Motomi enjoys sleeping, tea ceremonies, and reading Haruki Murakami.

Queen's Quality

Vol. 15
Shojo Beat Edition

STORY AND ART BY
KYOUSUKE MOTOMI

QUEEN'S QUALITY Vol. 15
by Kyousuke MOTOMI
© 2016 Kyousuke MOTOMI
All rights reserved.
Original Japanese edition published by SHOGAKUKAN.
English translation rights in the United States of America, Canada, the United
Kingdom, Ireland, Australia and New Zealand arranged with SHOGAKUKAN.

ORIGINAL DESIGN/Chie SATO+Bay Bridge Studio

English Adaptation/Ysabet Reinhardt MacFarlane
Translation/JN Productions
Touch-Up Art & Lettering/Rina Mapa
Design/Julian [JR] Robinson
Editor/Amy Yu

Printed in the U.S.A.

Published by VIZ Media, LLC
P.O. Box 77010
San Francisco, CA 94107

10 9 8 7 6 5 4 3 2 1
First printing, September 2022

viz.com

shojobeat.com

QQ Sweeper

Story & Art by
Kyousuke Motomi

By the creator of *Dengeki Daisy* and *Beast Master!*

One day, Kyutaro Horikita, the tall, dark and handsome cleaning expert of Kurokado High, comes across a sleeping maiden named Fumi Nishioka at school... Unfortunately, their meeting is anything but a fairy-tale encounter! It turns out Kyutaro is a "Sweeper" who cleans away negative energy from people's hearts—and Fumi is about to become his apprentice!

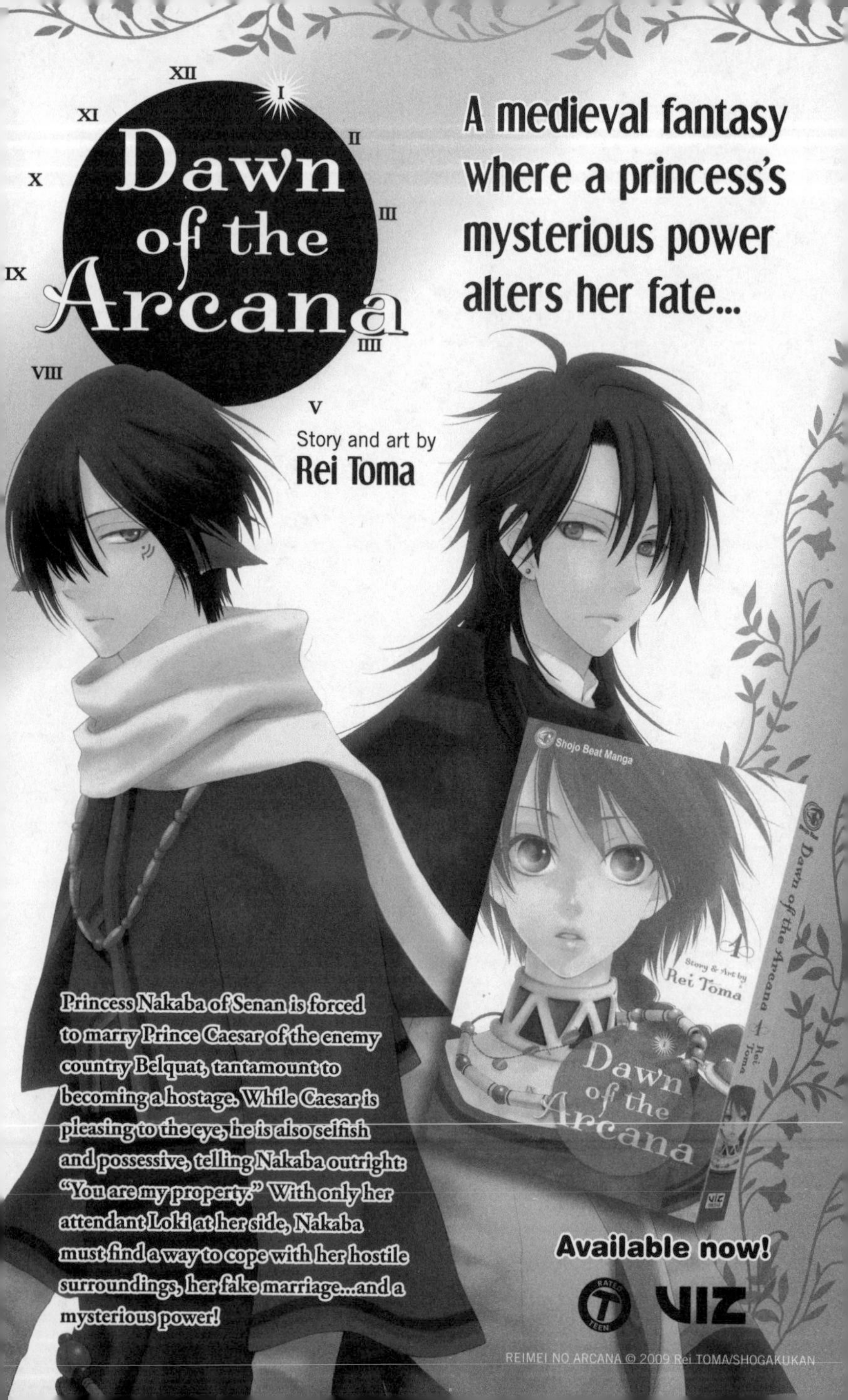
Dawn of the Arcana
A medieval fantasy where a princess's mysterious power alters her fate...
Story and art by
Rei Toma
Princess Nakaba of Senan is forced to marry Prince Caesar of the enemy country Belquat, tantamount to becoming a hostage. While Caesar is pleasing to the eye, he is also selfish and possessive, telling Nakaba outright: "You are my property." With only her attendant Loki at her side, Nakaba must find a way to cope with her hostile surroundings, her fake marriage...and a mysterious power!
Shojo Beat Manga
1
Story & Art by
Rei Toma
Dawn of the Arcana
Available now!
RATED T TEEN
VIZ
REIMEI NO ARCANA © 2009 Rei TOMA/SHOGAKUKAN

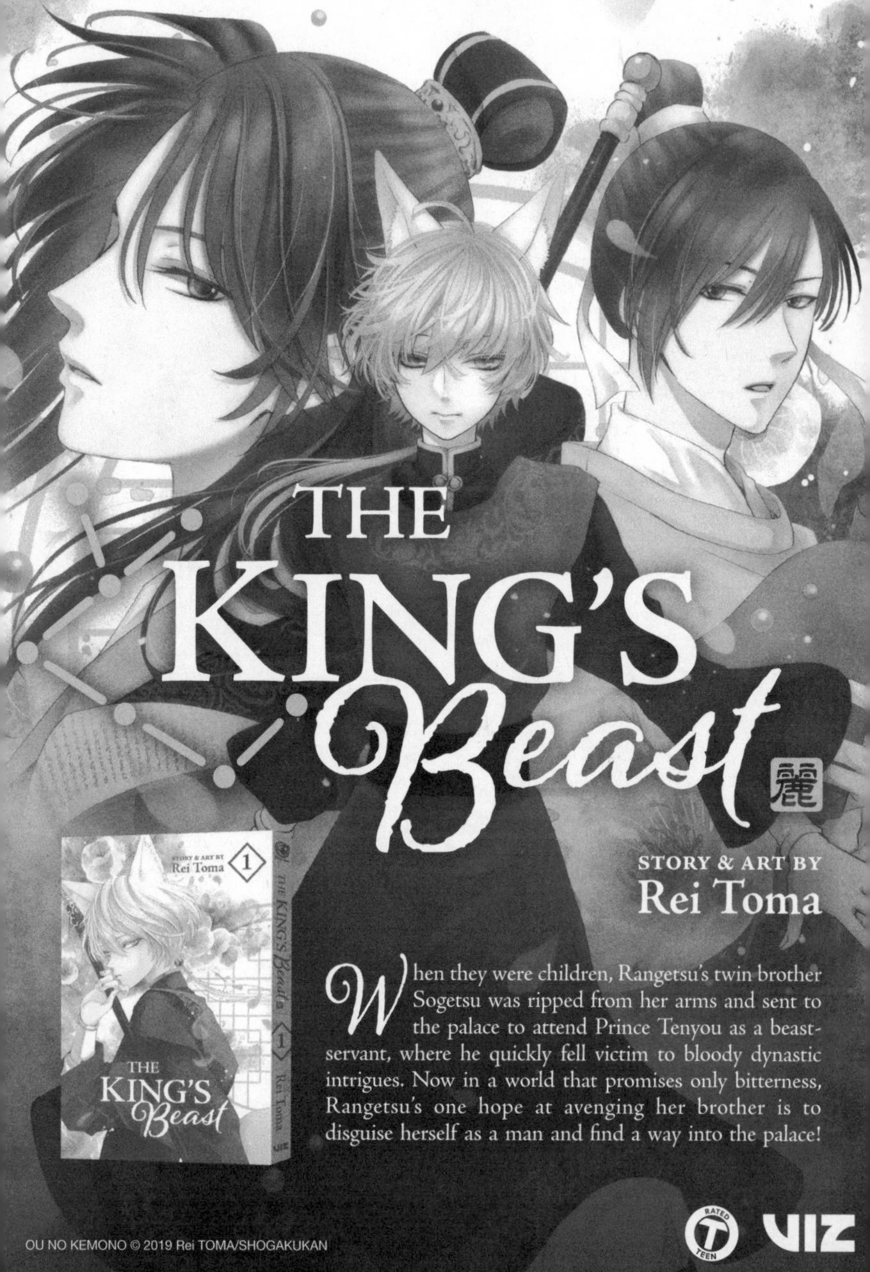
THE KING'S Beast
麗
STORY & ART BY
Rei Toma
When they were children, Rangetsu's twin brother Sogetsu was ripped from her arms and sent to the palace to attend Prince Tenyou as a beast-servant, where he quickly fell victim to bloody dynastic intrigues. Now in a world that promises only bitterness, Rangetsu's one hope at avenging her brother is to disguise herself as a man and find a way into the palace!
STORY & ART BY Rei Toma 1
THE KING'S Beast
RATED T TEEN
VIZ

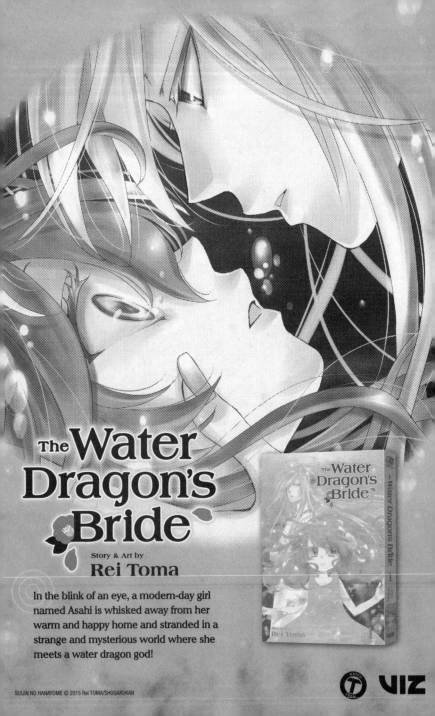

The Water Dragon's Bride

Story & Art by
Rei Toma

In the blink of an eye, a modern-day girl named Asahi is whisked away from her warm and happy home and stranded in a strange and mysterious world where she meets a water dragon god!

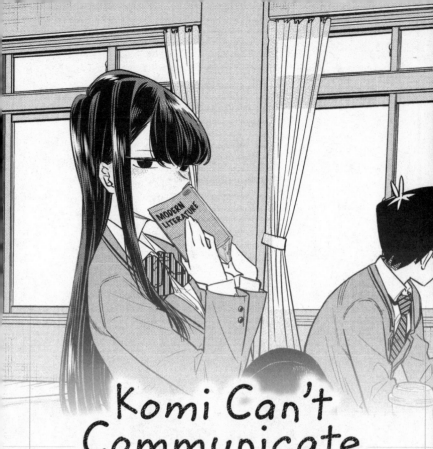

Komi Can't Communicate

Story & Art by Tomohito Oda

The journey to a hundred friends begins with a single conversation.

Socially anxious high school student Shoko Komi's greatest dream is to make some friends, but everyone at school mistakes her crippling social anxiety for cool reserve. With the whole student body keeping its distance and Komi unable to utter a single word, friendship might be forever beyond her reach.

This is the Last Page!

It's true: In keeping with the original Japanese comic format, this book reads from right to left—so action, sound effects, and word balloons are completely reversed. This preserves the orientation of the original artwork—plus, it's fun! Check out the diagram shown here to get the hang of things, and then turn to the other side of the book to get started!

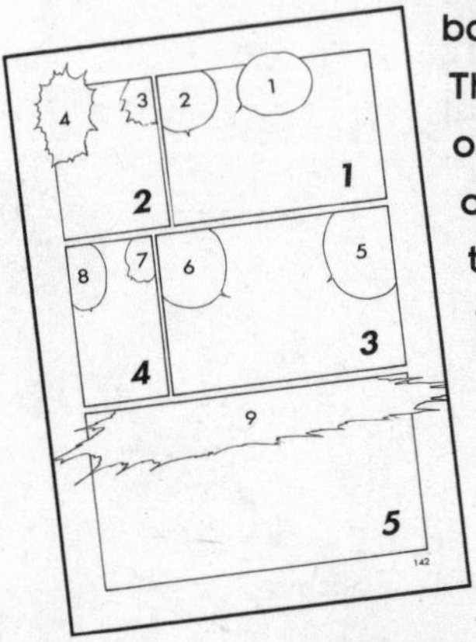
1
2
3
4
1
2
5
6
7
8
3
4
9
5
142

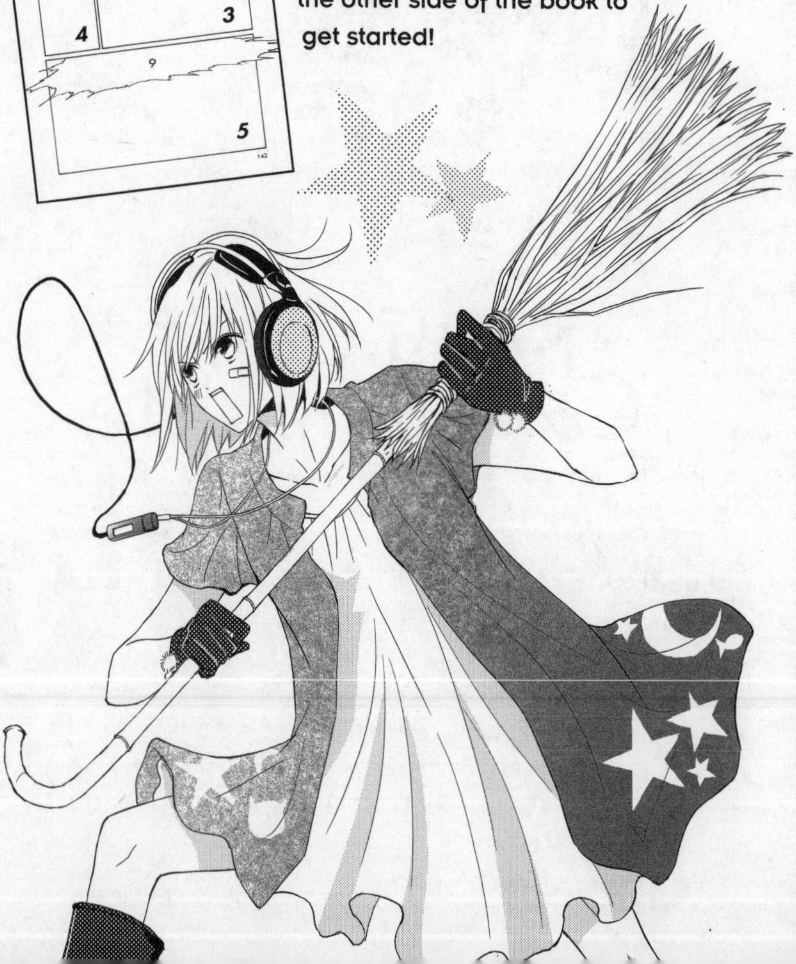